*St Antony's Series*
General Editor: **Richard Clogg** (1999–), Fellow of St Antony's College, Oxford

*Recent titles include*:

Felix Patrikeeff
RUSSIAN POLITICS IN EXILE
The Northeast Asian Balance of Power, 1924–1931

He Ping
CHINA'S SEARCH FOR MODERNITY
Cultural Discourse in the Late 20th Century

Mariana Llanos
PRIVATIZATION AND DEMOCRACY IN ARGENTINA
An Analysis of President–Congress Relations

Michael Addison
VIOLENT POLITICS
Strategies of Internal Conflict

Geoffrey Wiseman
CONCEPTS OF NON-PROVOCATIVE DEFENCE
Ideas and Practices in International Security

Pilar Ortuño Anaya
EUROPEAN SOCIALISTS AND SPAIN
The Transition to Democracy, 1959–77

Renato Baumann (*editor*)
BRAZIL IN THE 1990s
An Economy in Transition

Israel Getzler
NIKOLAI SUKHANOV
Chronicler of the Russian Revolution

Arturo J. Cruz, Jr
NICARAGUA'S CONSERVATIVE REPUBLIC, 1858–93

Pamela Lubell
THE CHINESE COMMUNIST PARTY AND THE CULTURAL REVOLUTION
The Case of the Sixty-One Renegades

Mikael af Malmborg
NEUTRALITY AND STATE-BUILDING IN SWEDEN

Klaus Gallo
GREAT BRITAIN AND ARGENTINA
From Invasion to Recognition, 1806–26

David Faure and Tao Tao Liu
TOWN AND COUNTRY IN CHINA
Identity and Perception

Peter Mangold
SUCCESS AND FAILURE IN BRITISH FOREIGN POLICY
Evaluating the Record, 1900–2000

Mohamad Tavakoli-Targhi
REFASHIONING IRAN
Orientalism, Occidentalism and Historiography

Louise Haagh
CITIZENSHIP, LABOUR MARKETS AND DEMOCRATIZATION
Chile and the Modern Sequence

Renato Colistete
LABOUR RELATIONS AND INDUSTRIAL PERFORMANCE IN BRAZIL
Greater São Paulo, 1945–60

Peter Lienhardt (*edited by Ahmed Al-Shahi*)
SHAIKHDOMS OF EASTERN ARABIA

John Crabtree and Laurence Whitehead (*editors*)
TOWARDS DEMOCRATIC VIABILITY
The Bolivian Experience

Steve Tsang (*editor*)
JUDICIAL INDEPENDENCE AND THE RULE OF LAW IN HONG KONG

Karen Jochelson
THE COLOUR OF DISEASE
Syphilis and Racism in South Africa, 1880–1950

Julio Crespo MacLennan
SPAIN AND THE PROCESS OF EUROPEAN INTEGRATION, 1957–85

Enrique Cárdenas, José Antonio Ocampo and Rosemary Thorp (*editors*)
AN ECONOMIC HISTORY OF TWENTIETH-CENTURY LATIN AMERICA
Volume 1: The Export Age
Volume 2: Latin America in the 1930s
Volume 3: Industrialization and the State in Latin America

Jennifer G. Mathers
THE RUSSIAN NUCLEAR SHIELD FROM STALIN TO YELTSIN

---

St Antony's Series
Series Standing Order ISBN 0–333–71109–2
(*outside North America only*)

You can receive future titles in this series as they are published by placing a standing order. Please contact your bookseller or, in case of difficulty, write to us at the address below with your name and address, the title of the series and the ISBN quoted above.

Customer Services Department, Macmillan Distribution Ltd, Houndmills, Basingstoke, Hampshire RG21 6XS, England

# Russian Politics in Exile

## The Northeast Asian Balance of Power, 1924–1931

Felix Patrikeeff
*Lecturer in International Politics*
*University of Adelaide*
*Australia*

palgrave
macmillan

in association with
St Antony's College, Oxford

© Felix Patrikeeff 2002

All rights reserved. No reproduction, copy or transmission of this publication may be made without written permission.

No paragraph of this publication may be reproduced, copied or transmitted save with written permission or in accordance with the provisions of the Copyright, Designs and Patents Act 1988, or under the terms of any licence permitting limited copying issued by the Copyright Licensing Agency, 90 Tottenham Court Road, London W1T 4LP.

Any person who does any unauthorised act in relation to this publication may be liable to criminal prosecution and civil claims for damages.

The author has asserted his right to be identified as the author of this work in accordance with the Copyright, Designs and Patents Act 1988.

First published 2002 by
PALGRAVE MACMILLAN
Houndmills, Basingstoke, Hampshire RG21 6XS and
175 Fifth Avenue, New York, N.Y. 10010
Companies and representatives throughout the world

PALGRAVE MACMILLAN is the global academic imprint of the Palgrave Macmillan division of St. Martin's Press, LLC and of Palgrave Macmillan Ltd. Macmillan® is a registered trademark in the United States, United Kingdom and other countries. Palgrave is a registered trademark in the European Union and other countries.

ISBN 0–333–73018–6

This book is printed on paper suitable for recycling and made from fully managed and sustained forest sources.

A catalogue record for this book is available from the British Library.

Library of Congress Cataloging-in-Publication Data
Patrikeeff, Felix.
    Russian politics in exile : the Northeast Asian balance of power (1924–1931) / Felix Patrikeeff
        p. cm.
    Includes bibliographical references and index.
    ISBN 0–333–73018–6
    1. Russians – China – Manchuria. I. Title.
DS731.R9 P37 2002
951′.80049171–dc21                                                                2002019597

10  9  8  7  6  5  4  3  2  1
11  10  09  08  07  06  05  04  03  02

Printed and bound in Great Britain by
Antony Rowe Ltd, Chippenham and Eastbourne

# Contents

| | |
|---|---|
| Acknowledgements | vii |
| Map 1   A political map of Manchuria | ix |
| Map 2   Harbin | x |
| A Note on Transliteration | xi |
| Introduction | xii |
| 1   The Birth of Politics in Exile: Russian Settlements in Manchuria and the Question of Imperialism | 1 |
| 2   The Soviet Union, Northern Manchuria and the Civil War: Aspects of Interplay and Separation | 21 |
| 3   Liberation and Exile: the Paradox of Russians in Manchuria and China | 29 |
| 4   Politics on the Ground | 52 |
| 5   An Economy on the Brink | 65 |
| 6   The 1929 Crisis | 80 |
| 7   Decline into Oblivion, 1930–31 | 104 |
| 8   Manchuria and the Geopolitics of Myth | 121 |
| Appendix | 132 |
| Notes | 135 |
| Select Bibliography | 205 |
| Index | 220 |

# Acknowledgements

A study that requires a diverse range of materials is very much dependent on co-operation and skills of librarians and archivists in a number of institutions. I have, without exception, received great assistance in my work at the various libraries of Columbia, Harvard, Hawaii, Hong Kong, New South Wales, Oxford, Stanford and Sydney Universities, as well as the British Library and the New York Public Library. Of particular note, however, have been the staff of the Hoover Institution on War, Revolution and Peace, who provided me with expert guidance on its rich holdings and a most congenial environment in which to conduct research; in particular I have quoted from the Vladimir D. Pastuhov collection, Box No. 3, Item 20 of 14 May 1932 (the author gratefully acknowledges that the appendix on p. 132 is a reproduction of this). Similarly, the staff at GARF, the University of Communications, St Petersburg (where I spent a most useful and agreeable time as a visiting fellow) and the Hongkong & Shanghai Banking Corporation (HSBC) Archives in Hong Kong, through their assistance and patience, have done much to enrich this book. Librarians at St Antony's College, Rosamund Campbell and Jackie Wilcox, had, from the beginning of my work on Manchuria, provided help and good cheer that was much appreciated, and is gratefully acknowledged here. So too is the support of the Warden and Fellows of St Antony's, where I spent some of my most enjoyable years (both as a postgraduate student and a Senior Associate Member). Conducting research in as many locations as this study has required is an expensive business. Grants from the Cyril Foster Fund, Oxford University, the University of Sydney, the Department of Politics and Faculty of Humanities and Social Sciences, University of Adelaide have helped me greatly in this respect. Jill Barton and Rob Lovell, in addition to their encouragement, gave me a welcome opportunity to conduct research in Russia.

My thanks are due to a large number of people who helped me reach the end of this long journey. The various individuals who have provided me with time, advice, interviews and materials are too numerous to mention by name. Most are cited in the bibliography and their contributions have been invaluable. Indeed, the Russian '*Kitaitsy*' (as the Russians who had lived in China are sometimes known) now resident in America, Australia, Britain and Hong Kong were wonderfully generous in the time and effort they devoted to my queries. Of particular note here are Shura Lutai and the late Alexei Petrovich Zanozin, who provided me with a remarkable insight into the pathos of what it was to be a Russian in North Manchuria, and the redoubtable Tanya Drizul', who read the entire manuscript, provided numerous comments, criticisms and, thankfully, steered me away from producing a few clangers. Her enthusiasm for things Russian was infectious and remarkable grasp of detail concerning Manchuria reassuring. Intellectual sustenance of a specialist sort has come from a number of importance sources. Rosemary Quested has figured prominently in this respect, and has been most supportive of my work, as have Patricia Polansky, the remarkable bibliographer of Russians-in-Asia, and John Stephan through his elegant prose and thought on this area of study, as well as comments on my early work on Manchuria. The help of Alan Birch, Mark Elvin, Thomas Wong and the late Dick Storry has been of great value, as has that of John Perkins, who have provided me with this, as well as commentary on portions of my work. Michael Kaser and Alan Wood read the full study, recommended it for publication and provided detailed criticism and a degree of wisdom which has made the historico-political and economic focus sharper and the prose more readable. I am very grateful to them both. My greatest debt, however, is to Harry Shukman, whose contributions to my work and skills as a researcher and writer have been inestimable.

I would also like to acknowledge the efforts and patience of my publisher, Palgrave Macmillan, in guiding this book through to its completion. In particular, I would like to thank Alison Howson, the Senior Commissioning Editor (Politics and International Studies), Kerry Coutts and my copy-editor, Ann Marangos for their respective contributions to the book. Needless to add, any infelicities of fact or interpretation are solely my own.

As with any task of writing, the intangibles are often as important as the tangibles. George Hayim and the late Ezekiel Abraham gave me valued support. Sue Johnson bore the early stresses and strains of converting research to prose, and Anne Nicolaou the at times problematic 'dotting of the I's'. Julie Burton, Marieke van Hoeve, Alan Pordage and Hans Stoeve made the process of writing that much easier with their friendship and most welcome humour. Barbara Shukman has, through her cherished friendship, given me more peace of mind and motivation than she will realise. My Mother, Nina Patrikeeff, has unfailingly borne the necessary (and at times unnecessary) delays associated with finishing the book. Without her unstinting faith in me and her self-sacrifice, this study would not only have remained unfinished, it would never have been started. I owe her more than I can over hope to repay. Finally, my Grandfather and Grandmother, Petr Nikolaevich and Elizaveta Mikhailovna Patrikeeff, sadly, did not live to see the final work. The former's memories of both the broad picture and detail of Manchurian affairs, and the latter's reminiscences of an exotic Harbin existence first led me to the study of Russian life in Northern Manchuria. This book is dedicated to their memory.

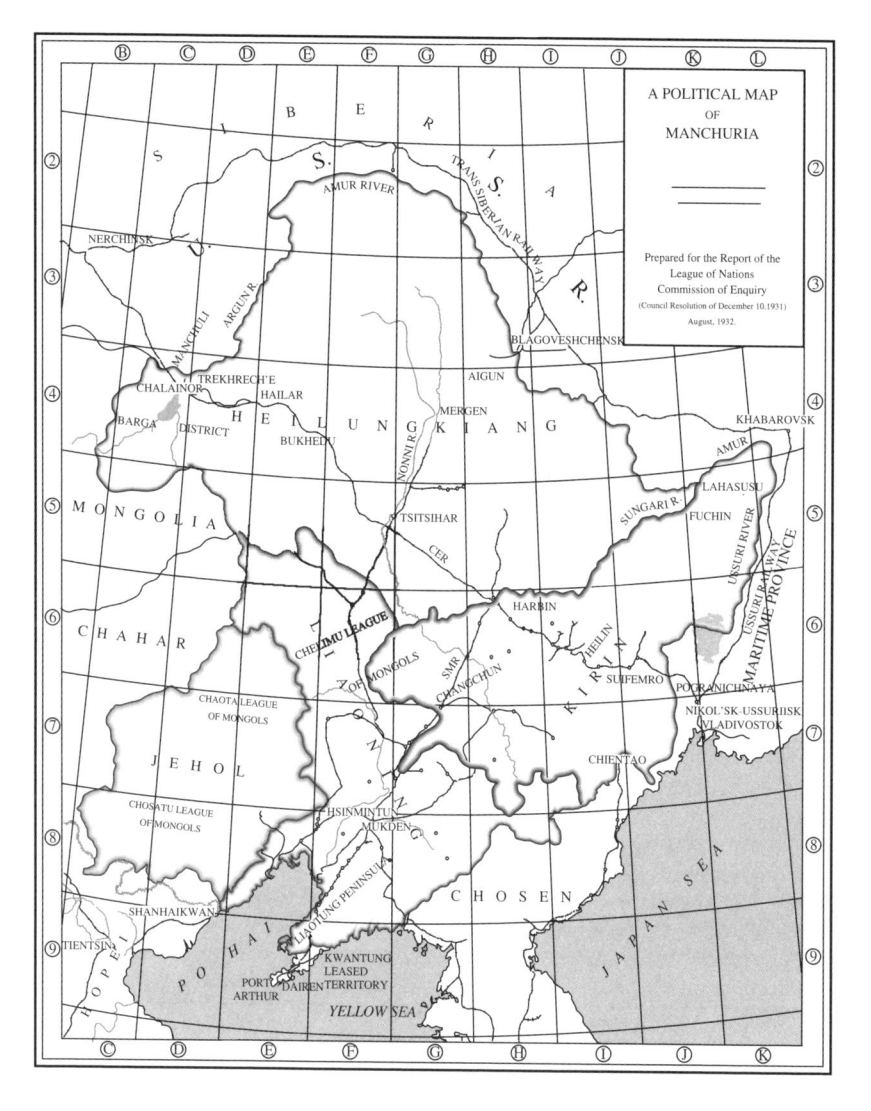

**Map 1** A political map of Manchuria

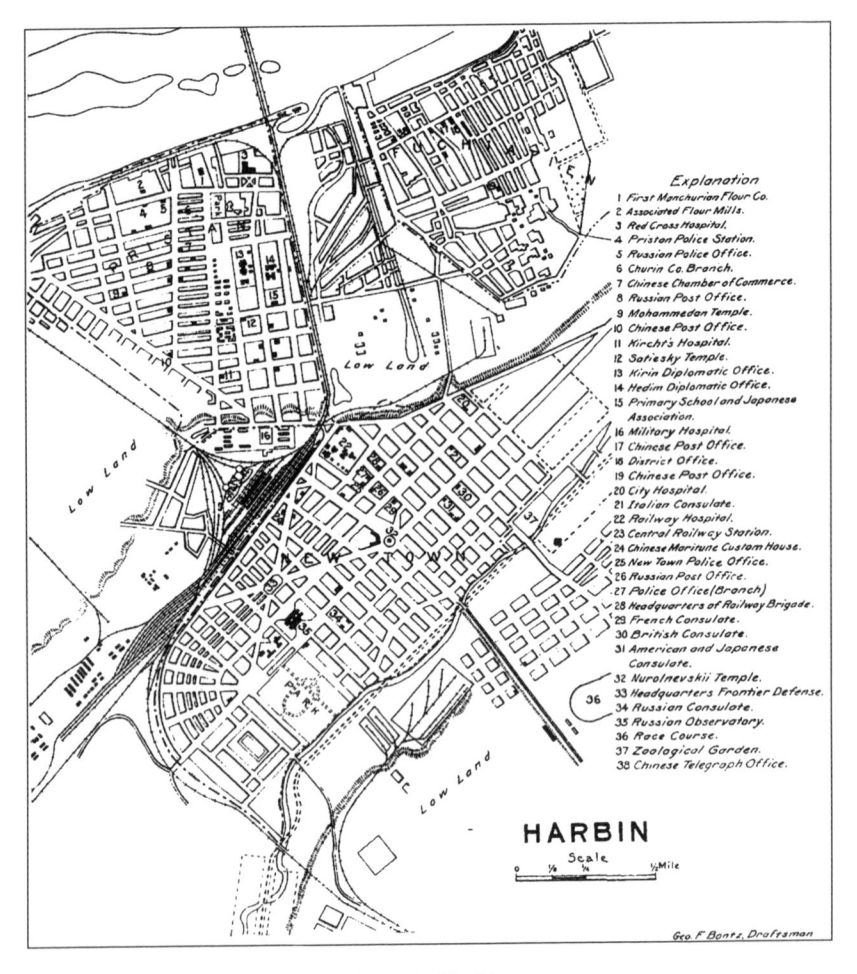

**Map 2** Harbin

# A Note on Transliteration

I have employed the Library of Congress form of transliteration for the Russian, with the exception of commonly recognised names that have entered into normal usage (e.g. Trotsky rather than Trotskii), and occasional adjustments for *émigré* usage. With Chinese names and words, I have opted for the Wade-Giles form. I have done so for two reasons. First, as the study is locked very firmly in the Republican period of China's history, the use of Pinyin (now generally, although by no means universally, acknowledged as a standard form – see W.A. Shibles, 'Chinese Romanization Systems: IPA Transliteration', *Sino-Platonic Papers*, No.52, November 1994), would cause problems with names such as Chiang Kai-shek and the Kuomintang, which have been quite resistant to change and, in any event, appear throughout the English-language material used for this study. Secondly, Russian transliteration of Chinese words/names is often opaque through both Pinyin and Wade-Giles, although it appears closer to the latter. It seemed more sensible, therefore, not to add a further level of difficulty for the reader by opting for a third form of transliteration.

# Introduction

The years 1924–31 constitute an important period in the history of Manchuria, representing a time of turmoil that draws in the tail end of the Russian civil war, the Chinese civil war and the evolution of a complex set of relations between the three principal powers in the region: China, Russia and Japan. Much of the attention has, in this last respect, been devoted to the competition of these powers over the railway system in the region, and notably the Chinese Eastern Railway (CER) in Northern Manchuria. Beloff, Tang and others[1] have helped to establish the CER as the core to the understanding of the politics of the region. While this is undoubtedly an important area for scholarly investigation, such study has tended to leave lacunae in our understanding of the Manchurian problem in the interwar period. Three elements stand out in this regard. First, the nature of politics within the broader Russian community in the region and its influence on that period. Secondly, the interplay of politics and economics there. Thirdly, the place (and interpretation) of the 1929 Sino-Soviet Conflict. Puzzling with respect to the last of these is the question why the Soviet Union, having been so successful in re-establishing its rights on the railway and Northern Manchuria as a whole as a result of its military action in that year, should have been offering the CER for sale just two years after its resounding military and diplomatic victory. The inability of existing scholarship to answer this question fully and satisfactorily is a major concern for the present study.

The conventional approach, which stresses the importance of the events of 1931–33 and the seizure by Japan of full effective power in Manchuria as a whole, has had important consequences in this regard. Above all, it led to the belief that it was in 1931 that the political ante was raised in the region, and the open tripartite contest for the control of Manchuria began. This has been an approach that has not varied very much from the early commentary of writers such as Sherwood Eddy, who recounted how he had '...come into fresh contact with all three powers which are contending for Manchuria – Russia, Japan and China'.[2] A similar slant can be seen in subsequent work on the subject, reinforcing the impression that 1931 was the *annus terribilis*.[3]

This study argues from a somewhat different perspective: that by 1931 Manchuria had already become a two-cornered struggle, with the 1929 conflict, ostensibly a great Soviet triumph, ironically spelling the demise of the Soviet presence in its northern portion. The argument here is one in which the confluence of the sustained – and bitter – struggle between Soviet interests and those of Russian *émigrés*, together with the political/military and economic crises (in the case of the latter, both that which was generated by the political situation in Manchuria itself, and the onset of the depression experienced by the world economy), played a key part in hastening and intensifying this process. Brought to a state of ruin were not only the sustained, and markedly successful, Soviet efforts to build up an economic presence in Northern Manchuria, but also its principal *institutional* claim for that presence: the CER itself. With the logic of an economic presence gone, the study argues, so too was that of the political. All that remained was for the Soviet Union to secure the best possible financial result from the sale of the railway, which it did, with a final telling swipe at the Russian *émigré* community of Northern Manchuria.

The study approaches the subject by looking at it in the context of the nature of Russian, and then Soviet, presence in Manchuria, paying particular attention to the matter of the interpretation of Russian/Soviet imperialism. The conclusion here is that its character may be interpreted as *bezalabernyi* (slovenly, disorderly), resulting in the creation of a Russian community that was consistently at odds with central policies. Whereas in the tsarist period this principally took the form of dissonance on economic policies, this was subsequently replaced by political schism (after the Russian Revolution), which found an increasing outlet – much at the expense of Soviet interests – in the economic sphere. Examined then is the crystallisation of Soviet attitudes and policies resulting from the place that Manchuria occupied in the Russian civil war; a period, the study suggests, that was to bring the area to the fore in Soviet thinking on questions of regional security and its relations with its neighbours in Northeast Asia. Such thinking is explored in Chapter 3, in which it is proposed that what we see emerging is a paradox in Soviet policies in Manchuria and China proper. The conventional view of a single, homogeneous line of Soviet policy is questioned. This, the book argues, was far from being the case, with a very clear division being in place between the ideologically charged policy the Soviet Union maintained in China proper, and the more conservative, pragmatic approach adopted in Northern Manchuria itself. The two, finally, showed themselves to be incompatible, with China seeing Soviet 'policy', as represented in Northern Manchuria, as a continuation of familiar forms of imperialism, while Manchurian authorities looked upon activities in China proper as an indication of Soviet 'revolutionism' in their own area. Chapter 4 examines this dichotomy in the context of the Manchurian situation, while Chapter 5 discusses the character of the North Manchurian economy, depicting the rise of the Soviet presence in this in the period 1924–28; roughly the years in which Soviet 'revolutionsim' was at its height in China proper. Chapter 6 provides an analysis of the 1929 Crisis. Looked at in this chapter is the nature, and significance, of the military action, with particular attention paid to its impact, both in establishing the Soviet Union's prestige as a regional power, and, coincidentally, in bringing on an early collapse of the North Manchurian economy. Highlighted in this chapter is the irreparable damage done to the Russian 'spine' of that economy; a theme that is further developed in Chapter 7, which examines also the swift decline in the Soviet Union's fortunes, and indeed those of the Russian *émigré* population too in the period 1930–31. With the raison d'être for its presence fatally undermined, Harbin's Russian community became even more polarised, with its more radical views finding shape, finally, in its contributions to a Japanese-guided Manchukuo and dreams of empire. The final chapter discusses these *émigré* aspirations in the broader geopolitical context of Northeast Asia and its distinctive history, concluding that these were only one element in the emergence of the 'geopolitics of myth' and the rise of a hegemonic Japan.

# 1
# The Birth of Politics in Exile: Russian Settlements in Manchuria and the Question of Imperialism

The important period of Manchurian history commences in the thirteenth century, when Genghis Khan overran the Chin Dynasty. Under Mongol rule, Manchuria was devastated and it was not until the start of the seventeenth century that the populace of the Ussuri region was able to show the first signs of recovery. Soon afterwards, however, the Manchus began to bring their sister tribes under their control and seized the power of a declining Ming Dynasty (1368–1644). At this time, moreover, the Manchus brought along related tribes from Manchuria into China proper for further conquest and enforcement of their rule.[1] Even by this stage, one could observe the existence of a deep-seated, if stormy, relationship between the affairs of China and Manchuria. E.G. Ravenstein, in his *The Russians on the Amur*, concluded that in this respect 'We find the destinies of Manchuria almost uninterruptedly connected with those of China',[2] adding that the Manchurian tribes[3] '...prefer conquest in the south, rather than to rely upon their own strength, and to found an independent empire in Manchuria'.[4] It is because of this curious relationship that the Chinese historian Li Chi was able to conclude that:

> Manchuria's history is...only a part of Chinese history... [because] ...it is impossible to relate the history of Manchuria by itself. Events in Manchuria are but reflections of the happenings in China proper: the Chinese domination in the Northeast, the nomadic invasions, the uprisings and downfall of the various tribes are all phases of Chinese history in general.[5]

However, it was only under the Ch'ing Dynasty (1644–1911) that Manchuria assumed a new status, and one which was closely tied with China proper. It became, under the Ch'ings, the home of the imperial house.[6] Under this dynasty the Manchus ruled an empire of unrivalled proportions, controlling

China itself, Manchuria (to the watershed north of the River Amur), Mongolia, Sinkiang, Tibet and Formosa.[7] They were, in fact, fulfilling the aims of their nomadic ancestors in holding sway over the entire area of China. However, as Owen Lattimore points out, a process of transformation was taking place too, with the cultural division between ruler and ruled becoming far less distinct:

> Owing... to the fact that each alien dynasty, as it matured, became more and more Chinese, the reflex action of Chinese culture north of the Great Wall was never lacking. Invariably the conquerors took over the Chinese dynastic model for their ruling families and Chinese forms of government for their new territories; and gradually losing the characteristics of conquering aliens, became essentially a Chinese ruling class.[8]

Lattimore views this, together with his suggestion that long before the Manchu conquest of China 'the largest numerical element in the Manchu armies must have been Chinese',[9] as an indication that the Manchu conquest of China was an early civil war:

> The Manchus, for their part, had taken on a thoroughly Chinese colour. Their two emperors who ruled from Mukden before the entry into China were emperors in the Chinese manner. It is not too much to say that the final Manchu conquest of China was less an alien invasion than the triumph of the strongest regional faction in a colossal civil war.[10]

However, while this depiction of the drawing in of Manchus and Manchuria itself into the Chinese sphere is reasonable enough, to it must be added one other factor; a factor which is crucial to our understanding of the balance of political and economic power in the region. While the Manchu Court had looked upon '... Chinese civilization as something to aspire to',[11] it also perpetuated a perplexing policy barring Chinese emigration to Manchuria. The effects of this policy were to be felt most severely after the Manchus themselves migrated *en masse* – as officials – to China proper, leaving Manchuria (with the exception of an old Chinese settlement in Liaotung) largely depopulated. To correct this potentially troublesome situation, the Manchu Court issued an edict in 1665 which encouraged Chinese settlement in the region.[12] However, within eight years this policy had been reversed and the Chinese were again forbidden from settling beyond the settlement of Mukden. In 1776, the Emperor Ch'ien-Lung gave political and cultural form to this policy by proclaiming in an edict that 'Shengking and Kirin are the home of the dynasty. To permit immigrants to settle down there would greatly affect the Manchu mode of life. ... Let ... orders be given out that immigrants are forever prohibited from entrance'.[13]

The reasons for this policy may be seen as having been threefold. First, the Imperial House wanted to maintain a monopoly of Manchurian trade in pearls, ginseng and fur. Secondly, the early Manchu emperors may have desired to keep their race at least notionally pure. Thirdly, the Manchus appear to have placed great store in *feng shui* (geomancy) and therefore did not want the proliferation of Chinese tillers on their native land. The final point is supported by the fact that the last ban on Chinese landownership in Manchuria was not lifted until 1905.[14] Thus, Manchuria may be seen as virtually a Manchu patrimony.

That Chinese settlers were barred from entry into Manchuria did not mean that there was *no* migration. Illegal entry during the second half of the nineteenth century, for instance, intensified considerably, despite the legal–administrative measures that were in place to prevent it.[15] Eventually, in the aftermath of the Taiping Rebellion of 1850–64, the Manchu administration was forced to acknowledge the *fait accompli* of limited Chinese colonisation. However, as Tang so rightly puts it, '… [this decision] which could have fortified the border and perhaps discouraged Russian advance into Manchuria, came almost a half century too late'.[16] It was too late because by 1860, when the colonisation of Manchuria had become a '…vital matter of policy',[17] China had already conceded some 350000 square miles of territory north of the Amur and east of the Ussuri to Russia.[18] In the half century that followed, the urgency of Chinese colonisation became even more evident, while the Chinese government's policies were seemingly out of step with this, not being able to make any genuine headway in using colonisation to demonstrate Chinese sovereignty in Manchuria. For example, in 1860, after the cession of land to Russia, the rich virgin plains of the Hu-lan River to the north of Harbin were opened to Chinese immigrants. The following year, a fertile area in north-western Kirin was made available too. After the Sino-Japanese War of 1894–95 and the Russo-Japanese War of 1904–05, attention to Chinese colonisation of the region was redoubled, with the matter being viewed as an '…even more urgent national concern'.[19] In short, while the foreign powers, and notably Russia and Japan, were in the process of aggrandising political and economic power in Manchuria, the Chinese authorities were frantically seeking to establish large-scale forms of habitation in the region.

Chinese colonisation of Manchuria, and particularly the accelerated form that came into being after 1860, gave rise directly to the importance, both in political and economic spheres of Manchurian life, of the northern warlords. Many of the Chinese migrants coming to the region were 'sponsored' by this elite[20] and thereby entered into what amounted to feudal ties with these new 'lords'. The capital derived by some of the warlords through these ties was sown into a number of areas of enterprise, including commercial agriculture, money-lending and banking. Others used their positions to invest in pawnshops and grain exchanges too.

It was principally through such means that Marshal Chang Tso-lin,[21] the leading warlord in Manchuria during a part of the period covered by the present study, came to own the *Sanyu Public Oil Company* at Hsinmintun, and the *Sanyu Grain Company, Sanyu Pawnshop* and *Sanyu Bank* in Mukden.[22] Through their parallel rise in the economic and political spheres, the warlords became a major force in the Manchurian arena; more so, in fact, than the central Chinese government.

There is a further implication to be gleaned from China's attempts to populate the region with its own people. The influx of vast numbers of settlers created a substantial consumer market, demand from which indigenous industry could not satisfy. Thus, while Manchuria was rich both in agricultural produce and mineral deposits, which were duly exploited by a variety of Russian, Japanese and other foreign firms, the following report from Shirani Takeshi (the Kwantung Civil Governor) attests to the state of manufacture of consumer goods in Manchuria. As late as 1909, he reports, '...although Manchuria possesses a population of forty millions, not a single piece of clothing worn by the inhabitants is manufactured in the province. All textiles required by the people are imported either from South China or from Japan'.[23] What may be seen in Manchuria, therefore, is a tremendous potential for the development of both industry and entrepreneurship.

As early as the middle of the seventeenth century, 40 years before the era of Peter the Great, Russia had demonstrated an interest in the Far East. Following Vasilii Poiarkov's and Erofei Khabarov's Cossack 'expeditions',[24] Russia had expanded its power eastward to the Amur basin. Moreover, these Cossack ventures into the Amur region of the Manchu Empire, and many of which were marked by '...treacherous and cruel behaviour towards the natives',[25] were not countered by the Manchus, as Ravenstein explains:

> The tribes living there partly acknowledged Manchu sovereignty, but the Manchu, still occupied in the consolidation of their power in China, were not in a position to protect their subjects against the ravages committed by the Cossacks, and only in 1651 we find them actively engaged in the wars against the Russians. It was reserved to the great emperor Kang-hi to expel the enemy, and force him, in the treaty of Nerchinsk, to evacuate the regions of the Amur.[26]

The episode that brought the Manchus and Russians to direct confrontation was the Manchu siege of the fortress town of Albazin. This prompted a Russian proposal to negotiate a peaceful resolution of all boundary questions with the Manchu Court. Negotiations followed shortly afterwards. The Treaty of Nerchinsk was concluded on 27 August 1689. By its terms, a long-needed frontier line was drawn and the Russian encroachment was halted for almost a century and a half.[27]

In the century following the Nerchinsk agreement, the Manchu Dynasty attained the peak of its power, yet its officials paid little attention to the defence of its Northeastern frontiers. In fact, the centre of border defence was moved inwards, first from Aigun to the left bank of the Amur, then to Mergen, then to Tsitsihar. Boundary inspections took place only once a year in some areas, once every three years for others, and not at all in the more remote areas. Russian peasants and Cossacks, following in the footsteps of the Chinese frontier inspectors, were therefore able to hunt game in these areas and collect tribute from local residents.[28]

G. Vernadsky suggests that '... if Peter [the Great] had lived longer, he would have tried to reach India. At the same time he secretly dreamed of opening a way to China as well'.[29] Neither Peter nor his successors, such as Catherine I and II and Alexander I, was able to achieve these ambitions. It was only during the reigns of Nicholas I and Alexander II, in fact, that Nikolai Nikolaevich Muraviev, the Governor-General of Eastern Siberia, was able to secure the Amur region for Russia: 'The Amur had virtually become [only a few months before the signing of the Treaty of Paris in 1856] a Russian river, and it was only necessary to obtain the nominal sanction of the fait accompli from the Chinese'.[30] On 19 March 1857, Alexander II gave imperial sanction for the establishment of military colonies, consisting of Cossacks and their families, on the left bank of the Amur. Interestingly, D.J. Dallin describes this colonization as '... a compulsory resettlement and its results, when they became known in the European part of Russia, were anything but encouraging as far as further immigration was concerned'.[31] Most of the Cossacks had been 'recruited' from the peasantry registered at Nerchinsk under a conversion programme proposed by Muraviev in 1851.[32] This resettlement was sanctioned on 16 May 1858, when the Treaty of Aigun was signed, with Russia being ceded the left bank of the Amur down to the Ussuri and both banks below the Ussuri.[33] Five days later, Muraviev, at a church parade, addressed his troops in the following way: 'Comrades, I congratulate you! We have not laboured in vain; the Amur now belongs to Russia!'[34] He had, moreover, achieved this, as a Russian scholar later put it, 'without gunpowder or smoke'.[35] But Muraviev, in declaring the limits of empire in such unequivocal terms, was unable to catch a further dimension of imperial outstretch that Ravenstein was to recognise in 1861:

> On the Amur and Ussuri... the boundary line does not bear the stamp of permanency. Russia holding one bank only on these rivers, while China holds the other, may at any chosen time furnish its neighbour with fertile cause of dispute, and when the time comes the huge Chinese empire tumbles into pieces; the whole of Manchuria with Leaotong [Liaotung] must become the prey of Russia.[36]

This opportunity was to present itself, if in a somewhat illusory form, with the launching of the enormous Trans-Siberian railway project in 1891. Troops, in the form of the Transbaikal Army,[37] were ready at hand to enforce Tsarist policy in Manchuria, whilst potential settlers, who were living a miserable existence on newly acquired territory,[38] were also near enough to be drawn from in future projects involving Manchurian territory.

Alexander III was not to live long enough to see Russian activity in Manchuria on the scale of its involvement in the *Kitaiskaia Vostochnaia zheleznaia doroga*, or CER venture. Nonetheless, during his reign we can see a rapid change in Russia's imperial interests. Germany, for instance, attempted to encourage Russia to shift its attention from the Balkans and the Near East, to the Middle East and Far East, thereby postponing any friction between Russia and Austria. Because of the worsening relations with Britain over Afghanistan in 1891–92, it was natural enough that Russian sights should narrow further to only the Far East. An example of Alexander III's imperial ambitions in this respect become evident in 1893, when a Mongolian, Dr Badmaev, by most accounts a shadowy character, received two million roubles from the Treasury to allow him to establish private companies at Chita.[39] At about this time we also notice a growing closeness between Russia and China.[40] It is evident that this 'peaceful penetration' of China was part of a grander scheme – incorporating the Trans-Siberian Railway – of the Tsar's influential Minister of Finance, Sergei Iul'evich Witte; a scheme which rapidly unfolded in the aftermath of the Sino-Japanese War of 1894–95.[41] Alexander died before the Treaty of Shimonoseki ended the war between China and Japan, but in his report to the new Tsar, the Russian Foreign Minister, Prince Lobanov-Rostovskii, made it clear that Russia's role in the region was to continue to find form suitable to it: 'Our goals may be seen as two-fold: securing an ice-free port on the Pacific Ocean and the annexation of a number of areas in Manchuria, which would be essential in making the construction of the Trans-Siberian Railway easier'.[42] Witte was of a like mind with Lobanov-Rostovskii. A major concern for him was, moreover, how to maintain the integrity of a region in which Russia had a growing interest; a characteristic displayed in Witte's reflections on the signing of the Treaty of Shimonoseki and the cession of Port Arthur and Liaotung Peninsula to Japan: 'This agreement appeared to me as being unfavourable to the interests of Russia. From this, however, arose the question: what would be an appropriate response?'[43] The answer came six days after the signing of the treaty, when the Triple Alliance, comprising Russia, France and Germany, made a dramatic intervention in Sino-Japanese affairs. The Alliance 'advised' Japan to surrender the Liaotung Peninsula to China in return for a heavier indemnity. Furthermore, Port Arthur, if left under Japanese control, would pose a '...constant threat to China's capital and make the independence of Korea illusory, and it would be a permanent obstacle to the peace of the Far East'.[44] Thus Japan, which at the time stood alone, had to relinquish both acquisitions. Importantly, both once again became potential areas for Russian involvement. Some Chinese statesmen, interestingly, regarded Russia's part in the intervention as constituting a sign of '...her faith and righteousness'.[45] The Chinese plenipotentiary Li Hung-Chang saw a different motive behind Russia's actions. His misgivings, as it happened, were well founded. During the talks in St Petersburg on the proposed railway, Witte outlined plans for a monopoly of railways in Manchuria; a monopoly to be placed under the jurisdiction of the Russo-Chinese Bank.[46] Li Hung-chang responded angrily to Witte's proposal, as a contemporary account of the meeting showed: '[Li] could not refrain from making scenes in the presence of his fellow-negotiator, or to angrily declare that this agreement "would leave Manchuria under the control of the bank".'[47]

The terms of the agreement arrived at in St Petersburg allowed for the creation of a 'private' company which would control the affairs of the CER. But as Witte was later to recall:

> Li Hung-chang categorically refused to accept my proposal that the construction of the railway be undertaken by the Treasury, or that the railway belong to the Treasury and the Government. Consequently, it was necessary to form the Chinese Eastern Railway Company, which, of course, was, and in fact is to this day, under the full control of the [Russian] government.[48]

In the railway contract drawn up in 1896, the same year as the St Petersburg agreement, one of the clauses stated that '...the Company will have the absolute and exclusive right of administration of its lands'.[49] Russia's position in Manchuria was further strengthened when, in Peking in 1899, it reached an agreement with Britain on the question of railway construction. 'The significance of this proviso', a contemporary Russian commentary concluded, 'will instil both surprise and fear in local rulers; the suggestion being that our long-standing enmity towards England is at an end, and what remains for China is, henceforth, to comply unquestioningly to our demands, as well as those of England'.[50] Moreover, Russia had already secured the Liaotung Peninsula on leasehold and seized Port Arthur and Dairen in the year before.[51] Thus, by 1900, when the *I Ho Ch'uan*, or the Righteous and Harmonious Boxing Order, began what was to be known as the Boxer Rebellion, Russia was able to mobilise its troops and enter Manchuria to 'protect' its nationals' interests there, paying scant attention to the correctness of such an action. In fact, General Kuropatkin, the Russian Chief-of-Staff in the Far East, saw this as an unparalleled and fortuitous opportunity; an observation he quickly made known to Witte. 'It is imperative', Kuropatkin advised, 'that, taking full advantage of the present opportunity, we seize the whole of Manchuria'.[52] The recipient of these remarks was far from convinced of the necessity to take advantage of such a 'windfall'. Of the situation that had emerged as a result of the troubles, he observed that 'Our forces conducted themselves in a totally arbitrary way; that is, they behaved as an enemy would behave on captured territory, and moreover Asian territory'.[53] Witte's conclusion concerning this episode was unequivocal: 'It was in this way that the ground was laid for an eventual catastrophe'.[54] It was, as Witte had reflected, to end in disaster. The proliferation of Russian troops simply added to Japan's ill-will with regard to the South Manchurian Railway, a CER branch line that was rapidly reaching completion: 'The South Manchurian Railway was conceived in sin. ... The Japanese regarded this Russian railway thrust into South Manchuria as a "dagger pointing at the heart of Japan"'.[55]

Russia had in the first three years of the new century achieved the predominance in Manchuria which Ravenstein had envisioned some 40 years earlier. However, it was a position that was short-lived. In the 1904–05 war against Japan, Russia was to lose its 'dagger' in Southern Manchuria. Its policies in this conflict were, moreover, to be the cause of cleavage with the Russian settlements in Northern Manchuria, and notably in the nascent Harbin, where 'no sooner had Russian forces entered Manchuria than there arose a duality of power [with local authorities] in connection with the policy of the Russian government in China'.[56] These settlements, largely composed of Russians employed by the Railway, had within three years of their arrival in Manchuria established good working relations with Chinese authorities and populace alike. Moreover, Witte observed, they had already accumulated sufficient understanding of local conditions to realise the need for peaceful co-existence with the Chinese inhabitants of that region.[57] In his memoirs, Witte concluded that 'the entire administrative wing of the railway, all railway workers, together with frontier and security guards advocated a policy of peace'.[58]

Although it was intimately tied to the Russian government, the CER had, it should be noted, a fair degree of autonomy with respect to the general conduct of Russian affairs in Northern Manchuria. As early as 1904 we find that the interests of the CER and the government at St Petersburg do not necessarily coincide. In that year, Harbin was designated as a northern base for the Russian war effort against Japan.[59] Large numbers of wounded soldiers were sent there from the front. Due to the early stage of the town's development, there was a shortage of housing. With the needs of the Russian army's medical wing having been added to the existing problem, a crisis quickly emerged; a crisis that the CER management was not in a hurry to resolve:

> There developed a complex and stubborn struggle over the newly-completed administrative buildings: the railway management only begrudgingly assigned these to the needs of the sick and wounded, and

to secure the use of even one building for use as a hospital required immense effort.[60]

Even at the early stages of North Manchurian development, the CER stood out as something of a colossus both in economic and political terms. For the years up until 1914, it had absorbed an estimated 182 million gold roubles in subsidies from St Petersburg.[61] By the same year, the company employed over 20000 people, the majority of these being Russian.[62] An idea of the scale of CER operations at this time is that in the nascent town of Harbin, the Central Administration employed over two thousand members of staff, housed in one building, the maintenance of which was in the order of $2 million per annum.[63] As might befit such an overarching local institution, the CER's influence extended deep into the region's politics, assisted greatly by the peculiar form of extraterritoriality that had been written into its statutes As one Chinese commentator observed: '[Before] the Revolution [of October 1917]...the whole zone traversed by this road [i.e. the CER] was alienated from China and converted into Russian territory. The manager of this line was the virtual monarch of all he surveyed, and there was none to dispute his authority'.[64]

The municipal administration of Harbin, on the other hand, was much like that of provincial towns in Russia itself, and therefore, wrote one local critic, suffered the same defects so painfully obvious in the former:

> Chronic deficits, the lack of funds for even the most urgent of needs, the unsatisfactory nature of the municipal budget, absenteeism amongst officials and a general apathy in matters concerning city affairs. Interest in the latter is only shown in the form of regular protests against taxation intended to buttress the city coffers.[65]

However, the municipal administration, or the *zemstvo* as it was known in Harbin, differed from those to be found in the treaty ports such as Shanghai in China proper in that it was not allowed to exact funds through either land taxes or customs duties.[66] After the Treaty of Portsmouth (signed by Japan and Russia in 1905, and formally ending hostilities between them) opened Harbin as a treaty port and foreign nationals began to trickle into the city, the latter expressed their desire to see the introduction of a system of municipal administration similar to that in other treaty ports. But as a local Russian newspaper concluded: 'to the wider circle of the Russian public, those principles upon which was built this form of self-government and budget appear as *terra incognita*'.[67] Interestingly, the same commentator, having compared unfavourably the state of Russian municipal administration with even the treaty ports, mildly admonished the Chinese inhabitants of Harbin, concluding that 'it is surprising that the

Chinese of Harbin do not value the equality proffered to them in the area of municipal administration'.[68]

By the terms of the original railway contract signed in 1896, the CER was to receive *gratis*, or in some areas upon payment of an annual rent, all lands '…actually necessary for the construction, operation and protection of the line'.[69] The Russian 'tenants' subsequently interpreted this wording in the broadest possible sense. Besides the land one hundred feet on either side of the railway track,[70] the company acquired large tracts encompassing the various stations too. Such a broad interpretation of the agreement in effect gave rise to the towns, of which Harbin was the most significant.

The settlement at Harbin, which was founded in 1897,[71] boasted a population of nearly 60 000 people on the eve of the Russo-Japanese War.[72] Of this total, about 20 000 were Russian.[73] There was a predominance of railway workers, with the merchant class and military making up a large proportion of the remainder.[74] The town itself could be divided into three main areas, the first being *Staryi Kharbin* (Old Harbin). This had been the original Russian township, largely made up of the luxurious villas belonging to the engineers who had constructed the CER.[75] Old Harbin went into rapid decline upon the completion of the railway, and even at its height had only 10 per cent of the total population living there.[76] It was located some nine *versts* from the main station.[77] Much nearer the centre of the settlement was the *Pristan'* (or Quay) area, so-called because of its proximity to the River Sungari. Here, over 30 per cent of the total population of Russian Harbin lived in conditions not dissimilar to those of a North American frontier town. The streets were unpaved, deeply pitted and covered in a layer of fine yellow dust which would swirl into suffocating clouds during the dry season, but turn into a thick, immobilising mud after the torrential rains of the wet season.[78] A unique intertwining of Chinese and Russian cultures was to be found in the Pristan' area, in an atmosphere filled with the vitality of a thriving, bustling community. Hawkers peddled their cooked food to Chinese workers – many of whom would crowd into Pristan' from nearby Chinese settlements during the day, and return to their homes after dark – while Russians frequented their local *stolovye* (restaurants). In this crowded district were to be found market stalls, baths, Chinese theatres, inns, food stores and 'one commercial company after another [mainly steam mills]'.[79] Accommodation was hard to find, and as a result rents were high.[80] As with most communities of this type, *Pristan'* initially lacked adequate planning and sanitation. For some, these characteristics were almost too much to bear. Polner, for example, noted of this area that: '[it] is abominable. Here are commingled the worst features of Russian and Chinese settlements; all the excesses of Russo-Chinese civilization'.[81] He does, however, accurately identify a meeting point for some of Harbin's less reputable residents at that time. Within a few years, Pristan' proximity to the river had helped to transform the district into Harbin's main business centre;[82] its less savoury reputation having passed on to other, newer suburbs of Harbin, notably the Modiagou area, which was, by the 1930s, a haven for criminal activities, and especially kidnappings.[83]

The third Russian district in this early period was New Harbin, or, as it was later known, *Novyi Gorod*. This was the 'aristocratic' sector of Harbin, boasting of paved roads and even '...the occasional wooden pavement'.[84] Here there was a proliferation of two-and three-storey stone houses as well as 'the wooden houses of the railway staff; extremely elegant homes, bordered with verandas and balconies, luxuriant greenery hiding them from the gaze of passers-by'.[85] It was in New Harbin that the chief administrative complex of the city (including the CER management building, the post and telegraph offices and the headquarters of the Border Patrol) was located. These, along with the newly constructed central railway station and hotel, were structures that stood out in relation to the development of the settlement as a whole. As Polner observed: 'Striking in their splendour...[t]hese buildings captivate the beholder by their blatantly decadent contours, their grandiose character. The town grows before our eyes and woods still line many of the construction sites'.[86]

If, leaving aside the immense cost of the CER itself, we consider that these grand edifices were built at considerable expense to the company that had been formed a few years earlier, we begin to see a certain *raison d'être* to this extravagance, namely: to impress upon the Chinese authorities the permanence of Russian involvement in Manchuria. As Weigh quite rightly concludes: '...it was the intention of the Russian authorities to make the expenditures as high as possible so that it would be impossible or unprofitable for China to recover [the CER]'.[87] Among the first of the ornate structures in this area were men's and ladies' schools of commerce, with their respective halls of residence;[88] an image telling of the long-term intentions of Russian policy and, ironically, ultimately revealing flaws in the same, as is discussed in later chapters.

By 1904, the other important Russian settlements in Northern Manchuria were parochial by comparison with Harbin itself. Hailar, which was a centre for one of the major CER auxiliary enterprises and the timber industry, and Tsitsihar were both small Chinese communities which grew in importance only with the advent of the railway. The principal functions of these towns, other than in small-scale import/export ventures, were largely limited to those connected with the railway's own activities. As a Harbin scholar observing the economic history of Tsitsihar noted, the Russian attempt to introduce a textile industry to the town showed some signs of expansion 'only recently'. The reasons for the slow growth, he suggested, was that 'the Chinese are not yet sufficiently accustomed to it, hence the lack of demand for its products... . However, we can look forward to the industry expanding fairly rapidly if rational measures are adopted for such development'.[89] While the industries waited to 'take off', commercial activities, other than those directly related to CER business, consisted of small import/export trade, including imports of Russian sugar, soap and candles. The same writer noted that 'Russian styrene candles are very popular with the Chinese because they burn more cleanly'.[90] Exports from Tsitsihar were largely limited to raw agricultural products, and particularly cereals such as oats and native grains such as *mi-tsu* and *siao mi-tsu*.[91]

The Russo-Japanese War in its wake brought developments to the Russian settlements that are important to the understanding of the Russian presence in Northern Manchuria in the 1920s. The immediate, and most significant, result was that Harbin was formally transformed into a treaty port proper. Soon, Hailar and Tsitsihar too saw the arrival of foreign entrepreneurs, who were quick to provide stiff competition for Russian traders in those towns. As Polner points out, one of the most aggressive groups in this shift was the Japanese. 'At the present time', he wrote in 1909, 'the Japanese are employing all means to spread their manufactured and other goods'.[92] The feeling of vulnerability that the forced opening up of the local economy brought with it was aggravated further by doubts about the ability of the Russian government to defend the Manchurian Russians and their interests. Polner refers, for example, to his own sentiments at the time Port Arthur fell to the Japanese on 22 January 1905. 'In the course of the war', he writes in prose tinged not with a little bitterness, 'the uselessness of armaments which, on paper, the army possessed fast became obvious; so forcefully clear, in fact, that not a single intelligent observer could delude himself for long'.[93] From his distant vantage point in London, Lenin wrote of the events in Northeast Asia that it was 'not the Russian people but Absolutism [that] has suffered a shameful defeat. The Russian people has won by the defeat of Absolutism. The capitulation of Port Arthur is the prologue to the capitulation of Tsarism'.[94] Lenin's conclusion may certainly have reflected the situation in Russia proper, but for the Northern Manchurian Russians it was already the first act. The 1905 Revolution that came within a week of Lenin having made his pronouncement, had a ripple effect on Northern Manchuria, with a series of strikes taking place along the length of the railway.[95] To the Tsarist officers based in Harbin, the radicalism of the city was overwhelming at that point. As one of these officers, General Linevich, described, Harbin had become a '...city resembling a nest of various types of revolutionaries and agitators...'.[96] And indeed there was considerable agitation taking place there, with leaflets being distributed in considerable quantities among the rank and file of the Russian troops based there. But much of this activity was taking place within the army itself.[97] Judging from the evidence to be found in the Russian popular press in the region, the civilian population had preoccupations other than revolutionism, however. Indeed, the war and revolution had been instrumental in bringing into question the nature of Russian presence in

Northern Manchuria, and particularly any imperial ambitions that had burnt so bright in the thoughts of the likes of Ravenstein and Kuropatkin:

> In our government's brighter days, we heard the famous words: "Where the Russian flag has been raised, there it will always fly". However, in Manchuria we live under entirely different conditions. Here, the Russian flag has never been raised to mark the annexation of this territory. Here, our tasks could never stretch beyond the limits of simple commercial interests.[98]

The fears that were generated by such debate and commentary remained pronounced in subsequent years, with the invasion by foreign companies into economic territory once seen as the preserve of Russian trade being shadowed by the potential of a further thrust by Japanese forces from their new sphere of influence in Southern Manchuria. Such was the fear of a resumption of hostilities in the years after the Sino-Japanese peace treaty that local press commented on 'the newspapers of Western Europe and Russia informed us daily of the hundreds of Russian businessmen fleeing in fright from Harbin and the Priamur region'.[99] The echoed sensationalism of reports such as this were, indeed, to become the regular intellectual and political diet of the Russian population of the region.

On the eve of the outbreak of the 1917 revolutions in Russia, Harbin had rapidly increased its lead (both in size and importance) over the other Russian communities in Manchuria. By then it had a population of well over 30 000 Russians;[100] a figure that would shortly be augmented by the flight of over 14 000 refugees during the revolution and early stages of civil war.[101] By the late 1920s, as Lattimore quite accurately observes, '...the Russian population in Manchuria, while important in numbers, is chiefly concentrated at one point, in Harbin [and is] ... markedly urban'.[102]

This characteristic of the North Manchurian Russian community was to acquire increasing importance. With the steady trickle, and the occasional wave, of illegal immigrants crossing the border, and with every internal and international crisis that seized the Manchurian region creating smaller instances of internal migration, the prominence – and population – of Harbin grew. One has to note, however, that this growth was neither balanced nor, for the most part, desired. By acting as a magnet for rootless refugees from Russia itself and internal migrants who were fleeing from the excesses of the local Chinese authorities or military, and seeking ostensibly temporary sanctuary in the city, Harbin developed a voracious appetite for rumour, which, ironically, was both triggered and satiated by transient Russians. It was a feature of life in the city that hardly pleased the politically cautious, who realised, of course, the effect that interminable swings of mood, information and misinformation would have on their own lives and morale.[103] Moreover, whereas in other well-established, older cities, such flows of humanity would be physically and socially more easily absorbed, Russian Harbin was little over twenty years old when the flood of emigrants began in 1917.[104] If one were to include its unwilling participation in the Boxer troubles and, beyond that, the Russo-Japanese War, the city had spent most of its formative period in political turmoil.

Russian economic penetration of China therefore serves as something of a riddle. In terms of sheer scale and audacity, the misguided attempt to create a 'Yellow Russia'[105] in China's north-eastern corner surpasses anything that other European countries dared dream of in conducting their commercial affairs from the 'little Europe' of the concessions and colonies dotting the China coast.[106] Yet Russia's sprawling railway zone (with its areas of free trade and showpiece settlements) had its beginnings in a treaty system founded on fairly equal bases[107] and spawned little of the entrepreneurial thrust normally associated with the China trade. These contradictory images of the origins and course of Russian economic imperialism have resulted in inferences of it as a distinctive entity. Mark Mancall, in juxtaposing the Kiakhta and Canton trading systems, observes of early commercial relations at Kiakhta, one of two settlements to which border trade was limited under the terms of the Kiakhta Treaty (1727):

> The Russians did not seek entry into China [through the Kiakhta System]...nor to force concepts of free trade on the Chinese, concepts the Russians themselves held, at best, only weakly; the Chinese, in turn, did not insist on the all-importance of Chinese customary forms of this intercourse, as they did in Canton.[108]

To this image of harmony might be added that of Rosemary Quested's 'Matey' Russian imperialist as a phenomenon quite separate from his more imperious counterparts:

> It may be hypothesised that, notwithstanding the evidence for increasing racial seclusion after the Russo-Japanese war, the Russians could still thereafter mix better with Asians at certain levels – usually when it was politically or commercially desirable – than other Western imperialists of this period.[109]

The question then is whether Russian imperialism should be interpreted as an innately benign form, and if so is this conclusion entirely compatible with the obvious (and professed) scale and scope of its undertakings in Manchuria? In the end, the peculiarities observed in the Russian presence there may have to be explained not by a search for innate characteristics of the Russians themselves, or their trading relations, but by such factors as the effect of physical distance, absence of a consistent policy and the failure to integrate economic activity sufficiently with political objectives. Rather than 'matey' imperialism, a more suitable epitaph to the Russian phenomenon in Manchuria would be *Bezalabernyi* Imperialism.[110]

While the style of Chinese relations with Russians may be regarded as qualitatively different to that of their relations with other powers, the restrictions on the freedom of Russians to trade outside the immediate zones of advantage were similar to those governing other Western states.[111] Had Russia desired to do anything to improve these trading terms, it is unlikely that it would have had the means to pressure China into improving them.[112] The Russian Empire's Far Eastern limits were strained enough with the problems of securing and developing Siberia and the Maritime Province. The imbalance in China's favour is most graphically demonstrated by attempts at colonisation undertaken by Russia and China of the Russian Far East and Manchuria respectively. In the 300 years of Russian rule in Siberia, the population there had barely reached 15 million by the outbreak of World War I. In Manchuria, on the other hand, the population had increased six-fold in less than 30 years.[113] By the 1920s the results of this were further reinforced: the Russian territory, although able to support its own food production, was almost completely dependent on European Russian for its food supplies, supplemented by Manchurian exports of grain and cattle. Manchuria, on the other hand, was by then producing food for its own needs, plus surpluses (particularly wheat) for export.[114] The link of steel, which was to draw together the Russian Far East with the fertile plains of North-Eastern China into a single productive entity, instead served as a brittle bridge spanning an underdeveloped Siberia.

In Manchuria itself, the factor of distance, both historical and physical, worked against the Russians in that it allowed them, at least initially, the freedom from commercial competition that the treaty ports and China proper would not. Under the sheltering wing of the Ministry of Finance, the pockets of 'Russianness' were allowed to take root, but not long enough to blossom fully. The insularity of the Russian presence is best demonstrated by its response to forays by Western firms into the Manchurian markets in the early 1900s.

When an Anglo-American tobacco firm sent a network of agents into Northern Manchuria with advertising posters and free samples of cigarettes to carry out a sales campaign, they encountered a market still served by large quantities of Russian tobacco products. It was noted that the rival products they encountered were cheap cigarettes with brand names such as *Siren'* and *Kazakh*, which showed no signs of conforming to the tastes or needs of the Chinese market. Also, Russian *Papirosy*, the Russian versions of cigarettes, were seen to have a limited market as the Chinese regarded them as a way of using less tobacco.[115] That the Russian manufacturers and traders of these goods could be so far out of touch with sensitivities of the local marketplace seems to reinforce the view that there was a distinctiveness to

Manchurian society, but at the same time there were strong elements of ethnocentricity present in the Russian outlook from the start in this environment. That they came into sharper focus with the Russo-Japanese War seems to be a function of the shock imparted by the war on the Russians in Manchuria. Their extended claims both to 'Russianness' and their local 'colonial' status served simply to draw them closer together as a community in bringing their pleas to the attention of the Russian government. It was largely an attempt to revive the shelter provided earlier by Witte's 'paternal capitalism'. The war forced the Russian community in Manchuria to retrench, consolidate on the advantage provided by the CER, and begin to think about commerce on a broader, more keenly contested scale.[116] Along with the sense of siege and isolation experienced by the native Russian population came a flood of criticism of local Russian trade, of the gap between European Russian manufacture and the Chinese markets, of the untapped potential that Manchuria represented as a centre of trade.[117]

Witte's vision of a gradual development of Russian commercial interests in Northern Manchuria, taking the line of least resistance in dealing with the Chinese authorities, may have had a chance to take shape, had the Finance Minister's power base not been usurped by the more threatening and belligerent Bezobrazov clique in 1903. To his credit, Witte saw the brittle and fragile nature of Russian economic activity in the region. He saw that progress could only be achieved through 'patient, long-range policy, dependent on a feeling of security for the morrow...'.[118] and that the adoption of the militaristic forms of Western imperialism could only endanger the evolution of an enduring Russian edifice in the Far East. Combined with (and contributing to the success of) the harder political line that replaced Witte's blueprint was the sudden fall in investment provided by Russian heavy industry. After the slump of 1900, industry could no longer supply the funds that flooded eastward in the 1890s. Even if the funds were available for the further development of the Russian Far East, the political opposition to such investment would have been great, if not prohibitive.[119]

In its place was the short-sighted policy of consolidation and rule in the image of a quasi-military outpost. The new policy was disdainful of Chinese fears, Japanese aspirations, and Western commercial jealousies.[120] More importantly, it was oblivious to the inability of a fragile Russian infrastructure in China – created with the long term in mind – to resist the short-term onslaught of anxious neighbours and rivals. Investment in the railway continued to grow steadily, but this became viewed largely in strategic terms. This investment, in spite of its scale, provided little encouragement to Russian commercial flair or the conquering of new markets. A report from an agent of the Ministry of Trade and Industry, commenting on the state of Russian trade in the province of Kirin, observed that Russian goods there were plentiful, but that there was not a single Russian warehouse in the settlement. He also noted that the CER ran a commercial agency there which was open only during the summer months. 'It would be useful', he concluded, 'to open the premises in the remaining months as a repository to Russian trade for samples of our goods, by which Chinese buyers could decide on orders'.[121] By 1914 the CER had become bureaucratised and estranged from the task of spreading Russian commercial influence in Manchuria. Instead it competed (with razor-sharp margins) with the South Manchurian Railway for primacy as a conduit for Manchurian exports.[122] Harbin, rather than being the centre of Russian economic influence and the main distribution point for Russian goods for the whole of China, had become a processing centre for Manchurian raw materials destined for transhipment through Russia itself.[123]

The inability of Russian exporters, local Russian businesses and the railway to work hand-in-hand had led to lost chances and unrealised commercial potential in the areas opened by the railway, where Russia had a clear advantage. It was a state of affairs that forced the Harbin Stock Exchange Committee to publish a plea to the Russian authorities for decisive measures to be taken in support of its trade and traders in Manchuria. The pamphlet registers a sense of isolation and a feeling of desertion felt by the 'native' Russian population of Manchuria. It points out that trade and industry came into being in Manchuria 'at a time when Russia's goals were completely different [and] all forms of enterprise were encouraged by representatives of the Central Government, many of whom had visited the Far East'.[124] In a situation where the Russian share of Northern Manchuria's import market is inexorably slipping, the committee points to Southern Manchuria 'where everything is organised with such calculation that monopolies in all fields of economic activity belong solely to Japanese interests'.[125] This yearning for a return to Witte's priorities of 'trade and industry always in front'[126] disguises slightly the fact that Witte's scheme for extending Russian economic control through Manchuria, and indeed North China down to Peking, always had at its heart expansion via the CER and the Russo-Chinese Bank and not the direct furthering of Russian traders' interests *per se*. This policy had not altered significantly once Witte had lost the reins of effective control of Russian Far Eastern policy. What had developed, and the committee's comments seem to underline this, is the growing divergence in outlook between the CER, the Bank, and Russian commerce and industry in the region.

Once the idyll of the sheltered formative period had been shattered by the Russo-Japanese War, the Russians in Northern Manchuria were forced, mainly by commercial pressures from the south, to take stock of their role in the Far East. Although they continued to see themselves as a Russian colony, it became increasingly clear that their success would depend on individual commercial initiative rather than as the favoured charges of Russian policy in North-Eastern China. Given the wide range of enterprise and trade that the Russians explored,[127] it might have been concluded that there seemed to be no shortage of such initiative or an eagerness to prosper. Why this corpus of entrepreneurship did not take root may be explained by the unwillingness of the Russian authorities to shift their focus sufficiently from the CER to small-scale commercial presence as a basis for the spread of Russian economic influence. In spite of the triumph of Bezobrazov's crude form of economic imperialism over Witte's 'gradualism' as the basis for Russia's Far Eastern policy, a distorted form of Witte's dictum of 'railway and bank first' remained at the core of the scheme of development for Northern Manchuria.

The imbalance in this policy came into sharpest relief in two main areas: the chronic shortage of capital that plagued Russian businesses in the region, and the failure of European Russian manufacture to make sufficient inroads into internal markets there. Both created grave, and ultimately insurmountable, weaknesses in Russia's economic hold on Northern Manchuria. The paucity of capital was the result of the Russian authorities' inability to see past the strictures of a rigid finance structure (which placed emphasis on CER/Bank-generated enterprise) to the cultivation of a more broadly based network of credit institutions. This situation was not eased by foreign banks operating from Harbin, whose attitude to Russian business – in anything other than soya bean exports – was at best cautious. In the case of the HSBC, which became the most powerful of the banks through its early involvement in the bean trade,[128] substantial borrowing was made extremely difficult for almost all Russian businessmen. For many of the larger Russian business houses, their unavoidable financial entanglements with the CER became increasingly a liability. The railway would often deal in pronotes with these companies, which in turn attempted to use them as security with banks. The banks' attitude to such forms of guarantee, particularly after the 1917 Revolution, grew more cynical: 'These [pronotes] are only paid at due date when there is any cash in the till, which is akin to when the moon turns green'.[129]

For smaller Russian firms wishing to deal in goods in the interior, the chronic lack of funds meant that their operations had to be run on a shoestring, with very little room for miscalculation. The traders' position in this respect was not helped by the tangle of customs duties, agency administrative charges, and differences in forms of payment that were involved in moving goods inland. In Kirin province after 1908, for example, the duty on vodka was silver-based, while that on tobacco remained in local bronze currency.[130] More perplexing still was the fact that duties in Manchuria as a whole had the habit of appearing in sudden, quite unexpected ways.[131] If these extra costs were not provided for, or could not be met, the shipments would be confiscated, thus tying up stock and capital. Besides the straightforward scheme of duties (there were over 120 main categories by 1922[132]), the conduct of trade was made more difficult still by the cost of indeterminate obligations of provincial governments to the central government in China and the random imposition of 'military taxes' by local military authorities.[133] To this must be added the difficulties experienced by traders in securing a steady flow of suitable merchandise from sources in Russia, which were largely indifferent to trade in Northeastern China. This was an area in which the Russian authorities could have done more but failed to intervene. Furthermore, there was little encouragement by the Russian authorities of its own industries and traders to adopt more aggressive methods in defending existing, or developing new, markets in the region. In 1913 Russian exports of kerosene to Manchuria fell dramatically after a major Russian exporter had reached an agreement with the Asiatic Petroleum Co. not to compete with Standard Oil in South Manchuria. Not only did this cause a fall in the total Russian export of kerosene, but, as a government agent for trade put it: 'This hasn't prevented American kerosene from making greater and greater inroads into the Northern Manchurian market'.[134]

By World War I Russia's share of exports to China stood at a meagre 3.8 per cent of the total, compared with 3.48 per cent in 1910. After a brief rise to 4.8 per cent, with the Russian Revolution the figure fell below 1 per cent.[135] Even in Manchuria itself, Russia's share of the import market continued to rise only in value; its overall share had, as early as 1912, fallen to 17 per cent.[136] So serious were the problems of solvency (and the predicament of Russian imports) that the few years before the Russian Revolution were littered with pleas to the central authorities in Russia on behalf of Russian business in North-Eastern China, and notably Northern Manchuria. The Stock Exchange Committee of Harbin, for example, in their petition suggested five measures to bolster Russian business in the region. All five points concerned the creation of credit institutions.[137] The pleas went unheeded, and Russian interests were left at the mercy of foreign capital to conduct business on the brink. Funds, when they could be found, came in the form of short-term loans at prohibitively high interest rates.[138]

The contradictory characteristics in the relationship between Russia and its Manchurian 'colony' stood in direct contrast to Japanese policy in Southern Manchuria. There, investment was matched by a balanced combination of encouragement of, and shelter for, enterprise and entrepreneurial thrust, backed by a well-organised banking system and home industry. This combination, by contrast, was particularly potent in its ability to seize opportunities in markets and the purchase of troubled foreign enterprises. Gerasimov gives a vivid example of how the Japanese were able to employ 'roving capital' to its fullest effect. The Shcherbin Distillery at An'da Station was subjected to an unexpected military tax of 10 000 Tsitsihar Dollars. The owner and his partner could not raise the money and were consequently imprisoned. They had no choice but to sell the enterprise to Japanese interests at a substantial loss.[139]

To have expected a similar pattern of penetration and consolidation from Russian policy is, perhaps, unrealistic. The Russian trade policy in Manchuria conformed closely to the country's general attitude toward trade. Before 1914, the Russian government involved itself little in trade, and foreign commerce was conducted according to principles of private trade, with the state simply concluding trade arrangements and operating customs duties. It was not until after that year that the state involved itself actively in the country's foreign trade, while the first attempts at foreign trade planning, organised large-scale stockpiling for exports and purchase of imports came only with the revolution of February 1917 and the establishment of the Provisional Government.[140]

The revolution brought virtually a complete collapse of trade figures. Hardest hit, in this respect, was the steady evolution of Vladivostok as a conduit for Manchurian exports. Before World War I nearly 80 per cent of exports were via Vladivostok and the Russian land frontier at Manchuria Station (Manchuli). By 1920 its position had been taken by Dairen, which was handling 80 per cent of exports and had tightened its grip further on imports.[141] Siberia, which had been dependent on food supplies from Manchuria, became more so. Demand for grain frequently sent this commodity rocketing in price.[142] The black market, which had quickly re-established itself after the closure of the 50-verst duty-free zone in January 1913,[143] developed momentum as the Russian side of the border drifted into a chaotic state. There was also an economic counter-penetration of Russian territory. This culminated in the extension of foreign capital into the Siberian and Maritime regions: the intervention in 1918 was an ideal time to consolidate financial services for exporters in Vladivostok itself. The potential that the HSBC, for example, saw in the port was evident as late as October 1924, when a Bank official wrote: 'Everything seems to point towards Vladivostok becoming the commercially important port foreseen by its original founders. The great drawback is the uncertainty of the political situation'.[144] The HSBC operation in Vladivostok was to endure well into the Soviet era.[145] With the sharp rise of the Manchurian bean trade, the importance of keeping lines of finance and communication open between Manchurian trade and Vladivostok became a matter of semi-official policy on the part of the Soviet government.[146]

# 2
# The Soviet Union, Northern Manchuria and the Civil War: Aspects of Interplay and Separation

Vital to an understanding of the fortunes of Russians in Northern Manchuria in the period in question are the effects on it of the Revolutions of 1917, which effectively cut the Russian community in Manchuria from the country as a whole and created a sizeable diaspora in the course of that year. However, as Rosemary Quested and other scholars of the region have noted,[1] the Manchurian Russians' contribution to the history of the Revolution is a marginal one; a 'Russian revolution in miniature'.[2] Far more important to an assessment of the Manchurian Russians' role in the region, and indeed their lasting contribution to the geopolitics of Northeast Asia, is their part in the subsequent Civil War, and notably in Siberia and the Russian Far East; a role, arguably, which has been underplayed because of the relative non-event that the Russian Revolution itself represented in the region.[3]

The Civil War in Siberia and the Russian Far East is itself a complex subject that has been looked at in surprisingly straightforward ways. There are the classic studies, dealing with the rudiments of the War.[4] There are also more recent accounts, which have gone some of the way in exploring a few of the more intriguing aspects of the conflict.[5]

This is a curious state of affairs. The turning around of the situation in Siberia was vital to the success of the Bolshevik revolution. It was also the most complex of political, social and economic environments for the end game of the revolution to be played out in. Between 1896 and 1914, over four million settlers had flooded into Siberia, helping to make it one of Russia's more important agricultural regions.[6] Sown areas there rose by 122 per cent in the 20 years before the Revolution, with three-quarters of the annual harvest being marketed. Trade in furs, wool and meat, together with growth in metallurgical, service and food processing industries, added to Siberia's economic status.[7] Population in the larger towns (Tomsk, Irkutsk, Omsk, Vladivostok, Chita and Novonikolaevsk [now Novosibirsk]) grew by between 100 and 800 per cent in the same period.[8] Despite the rapid growth in urban population, however, the region remained predominantly rural (estimates suggest that the latter made up between 97.2 and 97.5 per cent of the population). This economic and social mix was reflected, understandably, in the politics of the region. Aside from the strong undercurrent of separatism that existed,[9] and continued to do so throughout the Revolution and Civil War, the mainstream Russian political parties presented in Siberia/Russian Far East found their work there hard going. The Socialist Revolutionaries (SRs) and Kadets were by far the most popular of the Russian political parties, with the Bolsheviks well behind (in the elections to the Constituent Assembly in November 1917 the Bolsheviks gained only 10 per cent of the votes[10]). And yet even the more popular parties were highly vulnerable in Siberia. The SRs' proposals for socialisation did not conform with the aspirations of the Siberian peasantry, while the Kadets' opposition to regional autonomy did little to raise their own standing.[11] Channon observes that '...a small working class, few really poor peasants, very few large landowners and a small intelligentsia...' was hardly a sturdy power base for the Bolsheviks in 1917.[12] He is quite right. However, one could go further by suggesting that it was difficult political terrain for other political groupings too, and this was well demonstrated in the course of the Civil War, when the shifts of power and allegiance were labyrinthine in character.

This alone should have provided scholars with ample reason to further explore the subject. Instead, we face the curious situation of not being able to accurately say how many separate governments and administrations there were in the region after the collapse of Bolshevik control in the summer of 1918,[13] let alone fathom the intricate web of relations that emerged between them and the other interested parties in the conflict. Tackling the subject is made no easier by the bulk of work on the Civil War in Siberia having come from Soviet scholars, who look at politico-economic questions in isolation from the military campaigns.[14] Nor, for that matter, by the difference in opinion as to how we are to conceptualise the region itself.[15]

The result of these factors is a framework that is, more often than not, made up of some clear dates or landmarks, but with little that would guide us to an appreciation of the full canvas of the war in the East, or the magnitude of its long-term effects there.

Even work such as Channon's, illuminating as it is, falls remarkably comfortably into the periodization and form which have characterised the study of the Siberian conflict for over 60 years. He discusses the rapid collapse of Bolshevik power in the major cities (and, by extension, in the countryside, where support for the Bolsheviks was weak to begin with) by the midsummer of 1918, the landing of Japanese troops in Vladivostok a few months earlier, the revolt of the Czech legion in May 1918, the formation of the Provisional Siberian Government (PSG) at Omsk in June–July, the

Ufa Conference in September and the last attempt to form an all-Russian anti-Bolshevik authority from below. According to such an interpretation, the PSG soon failed, as did the Directory. In their place, a military dictatorship under Kolchak takes control. In early 1919, the White forces were in a dominant position, with between 200 000 and 300 000 men; by the summer and autumn of the same year, however, the Bolsheviks began to secure victories. The reasons usually given for the dramatic reversal of fortune? Kolchak's seizure of power had done nothing to change the nature of government in Siberia, as it was already, in essence, a military dictatorship. Kolchak himself was hated by the left, had no support from the Bashkir minority, or the Orenburg and Ural Cossacks. And while his lines of supply were steadily choked, red partisans began to amass their forces (100 000 by the autumn of 1919). In November 1919 Omsk fell, and in March 1920 the Red Army had reached Irkustk and had effectively gained control of all central Siberia to Lake Baikal. By that time Kolchak had been handed over to the Bolsheviks, tried and executed.[16]

Bolshevism, however, required two and a half years after Kolchak's death to gain full ascendancy in Siberia. The Far Eastern Republic (FER) – established in 1920 – nominally controlled territory from Lake Baikal to the Pacific for that period. In addition, the troublesome Ataman Semenov and his forces (operating from Chita) and the infamous Baron R.F. Ungern-Sternberg (based in Urga [later Ulan-Bator]) continued to take the battle to the Bolsheviks, being silenced only in late 1920 and early 1921 respectively.[17] For the next 18 months, the Russian Far East remained the site for confrontation between White survivors, the FER and the Japanese garrison. In early 1922, there was the last gasp effort from General Diterikhs, followed by the recapture of Khabarovsk by the FER. In October 1922, the Japanese garrison departed, remaining Whites fled into Manchuria and Korea and Soviet forces entered Vladivostok. In November, the FER was absorbed by the Russian Soviet Federative Socialist Republic. At this point, as Channon concludes: 'The Civil War was for all intents and purposes over; Soviet power was now established from the Urals to the Pacific, and the whole of Siberia once more reverted to the centralised control of Moscow'.[18]

What is depicted in such studies, therefore, is the ebb and flow of power; quite regular in character, and essentially a contest between Red and White. When regional variations have to be taken into account, it is generally in the context of whether the leaders/military chiefs are co-operative or unco-operative with the 'central' authorities. Thus, General Khorvat, the first manager of the CER and a self-styled autocrat of the Russian railway zone in Northern Manchuria (three years of pressure from Moscow were required to dislodge him from his position with the CER),[19] is generally seen as a military leader who remained on the periphery of the war, providing little more than nuisance value to either the Red or White forces.

Atamans Semenov, Annenkov, Dutov, Kalmykov and the Baron Ungern-Sternberg too, although they play a key role in perpetuating the Civil War in the Far Eastern Region, are generally drawn as marginal characters.[20] The conventional view of their contribution to the history of the civil war is one of military remnants of the main conflict, who would be mopped up in Manchuria and the other areas of Asia and the Russian Far East they operated from once consolidation of power in European Russia had been achieved.[21]

In piecing together a revised view of the Civil War in Siberia, and its effect on the politics of Northern Manchuria, one of the more important steps is, indeed, to re-evaluate the place of these 'fringe' elements on the greater canvas.

Khorvat, with his be-uniformed Tsarist General's appearance and grand, bushy beard and moustache, could quite easily be seen as a quixotic personality, and his ambitions of becoming the supreme ruler of Russia from a seat of power in Vladivostok a whim of the deluded.[22] Even his long hold on power in Manchuria can be explained away in terms of China's wish to play the 'railway card' in dealing with the nascent Bolshevik government.

A similar portrait of eccentricity, although somewhat more sinister in character, can be produced for von Ungern-Sternberg, with the phantasmagorical political programme he produced for a Russo-Asiatic state (taking in parts of Siberia, Mongolia and China) perhaps being regarded as the effect of exile on the desolate Mongolian plains.

Such a view might be appropriate if the influence they generated was of an illusory nature too. This is difficult to establish. In the case of General Khorvat, even after he was forced out of his role in Manchuria and took on the seemingly sedentary function of the titular headship of the Russian emigration at Peking, his influence was apparently considerable. Correspondence as late as 1929 recounts how Khorvat was enjoying 'great success and trust' during his visit to the United States in the wake of the Soviet action in Manchuria a few months earlier. 'He will', the writer says, 'be given strong help in the struggle'.[23] With von Ungern-Sternberg, the Red Army experienced considerable difficulties in dealing with his forces and his flexible, often improvised methods.[24] This led to the hardening of territorial delimitations in Mongolia, and the formalisation of these in the guise of the Soviet Outer Mongolian Republic (thereby helping to neutralise a potentially troublesome launching-point for anti-Soviet forces).[25]

A more difficult question still was what was to be done with the Ataman Semenov, who in the period 1918 to 1921 launched a number of attacks on the Red Army. The earliest of his actions were, indeed, from a combination of locations: near the Mongolian border, from Manchuria and Zabaikal.[26] His movements into and out of the Russian Far East became a torment for the Red Army Command, and especially so given his enduring relationship with Japanese interventionist forces.[27] The spectre of his presence in the Russian

Far East was made all the more worrisome for Soviet strategists because after Kolchak's execution, Semenov commanded – at least nominally – 12 divisions in a variety of locations throughout the Far East.[28]

Collectively, Atamans Semenov, Dutov, Kalmykov, Annenkov, together with von Ungern-Sternberg and General Khorvat, represented the full chimerical nature of the Russian Far East, together with its relationship with Northern Manchuria, in the period of the Civil War. Despite the relatively small forces at their disposal,[29] this group's military campaigns were tenacious and frequently bitter affairs. Moreover, the creative use of regional politics and borders by these military leaders, as well as their intimate understanding of local conditions, made their excoriation a most difficult task.[30] Their activities in the Far East were, arguably, instrumental in shaping a number of key aspects of Soviet policy in the Siberian/Soviet Far Eastern regions for decades to come. Contributing to the formulation of this policy was the mystique – to the point of becoming an element of folklore – that grew around these actors in the course of the conflict. This aura developed through their military exploits, the often embellished stories these, and, in many cases, the atrocities committed by their divisions in the name of Monarchy, 'God and Gospel'.[31] The notoriety of these fringe actors, together with the iron discipline practised by them,[32] even achieved something of a celebrity status for them. In the case of von Ungern-Sternberg, for example, to this day a perverse reverence is expressed with regard to those who had seen or met with the notorious Baron.[33]

These Far Eastern fringe actors for the most part remained quite aloof from the White commands in the Siberian hinterland. Semenov, being a prominent case in point, maintained an independent stance for much of the time that Kolchak sought to consolidate the Siberian area. (It was only a few weeks before his handover and execution that Kolchak, finally, named Semenov as the overall commander of White Siberia[34].) What this in effect meant was that the Red Army Command had to pursue at least two distinct lines of policy in order to secure Siberia and the Russian Far East: on the one hand, it had to dispose of the major opponents such as Kolchak who, at least symbolically, occupied centre stage in Siberia, and, on the other, conduct a most complex initiative that emerged as a running conflict not dissimilar to a guerilla war in the Far East. In the latter case, the Bolsheviks' opponents would seek, and secure, sanctuary either under the sheltering wing of foreign occupation forces (as in the case of Semenov and the Japanese interventionist troops) or in adjoining states such as China, where they could regroup and plan fresh incursions. To this end, communications and intelligence that the major leaders of this military fringe had at their disposal were, given the very difficult terrain that they covered, remarkably good.[35] Furthermore, as many of them were quite young,[36] and in the case of Semenov and von Ungern-Sternberg well-financed,[37] there was also the prospect of their pernicious activities continuing for some years to come.[38] The nature of these awkward pockets of opposition, combined with the Soviet Union's own uncertain grip on its Eastern perimeter, resulted in greater attention being devoted to the region and the threats posed to the security of the long, and seemingly highly permeable, border.[39]

The pressures resulting from this complex political situation were revealed in a variety of ways, but most notably in the military context. A variety of approaches were adopted to secure what was, in essence, a nightmare to defend. The Soviet Union's difficulties in managing the disparate aspects of the conflict were reflected in the creation, merger and restructuring of military commands in the course of the years 1918–21.[40] Finally, in June 1924 we see the emergence of the Siberian Military District (SMD); the largest military district to be formed in the Soviet Union, and the earliest appearance of a full theatre command in the most extensive geographic context (taking in both Siberia and the Soviet Far East).[41]

Such an unwieldy organisational device was logical only from the perspective of a need to provide the semblance of homogeneous military authority across territories which had in the course of the Civil War demonstrated tendencies to autarchic behaviour and shown themselves to be vulnerable to encroachment. This overarching military command might be seen, in other words, as an attempt to bring borderlands under control in the face of the seemingly ever-present danger of White forces gathering in neighbouring foreign territories and using these as a springboard to wrest portions of the periphery from Bolshevik control.

The problem of consolidated White military action did not materialise, instead being restricted to stubborn, strenuous political agitation in major centres such as Harbin (in Northern Manchuria) and accentuated by the occasional confluence of this with anti-Bolshevik activity initiated by the Chinese authorities themselves, as in the raids on the Soviet Embassy in Peking in 1927 and consulate in Harbin in 1929.[42] However, the concerns regarding the danger that the White fringe actors posed were apparent in senior Soviet officials' thinking on the subject, notably in terms of the numbers involved and their interplay with Japanese interests.[43]

In 1929, the effectiveness of this security structure was tested by another major source of insecurity: the influence of other major players in the Far Eastern region, in this case China. By the summer of that year, Chinese authorities in Northern Manchuria were poised to seize complete control of the CER, which they indeed did in July.[44] The SMD was found to be unsuited to making a military response to this and the Soviet government was forced to dispatch the veteran Bolshevik commander Bliukher, who had already spent a number of years off and on in the Siberian/Far Eastern area, to take charge of a newly formed Special Far Eastern Army, the *Osobaia Dal'nevostochnaia armiia* (*ODVA*) to deal with this crisis.[45]

As will be shown in Chapter 6, Bliukher and the *ODVA* achieved a stunning victory against the forces of the Manchurian warlord Chang Hsüeh-liang, restoring the Soviet Union's share in the control of the CER. Given the disastrous effect that this victory had on the Manchurian economy (together with the Soviet share in it), as well as Japan's own fears for the region's security, one could ask whether the Soviet Union had not over-reacted.[46] If, however, the Soviet response is viewed in the context of the Bolshevik regime's experiences in the Siberian and Russian Far Eastern regions during the Civil War, it becomes somewhat easier to understand.

Broader implications for the Northeast Asian region as a whole flow on from such a re-evaluation of the Civil War. It may be more appropriate to see this period – as opposed to, say, the 1929 Crisis or, for that matter, the 1931 Mukden Incident and the creation of Manchukuo – as the true point at which the various regional actors were set on the collision course that was to become so apparent in the 1930s. After a brief flirtation with revolutionary idealism, China's relations with the Bolshevik government, for example, cooled remarkably quickly. To a great extent this must be seen in the context of Bolshevik fears for the Russian Far East at the early stages of the Civil War; notably through the frustration generated by Khorvat *et al*.[47] The repeated venting of such frustration was, understandably, regarded by the Chinese authorities as an affront to China's sovereignty, and brought into question the Soviet Union's own attitude to its neighbour.

On another front, of course, was Japan. While it adopted a curiously reticent role in Eastern Siberia during the Intervention (its forces not moving to the front lines in support of Kolchak, for example), Japan nonetheless contributed to the Bolsheviks' understanding of the meaning of the triangular relationship between Russia, China and Japan in Northeast Asia, and the Russian Far East's part in it.[48] Moreover, for the Japanese militarists, the lessons regarding their own interests in Northeast China were there too. Given the bewildering character of politics the Japanese military experienced in the Russian Far East, it is perhaps not altogether surprising that they should have wished to tighten their grip on the situation in Manchuria soon after the Bolsheviks had shown that they were victorious in the Siberian and Far Eastern theatres of the Civil War. One of the ways of doing so was to provide encouragement and support to Russian *émigré* political and paramilitary organisations in the region.

The attention that the Bolshevik centre devoted to the Siberian/Russian Far Eastern areas, and *émigré* activity in contiguous territories, translated into a heightened concern for regional security. The earlier-mentioned creation of a Soviet Outer Mongolian Republic to counter destabilisation in that area is one such example. Such territorial concerns increased the Bolshevik central leadership's already considerable suspicion of the motives of neighbouring states. Stalin, for example, remained most uneasy, if not obsessive, about Japanese activities in the region;[49] an attitude largely shaped by the Japanese part in the Civil War in Siberia and the Russian Far East. Thus, when the Japanese Kwantung Army 'privately' took control of

Manchuria in the wake of the Mukden Incident of 1931 (itself to a great extent precipitated by the routing of Chinese forces by the *ODVA* during the Sino-Soviet Conflict two years earlier), the Soviet Government reacted firmly. Between 1931 and 1935 the Soviet Union virtually tripled its ground strength (with corresponding increases in air and naval forces) in the areas bordering the new puppet state of Manchukuo and the Mongolian People's Republic.[50] This increase contributed steadily to the build-up of tension between the Soviet Union and Japan, finally resulting in a number of cross-border incidents in 1938–39 and the steady slide of the Far East into the broader international conflict.

In the early 1920s, these foreign policy considerations were in their formative stages. The Soviet Union's general preoccupations were to initially show themselves in two broad policy lines. The first, and arguably most important, of these was the need to lead a 'divide and rule' policy in China. In effect, this meant maintaining the division between Manchuria and the rest of China, thereby, finally, providing support for two seemingly antagonistic groups in China's body politic: younger, progressive elements in China's southern provinces, and the older, more reactionary, warlord cliques in Manchuria.[51] The methods employed by the Soviet Union in pursuing this dual line were successful, indeed ultimately possibly too much so.[52] The second involved the concentration on developing Soviet strengths in Manchuria itself, namely the railway and the local Russian-led economy. Success in this latter respect would help to further buffer the Soviet border regions and, simultaneously, allow the undermining of *émigré* status, and power, in Manchuria.

But if the role of the fringe White military leaders was to focus the Bolshevik government's foreign policy and to give body to its view of the disparate elements of the complex politics of the Far East, the effect was, understandably, quite marked on the Asian side of the border too. Nowhere was this crystallisation of policy more evident than in Soviet attitudes towards the Mongolian and Manchurian borders and administrative questions within the CER Zone. The Karakhan Declarations of 1919[53] had, in the spirit of Bolshevik internationalism, put forward policy lines which suggested a new era of political openness and egalitarianism for Sino-Russian relations and the region as a whole. Less than two years later, these pronouncements had transformed into preoccupations with border questions and the forceful retrieval of Russian rights in the CER Zone. By 1924, the latter had begun to assume an image of power politics all too familiar to China in the course of its modern relations with the Great Powers. For Japan, the new politics suggested a counterthrust that was to begin to encroach upon its own spheres of influence in the region. As this counterthrust was a combination of power politics and a sustained, and uncomfortably vigorous, ideological campaign, the effects of the new Soviet outlook posed a threat not only to Japanese interests on continental Northeast Asia, but to its own national heartland.[54]

# 3
# Liberation and Exile: the Paradox of Russians in Manchuria and China

One of the most significant factors deriving from the collapse of Tsarism concerned the legal status of Russians living on Chinese territory. Until the revolution of February 1917, Russians had, along with other foreigners in China, enjoyed the advantages of extraterritoriality.[1] However, with the overthrow of the Tsar, and until the Sino-Soviet Treaty of 1924 finally clarified the situation, there was, at least as far as the Chinese authorities were concerned, no legally constituted government in Russia which could be held responsible for its nationals, '...[hence] the Chinese had to adopt a novel scheme of administration of the Russian population in China at large and principally in the Chinese Eastern Railway Zone'.[2] In connection with judicial procedure in the CER Zone, for instance, the Chinese authorities ruled that while the legal process was to transfer to Chinese control, Russian advisers (most appointed from the ranks of retired judges, public prosecutors and lawyers) would be allowed to help in legal questions involving Russians, but that these professionals would not be permitted to participate in the court sessions themselves.[3] Furthermore, the Chinese authorities continued to recognise the Tsarist representative at Peking, who continued to represent Russian interests even after the October Revolution had taken place, and this despite two telegrams from Trotsky demanding his immediate recall.[4] Even after Soviet Russia and China had arrived at an accord, the Russians who were forced, or chose, to remain stateless were subject to Chinese law, and therefore outside the purview the Soviet Union's authority.[5] Ironically, the Soviet Union made the situation more difficult for itself through the distinct evolution of the ethics in its foreign policy. In the early, chaotic period of its relations with the outside world, the Bolshevik government had reserved the right to intervene beyond its borders, as is so graphically shown in Lenin's justification of his country's war against Poland in 1920:

> Wars of defence [and]...wars of conquest [are]...words which lost their meaning long ago, words of petit bourgeois pacifism.... We would be

not only fools but even criminals if we promised never to commit acts which could be considered aggressive in a military-strategic sense.[6]

With the rise of Stalin, and the beginnings of a preoccupation with maintaining rather than defining the Soviet Union's borders, the class analysis in international relations was to be reinterpreted into a less pointed form. In his *Marxism and the National and Colonial Question*, Stalin expressed this in a typically revisionist fashion. 'Only the people themselves', he stated unambiguously, 'have the right to determine their fate; *nobody may interfere forcefully in the life of a people....* The nation is sovereign and all nations are equal'.[7] Typically, such a sweeping restatement of socialist ethics led not only to a characteristic ring of hypocrisy (the Soviet Union, at the time of the restatement – that is in the early 1920s – was seeking to regain the markedly unequal rights that Tsarist Russia had enjoyed in Northern Manchuria before 1917), but also, and equally typically, it made the lives of Soviet operatives in China very difficult indeed, as the memoir of one young, idealistic representative of the new Soviet regime then residing in China makes clear.[8]

George F. Kennan summed up the inherent difficulties in the area of Far Eastern diplomacy by saying that 'the entire vocabulary of Western politics and historiography is inadequate as a means of understanding and describing the political realities of the Orient'.[9] Soviet policy in China and Northern Manchuria at first attempted to cut through this Gordian Knot by employing an often contradictory combination of Socialist morality and power politics, and subsequently became entangled in it through the adoption of *realpolitik*. This transition, and entanglement, serves as a backdrop to the unfolding of Russian politics in the period 1924–31.

In a letter to Canadian Immigration officials in the early 1920s, F.J. McLure, a passenger manager of the Robert Reford Shipping Company, branded the swarms of refugees entering Manchuria as being a 'useless ex-officer class, composed of men who either did not know how to work or do not want to work'.[10] His acerbic comment on the nature of Russians crossing the border was not untypical of the attitudes expressed by the foreign residents of Harbin, many of them in positions of authority and influence in countries which might have served as destinations for the Russian refugees.[11] Such comments often resulted from impressionistic encounters with the bustling nature of Harbin street life, where new arrivals would appear as if from nowhere, often with no money or contacts and little idea of what they might apply themselves to in this strange Russian town in the middle of nowhere.[12] A number of these arrivals were of an ex-officer class, and some, indeed, had to live by their wits.[13] However, many more were reputable petty bourgeois, workers and peasants,[14] but who came to be tarred with the same brush, thereby at times resulting in impossible barriers being placed in their way when applying to emigrate to new homes in countries such as Canada and Australia.[15] The majority of over 30 000 refugees who crowded into Manchuria in the course of the post-revolutionary period were peasants,[16] many having begun their treks from their abandoned lives as wheat farmers in the Volga region and Western Siberia; others came from Eastern Siberia '…crossing the River Argun, driving their cattle ahead of them'.[17] Many of the peasant families, once they had entered Manchuria, remained in the vicinity of the border, establishing small, homogeneous farming settlements on the fertile plains of northernmost Manchuria.[18] Despite the numerous obstacles that stood in their paths in re-establishing their lives and livelihood, notably from the punitive taxation regime imposed upon them by the local authorities,[19] within a relatively short time they were, at the very least, able to eke out a living. Other peasant families penetrated somewhat farther inland, establishing a settlement which came to be known as *Trekhrech'e* (Three Rivers). There, the soil was found to be much like the Black Earth region in European Russia and, therefore, highly suitable for the creation of agricultural enterprises. By the early 1920s, this community was a thriving centre of Russian life in the region, and highly respected for the quality of its dairy herds.[20] Many of those who settled in this area were the *Starovery* (Old Believers), for whom this had been the second period of resettlement (the first having been after the Great Schism in the mid-seventeenth century, when families had moved from European Russia in order to continue to practice their branch of the Orthodox faith and morally rigid lifestyle).[21]

Deeper in the Northern Manchurian hinterland were scattered further small, isolated settlements of the *Starovery*; their local village economies somewhat different to the larger settlements discussed above, but the social characteristics and, above all, moral strictures the same. One such village was *Ozero* (Lake), so named because it was on the shore of a lake – also known simply as *Ozero* by the villagers – on the Manchurian Taiga.[22] It was made up of a small cluster of families, each of them with a large number of children.[23] The chief occupation (and in fact the *only* occupation) in the *Ozero* was trapping. The men of the village would capture and sell tigers to zoos. The village was self-sufficient in all forms of food, with the exception of flour, which, together with a few other supplies and luxuries, of which there were very few, had to be brought in across the frozen lake during the winter months. As with some of the remoter villages such as *Ozero*, the settlement did not encounter any Chinese until after 1949, when the new Communist authorities began to send native and Korean settlers to racially 'dilute' it.[24] Education in the settlement consisted of a single teacher who would spend the winter months in *Ozero* and the summer in another distant village. Children who required broader, more specialised, education (of whom there were very few) would have to move to the major settlements on the railway. Medicine was, likewise, restricted to very basic forms.[25] Villages that were less isolated had greater commercial activity, with fur-trapping augmenting their otherwise self-contained economies.

Although farming-related activities accounted for a considerable number of refugees' futures, a proportion of those who found themselves in Northern Manchuria were absorbed by commercial activities located in and around the other major settlements of Hailar and Tsitsihar. As early as 1909, Russian economists in Harbin had remarked upon the poorly developed state of the Chinese timber industry in Manchuria. One such report concluded that '[t]here are no Chinese timber specialists [in Manchuria], the industry being managed by ordinary bureaucrats. As they do not have a specialist understanding of the industry, it is impossible to place them in responsible positions [in it]'.[26] Russian business soon found its niche in this industry. By the start of the Russian Revolutions of 1917, the Vorontsov Brothers had already generated a thriving Russian timber business near Hailar. They achieved this in two steps. The first was to conclude an agreement with the local authorities to allow the firm to fell trees to a distance of 1000 kilometres around Hailar. The second was to conclude an agreement with Russian contractors, who had '...quickly formed workers' *artel's* [co-operatives] for felling in the Taiga region and the transport of sleepers and logs to the banks of the river'.[27] The Vorontsovs' monopoly in this industry was relatively short-lived, however, as smaller rival firms sprang up in most of the settlements along the CER. Later, the Skidelskys, one of the most prominent of the commercial/industrial families in Northern Manchuria,[28] joined this area of economic activity too. Many of the Russians seeking refuge in Northern Manchuria found their way into this industry, which was arduous, but well remunerated.[29]

In Hailar there were also wool-washing plants, operated by the CER and She-ki Company, the latter being a private business concern operated by Chinese businessmen. After processing, the wool was exported principally to the United States.[30] These companies were also involved in fur-trading in the Hailar area, with similar operations outside of Tsitsihar. Hunting therefore served as a key activity in the region served by the northwestern line of the CER. As a newspaper published in Harbin depicted it, this industry '...supported the subsistence of an entire army of professional hunters. By the 1930s, the wool and fur trades had absorbed a significant number of immigrants into their respective labour forces'.[31]

In referring to these 'success stories', we must be mindful of the fact that while the numbers of immigrants absorbed by these industries and localities were significant, they represented a figure far short of the requirements of the flow of humanity that came from Russia. Prince Alexander V. Golitzin, the Commissioner of the Russian Red Cross in Harbin, and Captain Robert P. MacGrath, the Executive Secretary of the Russian Refugee Relief Society of America, estimated that some 16000 refugees wished to emigrate at that stage.[32] Of this total number, only 1500 had the necessary money even to be considered for visas to host countries, notably the United States and Canada. 'The remaining 14500,' the report continued, 'had no money'.[33] Their problems were compounded by the fact that a further 170 000 Russian refugees who had fled to Constantinople also wished to emigrate.[34] On top of this were the doubts cast on their character and readiness to work. Both *Russkoe Slovo* (*The Russian Word*) and *Kharbinskoe Vremia* (*The Harbin Times*) warned against '...a haphazard type of recruitment, insisting that refugees should be organised into small associations...'. Only those who agreed to such a scheme, and 'showed reliability and loyalty...[should] be permitted to emigrate'.[35] As a consequence, by 1926 Canada had allowed entry to fewer than 1000 Russian refugees from Manchuria.[36] The United States and Australia were similarly cautious in their willingness to accept the Manchurian Russians.[37]

And what of the thousands of others? It is here that we learn of the 'wandering Russian'; the rootless, stateless refugee who suffers the privations of his or her status, and who seeks shelter in one or other of the international settlements dotting the Chinese coast. While their numbers were relatively small,[38] with most of the *émigrés* preferring to remain within the confines of more parochial areas in Manchuria or in conditions of chronic unemployment in Harbin itself,[39] their role was one of heightening tensions in China proper in a measure far outweighing their numerical presence.[40] Some, looking for employment, and sometimes fortune, were individuals who would seek work as members of the Volunteer Corps in Shanghai,[41] or, on occasion, transforming themselves from 'rootless cosmopolitans' who had forsaken the land of their birth to ones who, ironically, came finally to work for it.[42]

Others still plumped for a less politically ambiguous role. Rather than becoming soldiers of fortune, they committed themselves to political causes that would, at least indirectly, wound the country from which they had fled. These 'White Guardists', as they came to be known, were regarded by Soviet officials as mercenary bands roaming the Chinese countryside. As one such official recalled in her memoir, these groups were eagerly assimilated by Chinese generals, although life was not easy for them in these armies:

> Chang Tsung-ch'ang was especially willing to take Russian White Guards into his service but the life they led was not a delight. According to the Chinese militarist tradition they were not to paid their salary for months at a time. People gave way to despair and committed suicide. The recruiters kept on supplying new mercenaries, employing deceitful practises to attract even adolescents.[43]

*Émigré* sources, on the other hand, frequently attributed to these men a dedication and courage of partisans waging planned, clandestine operations (both on Chinese and Russian territory) against the Soviet Union.[44]

The role of the *émigrés* in these and other efforts to subvert and embarrass the Bolshevik government in Moscow found form not only in military affairs, but also in less direct forms of aid, provided to elements in China which sought to discredit Soviet involvement in that country's political affairs. The most sensational of these was their contribution to the orchestrated raids on Soviet consulates in Canton and Peking in 1927;[45] raids which resulted in the ignominious withdrawal of the Soviet advisers from China. The raid on the Soviet Consulate in Peking, instigated by the Manchurian warlord Chang Tso-lin, occurred on 6 April 1927. Following this action, the Peking Commission, which investigated the papers allegedly seized on the Soviet Consulate's premises, released for publication sections of a document entitled *Instructions to the Soviet Military Attaché*, which included the following directives:

2) It is imperative that there be organised anti-European riots on territory occupied by Chang Tso-lin's forces.
3) It is imperative that Chang Tso-lin be discredited and that he be represented as a hireling of the international capitalist and imperialist... [document burned at this point] an obstacle to the Kuomintang in its efforts to free China from [economic] dependency.[46]

Almost three weeks after the raid, Randall Gould, a staff correspondent for the news agency United Press, issued a dispatch in which he claimed that 'The White Russians... had manufactured the[se] documents, even to the point of carefully burning their edges with matches'.[47] Moreover, On 6 May 1927 the official Soviet mouthpiece *Pravda* published more specific accusations against the *émigrés*, charging that '...Russian White-Guardists were experts at making counterfeit anti-Soviet documents', and made reference to their 'close collaboration' with the Ankuochün[48] as proof of how the forged documents could have been smuggled onto consulate property.[49] To complicate matters further, evidence also came to light which suggested that these captured documents, which received such wide publicity in Western press in China, may, in fact, have been genuine after all; the implication thereby being that the *émigrés* had been used as a scapegoat to direct the international community's attention away from Soviet policy in China.[50]

While the intricacies of such conjectures may be pursued *ad infinitum*, there are two main conclusions that can be derived from this episode, which signalled the start of the rapid eclipse of Soviet influence, and indeed presence, in China proper. The first is that it is in some respects immaterial whether *émigrés* were actually involved in the falsification of Soviet documents, so long as there existed reasonable grounds as to why they should be *perceived* to have been engaged in this activity; a perception that thereby dragged them irretrievably into the labyrinthine politics of China in the late 1920s. The other is that it elevated their actions to the uppermost level of political activity in China and Manchuria; a role that, even if it was not reflected in fact, nonetheless gave them an image of being a force to be reckoned with. In the case of the Soviet Union's attitude towards the *émigré* community in China, the events in 1927 had the effect of strongly reinforcing the fears that had emerged in the course of the civil war (discussed in Chapter 2), adding to the existing concerns of localised destabilisation in the Russian Far East the spectre of a growing *national* political influence in China and Manchuria as a whole. Grounds were thereby created for a redoubling of efforts on the part of the Soviet Union to eradicate this political scourge; opportunity for which – at least in the Manchurian theatre – was to appear two years later. In the meantime, attention was, understandably, drawn to the further undermining of the economic and political position of the Russian *émigrés* in their principal sanctuary of Harbin.

In terms of the broader context of Sino-Soviet relations, however, the issue of the materials supposedly found on the premises of the Soviet Consulates is of interest to explore. As suggested earlier, the raid on the Peking mission marked a dramatic slip in Soviet fortunes in China. This downturn was, above all, an indication to observers of the Chinese situation that the Soviet influence on Chinese affairs was at last on the wane. Chang Tso-lin's intervention in Peking was associated with summary justice for many Chinese nationals who had collaborated with Soviet citizens there.[51] But the Manchurian warlord's actions paled by comparison with the treatment Chiang Kai-shek's faction had meted out to his former Communist allies in Canton just a fortnight earlier. The right wing of the Kuomintang had swiftly gained ascendancy, and seemed, for the first time, to be moving closer to the arch-conservative politics practised by Chang Tso-lin's government in Manchuria. What had been a slow squeeze of the Communists since they had accepted the so-called 'eight limitations' at the Plenum of the Central Executive Committee of the Kuomintang[52] almost exactly a year earlier suddenly turned into a sharp and bloody rout; a veritable *coup de grâce* for the Soviet Union's doggedly, and one must add blindly, loyal Chinese comrades. On 12 April 1927, Chiang Kai-shek ordered that all Communist leaders in Shanghai (where he had moved from Canton 12 days earlier) be arrested as first measure for what was euphemistically called an urgent 'purification of the [Kuomintang] Party'.[53] This instead served as a signal for a witch-hunt and mass slaughter of all Communists in the city.[54] In August and December similar bloody purges occurred in Nanchang (in Kiangsi Province) and Canton respectively.[55]

Why the Chinese Communist Party (CCP) would have accepted the demotion is generally seen as symptomatic of a political struggle taking place in Moscow; a struggle that had begun as early as 1923, when Trotsky proclaimed his 'New Course' for the Soviet Union and, in relation to foreign affairs, expressed his dissatisfaction with the Politburo's motion instructing the Chinese Communists to join the Kuomintang. After a stormy power struggle in Moscow, both Trotsky's 'New Course' and his stand on the issue of the CCP's cohabitation with the Kuomintang had been totally defeated by 1927, with the Stalin-Bukharin faction emerging triumphant on both issues. This faction's line on both Soviet policy in China and the Chinese party's path was quite explicit. 'Our most immediate perspective,' announced Bukharin in a speech at the Seventh Plenary Session of the Comintern in November 1926, 'and our most immediate aim in China...is the defeat of the imperialist enemy...'.[56] Bukharin's pronouncement was shorthand for the necessity of the CCP and KMT remaining as a single wedge in China's conflict with imperialism. Six months later, Bukharin's words, and the Stalin-Bukharin line on China, lay in tatters, whilst Trotsky's early pronouncements on the folly of merging the CCP and KMT[57] might have reverberated about the corridors of the Kremlin, had he himself not been in terminal political decline by this time. As a result of this costly error in judgement, and stubborn adherence to a perversely utopian policy line, the argument runs, the Chinese Communist Party was devastated and the Soviet Union's own formidable team of advisers in China imperilled. And, indeed, on 27 July 1927, Mikhail Borodin, the chief Soviet adviser, confidant to Sun Yat-sen in happier days and a man for whom contemporaries reserved such superlatives as 'physical magnificence' and waxed lyrical about his 'massive authority',[58] left China via the Gobi to Ulan Bator. He had to avoid Shanghai, his most natural point of exit from China, because '...the entire...police force, Chinese and foreign, was running its legs off looking for [him]'.[59] The rest of the force of Soviet advisers were soon to follow his uncomfortable lead. At the time of the Soviet advisers' departure from China, Chang Tso-lin had reached the apex of his power. His actions in Peking had established his prominence in China itself, while in Manchuria he had, with the help of the Japanese, already come to rule supreme. Thus, we are to conclude that the pincers had closed, catching a Soviet Union which had pursued a well-defined policy, even if it was nothing short of folly.[60]

Where this depiction of the Soviet policy falls well short of providing a satisfactory image of the politics in China in the crucial years of 1924–8 is precisely in that it represents a unitary line of foreign/Comintern policy. It does not differentiate sufficiently between China and Manchuria in its analysis; neither in the politics conducted in the two areas, nor in the character of Soviet policy pursued in them.

Part of the problem with the homogeneous image we associate with the Soviet presence before mid-1927 is its linkage with competence: generally, the picture is one of Soviet agents whose deliberate policy and actions may, due to the distortions imposed by Moscow, be *misguided* but always coherent. To an extent, this may have been the result of some of the key personnel who had, in the case of the chief figures Borodin, L. Karakhan and V.K. Bliukher, public images which were larger than life.[61] Mentioned earlier were some of the descriptions of Borodin, who, quite appropriately, was regarded as something of a sophisticated Bolshevik 'man-of-action', whose activities in Southern China were tireless and effective.[62] There was also Karakhan, a skilled and wily diplomat who, from his position in Peking, had steered the grander ships of strategy and ideology in the country as a whole.[63] And, finally, Bliukher, a military strategist of great talent who had overseen the formation of Chinese revolutionary forces and, concomitantly, of course, a Soviet military strategy. This formidable triumvirate came to embody Soviet Policy in China (and by extension in Manchuria too), earning even an adversarial respect from its opponents.[64] As late as 1930, and long after the trio had left Chinese territory, they were held responsible as a group for political de-stabilisation occurring in China *and*, virtually in the same breath, Manchuria too. In January 1930 the conservative *China Weekly Review* wrote the following on the Sino-Soviet conflict in Manchuria: 'These agents of Bolshevism, Galen [i.e. Bliukher], Karakhan and Borodin and the senior leadership in Moscow, together with their agents, employed all the "imperialist" methods that they had renounced only three years earlier'.[65] Nowhere was this more clearly visible, the article argued, than in Northern Manchuria in the 'past few months'.[66] There, the 'true face of Bolshevism', the writer went on, made itself known at a time when Soviet agents were preaching altruism and non-aggression in Central and Southern China.[67] Hopelessly entangled in this article is the former, revolutionary rôle of the three advisers (an image taken from their pre-1927 activities while still in China) and an assumption of a unitary, and consistent, nature to Soviet policy in Manchuria and China proper.

The weaknesses of such an argument, it may be added, are present not only in the uniformly conservative, and ideologically charged, English-language China Coast press, but also in subsequent scholarly analysis. A good example of this can be found in the writings of Allen S. Whiting. Quite astutely, the latter asks whether it is accurate to speak of a single Soviet *policy*. Looking at the period 1917–24, Whiting observes the chaos associated with a multi-stranded policy (or, perhaps, *policies*). 'Various factions within the Communist International', he argues, 'penned interminable polemics, arguing the means of adapting Marxist theory and Leninist tactics to turbulent, peasant-dominated China'.[68] He observes that in the period in question Profintern[69] argued the need for a dilution of radicalism in favour of winning the support of bourgeois-led independence movements. Narkomindel,[70] on the other hand, pursued a zigzag – but nonetheless determined – course aimed at establishing Soviet Russia's place in the Far East, regardless of the means required to achieve this.[71] To this point Whiting's interpretation is illuminating, giving the impression that the revolutionary and diplomatic fronts in China '…sometimes worked separately and at cross-purposes, [and] sometimes remained distinct but parallel'. However, he then concludes the argument by suggesting that it was the *merger* of the two fronts '... *in 1924* [which] placed Soviet Russia in an ascendant position in the Chinese Revolution'.[72]

It must be said that Whiting's argument does take us many steps ahead of the undifferentiated analysis offered by the China press, as it suggests that Soviet involvement, at least until 1924, was far from being clear-cut. One has to ask the question, however, as to whether the fronts *had* merged in 1924 in the fashion suggested by Whiting. A more recent study by Bruce A. Elleman approaches the whole question somewhat differently, concluding that by May 1924 the Peking Ministry of Foreign Affairs *knew* that the Soviet propaganda of equality and anti-colonial fraternity was little more than a smoke-screen to hide an otherwise quite venal intent on the part of the Soviet state '... merely to expand [its] power... [in] China'.[73] The Chinese authorities, Elleman continues, chose not to release the proof upon which this certainty was based because it suited China to prevent the international community from regarding it as having been duped by the Soviet government, and to forestall the latter's use of a secret protocol by which the bilateral agreements signed by the two countries could be suspended. Furthermore, he concludes, it suited Chinese officials to perpetuate the myth of their country's relations with the Soviet Union because this placed '... enormous pressure on the capitalist countries to eliminate their own unequal treaties with China'.[74] However, while such an interpretation is plausible if seen entirely from a unitary Chinese perspective,[75] it fails to take into adequate account the strength of the rival loci of power emerging on the peripheries of China. Given the strength of warlords such as Chang Tso-lin, one has to ask the question of how much in control *were* the central authorities in playing out such a intricate deception? Furthermore, it does not provide sufficient scope for the recognition of the evolving, and intriguing, dualism of Soviet policy in China.

It could be argued that it was *precisely* in 1924, with the signing of separate agreements between the Soviet Union and the Chinese authorities at Peking and Mukden, that Soviet policy appeared at its most diversified and complex (indeed, often contradictory) rather than the monolithic, single-minded form generally portrayed. On the surface, conventional diplomacy and revolutionism may have merged to suggest that what was being promoted was the 'united front' line that the Stalin-Bukharin policy eventually came to represent. Such a view would be supported by the impression that Soviet policy had achieved a universal system of workable relations within the Chinese body politic; a spectrum that ranged from an 'understanding' with the most conservative of the warlord leaderships, to the influence over radical elements of the KMT and, of course, the seemingly direct – and full – control of the CCP.[76] Rather than the coherent, rational linkage that this suggests, the 'merger' that lies at the heart of such a reading may be one characterised by differentiation and deep contradiction.

The Soviet Union's signing of virtually identical agreements with the Peking and Mukden authorities over the CER was seen by friend and foe alike as something of a coup. As important, however, was the image of the proletarian state speaking with one voice on matters of its China policy. Even Trotsky appeared to fall into line when he hailed the amicable settlement that had been arrived at between Moscow, Peking and Mukden, claiming a '...major moral victory over the imperialists'.[77] By extension, of course, what he was also hailing was the restoration of Soviet Russian quasi-colonial *rights* in Manchuria; a development which in itself should have given food for thought regarding the existence of any coherent Soviet foreign policy doctrine in China. Put in another way, one could conclude that even if the Soviet Union was speaking with one voice over China, it was one which was dissonant and garbled. The Manchurian agreement may have been amicable, but it was one that, perforce, had been reached between three separate political entities over a single piece of territory, which, ultimately, belonged to only one: China. Thus, while the Soviet Union may have been able to comfortably differentiate between the 'businesslike' guise it had adopted in Manchuria and the more radical line it continued to pursue in China proper – in itself an indication of an important contradiction in Soviet policy in China, one could argue – in its own mind, the impression this left with others is one that is less than logical. Understandably, the contradictory nature of the novel Soviet policy quickly drew sceptical and critical commentary. One correspondent noted that the Soviet Union, in resuming its involvement in Manchuria, occupied a strong position: given the poor state of the Chinese treasury, the clause it contained allowing China to eventually purchase the CER from the Soviet Union was unlikely to be invoked.[78] At the same time, moreover, the agreement made it impossible for other foreign powers to take up the Soviet interests should China be unable to do so.[79] Not with a little irony, the writer noted that this tightly formed legal phraseology was in sharp contrast to the more generous verbal outpourings of the agreement's chief Soviet negotiator just a few months before the accord was reached. 'The agreements reached with the international powers', Karakhan was reported to have announced in greeting the Chinese premier at a banquet commemorating the anniversary of the October Revolution, 'should not only be looked at afresh, but torn up and destroyed'. And even with the agreement in place, and the red Soviet flag rising above the Soviet Mission in Peking, the new Soviet Ambassador Karakhan ('the Elder of the Diplomatic Corps'), triumphantly announced:

> This flag reminds us not only of the first occasion in human history that power has transferred into the hands of the workers and peasants, but also of the coming struggle against global oppression. This is why the peoples of Asia welcome our flag as an emblem of their liberation and national independence.[80]

Such revolutionary 'fire and brimstone', while being in keeping with the line advocated in Southern China, was, as the journalist so pointedly shows, difficult to square with the situation in Manchuria itself, where a more temperate line was required.

Looking more closely at the character of relations on the ground in China and Manchuria respectively, we find that, indeed, there are substantial differences in the policies conducted in the respective areas. 1924 marks the rise of the 'corporate communist' in Manchuria, more concerned with outperforming the foreign capitalists than subverting them, while in China proper the mood is characterised by an increased revolutionary bravura that heads steadily to confrontation and crisis.

These tendencies were reinforced by the character of personnel present in the respective regions: if there was a uniformity of policy coming from Moscow, this did not necessarily extend to the nature of the people executing it. Karakhan, Borodin & Bliukher were charismatic, inspirational, brilliant. Thanks largely to the coverage that they received from the China foreign-language press, they became larger than life, ubiquitous and, most important of all, seemingly perfect in their subversive activities. This may have, in part, been due to the all-too successful work that Borodin and Karakhan carried out in self-promotion in their early years. Borodin's influence, for example, was described in the following way in a contemporary account by the writer O.M. Green in his *The Story of China's Revolution*:

> Borodin's achievements as High Political Adviser (to which office he had been appointed by Dr. Sun) are the most extraordinary in that he never learnt to speak Chinese, nor did he ever thrust forward. He attended all the meetings of Dr. Sun's directorate, but very rarely took part in the discussions. Yet in some manner known only to himself he swayed the doings of the Party exactly as he pleased. General Chiang Kai-shek, who was now coming to the front as head of the Whampoa Academy for military cadets, never trusted the man, and once, during a temporary absence of Dr. Sun, tried to arrest him.[81]

Green's account is interesting in many respects: it shows, as this excerpt suggests, why Borodin would have been less effective on the field (his inability to speak Chinese would have made it nearly impossible to act as a popular leader in China), and why we should consider that his position within the KMT alone, and even at this early stage, was precarious (as is suggested by the unexplained enmity that Chiang Kai-shek held for him virtually from the start). And yet, he is the consummate political agent; in this case seemingly guided by court politics as much as by Bolshevik principles. In less balanced accounts, and notably those published by the China press, he and the other Soviet advisers could do no wrong; instigating, guiding and controlling every conceivable disturbance in the troubled

Chinese polity. Weighty analyses came from commentators such as Captain Eugene Pick ('Late of the Red Army Intelligence Service in China'), who observed that:

> [E]ver since Borodin's influence in 'Nationalist' circles has amounted to anything, he has wired the fullest possible reports upon the situation and his activities, and it has been Moscow's custom to telegraph instructions every other day in diplomatic code through the consulates, with daily messages in critical times. When they were decoded Borodin usually showed them to Eugene Chen (the Republican Minister for Foreign Affairs), who was expected to act upon them, but they sometimes contained comment upon the Chinese which Borodin had to withhold.[82]

Communist plots were, according to coverage in the same China press, in evidence everywhere. Pick describes how Soviet representatives were holding sway over the anti-foreign troubles in Hankow. Conflict arose there between Chinese coolies working on dockside in the Japanese Concession and Japanese sailors. 'Local Reds' (both Chinese and Russian), wrote Pick, proceeded to '...make the most of the incident and to provoke such a situation as resulted in the surrender of the British Concession...'.[83] The account of this localised dispute then assumes a broader dimension:

> But Moscow, adhering to its fixed policy of concentrating on one Power at a time, interfered with explicit orders. In the thick of the campaign against the Japanese, May 4, telegraphic instructions came through Koubiak in Habarovsk and the Shanghai Consulate-General, to stop at once any agitation against the Japanese that had started and to put an end to whatever friction there was by any and all means. Hankow was ordered to agree to any settlement demanded by Japan and to take drastic steps against the mob leaders if they were out of hand. ...If the Japanese demanded that the pickets should be disbanded, the Wu-Han Government was to agree at once. The public will understand from this how it happened that this incident was so quickly and easily adjusted.[84]

In the course of the period the Soviet advisers were active in China and Manchuria, this direct relationship and all-pervasive image of Bolshevism in the country reached a rarefied and universal form that would have ascribed *any* disturbance, in a country itself rife with social inequalities and frictions, to the influence of Moscow and the Bolshevik credo. Signs of this process were, indeed, evident early as September 1923, when *The China Advertiser* in Tientsin asked the rhetorical question '...what is Bolshevism?' In answer to this question, the newspaper reasoned:

> In essence [Bolshevism] is simply class war. Those who have nothing are stirred up to rise against those who have something and take it from them, while if it is necessary to kill the victims in the process it does not

matter. It is simply the attempt of daring and needy adventurers to [seize] the reins of power by shooting, or scaring away, the previous occupants of public office and taking their place, after which they control public affairs in the way which best suits their own interests.[85]

Chinese Nationalists, anti-colonialists, Chinese Bolsheviks, Soviet advisers and the prairie-fire-like mob politics that characterised the China of the 1920s thereby overlap and merge into a single spectre. The all-encompassing ideology and the means of implementing it were assumed to be (and more often than not *depicted* as) perfectly efficient.[86] However, can such a straightforward view be sustained in light of the experience of Soviet agents in China?

There are a number of levels to address in answering this question, even if one were to assume that Soviet activities in China and Manchuria worked as a coherent whole. The first is to observe the physical environment within which the principal Soviet advisers worked in the southern provinces of China. Far from the neat – albeit apocalyptic – pattern depicted in the China press, this was a maze in itself. In writing of Canton at the time Borodin was in the ascendancy, commentators suggested that the southern city was something of a Tower of Babel in which it was possible to become impossibly lost. It was, the commentary shows, hard to find two individuals in Canton who could agree on anything.[87] This was, moreover, the base of operations for the Chinese political party – and government – he was advising, suggesting that the environment here would have been the friendliest and most secure, comparatively speaking, that Borodin would have expected to have encountered in China. Conditions elsewhere in the country were far more difficult, as Vishniakova-Akimova records of Shanghai in her memoirs: 'The Shanghai White Guard community often attacked [the Soviet Consulate] building, enjoying the non-interference of the British police. Embassy employees and their families had to drive the attackers off unaided'.[88] Sporadic attacks on Soviet consulates and personnel were complemented by forms of surveillance that ranged from the formal to the bizarre.[89] Post coming to the missions from the Soviet Union was censored by Chinese authorities from as early as 1923.[90] Under these conditions, much of the contact between the various Soviet diplomatic stations around China had to be carried out by couriers, who were often the more senior – and strategically important – Soviet officials themselves; a method which was in itself fraught with difficulty and not just a little danger.[91] The inefficiencies that this scramble engendered were reflected in the often breathless movements of Borodin himself, with periods in Canton, to Shanghai, to Peking, to Hankow, interspersed with visits to Moscow.[92] With each move, Borodin found himself having, in each case quite literally (if Pick is to be believed), to re-create an image of himself at the previous location. After the arrival of Chernykh, the new courier at Peking, and the official who was to succeed Borodin at that mission, '... it was Borodin's duty to outline for him the major points of every note that he was supposed to write'.[93] At the time of the raid on the Peking Embassy, Chernykh was in Peking whilst Borodin was in Hankow. Characteristically, communications between them was by courier, in this case a man named Eitingon,[94] who himself had only recently arrived in Central China after an earlier posting in Manchuria. Eitingon was in Shanghai, carrying instructions from Borodin to Chernykh, when he heard news of the raid on the Peking Embassy.[95] In other words, communications between Hankow and Peking, Borodin and Chernykh had been non-existent for much of that critical period.

The staff who worked with the more charismatic and prominent Soviet advisers such as Borodin, must also be taken into account in this assessment. Political constraints, such as those discussed above, prevented the latter from being joined by agents of similar calibre and prominence. Borodin especially, therefore, was encouraged to cover far more territory than was good for his own political survival in China, leaving less *adroit* 'images' of himself in the various places he could not physically be. Thus, while the China press reported '...literally scores of expert Russian Tcheka agents [being] imported, their names and passports changed in Harbin in a forgery mill, and sent to every big Chinese industrial town...',[96] even if these reports were entirely true, such agents would have had to be completely anonymous individuals; their faces and professional histories not being recognised by the intense scrutiny of the Chinese authorities, Maritime Customs and, especially, the hypercritical Russian *émigré* community in Harbin itself.

Furthermore, as suggested earlier, the pressure on these agents was immense. The ideological drive, and physical stamina, of the triumvirate of Borodin, Karakhan and Bliukher was unlikely to be as evident in the personnel joining them. The commitment, personality and flair of this small group were, however, in many respects the key factors in drawing these individuals closer to the heart of Chinese politics; to the point, indeed, of eliciting from the China press comments such as General Galen (Bliukher) earning more respect from the Chinese 'nondescripts' (soldiers) than the latter held for either Chiang Kai-shek or Sun Yat-sen.[97] And yet even Bliukher was, by the end of the period, reportedly in a state of nervous collapse in Hankow,[98] leaving Borodin as the Soviet 'wire-puller' in China.[99]

If the experiences of other Soviet representatives in China are examined, a different, far more brittle, picture emerges. In many cases, these were the personalities of grey 'assistants', driven, and more often than not dragged down, by preoccupations of a less inspirational sort than we normally encounter in the public persona of either a Borodin or Karakhan. When, at a rally in Hankow in December 1926, Borodin announced that 'The (Chinese) revolution was...half through',[100] for many of his comrades there was little inspiration, or energy, left to drive them through the 'second half'.

In this respect, the case history of M. Hassis, a Soviet official who became Soviet Vice-Consul in Canton in 1925, and executed by Chiang Kai-shek's Secret Police after the abortive rising in that city in 1927, is illuminating. Born in 1896 in the province of Ekaterinoslav, and displaying a typical careerist path of development,[101] Hassis had by the time he reached this position shown little sign of making anything more than a functionary's contribution to the Chinese Revolution. Notes in his personal file show him to be a man far older, and frailer, than his 31 years would have suggested. By 1926, after only two years in China, he was diagnosed as suffering from severe ulcers and residual amoebic dysentery. As early as 1924, however, he had already complained of ill-health, having been granted permission to spend some time at a sanatorium in the course of that year. Emotionally too Hassis's mind was far removed from the problems of China. He was plagued by matrimonial troubles, having been divorced from a wife who herself was a 'complete cripple' (suffering from a badly neglected case of infected swelling), but nonetheless contested protracted alimony actions against him in various courts in Moscow. It was clear too that Hassis had been secretly sending money to their daughter Lina.[102] Curiously, nothing is said in the report of his work as a 'revolutionist'. Similar – if perhaps less poignant – cases can be found with other Soviet officials serving in China; individuals with hearts much removed from the fervour of revolutionism, and located in a distant, and by all indications foreign, land. Their contributions were ultimately little more than the frantic business they were obliged to conduct, and, at times, as with Hassis, their wretched, alienated lives.

Lines of weakness too are in evidence when we look at the Soviet policy itself. If the Soviet Union spoke with a single voice after 1924, this was one in form only. The content of what that voice espoused was itself open to question. Borodin himself may have agreed with the Stalin–Bukharin line which he had to interpret on the ground in China, but there were reservations even in his own mind about its suitability. His correspondence with Moscow, according to Green's account, showed that his experience in China had led to two 'all-important facts' which his masters were unwilling to entertain: '... Sovietism *à la* Moscow must be modified to suit Chinese tastes...', and that the East could not be hurried.[103] 'If Moscow had been willing to listen to Borodin', Green argues, 'it is possible that he might have succeeded in bringing China completely under Russian control, at least for a time'.[104] Such a view, in addition to not taking into account the earlier-mentioned poor relations that had at an early stage developed between Chiang Kai-shek and Borodin[105] (relations which would in themselves have suggested that the latter's days in Chinese politics were numbered), also reveals a fundamental gap between Borodin and Moscow, and one which was never more than papered over.[106]

But the problems in the 'unified' Moscow line went somewhat deeper than even this representation of dissonance. What Borodin was seeking to do, under instructions from Moscow, was to create a united front, thereby drawing in a diverse range of political views. A united front, however, is also normally intended to fragment and isolate component parts of the opposition, not to provide them with cause to group more closely together.[107] And yet this is precisely what Borodin's interpretation of Moscow's policy line resulted in. His address at a rally in Hankow in December 1926 has already been referred to earlier. At this rally, Borodin reached the pinnacle of his revolutionary oratory, referring to the half-completed Chinese revolution and warning that the remaining half was the 'most important': the overthrow of the British and their ally Chang Tso-lin and the Fengtien Party.[108] 'When this is accomplished,' he promised, 'the country will be peaceful and prosperous'.[109] Such rhetoric was in itself conducive to the British, Chang Tso-lin and his Japanese backers (with whom the Soviet Union had been at pains to co-exist peacefully) and the Russian populace of Manchuria wondering if there were not grounds for a broad oppositional front to such an ominous Soviet threat to their respective positions. However, in the course of his stay in Hankow, and possibly buoyed by the disputes taking place there at the time, Borodin went further still, drawing in the rest of the foreign powers in China, as well as the country's vulnerable middle class. 'The trouble with your businessmen', he announced provocatively in an interview with the Reuter Agency, 'is that they don't read our Kuomintang literature. They take the Treaty Port newspaper with their breakfast and then they go on to the racecourse. Perhaps later on they read a book about the Manchu dynasty. Thus they live in a permanent atmosphere of misconception and eventually the old Colonial complex reasserts itself'.[110] Such pronouncements – so reminiscent of the ripe imagery of a Trotsky in the Russia of 1917 – may have been acceptable in the chaotic atmosphere of a politically unstable Hankow, but they fell far short of steering his country's policy further around the intricate political map of China, which included a Manchuria, where business, 'Treaty Port newspapers over breakfast' and racecourses were far closer to Soviet *desiderata* than was revolutionary upheaval. For those other than the anti-imperialists, however, outpourings such as this were threats of a furtherance of instability (indeed, of a permanent revolution) and, in effect, a call to arms to the disparate elements opposing the 'bolshevisation' of China. For Mukden – and despite any words or policies of conciliation and cooperation – this was a call for further friction and destabilisation. In light of this, but without specific reference to it, Japan could do nothing but wonder whether such language indicated a possibility of its position being undermined in Manchuria and China as a whole;[111] especially so with the Soviet Union's principal political figure in China warning that '...[the northerners] are as good as defeated. History has condemned them and all that remains now is to bury the corpse'.[112]

The corpse was far from ready to be buried. Chang Tso-lin, with the aid of the Japanese in Southern Manchuria, was in the ascendancy. If he needed any reason to doubt Soviet sincerity in maintaining equal relations after the signing of the Mukden–Soviet agreement over two years earlier, Borodin and his cohorts provided more than adequate grounds for such suspicions. Ironically, in Northern Manchuria the situation was one that should have provided the Mukden authorities some confidence with respect to the possibility of long-term, constructive relations with its co-signatory. There, the nature and activities of Soviet operatives was far removed from that of their counterparts working in the more militant atmosphere of Southern/Central China. Both the diplomatic representatives and heads of the CER – these were to be viewed as officials of comparable standing – were far more conservative in their activities and public utterances. For the most part, what we see in Northern Manchuria is the work of bona fide managers rather than political activists.[113] One could, of course, argue that the political climate in Manchuria was not suited to the more fiery approach discussed earlier, and that natural inclinations of the Soviet senior staff were severely tempered by the suspicion they would have encountered from the Chinese authorities; suspicion compounded by the hostility of Russian *émigré* circles.

Such a perspective is supported by the unhappy experiences of some Soviet personnel who had lived and worked according by stricter ideological lines before they were stationed in Northern Manchuria. An example of such an individual is the unfortunate M.M. Lashevich (whose history is discussed below), for whom any inclination towards more radical thought and action was unnaturally, and painfully, stifled by existing political conditions. For individuals such as these, the process of immiseration might have been slowed if in their own spheres of operation in Manchuria they saw evidence of political activity that, even if not blatantly so, dovetailed with the China policy that Borodin and his group of advisers/consuls were employing in China proper. Despite the existence of numerous accounts of Soviet subversion in Manchuria, many of these must be attributed to the *émigré* rumour-mill or the Chinese authorities' attempts to discredit Soviet motives in Northern Manchuria.[114] Even the papers allegedly seized in the course of Chang Hsüeh-liang's raid on the Soviet Consulate in June 1929 failed to provide conclusive linkage between the two areas of political activity.[115] Indeed, the only clear, consistent line of openly political policy that the Soviet authorities conducted in Manchuria involved the excoriation of *émigrés* from the CER; a policy which was itself, ironically, to be an important contributory factor in the breakdown between Soviet and Chinese relations in 1929.[116]

The image of a unified policy is too neat in another respect; one that is vital to an understanding of the relationship between Manchuria and China, and Soviet involvement in both. Even in Southern China, the Soviet advisers' part was less than clear (certainly sufficiently so to cast doubt on whether or not policies laid down by Moscow *could* have been translated directly into its politics in China). Links between South and Central China were made very difficult for Soviet emissaries by Chinese and foreigner alike. Upon close examination, the relations between Soviet officials in South/Central China and Manchuria seemed hellishly difficult to sustain. This meant, in effect, that even if the Soviet operatives in the respective areas were like-minded – which was far from certain – maintaining the cross-links necessary to implement a unified policy was remote possibility; a situation made no easier by Borodin's broadly confrontational statements.

As Jacobs, Borodin's biographer, observes: '[v]irtually every chronicler of that period [the 1920s] – Wuhan or Nanking KMTers, Stalinists, Trotskyites, Chinese communists, dissident Chinese communists, liberal journalists, conservative journalists, and permeations and hybrids of each...' felt the need to make a summation of the Chinese Revolution of the 1920s.[117] Of central interest to each of these was the rôle of Soviet policy. 'To some,' Jacobs concludes, 'Soviet policy was blameless; to others it was the incarnation of evil and perfidy'.[118] But in most, if not all, cases it was seen as a unified policy. A full and relatively persuasive account of an otherwise highly confusing policy is provided by Whiting when he writes:

> Borodin worked diligently in Canton, reorganizing Sun's party. Ultimately he managed to forge the varying elements that composed the Kuomintang into a fighting force with a discipline and organization unknown in Revolutionary China... [B]y mid-1924, the influence of the Russian advisers in Canton reached its ascendancy. The First Kuomintang Congress in January, 1924, marked not only the full joining of the Chinese Communist Party and the Kuomintang movement but also the emergence of a new spirit of anti-imperialism coupled with proletarian and peasant participation in the political and military apparatus. Karakhan took this opportunity to send another congratulatory letter to Sun, but the Chinese leader's reply of February showed his anxiety over the negotiations in Peking. As 'President of the Chinese Republic', Sun pointed out that since Russia now enjoyed *de jure* recognition from Great Britain, it no longer needed to be satisfied with the 'non-representative, anti-nationalistic, and pro-foreign capitalist body' in Peking. The best course for Karakhan to follow would be to establish formal relations with Canton. Such was not the design of the Narkomindel strategist, however. Peking was still available to sign away China's interests in Outer Mongolia and Manchuria, and it was to be utilized accordingly. The Sino-Soviet treaty of May 31, 1924, was the result.[119]

This account, however, suggests that if such a carefully-constructed exploitation of a bewildering range of Chinese factions took place, the ultimate goal was one of advantage gained via *realpolitik* rather than ideologically driven policy. And yet, following the 1924 treaty there was every indication that the Soviet personnel in China proper pursued a markedly ideological line, which tended to ignore the finer points of the political lie of the land and, as was demonstrated earlier, tended to act *against* Soviet interests in Manchuria.

Looking at the official Soviet representation in Manchuria, we find that an intriguing pattern emerges. Because of its sensitive situation, the Harbin Consulate maintained a position that was opaque, taking no part in activities in commercial circles or interaction with the foreign presence (which in itself provided grounds for the circulation of wild rumour concerning its genuine activities).[120] Outside the sensitive centre of Harbin, however, Soviet officials were not only open to contact with the foreign and merchant presence, but virtually at one with it. A case in point is that of Geitsman, the Soviet Consul at the small border settlement of Manchuli, where J. Gibbes served as Assistant in charge of Sub-Port for the Maritime Customs. Despite the fact that Geitsman had emerged from the 'old order' of Bolshevik ranks (having been sent manacled into exile in Siberia before the revolution[121]), his manner and activities suggested a less politically righteous nature than his southern colleagues. Wheeling and dealing with fur traders in the area (most of them Russian *émigrés*)[122] went on despite the ideologically strident face presented by Borodin, Karakhan and their associates in this period. His stay at Manchuli lasted almost two and a half years; a very long period in the context of other Soviet Consular appointments at the time.[123] In his role as consul, Geitsman developed very friendly relations with the international community there, largely through the regular round of cocktail parties that he attended. His relations were warm with local Chinese officials and, to an extent, the *émigré* community too.[124] Geitsman's behaviour obviously went a little too far in the direction of his bourgeois acquaintances and colleagues, for he was eventually recalled to Moscow (ostensibly on three-month leave, but, as the Customs Assistant noted in his monthly report, 'with very little chance of his returning'.[125]). His friend Gibbes was at the station to see him off and reported that '[h]e had quite a hearty send off, in fact – as he remarked to me on the platform – the only people who were not present were the working classes'.[126] At his farewell banquet some days earlier, the band leader had approached the Consul to ask if he should play the *Internationale*. Geitsman gave a '... very firm negative in reply ...'. Despite this, the bandmaster, possibly not believing what he had heard, burst into the strains of the communist anthem. 'Mr Geitsman immediately went up to [the orchestra] and said "who asked you to play it? Don't play that until you're asked", and the music promptly wheezed out'.[127] Such discretion was not limited to Geitsman's precinct alone. For some months a similar modesty had descended upon much of the Soviet activity in Manchuria. Gibbes observed in one of his reports that May 1 celebrations in Manchuria '... were the quietest since the Soviet Republic began to function... . This spirit now marks all Soviet functions'.[128]

Most important in considering the character of this Soviet presence is its marked contrast with the more aggressive, indeed inflammatory, tone employed by the Soviet representatives working in China proper, and the fact that these very different approaches were to be seen at work at virtually the same time. It must be said that there was a period after the Karakhan Declarations that the mood even in 'Soviet' Manchuria picked up in its militancy, but this was quite short-lived.[129] On the whole, the Soviet representatives in Manchuria appeared to be of a somewhat different breed. Even those who arrived in Northern Manchuria with a depth of idealism, or wealth of experience on the front line of Revolution, found their work constrained by the resistance encountered in Northern Manchurian Russian society, and the occasional fillip to the latter from Chang Tso-lin's government.[130] Application of revolutionary principles was hampered too through the imposition of symbolism which, in its quintessential Russian setting, at times had a tendency to appear comical, if not grotesque. J. Gibbes, in a report from May 1925, included the following abridged report from a Manchuli newspaper, accompanied by his own observation '[w]hether Manchouli is quite as red as it makes itself appear, I very much doubt; but it has accepted with gusto the new "Soviet religion"':

On the 17th May the ceremony of 'OCTOBRIN' was performed on eight infants – 3 boys and 5 girls – children of citizens who are true to the Communistic faith and who are, presumably, very bad Christians. As the first of its kind, the event proved an attraction to the curious who filled the local Railway Hall to its limits, the performance being carried out upon the stage with proper theatrical effects: – Babies in the wings OFF – An oration from the President and musical ovature (*sic*) 'International' by a brass band. Then the Grand Entry of Babies, who are baptised in floods of words for want of water or anything better. The ceremony ended with more 'International' and two older Pioneers at the salute shouting 'Be prepared' at the Babies, with the united group of Babies loudly weeping and wailing, severally refused the comfort offered by their parents and sponsors, over which the curtain SLOWLY falls.[131]

Contrary to Marx's dictum that history repeats itself, once as tragedy and once as farce, with respect to Soviet activities in China and Manchuria, the tragedy and farce manifested themselves virtually concurrently, in the process neither toppling a recalcitrant old order in China, nor converting a sceptical Russian public in Manchuria through what was in effect a combination of 'business as usual' and thoroughly unconvincing high (or low) theatre. Together, however, the contradictory characteristics at play made it difficult for the more dedicated functionaries in Manchuria to do much more than despair.

An example of this is in the form of more prominent members of the Bolshevik old guard despatched to Manchuria. The most illustrious in this category was Mikhail Mikhailovich Lashevich.[132] In the October Revolution, he had played an important role in facilitating the seizure of power by the Bolsheviks. On 23 October 1917 he had accompanied Trotsky to the Peter-Paul Fortress, where they succeeded in convincing its anti-Bolshevik garrison to transfer its allegiance to the Revolutionary Military Council. Had they failed, the fortress (with artillery overlooking the Winter Palace and 100 000 rifles in the armoury) would have served as a formidable command point for the Provisional Government's further resistance. Then on the night of the 25 October he was involved in planning (with Antonov-Ovseenko and Podvoisky) the capture of the Winter Palace as well as directing the seizure of the government bank, treasury, telegraph and post offices and the Pavlovsk Military Academy. Lashevich's contributions during the civil war had been no less significant. He was a commander (and a member of the Revoensovet) of the 3rd and 7th Armies, as well as those of the Eastern and Southern fronts. In this capacity, he contributed to the final defeat of Generals Kolchak, Denikin and Iudenich. From 1920 he served in the Presidium of the Petrograd Ispolkom and went on to become a member of Revoensovet and commander of forces in Siberia. In August 1921 he was transferred to the Revoensovet of the 15th Army and action in Poland. In the course of hostilities, he had twice been decorated with the Order of the Red Banner.

Although he had arrived in Harbin in late 1926 in partial disgrace, having devoted himself to the work of both the Leningrad Opposition and the Joint Opposition in the years before he was posted to Northern Manchuria,[133] his appointment there was at the lofty (and powerful) level of Vice-President of the CER, and came at a time when his proven skills and tenacity would have been at a premium. Indeed, Lashevich had been described as '...a good-natured, fat little fellow' who refused to be daunted by any problem set before him: if a solution could not be finessed, it could be forced. It was an attitude shared by many of the Bolshevik old guard in the years of improvisation during the revolution and civil war.

His new posting, however, proved to be a particularly cruel combination of political exile and delicate diplomacy. His task was to reinforce Soviet interests in a railway management already beginning to show signs of paralysis through the awkward combination of heightened Chinese nationalism, Japanese rivalry and Russian *émigré* hostility. With considerable tact and his normal tenacity, Lashevich succeeded in temporarily restoring a veneer of order to the operation of senior management in the CER, but, it seems, at great personal cost. As the contradictions began to mount (not least of which would have been those in Lashevich's own mind regarding his former role as revolutionary and his new part as something of a bourgeois negotiator), so too, seemingly, came depression and, finally, despair. In late August 1928 he committed suicide. The horror of his existence in Manchuria, with its Soviet pastiche, the drone of *émigré* hostility and Chinese suspicions, is well summed up in the scenes connected with the memorial ceremony and despatch of his body to Moscow. A Russian, who many years later arrived in Hong Kong as a refugee, remembered how *all* employees were required to attend the ceremony and to line the streets down which the funeral cortege would travel. The entire affair, the refugee recounted, led to '…many minor conflicts between Chinese Nationals, Russians and Soviet citizens. …Many tempers flare[d]…[and] especially with those who hated the sight of Lashevich, and, for that matter, all Soviet officials'.[134] The respondent's father, who was a CER employee at the time, recounted to him how he had entered a Russian café after the ceremony to find a Russian employee (one of those who had been granted Chinese citizenship) toasting Lashevich's demise. A pro-Soviet patron immediately physically launched into him.[135]

The picture of the Soviet presence in China and Manchuria that emerges from such glimpses is one that is both spatially and ideologically differentiated. Rather than the coherence suggested in the writings of scholars such as Whiting, Soviet policies, at least in their implementation, are characterised by confusion, contradiction, and for some of those implementing them, abject despair.

In the process, one must also ask the important question: what was the effect of this approach on the political situation in China and Manchuria? Arguably, the pursuit of the disparate lines had profound implications in this respect. By attempting to maintain a radical line in the Southern and Central parts of China, the advisers – and Soviet policy – encouraged the younger, more radical elements of the Chinese political spectrum there to storm the bastions of power. In parallel with this, however, Soviet officialdom worked at co-habitation with the old, reactionary militarist clique north of the Great Wall (a clique that normally stood in opposition to the young Nationalist China). The most stark result of these contradictory lines of practice was that the Soviet Union was systematically working to destroy the influence of the relatively young elements – 'educated in a fairly modern spirit' – in Manchuria itself.[136] In doing so, ironically, it was also undermining its own considerable position in the latter location.

# 4
# Politics on the Ground

At the time of the Soviet group's departure from China proper, Chang Tso-lin had come to reign supreme in Manchuria. His actions against the Soviet Union in Peking had extended his political influence well beyond the borders of his warlord fiefdom, reinforced, at least for a time, by the full backing of Japan. With the Soviet Union's China policy so clearly in tatters after the events in Peking, Canton, Hankow and Shanghai, together with the subsequent withdrawal of Soviet advisers from China, the focus shifted from fears of Soviet subversion in China as a whole, to actions in Northern Manchuria specifically.

In Northern Manchuria, it might be noted, the battle lines had been drawn quite early, but not between the Soviet authorities and Mukden. Aleksei Alekseevich Ivanov, the General Manager of the CER,[1] had in May 1925 announced that all persons holding neither Chinese nor Soviet citizenship would be relieved of their jobs with the company. The intention was, obviously, to rid the CER of all Russian *émigré* workers and to replace these with more ideologically reliable Soviet personnel. Crudely too, this measure might also have been taken to divide the Russian population of Manchuria by forcing politically acceptable stateless Russians to apply for Soviet citizenship, thereby cutting them away from their more stubbornly resistant fellow Russians.[2] The strategy backfired on its Soviet architects in two ways. First, the measure, while it had something to be said for it in terms of administrative efficiency (no management, after all, would wish to have a hostile core of workers in its labour force, and, given that the CER was to be a Sino-Soviet venture, it was logical that the Soviet side should be populated by Soviet nationals), was met by an equally rational – although unexpected – measure on the part of the Mukden authorities: stateless Russians working for the CER would be provided with Chinese nationality, if they wanted it.[3] Indeed, it provided the Mukden government with an opportunity to go even farther in garnering the support of *émigré* Russians. After giving the CER *émigrés* tenure of citizenship, Chang Tso-lin went farther still by permitting the formation of a Union of Chinese-national

Railway Employees, which was used to counterbalance the Union of Soviet Railway Workers (formed by the Soviet part of the CER management).[4] According to a Russian residing in Northern Manchuria at the time: '[t]o further shield Russians holding Chinese nationality from the tyranny of the Soviet railway administration, there was formulated a set of separate regulations and the Union was placed under the supervision of the Chinese members of the [CER] Board of the Directors, thereby circumventing the lower level of management, which was dominated by the Soviets'.[5] Secondly, and more importantly, the Ivanov legislation was, in effect, an open declaration of hostilities against the *émigré* Russian population of Manchuria. It must be remembered that many Russians who were living in Manchuria – including most of the Russians working for the CER – were *émigrés* by default, and not necessarily through carefully formed political choice. Ivanov's measures summarily lumped these Russians into the same category as those who had consciously expressed opposition to the Soviet Regime, either through action or implication. *Émigrés* were not only those who had become such because they had 'voted with their feet', so to speak, by crossing the Chinese border after 1917, but, equally, those who had been living there for some years *before* the Revolution. In sum, it created fresh antagonisms within the region's Russian community, as well as fuelling existing resentments and hostility. It also created a situation whereby Marshal Chang Tso-lin's Mukden administration became the unlikely champions for this community, despite the fact that life had not been easy for the latter under the same administration in the past (discussed more fully in Chapter 5).

To some degree, the hardening of the Soviet line appeared to be linked to the nature of Ivanov himself, who was not much liked in Manchuria.[6] His predecessor, Ostroumoff, had done much work in order to ensure the continuity of the CER's operations, and credibility with the businesses it worked with in Manchuria. An important component of this continuity was the recognition of pre-1917 debts that the railway carried. Before March 1917, debts had been covered systematically by the CER administration. From December 1917 to 1920, with links between General Khorvat's administration and Petrograd lost, debts mounted quickly and the financial situation became 'grave'.[7] In 1921, with Khorvat's grip finally wrenched from the CER, the debts transferred to Ostroumoff, who tackled these 'energetically,' as one local commentator noted.[8] He had to vacate his post on 3 October 1924. By the latter date the work that he had carried out toward the normalisation of the CER operations had been considerable, but the settlement of debts far from complete. On the basis of the USSR–Mukden agreement of 20 September 1924, the Soviet era was officially ushered in on the railway, with Ivanov installed as the General Manager, and Emshanov as his deputy. 'In many cases,' a contemporary commentary observed, 'the new management team disavowed any responsibility for the debts carried over from the period before 3 October 1924'.[9] The answer to questions concerning why this should have been the case was met with a blunt answer: '[they – Ivanov and Emshanov – did not have] the legal basis to do so'.[10] Thus debts to *émigré* Russian-owned companies, as well as the latter's commercial relations with the railway (which for many would have been the life-blood of their operations), were treated in a similar fashion to the stateless Russian employees of the CER itself. A clear statement of authority and a 'fresh' start appeared to be more important for the Soviet side of the joint-control than the efficient operation of their troubled charge, the CER. Regular newspaper articles on the subject of these outstanding debts were to serve as a steady reminder of the inability of Soviet railway officials to differentiate clearly between business and politics;[11] doubtless making embarrassing reading for the large number of Soviet companies and representative agencies that were rapidly developing their work in Manchuria. Such a hard line was an awkward one for the more liberal-minded Soviet consular representatives who were building up cordial relations in the region.[12]

Here too the issue of Soviet policies raises a number of questions, the chief of which was this compelling evidence of the existence – virtually from the start – of a desire to deal with the *émigré* 'problem' with a strong and forceful hand, much encouraged, of course, by the fears that had arisen during the civil war, as detailed in Chapter 2. However, this pragmatic political line had, in some way, to be squared with Soviet inclination to create a business-like, co-operative presence in the region. After all, as has been argued earlier, the Soviet agreement with Mukden was widely hailed as the epitome of just such a relationship between the radical and conservative partners. Both the attitude towards, and the treatment of, the *émigré* presence therefore stood as something of a key to the success or failure of this novel venture. The years 1924–28 were the crucial ones to the unfolding of this problem.

Here, one has to note from the outset that, despite the fearsome character of the civil war and the terrible hardships that 'White' and 'Red' alike experienced in the course of this conflict, the lines of demarcation between the two political categories are not altogether clear-cut on the ground in Manchuria. Indeed, they remained fluid during the conflict itself, making the Soviet policies that much more important to the political stability of the Manchurian area in the subsequent period of peace. There are many examples of this to be found in the descriptions of the civil war in Siberia, the Russian Far East and Manchuria, but these are particularly vivid in the recollections of the rank-and-file combatants, in whom, arguably, this phenomenon was most strongly present.

One such Russian, Alexei Petrovich Zanozin, who served with Ataman Annenkov in Siberia, Mongolia and Manchuria, recalled how surprised he was to have learned, after having heard numerous ghastly stories of how the skin had been stripped away from the backs of 'White' soldiers by 'Red' partisan bands, that 'White' soldiers had been slipping away for evenings of dancing and *liaisons* with women in 'Red' partisan camps nearby. At first he considered this to be nothing more than a fantastic rumour. Eventually, however, he noticed one of his own number slip away from the camp, returning some hours later that night. Curious about this, Zanozin decided to join him the following evening. He noticed that this sort of behaviour went on 'under the nose' of the their commander who, although not in favour of such antics, nonetheless did nothing to stop them. Upon reaching the 'Red' partisan area, he was astounded by the reception he and his comrade received. The partisans encouraged Zanozin and his fellow soldiers to '...take a woman and some land and settle down peacefully in the area'. Despite the fact that he did not take this advice, he went on visiting the partisan base. Evenings of 'wine, women and song' were supplemented by some furious card sessions.[13] The only logical explanation he could think of to explain this openness on the part of his – supposedly – sworn enemies was the possibility that the 'Red' partisans were especially keen on attracting Zanozin's division because of their 'enlightened sense of discipline and internal relations [between soldiers and officers]'.[14] And yet this too does not ring altogether true, given the reputation that the 'White' officers had – often deservedly – achieved in the region. Zanozin himself, in fact, remembered his division's stay in Vladivostok, where many of Annenkov's injured existed under 'horrendous conditions, lying on stone floors at the railway station and without much medical attention'.[15] He himself, having been lightly injured before his arrival in that city, learned that one of his 'White' commanders was staying at a local hotel, so he, together with another soldier, decided to visit him to plead for help for their fellow-soldiers. They arrived at the hotel to meet the officer, who they noticed was staying in '...very comfortable surroundings indeed'.[16] After protracted effort to convince him to act, all they managed to elicit was the cold response: 'All of us must exist under harsh conditions. I will do nothing for you'.[17]

But it was not from the broader 'White' command alone that Zanozin had experienced such affronts to human dignity. Within Annenkov's forces themselves there were reports of atrocities that simply strained comprehension, and encouraged soldiers to consider changing sides.[18] However, even experiences such as Zanozin's had not, in fact, compelled soldiers such as him to cross over to the Bolsheviks, or, in his own description, to 'neutralise' themselves when offered the opportunity to do so. Indeed, this question obviously played on the minds of the more thoughtful (and especially those who had not experienced Bolshevik 'excesses' at first-hand) for many years to come. They, like the many demobilised soldiers returning from the Western front in the course of the revolution and civil war, were at least potentially open to the humanistic appeals that the Bolsheviks had employed so successfully in their efforts to win the hearts and minds of their adversaries. In the end, one might conclude that had the Soviet authorities in Northern Manchuria not pursued hostile policies aimed, it would seem, at isolating, demoralizing and, ultimately, destroying the pocket of Russian settlement that had developed in the region, they might well have found ready allies in the task of building up a sustained Russian economic presence in the area. To the Soviet authorities men like Zanozin were potentially dangerous elements, whereas one could argue that they were first and foremost Russians whose political views could hardly be regarded as having been set in stone, at least when they first settled in Northern Manchuria. However, through the constant pressure brought to bear on the *émigré* community a balanced outlook and neutral position became more and more difficult to either sustain or, as in Zanozin's case, to so much as contemplate seriously.[19] Worse still, the Soviet actions forced a proportion of men, who might otherwise have possibly been able to co-exist with the new presence, into the opposition's camp. The opposition, on the other hand, became all the more alienated, and willing to take on ever more antagonistic positions. In a sense, therefore, Soviet behaviour encouraged the crystallisation of what had been feared, and what Moscow had sought to eradicate: something approaching a uniformly oppositional *émigré* body.

It is difficult to quantify the losses of good-will from amongst the ranks of Russians who were either neutral to, or perhaps even marginally inclined towards, the many virtues that the Soviet Union, at least in principle, represented. Whatever their number, they would have added to the critical mass of younger, more idealistic Russians who had been born or spent their childhood in Manchuria, and who, at least for a time, were inspired by what they came to regard the Russian Revolution as standing for. Of these younger Russians, moreover, some came from backgrounds which did not automatically make them averse to the Soviet Union. The families they came from were often a complex mix: a strong sense of individualism and political balance; traits which were visibly passed on to their children.

*Émigré* family histories often display some of the twists, turns and ambiguities that the Soviet presence represented to them in Northern Manchuria; often, in turn, inspiring and then deflating the idealists among them. Evident too was the complex psyche that emerged from the curious intellectual cross-fertilisation that had taken place, filled as it was with contradictions which only a politico-cultural environment such as Harbin's could have provided. In the five short years of its presence in Northern Manchuria, the Soviet Union had created many of what can be best described as 'half-baked patriots'. When we examine the psychological traits of these individuals, we find spirited, extremely bright adolescents who were politically partly conscious, to the extent at least that they were in favour of change, and possibly even to the extent of contemplating seriously the dismantling of the stifling old order. And yet their education and attachment to their own life-style would not permit a full acceptance of the events and social forces at play just across the border in the Soviet Union. Hence, their realignment could only ever have been a partial one. Families were frequently not altogether 'White' or 'Red,' and the forms of education experienced by children reflected this ambiguity, and most notably so in the way the latter approached learning and culture in Harbin. In talking about the positive contribution made by Soviet educationalists, views were clear-cut, with young people inspired by the achievements of the Soviet Union.[20] And yet, quite understandably, analyses of the politics of the region were strongly shaped by influences other than those of Soviet origin. Tertiary students would speak with pride about the notions and theories of the state produced in the discourses of leading academics at the *Iuridicheskii Fakul'tet* (Faculty of Law).[21] A Professor Ustrialov was an academic who was regularly singled out in demonstrating how far advanced Harbin was in this area of study.[22] And yet the same Ustrialov had, in fact, been one of the major personalities (together with the symbol of reactionary politics, Khorvat) behind Harbin's resistance and separatism in the course of the Revolution and Civil War.[23] Suffice it to say, in Harbin Marxist and bourgeois notions of – and preoccupations with – the state were at considerable variance too, although by the time the post-revolutionary generation of students came across these ideas, Stalinist orthodoxy was in the process of bringing these separate notions even closer together.

What we must also recognise about Harbin of this period, therefore, and quite curiously, is the existence of an environment conducive to the free association of ideas. In the case of some, the formation of their world view is one that can be quite logically traced; in the case of others, perhaps lacking broad areas of interest and learning, the world view could as easily be politically phantasmagorical. It is within the less critical middle ground that, in this brief period of political openness, the main struggle for hearts and minds took place between Right and Left. Ironically, the peculiarities in the formation of the students' political outlook meant that in many cases they would be forever lost to both ideological camps. Lost too, often as a result of their premature dispersal, or, if they stayed on, their neutralisation, was the considerable acumen and depth of understanding of the foreigners' life among the Chinese.[24]

The political climate that emerged in this critical period was, like its enigmatic actors, a complex one. In its way, the atmosphere of tension and heightened political feelings in Harbin was comparable to that experienced by the Soviet agents in China proper, although lacking in the sense of imminent danger that might have been felt in a place like Canton.

Harbin's own political conditioning had begun somewhat earlier, having been the focus for those running from Russia during the Revolution, but in particular the large numbers entering in the protracted period of the civil war. A refugee aphorism 'the further we go, the quieter it will be,' current during the tumult in Russia, was frequently adhered to, with Harbin serving as a *glush'* (wilderness) for many of those who crossed the border. The city, after all, had all the characteristics of old Russia, and with few reminders of what they had been running from. Bolshevik activity in the city in the course of the revolution and civil war was, as has been discussed earlier (in Chapter 2), minimal. A story circulated regarding the time that Military Headquarters for the Zaamur Region was finally dissolved and the Russian flag 'beneath which the CER was established' taken down, while the Bolsheviks stood by clapping.[25] *Émigré* society in Harbin had, moreover, nervously watched the closing of the tsarist Russian postal service in their region and the handing over of control of the local police to the Chinese authorities. They watched too the departure of General Khorvat for Peking and self-exile after his abortive attempt to establish an independent Russian Manchuria. In the face of all of these changes, *émigré* society stood powerless. Despite all of these changes, however, the city remained relatively quiet. In his memoirs, I.I. Serebrennikov relates the strange feeling he experienced in seeing the stream of humanity arrive to join this society and '...somehow become silent...beginning to live in their memories of the past and the uncertain, troubled hopes for a better future'.[26] The only form of solace, he observed, was in prayer. The churches had found a new vitality in these very difficult times, with choirs forming that would not be out of place in the biggest of Russian towns.[27] Although there was a chronic shortage of work in Harbin, and a persistent fear that Bolshevism was '...outrunning the runners, waving red flags and teasing as it ran',[28] many of the refugees refused to move on to cities such as Tsingtao and Shanghai, where work was more readily available. 'What will be, will be,' they said, 'but we will not move from Harbin. Enough, we've run enough!'[29] Such attitudes were to subtly change as it became clear to many that there was not likely to be a better future, and yet the stubbornness of 'enough is enough' still made the idea of moving away from Harbin unacceptable for many, even if this meant denying themselves work and a modestly comfortable existence. Therefore, in the course of the 1920s we see the emergence, and indeed rapid growth, of a hard core of impoverished Russians, for whom the potent atmosphere for political rumour and simple gossip provided one or the few heady forms of diversion.[30]

Many had reached Harbin with little or no money, and in later years came to eke out an existence in a city where accommodation was difficult to find and expensive. The more fortunate were able to seek the assistance of family, friends or simply acquaintances who had run ahead of them and were already able to establish a life for themselves. The majority, however, were not able to do so. Memories of the sacrifices that the soldiers had made for the 'White' cause during the terrible conflicts were remarkably quickly forgotten. Serebrennikov found this a difficult thing either to understand or accept. He asked a former soldier that he met on the streets of Harbin how many times he had been wounded: '"twenty-one," he answered in a quiet tone'.[31] The thought caused Serebrennikov to reflect sadly on their experiences in their new home:

> Many [of them] had followed their own 'way of the cross' from the Caspian to the shores of the Pacific Ocean, across the entire Asian continent. If only these Russian wayfarers had been talked about, written of in the newspapers at an early stage. Now, no-one sees anything special in them: 'So what,' they say, 'people ran, saved themselves – what is there to speak of?'[32]

In the years 1917–21, there had still been hopes of a military reversal in Russia, while in the following year or so some of those 'temporarily' residing in Harbin continued to look for a rising of the people against their Bolshevik oppressors. News throughout those years was greedily devoured: Wrangel's battles, the war with Poland, events in Soviet Siberia and the 'buffer' Far Eastern Republic, the Amur and the Maritime Province. Information 'from there', as the refugees came to call their former home, fed conversations and encouraged rumour. In order to satisfy the demand for information, local Russian newspapers at times published reports that raised spirits dramatically, and yet were based on the skimpiest evidence. In 1920 *Russkii Golos* (Russian Voice) published a note concerning a major peasant rising in Western Siberia. Despite the lack of detail, or authoritative confirmation, the article caused great elation in Harbin. The information for this story turned out to be from a commercial agent at Urga and from an 'official Chinese source'. With no further news arising about this 'uprising', disillusion descended upon those who were celebrating only a few days earlier. Much later, the true basis for the story emerged: there had been a small, localised rising in Tobolsk Province, which had been quickly suppressed by Soviet authorities. 'Its size, one had to think,' a commentator observed, 'increased in direct proportion to the distance [that Harbin] was away from it!'[33] This volatile political climate was to remain even after it was clear that the new government in Russia was not likely to either collapse or be overthrown. Gradually, instead of looking for good news to report of signs of the imminent destruction of the Soviet Union, the Harbin press turned to the close tracking of newly recognised socialist state's activities in China, and especially Manchuria.

Perhaps the most significant feature arising from the Russian *émigré* society's attention to its own immediate domain was that much of the politics that resulted from this assumed a populist character, but was not specifically steered by any of the experienced political leaders who had fled to China. Khorvat's departure to Peking left a sizeable gap in the formal political sphere. None of the men who one might have expected to have taken control did so. Indeed, in the case of the more illustrious of these, there was a very clear distancing occurring. Serebrennikov, who had been a senior member of the Government in Siberia and seemingly a most suitable centrist leader, was quick to forsake Harbin for Peking. Before him, Baron Staal'-Gol'shtein had done the same thing, using his considerable skills in Sanskrit to become a professor at Peking University.[34] While Serebrennikov dabbled in activities on the periphery of *émigré* politics in China for some time, Staal'-Gol'shtein steered well clear of any involvement in this, and had done so from the start.[35] In effect, therefore, this left Khorvat as the undisputed – but nominal – head of the Russian emigration in China, and by extension Manchuria, until he was dislodged from this role too by the newly recognised Soviet diplomatic presence in Peking.[36] The situation of the *émigrés*, ironically, mirrored that of the pro-Soviet members of the Harbin community for the period in question: neither had the benefit of clear, sophisticated political direction to draw upon.[37] However, both tended to focus on the many reports on the Soviet Union's acts of subversion abroad, but particularly those closer to home; work of people such as Borodin and Karakhan in China, and, in Manchuria, the ill-fated Lashevich. This steady, curiously disembodied (but nonetheless immensely embittering) conflict took place in as rarefied an environment as had been the response to the earlier-mentioned peasant rebellion of 1920 in Tobolsk Province.

The combination of idle hands, and often brains too, engaged in a process of 'intelligence-gathering' and the spreading of rumour, which itself was at times credible and at others fantastic, imparted upon Harbin not only the image of being the 'Paris of the North' and a thriving centre for trade and commerce, but also that of a political cesspool.[38]

The bitter struggle between the pro-Soviet and the *émigrés* unfolded in this period only in ways that the existing constrictions allowed it to. Without inspirational leadership, the contest was more often than not through rival organisations and informal groups, mixed with some 'traditional' forms of political outlet such as anti-Semitism.[39] The various forms of political contest frequently coalesced, as anti-Semitism was also prevalent among young Soviet toughs, many of whom were working in the CER machine shops.[40] Thus, often Jews often had to contend with not only the extreme Right in Harbin, but also the Left. Boris Bresler depicts this curious situation in the following way:

> Within twenty blocks there stood two buildings that symbolized the paradox of the situation. One building housed the local headquarters of KOMSOMOL (the communist youth organization) and the other the local headquarters of the Russian fascist youth organization, the BLACK RING. Their groups roamed the streets, not unlike the youth gangs of New York's Hell's Kitchen, and fist fights between Jews and their foes

were common. The Jewish youths were fair game for both sides, and had to learn to defend themselves as best they could (some better than others). For the KOMSOMOL, the Jewish kids were the enemy as 'dirty Yid capitalists,' even though most of the Jewish families were far from being rich. For the BLACK RING, the Jews were the enemy as 'dirty Yid communists,' even though most belonged to the Zionist youth organization *Betar* and were frequently called 'Jewish fascists' by some of their Jewish friends.[41]

For Chinese bystanders this must have been a sight, and indeed a concept, that was even more perplexing. For the Mukden authorities, however, the problem was not only to understand the politics that confronted them, but also how to *contain* it.

The solution, as befits the crude style associated with warlord politics, was, in the end, for the Mukden government to accumulate as much power as possible in its own hands vis-à-vis the Russian community. This was the case even when Chang Tso-lin was for a time (in 1920–21) on a weak footing relative to the other contending Chinese forces in the northern reaches.[42] Nonetheless, the Mukden authorities had, even through this turbulent period, continued to gather power within Harbin itself. By 1924, the Marshal's situation had improved considerably, and he began to act as something of a local patron to his Russian *émigré* subjects, giving them limited freedom of activity in the political sphere, and thereby seeking to turn them into dependable, loyal citizens. The success of his countermove against the Soviet effort to remove stateless Russians from the CER in 1924 helped him greatly in lifting his prestige amongst the non-Soviet Russians in Harbin.

Chang's scheme, however, did not result in quite the sense of calm that he intended. One of the main problems here (and, given the picture of hopelessness painted earlier of some sections of the Russian community, paradoxically) was the ability of the Russians to penetrate and lock into existing Chinese society. A notable, and ultimately perhaps even crucial, example in this respect was the Russians' ability to co-exist with the Chinese underworld, so significant to the functioning of Republican China in this period.[43]

In Manchuria the *Hunghutze* (Red Beards) grew to a stature and notoriety similar to the Triads in other parts of China (and who were important even to the Kuomintang in China proper).[44] Although originally the *Hunghutze* had been 'noble rebels' in the mould of other such groups in Chinese history, by this time they had lost almost all of the veneer of historical respectability[45] and were associated largely with more venal pursuits such as protection, extortion, robbery, kidnapping and murder. For the most part, they held sway outside of the settlements (see below), but from time to time carried out their illegal activities within them too, employing a very well-developed system of local contacts and operatives. Their networks were almost completely invisible to local authorities and foreigners (the richer of whom, together with their families, were popular targets for kidnapping) alike.[46] An incident a Harbin Russian recalled suggested why this was the case. In the 1920s this Russian, who was working as a commercial buyer at the time, on one of his buying trips encountered a camel train of about 80 animals carrying BAT cigarettes via Urumchi and Kalgan. Soon after he had seen it, the camel train was set upon by a party of *Hunghutze* and the tobacco products plundered. The authorities, at the behest of the company, sent out soldiers and policemen to trace the theft. 'For many weeks,' he remembered, 'the officials frantically criss-crossed the area to find the culprits and recover the goods, but with no result'.[47] The story ended with the Russian seeing a few of the policemen and soldiers involved in the search stopping and smoking some of the products from the very shipment that had been seized by the bandits.[48]

Among the measures that Chang Tso-lin adopted to collar the Russian community of Northern Manchuria was the introduction of a Russian wing to the local police force, although the latter was to be under Chinese control.[49] The measure was important not only for reasons of political control but, in an uninhibited commercial environment such as Harbin's, coupled with a large and fairly solid core of unemployed and impoverished Russians, the potential for Russian crime was considerable. However, it gradually became evident that the Russian police officers were as close to the bandits as were some of their Chinese counterparts.[50]

The formation, and firming, of low level relations such as these, together with the political sniping and brawling between various factions in the Russian community and the exertion of an increasingly tight grip on power in the region by Chang Tso-lin (emboldened enough to have sent his troops to Peking to raid the Soviet Mission there in 1927), presented a daunting image of Northern Manchuria in 1928 to at least one interested party: Japan. The latter had been building up its involvement in the region through a rapid increase in its involvement in the economy,[51] increasing its human presence[52] and had done much to carefully position its political place there.[53] Important too is the amount of intelligence that was being gathered on the ground in Northern Manchuria by a number of Japanese agencies and research institutes.[54] Information was compiled covering a myriad of economic, social, political and ethnographic topics, ranging from minutiae on Russian farming in the North Manchurian heartland,[55] to the activities of local councils/administrative bodies in Harbin, to the nature of Chinese prostitution in that city.[56] Such information-gathering was systematically supplemented by the surreptitious placement of senior intelligence officers in positions that could only suggest that they were there to observe and to gather information from Chinese and Russian officials during the latter's unguarded moments.[57]

For Japan, the political picture that was coming into focus in Northern Manchuria would have been particularly worrying, given the nature of its *modus operandi*. As a rule, the Japanese presence was marked by far more formalistic relations with the region and its political and social systems. There is little, if any, evidence of Japanese nationals becoming entangled in local lawlessness in the way, so clearly, the Russians were.[58] Based on their intelligence-gathering activities, the nexus of Chinese authorities and some of the less than morally upright Russian and Chinese residents, together with the increasingly complicated political situation that was developing between Chinese, Soviet citizens and *émigré* circles, the Japanese concern for both their future in the region, and the security of their own interests in Southern Manchuria, would have signalled a compelling need for *some* action to draw the region closer to Japanese authority. However, in addition to this, there emerged another disturbing image: since the signing of the Soviet-Mukden treaty in 1924, the see-saw struggle between Chang Tso-lin (egged on by his *émigré* supporters) and the Soviet Union for control of the CER Zone took on a protracted and messy character. Four years later, there was still no satisfactory conclusion to this thorny issue. If anything, the problem seemed to be leading to an open contest of wills between a warlord (with his increased prestige to nurture and preserve) and Moscow. Moreover, this was a contest of wills that saw the Marshal drawing closer to southern Chinese political voices and allies, as the seemingly co-ordinated efforts of Chang and Chiang Kai-shek in stemming the 'red tide' in Peking and Canton in 1927 suggested.[59] This too would have provided Japan with food for thought: virtually from the start its strategic thinking was of a Manchuria that was a separate political entity, uninhibited by the interests of China proper.[60] At this point, however, such a goal began to appear ever more remote. As one Russian correspondent in China observed at this time in a letter to the Paris-based publication *Dni* (Days), 'It will not be at all surprising if some sort of new, unexpected large page in Chinese history will unfold by the time this correspondence reaches you'.[61]

What unfolded came in the aftermath of the spectacular assassination of Marshal Chang Tso-lin on 4 June 1928. Chang's death occurred as his train, carrying the warlord himself together with all the governors of the northern province, a number of ministers in his government and most of his military leaders, was on the downward approach to Mukden, in a small tunnel where the Southern Manchurian Line met with the Peking-Mukden Line (about 5 *versts* from the southern capital). The charge that had been planted there went off with split-second timing, just as the middle three coaches of the Marshal's heavily-guarded train passed over it. The spot where the explosion took place was only a few hundred metres from a Japanese railway terminus, and therefore located in the Japanese zone, guarded by Japanese troops.[62] Tellingly, with regard to the veracity of

Harbin's Russian press, while the English-language *Harbin Observer* reported Chang dead, Russian-language papers in Harbin announced that the Marshal had survived the explosion, had undergone an operation and that '...his condition was improving'.[63]

Volgin, *Dni's* correspondent in Harbin, commented on the situation in a slightly different way to the voice of optimism in the Russian reports. 'Wasn't there in its design,' Volgin asked pointedly, 'the intention to create the conditions of crisis, breakdown, panic and anarchy?'[64] He continued with the following observation:

> Suddenly, and tragically, there was no was no authority, nor even an alternative [body of officials] to replace it. In its place, there is anarchy, the collapse of the remaining elements of the [Mukden] army etc. etc. Aren't these the best conditions for the inevitable intervention of an outsider and the declaration that their temporary interference [in matters of state] is in order to guard law and order, and to defend their material interests [in the region]?[65]

With, at a stroke, virtually the entire political and military leadership gone, there was no need for Japan to declare such intentions. It simply allowed a natural succession to take place from Chang Senior to his son Chang Hsüeh-liang, simultaneously taking an even closer advisory position in the 'court' of the new Marshal.[66] For the *émigré* community, its brief rise in political fortunes would have appeared to be temporarily blocked. In fact, this was the start of its final decline.

# 5
# An Economy on the Brink

The economic setting within which Russian settlement had taken root in Northern Manchuria was one shaped by the intertwining of the politics of railway and colonization. This was the inevitable result of Russia's continued imperialistic aspirations in Manchuria, foreshadowed by the Tsar himself in 1913, and which were to remain active until the chaos of revolution took hold of Russia. Together with this, there was also the muddled message that the new Soviet government was to convey in the first years of its involvement in Manchuria. As one prominent Chinese nationalist, Liang Ch'i-chao, put it in the mid-1920s:

> Is the Soviet Union an imperialist? I have no hesitation in answering: it is the crystallized product of imperialism; it is the big devil of imperialism.... The common saying is right; it is easier to change the landscape than the character.... The politics which the Russians play is always autocracy inside and aggression outside. They would not feel comfortable if they do not do so.... O Soviet Russia! Do you want to say that you are not imperialistic? The day on which you stop your activities in China will be the day we believe you. But, is this really possible?[1]

The principal means employed by the Central and Provincial Chinese leaders to counter this apparent imperialism, as has already been discussed in Chapter 1, was to step up the process of physical colonisation through the encouragement of millions of Chinese peasants to move into the provinces that made up Manchuria.[2] As the CER built up its arterial lines through regions which had hitherto been inhabited by nomads, as well as into areas and townships that the Manchu Dynasty had earlier reserved for its own needs, so the Chinese settlers moved into these newly opened lands.[3] The symbiotic nature of this process supplemented the masses of Chinese workers sent to the region by the Chinese authorities themselves for the construction of the railway; workers who then became a ready-made body of colonisers, as had been the central Chinese government's intention.[4]

The Chinese efforts at colonising Manchuria in this way were a considerable success, as the Chinese population of the region grew swiftly. In Helungkiang Province (with a total area of 224 944 square miles), the population grew from 408 000 in 1887, to 2 462 000 in 1914, to 5 321 000 in 1930.[5] In province of Kirin (with a total area of 103 379 square miles), the rise in population was even sharper, with the 1 063 000 population in 1891 rising to 5 617 000 in 1914, and 9 192 000 in 1930.[6]

While there was a dramatic increase in the population of Northern Manchuria, as is evident from these figures, the size of the population was nonetheless relatively low for the purposes of conducting an extensive colonization of Manchuria. More important than this, however, was the nature of the incoming peasants, which did not equip them fully for the pioneering life-style that they were to encounter in Manchuria. This was especially true of the traditional forms of farming that they brought with them; forms which were not entirely suited to the physical spread of the Manchurian *steppe*. Chinese farming methods were labour-intensive and the peasants reliant upon a close link with the markets in town centres.[7] The agriculture of Russian peasants, on the other hand, could, as a Harbin economist put it, 'flower at a distance from town centres'.[8] The same economist concluded that without the aid of a railway, Chinese agriculture would be able to expand only very slowly, 'that is to say, according to the thousand-year tempo that we have observed until now in the way in which China opens up its territories'.[9] It was, judging from accounts such as this, the Russian peasants and the native minorities (the latter with their nomadic/semi-nomadic existences) who were more suited to the geography of the region.[10] In addition, from contemporary Russian accounts, it appeared that the Chinese peasants streaming into Northern Manchuria were far from being well versed in modern forms of commercial agriculture. With a certain amount of frustration, agronomist P.F. Konstantinov posed the following question concerning the state of the Chinese peasantry in Manchuria in 1925: 'Who knows when it will be before Chinese fields tractors will not appear as some foreign monster, or when wooden ploughs and stone rollers will be exchanged for steel ploughs and threshing machines?'[11] While it was possible for the Chinese peasant to generate high levels of commercial agricultural output without the more modern forms, this 'primitivism' was to reflect unfavourably on the nature of the import trade in major centres such as Harbin, where it was consistently difficult, if not impossible, to forecast quantities of imports[12] and, more importantly, to observe a steady rise in such trade.

The nature of the Chinese sector of Northern Manchurian commercial agriculture was, therefore, both simple in its character and, in spatial terms, largely limited to the catchment area of the CER itself, or the areas that could easily be reached by water or cart transport. Russian agrarian enterprise, although not hindered by such factors, was also largely limited to the

CER 'corridors', but for very different reasons. With the Russians, the major constraining factors were: (a) the difficulties in raising capital for larger-scale enterprise; and (b) the increasing influence of the political factors.[13] As has already been observed, taken as a whole, in political terms the period 1917–24 was particularly severe for the *émigrés*. For Soviet citizens, on the other hand, a period of hardship commensurate with this was experienced by them in 1924–29 (and especially 1927–29). These political pressures, when they showed themselves in the local economy, may be characterised in two ways. For the Russian *émigrés* the scope of economic activity was affected by a dual constriction: the long-term Chinese constraints and the short-term efforts to limit *émigré* economic pursuits. For Soviet citizens, 1927 marked the start of a period of open persecution (moderating somewhat after the Soviet military success in late 1929), which was to spill over dramatically into the economic sector, as will be demonstrated in the next chapter. Furthermore, the informal areas of influence exercised by the *émigrés* assumed a more potent form at that time. Their important positions in the Chinese Maritime Customs (particularly as tidewaiters), for example, allowed them an enhanced potential to persecute Soviet citizens, and especially so when taken in conjunction with the growing stature of *émigrés* in the ranks of Chang Tso-lin's military, as the warlord's advisers, as well as activity in other military and paramilitary bodies. Moreover, Harbin emphasised and heightened the polarization already existing in the Russian settlements, with the emergence there of *émigré* groups such as *Soiuz Mushketiorov* (The Union of Musketeers), which, eccentric and innocuous as their names they may have seemed, imparted a most sinister impression on Soviet Russians.[14]

Thus, a relationship between Chinese and Russian economic spheres of activity, which by their very nature should have been complementary and thriving, instead came to be something of a twin burden on the CER. The railway had, in effect, both the spread of Chinese colonisation and the heavily constrained development of the Russian sector of the economy left as its areas of responsibility. Both, it must be added, were highly capital-intensive areas of activity for the CER, and both were a cause of capital overstretch.[15] The North Manchurian economist Gorshenin echoed this view in a 1926 article on the railway freight levels in Manchuria. In the course of this article he argued that when the future of the vast area of Manchuria was contemplated, it became clear that the SMR and CER should have produced a unified plan for the opening up of further tracts of land, based not on principles of competition but on the 'cooperative work of the railways'. In putting forward such a proposal, Gorshenin pointed to the logic of treating the South Manchurian, North Manchurian and Ussuri Railways as part of a single, homogeneous economic entity;[16] a logic which was not only sound in its own internal make-up, but also appeared to be an expression of exasperation at the pressures being brought to bear upon the CER itself.

An important focus in examining the Northern Manchurian economy in this period remains, then, the railway, the massive investment associated with it, and the economic 'index' which it set for the region. However, this should not be allowed to obscure the fact that even though the railway was of vital importance to a primitive colonial economic framework, the study of the CER should not replace, or drastically distort, the study of the broader economy.

On the Western seaboard of the United States in the early 1800s, '...one dominating subject of conversation among settlers was the need for improved transportation facilities'.[17] Much the same can be said of Manchuria. Transport was vital for rapid migration and colonisation, while the latter was, in turn, crucial to the facilitation of the rapid economic take-off of the region. This was a crucial theme in the debate over the future of Northern Manchuria,[18] and understandably so: without railway expansion, there would be little hope of exploiting vast tracts of virgin land and even less hope of implanting Western methods of agriculture and industry in the areas already peopled. The arterial format of the CER remained, of course, the vital force of the Northern Manchurian economy. But what was marked in its absence was a capillary rail/transport network that might force land prices upwards and generate capital internally in a broader area of the hinterland. Despite this, it is important not to lose sight of the fact that many millions of settlers, including large numbers of Russians, were finding their way into the hinterland without such a capillary rail system being in existence. It is vital, therefore, in looking at the nature of the economy at this time, to bear in mind the *general* underlying factor of an underdeveloped railway/transport network.

Such an approach emphasises both the strategic value of the railway,[19] and also its vulnerability; the value of the railway being very much dependent on the success of colonisation, the spread of commercial agriculture, the development of communications and, thereby, the increased influence and strength of the arterial network.[20] One of the best indicators of this curious combination of strengths and weaknesses was the nature of the CER auxiliary enterprises and their susceptible state,[21] leading to sustained, and increasingly frustrated, attempts by the CER to introduce diversification to the periphery's economy. Such a process was unlikely to succeed without considerable inputs of capital (both human and financial), which, as we have seen earlier, the CER was unable to provide. The alternative was to attract capital on the open market and in the enterprises' own right, which was an unlikely course for two reasons. First, the chicken-and-egg situation with respect to the sparse population, which meant that these operations could not survive on the basis of their own, thin markets. Secondly, the fact that merchants, and behind them the banks too, were increasingly looking to commercial agriculture (notably soya beans) for a quick profits; a tendency that helped to further eclipse the other areas of the economy. The slower returns provided by the work of venture capital was, for these reasons, far less attractive than the often windfall-like profits of commercial agriculture.[22]

The combination of strengths and weaknesses was highlighted by other factors too, notably the rivalries over railway construction,[23] and the difficulties thereby encountered in developing the railway network. In this respect, the central Chinese and Manchurian governments were unable to raise the necessary finances to markedly develop the transportation network in the region. In any case, where it was allowed to do so, the Chinese efforts were directed at *duplicating* the existing network, rather than extending the arterial lines that were already in place. In addition to this, however, were also the perennial weaknesses associated with road and river communications.[24]

In a sense, therefore, the railway was at one and the same time a manifestation of, but also a hindrance to, the development of sovereignty in the region. This meant that foreign companies were not able to achieve a level of success attainable in China proper, due to Russian opposition in Northern Manchuria. The Russians, on the other hand, were not able to achieve full economic and political hegemony without being in control of the process of colonisation and possessing the ability to tap this process in order to generate capital. And, finally, the Chinese were hard pressed to achieve full control of the periphery without playing into the hands of the Russians, or creating irrational elements in the economy (for example, the duplication of railway lines mentioned above), or achieving stability of colonisation (the numbers of Chinese migrants here were insufficient to secure firm political control of the region[25]). Ideally, the goal in this last respect might have been to quickly settle the incoming masses and thereby to create stable pockets of Chinese interest, linked very firmly to the CER's own areas of activity and development. Instead it came to be an area of tension and, ultimately, contest.

This was overwhelmingly a three-way struggle between China, Japan and Russia. The 'fault line' in the political economy of Northern Manchuria also served as a 'battlefield' for the contest; manouevres involving the rapid and controlled colonisation of the region, to allow the competing powers a firm claim the sovereignty over the area. Japan was, through the Russian presence in Northern Manchuria, temporarily blocked from embarking on a full-scale transplant of Japanese and Koreans there, although capital and commercial influence continued to grow in advance of Japan taking *de facto* and then *de jure* control of the region.[26] The Russians, on the other hand, in a sense hampered their own claims in this contest. The majority of Russians who came across the border were urban dwellers, with the Russian peasants who fled from Siberia not making up a sufficient critical mass to allow them to create agrarian infrastructure in the countryside, and thereby were unable to exploit local agricultural resources on anything but a localised scale. If anything, Russians tended to gravitate to a small number of established centres rather than founding a greater number of settlements, and thereby controlling greater geographical expanses; something that was in any event looked upon warily by the Chinese authorities.[27] The only major example of this form of development (and its potential) was *Trekhrech'e*,[28] but the latter was itself the subject of considerable political scrutiny, not the least of which being the threat it seemed to convey to the Soviet Union.[29] Soviet citizens were inhibited from entertaining any plan for a firm territorial foothold. The periphery was, on the whole, extremely hostile to Soviet presence,[30] while the cities were ideological hotbeds, with little chance of establishing full control as a result. Ideologically, therefore, any Soviet attempt to initiate formal colonisation would have been untenable; the exception to this being through the beleaguered medium of the CER itself.[31] Also, of course, there was the internal wrangling going on within the broader Russian presence, manifesting itself in Chinese restrictions (often with *émigré* assistance) on Soviet activities, and Soviet restrictions, in turn, on *émigré* activities throughout the period in question. This continuous infighting within the Russian community ultimately ensured the weakening of any claim (either *de facto* or *de jure*) by Russians to increase their economic activity.[32]

Although, strictly speaking, the Chinese were in the strongest position in this odd equation, for a number of reasons they too were unable to take complete control of the region, and incorporate it fully into the Chinese sphere of sovereignty. The most significant of these was, as suggested above, the inability of Chinese authorities to conduct methodical and stable policy of colonization of the periphery without locking this into the problematic railway question. In addition to this, however, was the central Chinese authorities' rivalry with the warlord administration of Manchuria and their failure to control adequately the formal and informal tax zones, which, being locally imposed, generally ensured that a linkage of the Chinese and Manchurian markets was uneconomical and administratively problematic.[33] Finally, into their own policies the central Chinese authorities had to factor the entangled 'Russian Question', as well as external pressure from Japan; the latter drawing in long-standing ideological confrontations between Japan and China.[34]

It might be noted that the difficulties experienced in conducting commercial activities were not restricted to only the Russians, Chinese and Japanese: to some degree all foreigners suffered in this economic climate. This was particularly the case in the hinterland, where local authority was wielded in an autarchic fashion, and was something to be dealt with in the most delicate fashion possible: deference had to be shown to magistrates, police, military, local officials, and heed taken of warlord ambitions.[35] But the Russians were especially vulnerable because they had no separate legal code to look to as a recourse; they existed and operated under Chinese jurisdiction. In this sense, therefore, the Russian merchant experienced very similar conditions to that of his Chinese counterpart, whose fortunes swayed like reeds in the 'gusts of wind' of local politics.[36] We have already seen that those working for foreign firms were the lucky few with both ease of mobility and legal protection. Those Russians who worked as pettybusinessmen, owners of small enterprises, or as locally-recruited staff, faced the full force of the more arbitrary facets of local politics.[37]

Given these conditions, the Russian proposals for Manchurian development might have been the best course for all parties concerned, but most notably for China, which might have ultimately been able to make a full and incontestable claim to sovereignty of the region, using the creation of a stable politico-economic infrastructure as the basis for this.[38] However, because of the overlapping economic and political factors in the development of Northern Manchuria, it gradually became clearer that such a course was not open even to China. Part of the problem here lay in the artificial division between Northern and Southern Manchuria.

While we have addressed the situation in terms of the Northern Manchuria, being our principal area of interest in this study, its economy cannot be examined to the exclusion of its southern counterpart, for which a great deal of this analysis holds. It was, after all, the 'dagger pointing at the heart of Japan',[39] the railway, which set the pattern of growth for these economies and, to an overwhelming extent, dictated the forms taken by their major crises. With the artificial disassociation of the blade from the handle of that dagger after the Russo-Japanese War, the more firmly established capital, Harbin, and the chief port, Dairen, instead of functioning as complementary points in a single unified economy, became rival centres of trade, commerce and industry. Quite apart from the obvious inefficiencies created by this duplication of function for the competing economic foci, and their respective catchment areas, each had its Achilles' heel: Harbin, although it served as a natural confluence, being the central 'knot' for railway and trade, was extremely weak as a port, having to employ the River Sungari, with its short and erratic navigation season, for the shipping of goods. Dairen, on the other hand, was an ideal port, but lacked the infrastructural development and the agricultural basin of the north.[40] Thus, the centres evolved and built up their respective 'spheres of influence' during the formative stage of the economies (roughly 1904–14), but the evolution was close and, in many areas, overlapped in the process of competition.

The creation of these parallel economies was particularly felt in the midto late 1920s, when, with the emergence of the Soviet Union as a trading force in the region and the subsequent attempt to build up Vladivostok as a transshipment centre, the 60 per cent share of freight handled by Dairen began to shrink.[41] Accompanying this was, for the Japanese interests, the looming threat of a larger scale integration of the North Manchurian region with Eastern Siberia and the Maritime Province. In the case of the latter, for example, exports to the province from Northern Manchuria had increased dramatically by 1927.[42] The appearance of vigorous Soviet trade activity contributed markedly to the North/South polarisation in an economy that was, by the mid-1920s, already taut.[43] By the latter part of the decade, this developed into a crucial issue: any slack that may have existed was fast disappearing, and a ceiling to further growth, without massive injections of capital, equally rapidly bearing down. Any major input of capital, however, would have had to come from the respective railway companies; an eventuality that was hardly likely in a situation where the South Manchurian Railway (SMR) was conducting a policy of undercutting CER rates, while the latter maintained its rates at a higher level from 1923 onwards, seemingly to tap the upward trend in agricultural production, and concomitantly devoting profits thereby derived to productivity and experimentation rather than capital accumulation. From 1925, the CER showed an increase in the sums allocated to maintenance of track and rolling stock to beyond the theoretical level of 15 per cent of the overall budget. An economist observing the railway's fiscal policy during the first half of the decade concluded: '...the economy of the CER must be handled most carefully and cautiously. The railway has to strive to obtain maximum profits and to limit to a minimum its expenses, because the demands of the coming years may absorb all its savings'.[44] The warning was remarkably accurate: in the years 1930 and 1931 the railway was severely tested and found wanting in precisely this respect.[45] Indeed, it was here that we see the CER was at the time caught squarely in the trap discussed earlier. For its further development, and to allow a significant level of capital build-up to occur, the company had to secure land concessions for the laying of feeder lines, thereby expanding its operations. However, in an acutely labour-intensive agrarian economy such as Manchuria's, the expansion of operations would not tap *existing* pockets of population and agriculture; it would simply encourage the colonisation of uninhabited territory, and, as discussed earlier, this would have brought into play some unwanted political factors too. Comprehensive development, therefore, would be a time- and capital-consuming, and politically most sensitive, process; none of which the company could afford by 1930. Despite these logistical problems, as a contemporary commentator put it: the CER could only have been saved through the combination of a '...rapid colonisation of the country[side] and by the development of industry and trade'.[46] The company had, of course, attempted in earlier years to fulfil the latter part of the equation by embarking upon a scheme of enterprise-creation and experimental farming, but in spite of this, the CER's fate still hinged on rapid and *extensive* colonisation. For such colonisation to take place, a communications network was required so as to allow a market-orientated peasant economy to take root. The equation, therefore, still necessitated an expansion of the area service by the railway.

Completing the dilemma for the management of the railway in this respect was the fact that the CER had been transferred to a 'purely commercial basis' of operations in 1921, and therefore had to show itself to be meeting this requirement in the conduct of its financial affairs.[47] Here, the various pressures discussed earlier came to bear, making it difficult for the railway to function on a commercial footing, and, more importantly, hindering its ability to act as a spur to regional development.

Such a reading should not suggest that the CER and Northern Manchuria experienced only hardships in the early stages. There were, of course, periods of prosperity too. These may be seen as developing in two major stages. The first began with the compression of legal and illegal colonisers into Northern Manchuria. This surge of settlers moving permanently to the north from the southern battlefields during the Sino-Japanese War, helped to build up the CER Zone.[48] However, by 1907, when the three North Eastern Provinces were formed (in effect 'Sinifying' Manchuria), the region was undergoing a financial slump, the CER being in debt and the Russo-Chinese Bank having initiated a credit squeeze. Besides the many bankruptcies, it was also a period of political reorientation, resulting from the loosening of the Russian grip on the local economy. During this period (roughly between 1906 and 1909), the cultivation of soya beans became a primary focus for Manchurian farmers, while foreign merchants learned and perfected their means and methods of bean export. From 1910 the cultivation of this 'useful bean', as the Hongkong & Shanghai Banking Corporation's (HSBC) representative in Harbin described it, received great impetus from a 'fearful scramble' for its export, with crops being sold twice over in some cases.[49] The next period was one characterised by the change in trading conditions caused by the Russian Revolution of 1917, the latter having further weakening Russian economic authority in the region. By 1920 the transition was complete and is vividly represented by the experience of the HSBC in Harbin, as one of its employees remembered it:

> Here at last came the opportunity for [the] Harbin Office to come into prominence in [the] Harbin commercial world. This opportunity was not lost and in spite of the continued depreciation of the rouble Harbin Office developed such activities by about the year 1920 that it was soon decided to build the bank's own building....[50]

The growth of the economy initiated by this change in conditions was fired by the convergence of a number of other factors which ensured that it was rapid and sustained: six years of good harvests, beginning in 1922, which led to annual surpluses in beans and most cereals;[51] a rapid rise in the prices of all bean products;[52] the constant 'priming' of the labour market, with an annual population growth of 3 to 5 per cent;[53] a significant decline in banditry.[54] These were augmented by a slight relaxation of credit conditions in a situation where, at least before 1924, there was little competition between banks.[55] Not surprisingly, export returns soared and were complemented to an extent by falling prices in the consumer sector, particularly in essential goods such as kerosene.[56]

In 1927, when Chinese cities were in the throes of severe economic contraction as a result of raging political strife drastically affecting trade and industry,[57] Northern Manchuria recorded progress 'more favourable than in the preceding two or three years',[58] with Harbin showing a 15 per cent rise in trade.[59] With the growth in trade and population – Harbin, for instance, had an increase of 33 per cent between 1923 and 1929 – there appeared hundreds of small firms in both the trade and service sectors.[60]

These tendencies, and particularly the concomitant rise in imports,[61] led a Harbin economist to surmise that what was occurring could be regarded as an improvement in the material condition of the peasant economy.[62] However, the yardstick he chose to employ measured not so much the material condition of Manchuria as a whole as that of the urban areas *to the relative exclusion of the peasant economy*. The latter had changed little, still comprised of a great proportion of 'poor farmers' (Chinese peasants with holdings of 10–20 *shan*), with over 50 per cent renting land under terms that were barely tolerable.[63] Sales of grain were perforce conducted through an intricate system of middlemen, taxes, short-term and high-interest loans, and advance purchases; the latter being the only way for a small holder or poor peasant to pay labourers and purchase seed or other requirements during the harvest. These factors, coupled with a strongly fluctuating currency (the *tiao*), left the seller with an actual return that had been reduced by over 40 per cent.[64] The Chinese farmer in Manchuria, it must be noted, was still better off than his counterpart in China proper, but negligibly and *perilously* so, as his economy was based on a market exchange of commodities and his fate increasingly at the mercy of market conditions.[65] The degree to which the indices of prosperity were permeating the peasant economy is accurately represented by the curious phenomenon involving the sale of ploughs in the Harbin area: during the 1926–27 agricultural season, 2500–3000 were sold off from old stock, encouraging a group of enterprising persons to import 7000–8000 more in 1928, but the expected sales did not materialise, with the result that Harbin found itself with an overstocked market in ploughs.[66]

In short: progress, development and prosperity in North Manchuria soon came to rest on the shoulders of a handful of large companies dealing exclusively in the major settlements, and working almost exclusively on building up the trade in soya beans.[67] Most banks, Chinese and foreign alike, refused as a matter of policy to finance any form of indigenous industry. Chinese banks preferred to concentrate on currency emission[68] as well as foreign currency and remittance operations, while foreign banks were involved more in foreign currency dealings and the handling of finance for the export of beans.[69] The foreign banks too, largely through the strain of competition, did involve themselves in the financing of industrial concerns,[70] and were therefore unable to provide the necessary support to boost a broader base for Northern Manchurian productivity, and in this respect suffered a similar fate to that of the CER. In fairness to these banks' commercial acumen, it must be added that Northern Manchurian industry, in absolute terms, but particularly by comparison with the export trade in soya beans, turned in mediocre performances *at best*. The chronic shortage of capital was most telling in the hinterland, where entire settlements rose and fell on the basis of a key source of capital emerging, and, in the course of a sudden slump, being unable to endure the drain on their limited financial resources.[71] Throughout Northern Manchuria, with agriculture making up over 85 per cent of the total value of production, industries – during this period of phenomenal economic growth – registered what was dubbed the 'darkest period in their history'.[72] Not only did this apply to provincial enterprises involving timber, coal, minerals, furs and skins, but even cereal-based enterprises. Flour milling, for example, began to exhibit signs of life only in 1927, after having suffered an initial slump in 1923; and the bean-processing industry, although on the surface quite lively, registering over one 100 per cent increases in production in the years 1922 to 1926, was 'fraught with dangers' and suffering from a shortage of capital.[73] In its impoverished state, Northern Manchurian industry as a whole was unable to generate sufficient fat to see it through an protracted lean period, such as the one it was to encounter in the early 1930s.[74] For most enterprises and businesses, especially those located in provincial towns, austerity had already left a familiar taste by then, having suffered the effects of local crises, and most notably of the Sino-Soviet conflict; the latter reducing turnover to about 40 per cent, and caused credit, together with banking, almost to disappear completely at the height of the conflict in the summer and autumn of 1929.

Against this general economic background for the period, however, we should trace the rise of Soviet fortunes in the Northern Manchurian market. For, despite the obstacles and conundrums which were thrown up by that market, Soviet methods appeared to be more than a match for these, as well as the foreign and Chinese competition Soviet companies encountered in the marketplace.

In Manchuria the process of establishing a Soviet economic foothold was tortuous, as evidenced by the difficulties encountered in wrenching control of the CER zone from the death grip of General Khorvat's 'regime'. The task was made no easier by the Soviet advocacy of a reconstruction of its activities in the area, '...but with new principles of co-operation with the Chinese rather than the pattern of exploitation set during Tsarist times'.[75] This formula would prove difficult to square with the exigencies of countering the practices of less altruistic commercial competitors in the region.

Equally, it provided a strong political weapon for the Chinese authorities in their efforts, between 1924 and 1929, to assume full control of the CER.

As we have seen, the conditions of re-entering North-Eastern China were exacerbated by the presence of a lingering element of opposition – that of the Russian *émigré* society – in an already complicated political fray. Many *émigrés* had experienced years of gradual impoverishment. Their numbers were bloated by large numbers of refugees finding their way across the northern borders of China.[76] Resources available to this political rag-tag, particularly the new arrivals to the Harbin area, were few; a factor which tended to heighten animosity towards their former homeland. Ironically, the increasingly hard times for the Russians coincided with the spectacular rise of the Manchurian economy. This is at least in part explained by the concentration of foreign banks on the bean trade, largely to the exclusion of many other forms of commercial activity that the refugees could engage in. The exports of beans, indeed export trade as a whole, was securely in the grasp of a small number of foreign (but not indigenous Russian) trading companies,[77] and little of the profit was ploughed back into Northern Manchuria. The polarisation between Soviet Russians and *émigrés* showed itself mainly in the atmosphere of mutual suspicion and recrimination. Institutional channels were available to the *émigrés* for their resistance to Soviet activities, the most important being their numbers in CER employment,[78] and those employed by the Chinese Maritime Customs.

This vexed political situation was to some extent fuelled by Soviet Union itself, having been quite slow in forming its new mechanisms of commerce and trade. Although the origins of a Soviet state monopoly and co-ordination of foreign trade may be traced to wartime conditions, with the introduction of a general foreign trade plan and the Supply Committee of the Ministry of Commerce and Industry, the initial steps taken by the Soviet government were tentative ones. Nationalisation of foreign trade was instituted on 23 April 1918, but there was no specification of which organisations were to conduct trade on behalf of the state. Nor was there any firm trade machinery devised until 1920, when decrees were passed transforming the Commissariat of Commerce and Industry into the Commissariat of Foreign Trade. It was only in October/November 1925 that joint stock companies, limited liability companies and syndicates were formed and the People's Commissariat of Foreign Trade merged with the People's Commissariat of Home Trade into a single People's Commissariat of Trade.[79] This realignment was mirrored in the pattern of trade with China, 1925 marking the first major expansion of trade (and particularly in Soviet exports) since 1916.[80] Although the rise was still well under the 1916 level, this belies the change that occurred in the style of trading that showed itself at about this time. However, once the new commercial mechanisms and institutions were in place, the transformation in Soviet trading methods was dramatic. Perhaps the most striking examples of the new entrepreneurial flair which appeared were those of *Dal'bank* and *Dal'gostorg* activities in the bean trade. In the case of *Dal'bank*, its operations began to show keenness during the liquidation of the Russo-Asiatic Bank. By the end of 1926 it had secured an active financial role in over half of Harbin's bean-oil refineries and bean mills, and by 1929 all bean processing operations in the entire region had at some stage received its credit.[81] *Dal'gostorg* had, within the space of a few years late in the 1920s, become one of five companies dominating the bean export trade.[82] Both *Dal'bank* and *Dal'gostorg* quickly came to show an aggressive commercial edge which had been the preserve of foreign banks and trading companies until then.

Such inroads into local commerce are particularly striking given the level of suspicion prevailing in China as a whole about the real motives of Soviet agencies operating there.[83] An opportunistic style of business was also to be seen in the activities of Soviet exporters to Manchuria, but here the results were less striking, with the general emphasis being on the import trade. Although the Soviet commercial initiative worked meticulously at preventing any political connotations being attached to its activities in Northeastern China,[84] the association with the exploits of Soviet advisers in China proper after 1925 was difficult to avoid. It allowed Chinese authorities greater leeway in exerting pressure on the Soviet position *vis-à-vis* the CER. As discussed in Chapter 3, this pressure, in turn, helped to reveal further anomalies in Soviet policy in China. When Soviet officials began to take a tougher line against the apparent Chinese encroachment on their rights within the structure of the Railway's management, the head of HSBC's Harbin Branch observed that 'Soviet Russia as the champion of foreign rights in China is something very strange and totally unexpected…'.[85]

No less difficult a task for the Soviet authorities was the problem they inherited from Tsarist Russia, namely how to incorporate their activities in Northern Manchuria into a general development of the Russian Far East. The Ussuri Railway, a system running parallel to the CER, remained underdeveloped and under-used. The territory through which it ran had natural resources, but their exploitation was difficult and costly. Only a branch line of the Ussuri (connecting Suifenho [Pogranichnaia] with Nikol'sk and Vladivostok) was found to be profitable,[86] and then only marginally so.[87] There were no straightforward solutions to this problem. Attention instead was increasingly directed to the further development of Vladivostok as an export point for Manchurian produce.[88] The growth of commercial relations between Vladivostok and Northern Manchuria was lucrative in the short term, but its foundations were not on safe ground. The enhanced commercial role of the port was based largely on the soya bean trade and was increasingly dependent on a smooth working relationship with the CER. The imbalance in this pattern of development eventually suffered a double blow. In 1929, as we shall see in the next chapter, the Soviet authorities were no longer able to maintain an adequate grasp of the situation in

Manchuria and resorted to a military solution. That in itself undermined the steady economic gain that the Soviet Union had enjoyed in the region since 1925.[89] The repercussions of the conflict on Northern Manchuria were severe. Foreign banks shut down their operations when hostilities broke out and did not resume their normal credit work until early the following year. By then the effects of the world slump had reached Manchuria. The commodity that suffered most was soya beans, with prices going down sharply until January 1931 when they were 135 per cent lower than in September 1929.[90] Even at these prices there were few buyers abroad. With the collapse of the soya bean trade, the CER's major source of revenue vanished. The Soviet Union had, through its successful military action in 1929, restored an active partnership in a crippled concern.

It is a fitting epilogue to this economic dimension of Russian presence in Northern Manchuria that this eclipse of Soviet political and economic influence there coincided with the start of a major export initiative by the Soviet Union. An intelligence report from Dairen warned in 1930 that in Manchuria:

> Even the foreign merchants with whose imports these goods compete, admit that the Soviet merchandise is of good quality considering the prices for which it sells, and, as a matter of fact, if the present situation furnishes an example of what Soviet Russia may be able to do when she shall have completed her ambitious industrial program, the foreign merchants in Manchuria are likely to find themselves facing the most serious competition which they have yet seen.[91]

Soviet exports to Manchuria had, in fact, begun to show a very steep rise after 1925, and notably in the late 1920s.[92] The Far Eastern Crisis of 1931, resulting in Japan's control of Northern Manchuria, hastened a political and economic process to ensure that this would not find an enduring form in the region. However, in Kinney's report is a faint echo of a response to the observations and suggestions made 17 years earlier on how a firm Russian grip on North-East China's economy might have been secured.

The year 1929 marked such a severe break, and had such a devastating effect on the locality that the more subtle differences in the roles of the Soviet Russians and the *émigrés* – and the use of political finesse – were all but submerged by the twin torrents of the military crisis and the economic depression. No longer was it a question of gaining local supremacy, but simply a basic struggle for survival; a struggle which eventually assumed a self-destructive character.[93]

The state of the Russian *émigré* portion of the economy, on the other hand, had been fairly bleak even by 1928. For the *émigrés* to thrive, or at least to achieve the security of economic 'tenure' in Northern Manchuria, it was vital for them to establish and to maintain a sufficiently strong position to ensure thoroughgoing political leverage in the region. For the Soviet Union, there was a supplementary task: the assertion of its presence, through an entrenched citizenry *and* the development of firm trade relations with the region. This it did steadily in the years after the near-complete cessation of trade with the onset of the Revolution and Civil War in Russia. So steady had this growth been, in fact, that it had prompted a number of commentators to raise an alarm, warning of Soviet 'penetration and infiltration'.[94] By 1929, the Soviet presence loomed even greater with the fairly constant stream of favourable reports on the development of the light-manufacturing capabilities of Soviet industry.[95]

In Northern Manchuria, however, the picture that began to emerge in the latter part of the same period was a different one: unfolding vistas of plummeting prices and of chaos in the business sector. In the process, Harbin quickly turned from a major financial centre in the Far East into a panic-stricken outpost of the world economy. The collapse was as complete as it was sudden. Deprived of the value of its chief export earner, soya beans, the finances of the city assumed a new image, one of a bubble. The speed of the collapse was, as we shall see, dramatic and enduring. Major changes took place as politics and economics blended, and history swept to its ultimate logical conclusion.

# 6
# The 1929 Crisis

Within a year of his coming to power, Chang Hsüeh-liang was locked in a struggle with Soviet interests in Manchuria. This was the result of his own indelicate manner and inept methods,[1] in combination with Mukden's attempt to deal with the visibly swelling Soviet economic tide, and by the time the crisis broke in the summer of 1929 political tide too, in the region.[2]

Examples of scholarship on the crisis and conflict of 1929 show a certain uniformity, and especially so in dealing with its consequences. Peter S.H. Tang, in his analysis of the 1929 Crisis, is content with stressing only one result of the conflict: that 'China', as a consequence of the Khabarovsk Protocol that ended the crisis, was in an ill-fated position, prostrated under the heel of the Soviet Union, because the protocol was 'conspicuously silent on the subject of Soviet propaganda',[3] thereby allowing the Soviet Union to interfere in Chinese internal affairs through the CER. E.H. Carr, on the other hand, attempts to show the broader strategic significance of the crisis by concluding that:

> The Red Army had shown the impotence of the Chinese warlords. The USSR had emerged as a military and diplomatic force in the Far East, and had forged links of common concern with the western Powers. It was a turning point in Soviet external relations.[4]

And finally we have James William Christopher, who, unlike either Tang or Carr, alludes to the importance of the crisis as a catalyst in the political equation of the region. Disappointingly, however, he fails to bring his analysis to its logical conclusion.[5] In brief, what is absent from these various interpretations is the socio-political dynamic of the situation. This apparent inability to delve a little deeper into the incident, at least beyond the bounds of simple diplomatic impact, results in shades of imprecision. Carr, for example, quite comfortably employs the notion of 'China' throughout his work on the conflict, while Tang avoids having to confront the unenviable task of explaining the intricacies of the political physiognomy of China and Manchuria by using blanket images such as 'China handing over power to local authorities'.[6] A somewhat more recent exponent of this line of interpretation, although on a more polemical wing, is Gavan McCormack, who goes as far as to suggest that there was no such a thing as Manchuria, the latter title being an imperialistic mask disguising the true face of the Three Northeastern Provinces.[7] How then are we to explain such phenomena as: the signing of two treaties in 1924, one with Peking Government in May and the other with Mukden in September; or the massive political and military tug-of-war along a north–south axis throughout the 1920s (so great, indeed, that military representatives of the foreign powers would invariably find themselves on the periphery watching gargantuan troop movements and the remnants of struggles[8])? Or that the Soviet Union secured no foothold in China proper as a result of her military victory? (In fact, within a year its political influence had all but died in Manchuria itself. The last is perhaps the most intriguing question of all, and one which orthodox interpretations cannot answer satisfactorily.)

One should not dwell too long on question of Manchurian 'differentness', although it is instructive with regard to seeing certain weaknesses in Western scholarship on the Manchurian question. One can hardly deny that Manchuria was part of China by this time; but largely through its own, and remarkably late, imperialistic efforts.[9] The ultimate result was something resembling a hastily sewn patchwork of stake-claiming on foreign territory. When we speak of Manchuria being very firmly part of China, the question (and, indeed, the analogy) which springs to mind is that when America was buying Alaska, was it purchasing Russian territory? Manchuria was home to a large number of indigenous minorities, all with aspirations and a deep mistrust of Chinese motives. The Barguts were leading a separatist struggle as early as 1911 against Chinese encroachment,[10] while the native Manchus – some 5 million strong in the 1920s[11] – were hardly dismayed at the fall of Chinese warlord rule in 1931, as one of their representatives made clear in an interview with a member of the Lytton Commission:

> He himself and his friends sympathised with the Manchukuo Government. They respected P'u Yi as their traditional emperor and they thought that life in an independent Manchurian state under his regency would give them better conditions than they had had in the Chinese republic. His people were rather conservative and had, for instance, in spite of pressure from ruling Chinese republicans, kept their old princes as before.[12]

The Manchu representative went further by suggesting that '…[he] was confident that a new state would keep to its promises and regain for Manchuria a state of prosperity where its people could be loyal to its government'.[13]

When Soviet troops crossed the border into Manchuria, the incursion drew no protest from these minority groups. Nor, surprisingly, and perhaps tellingly, did it bring forth the ire of the Chinese population there. Violent student outcry, so well known to the Japanese hierarchy which conducted military operations in China, did not materialise in this instance. Appeals to Chinese nationalism were, therefore, largely restricted to academic exercises, emanating *ex cathedra* from Nanking, concerning the illegality of Soviet actions.[14]

Ostensibly, the crisis sprang from the Chinese authorities' response to the gains made by Soviet Union in its attempt to regain full control of the CER. Moscow reasserted itself by overturning the agreements reached by the Soviet Union and Mukden and Nanking governments in 1924 (regarding the running of the railway and Soviet rights in Manchuria). The other cause, and one which the Soviet Union gave as a reason for its concern and, ultimately, military intervention, was the inability of the Chinese authorities to prevent White-guardist and warlord military intrusions into Soviet territory.[15] In fact, the crisis may be seen as the military response to a long history of Chinese attempts to displace Russian, and later Soviet, predominance in the Manchurian arena.[16]

The diplomatic prelude to military conflict was intricate, but may be summed up in a chronological sketch. In May 1929 there was a raid by the Manchurian authorities on the Soviet Consulate at Harbin, much like that on the consulate at Peking two years before. As as a result of the raid a number of Soviet citizens, including the General Manager of the CER and his assistant (Emshanov and Eismont respectively) were removed from their posts and, in some cases, arrested. Soviet retaliation took the form of the arrest of a number of Chinese citizens, including businessmen, in the Soviet Union. However, the Moscow's formal response came only on 13 July, in the form of a three-point ultimatum: (i) a conference was to be convened for the settlement of all questions concerning the CER; (ii) Chinese authorities were to cease at once all unilateral acts committed in respect of the CER; and (iii) all arrested Soviet citizens were to be freed immediately, and the rights of the Soviet citizens and institutions alike to be restored.[17]

Simultaneously, a note was issued by Karakhan, who was by then the Acting Commissar for Foreign Affairs in Moscow, personally warning the Chinese authorities of the consequences of their having frequently reneged on treaties he himself had helped to engineer, and which had been signed with both the Peking and Mukden Governments. On 19 July the Soviet Union severed diplomatic relations with China, suspending railway communication and 'inviting' Chinese diplomatic and consular representatives to leave Soviet territory. By 20 July all White Russians employed by the

Chinese Maritime Customs left Suifenho (over which Soviet military planes made frequent flights to demoralise the populace) and Lahasusu (where Soviet warships had their guns trained on the Customs House and the vicinity).[18] Moreover, *Dal'bank* began to transfer funds to New York at that time, the offices of Soviet companies in Harbin began to close and the German Consul-General was requested to take charge of local Soviet interests.[19] Between late July and the first week of August, there were negotiations between the two sides, with communications being sent by C.T. Wang, China's Minister of Foreign Affairs, as well as Chang Hsüeh-liang to Karakhan, calling for the initiation of talks, and agreeing *mutatis mutandis* to the Soviet demands. These communications were themselves the result of official discussions between representatives Boris Mel'nikov, the Soviet Consul General at Harbin, and Tsai Yun-sheng, Mukden's Commissioner of Foreign Affairs in Harbin, at Manchuli. What ensued instead, however, was a rather confused situation, with the Soviet Union refusing Japan's 'good offices' in settling the dispute.[20] But on 26 July the American consular representative MacMurray reported to Secretary of State, Henry Stimson that a meeting was in the offing probably to be held at Harbin, and that Soviet military 'demonstrations' would shortly cease (the meeting took place on 30 July).[21] However, and despite the prolongation of useful discussions between Mel'nikov and Tsai, Karakhan intervened with a note to the Mukden authorities, accusing the Chinese of 'bad faith'. This accusation stemmed from an apparent change from the original position adopted by China. Karakhan was, strictly speaking, right, although his intervention had in effect wrecked the grounds for discussion between Mel'nikov and Tsai. In the new Chinese position that Tsai had outlined (after consultation with Mukden), and that Karakhan had reacted so strongly to, the Chinese authorities: (a) failed to allow the USSR to appoint a new manager and assistant manager for the CER, and (b) instead of *status quo ante*, China proposed legislation based on the prevailing, and indeed changing, conditions. Karakhan concluded on an ominous note: 'A situation is developing that is pregnant with weighty consequences, the entire responsibility for which rests fully with the Mukden and Nanking governments'.[22] On 8 August, MacMurray reported to Stimson that General Boldyrev was appointed Commander of the Soviet Army of occupation and Beikker, a former director of the railway, was to serve as Chief of Staff.[23] Two days earlier, Bliukher, the former military adviser to the KMT, and N.E. Donenko, a member of the Revolutionary Military Council, were charged with the formation of the *Osobaia Dal'nevostochnaia armiia* (ODVA) by the Revolutionary Military Council (RMC). Bliukher was to be its Commander-in-Chief.[24]

Aside from isolated skirmishes in July, military action proper began on 17 August, with an 'official notification' reaching the Manchurian government of 10 000 troops and 30 guns attacking between Manchuli and Chalainor, with 50 Chinese soldiers killed in a separate incident at Manchuli itself on the same day. The attack on Chalainor is interesting in that 'either by design or fluke'[25] Chinese troops retreated some 400 yards to an entrenchment, which was well supported by machine gun emplacements, and as a consequence inflicted heavy losses on the Russian forces.[26] This was the last occasion on which Soviet forces suffered heavy casualties in the Manchurian conflict. In mid-October, Soviet vessels had forced their way up to the confluence of the Amur and Sungari Rivers (in the North East), and captured Lahasusu, shattering Chinese ranks and forcing their opponents to Fuchin, where the Chinese soldiers killed inhabitants who crossed their path and plundered all stores in the area.[27] The Red Army, on the other hand, took only military supplies and stores, but did not touch the civilian population or property.[28] On 16 October a public meeting was held in which the Chinese were invited to enlist in the Red Army and move with it to Khabarovsk.[29]

A tense, but relatively stable, period ensued until 17 November, when the main thrust into Manchuria began, involving the Transbaikal Group of the ODVA (comprising 10 divisions; but as the units were not on a war footing, the numbers were not more than 6033 infantry and 1599 cavalry). The stratagem was to divide the action into two stages, with a maximum emphasis on surprise, as it was to be again in 1945, but on that occasion against the Japanese (no smoking; no use of bullets, only bayonets; muffled wheels on vehicles).[30] The first stage was to sweep past Manchuli and to strike at the fortified region of Chalainor. Having captured the latter, the forces were then to wheel around and take the westward-facing fortifications at Manchuli by an assault from the East.[31]

With the exception of heavy resistance near Hailar, the plan was carried out quickly. By the morning of 20 November, troops had surrounded the township of Manchuria Station and the local *Tupan* was given an ultimatum, with two hours to decide his response. However, without waiting for a peace envoy, or the two hours to elapse, Stepan S. Vostretsov, the head of the Transbaikal Group, entered the city with several commanders and two autos; the remaining Chinese troops defending the settlement were too busy looting to interfere. The city itself had already been totally destroyed: not one window was intact and the streets were littered with abandoned weapons and equipment. The Chinese troops had begun their panic-stricken looting with the impact of the first bombs. Many soldiers had stolen civilian dress, including women's clothing and foreign dresses and bonnets.[32] The Russian forces gave chase to the routed Chinese army in an easterly direction to Bukhedu. In complete disarray, the Chinese soldiers moved towards Tsitsihar – even further East – plundering as they went.[33] Only 10 miles away from Tsitsihar, General Wan Fu-lin, who was charged with holding the bridge over the Nonni River, was able to stop them, shooting down hundreds of his own army, thereby preventing their entry into Harbin.[34]

The Soviet military campaign was a complete success: within 48 hours of the invasion, Chang Hsüeh-liang was ready to sue for peace on Soviet terms, and on 26 November had already acknowledged the Soviet demand that the three-point ultimatum of July be the basis for negotiation. On 30 November emissary Tsai left Harbin for Nikol'sk-Ussuriisk and there concluded a provisional agreement with Simanovskii (the representative of the Soviet Foreign Commissariat), and this was signed by the two men on 3 December. Two days later, once Tsai had returned to Mukden, Marshal Chang telegraphed his acceptance.[35] On 13 December Tsai arrived in Khabarovsk with plenipotentiary powers from both Mukden and Nanking governments and, finally, on 22 December affixed his signature to the Khabarovsk Protocol. In effect, the protocol restored peace along the border and *status quo ante* (to the 1924 position) to the situation in Northern Manchuria as a whole. All orders and instructions issued after 10 July 1929 were, thereby, declared null and void 'unless properly confirmed by the lawful board and administration of the railway'.[36] The Khabarovsk Protocol, unlike the initial agreement arrived at Nikol'sk-Ussuriisk, was not accepted by the Chinese authorities; a cause for further disturbance of the North Manchurian situation.

The Soviet performance was impressive, but particularly so with respect to its military. Russian forces were under strict instructions to inflict no damage on the non-military sector. The objectives were: the destruction of opposing armies; smashing of military fortifications and installations; destruction of prisons and the release of inmates. Special emphasis was placed on the requirement that there should be no destruction of hospitals, schools, cultural institutions and national shrines. Slogans employed in pursuing this line included: 'The Red Army – the friend of the workers of China'[37] The army was instructed, moreover, '...to ensure the highest degree of self-control with respect to all strata of the population, and especially the workers'.[38] Another aim of the Command was to '...forbid categorically the appropriation by military personnel of even the smallest things, as well as any purchases on enemy territory'.[39] During the campaign itself, there were meetings of political agitators with Komsomol members, and even 'socialist competition' between companies.[40]

During the month of occupation, Russian sappers demolished Chinese military installations and emplacements. Communist Party workers put up posters blaming the 'White Chinese Generals' of trying to trample on Soviet territory.[41] Propaganda, apart from posters, took the form of the Red Army trying '...to win friends' by its conduct. There were well-organised campaigns conducted by Communist Party agitators. As one commentary put it: 'Political life boiled over in the Chinese towns temporarily occupied by the Red Army'.[42] Efforts were also made to influence prisoners held in Chita: food for thought as well as for body was the order of the day for the representatives of local party, soviet and trade union organisations that met them.[43] This 'food' included the creation of a wall newspaper, *Krasnyi kitaiskii soldat* (the Red Chinese Soldier). These efforts soon paid dividends: within two days, 47 prisoners had filed membership applications for Komsomol, and 1 240 lodged applications to remain in the USSR.[44]

The Soviet military strike had been a sublime example of *voennoe iskusstvo* (military art), a major element of military science concerned with 'the theory and practice of preparing for and conducting military operations on land, at sea, and in the air'.[45] Indeed, one could go even farther by interpreting the action as a major stage in the development of Soviet Operational Art, which had been in gestation since 1927. The Soviet actions combined carefully measured use of depth and variety, co-ordinated in the fashion of a swift action designed to achieve the precise goal of '[a]n annihilating offensive under complex conditions' against enemy forces.[46] The Manchurian operation was also most important in that in its style, and in its disciplined achievement of seemingly very clear objectives, it had for the first time since the military humiliation of 1904 restored Russian military prestige outside its own territorial limits in the Asian region.[47] This, together with the extensive use of demoralising and confusing propaganda both through radio broadcasts and spread of printed literature, gave the Red Army the image of being an advanced form of war-machine.[48]

Taken as a whole, the Soviet campaign in Northern Manchuria convinced some Western observers of the Soviet Union's ability to demonstrate sophistication in military and diplomatic technique. One such observer, the British Envoy Sir Miles W. Lampson, summed up the Soviet tactical achievement in the following very full analysis:

> it is impossible not to pay a tribute to the extraordinary skill with which Russia handled the dispute. The restraint, the knowledge of psychology, Chinese and foreign, shown by the Soviet Government, and the manner in which their measures were adopted to the end in view and the means at their disposal were surprising. The situation with which they were faced in July, 1929, was one of which other Powers have had all too common experience – a forcible attack upon rights secured by treaty but which were represented as an infringement of China's sovereignty. An immediate invasion of Manchuria would not only have mobilised the whole opinion of the world against her and possibly provoked the armed intervention of Japan, but as a piece of 'imperialist' aggression it would have aroused the violent opposition of Chinese nationalism. If Russia had retaken possession of the railway by force in July (as events showed she probably could have done without difficulty) she would have placed herself in an awkward position. No further aggression on her part would have been tolerated by Japan, and the offensive would have passed into the hands of the Chinese, who, outraged by the affront to their national self-esteem and knowing that they had nothing more

to lose, would have had ample scope to exploit their favourite weapons and paralyse the railway by boycotts, agitations and strikes. Moreover, Russia's chances of political influence in China would have suffered a severe check.

As it was, by November the idea of the violation of Chinese territory had become so familiar that, when the Soviet raids were carried a stage further and assumed the proportions of an invasion, the adverse effect produced abroad was inevitably much diminished and it was generally realised that the chances of the affair developing into anything more than local hostilities were comparatively slight. On the other hand the Chinese in Manchuria, harassed and demoralised by raids, threats and ever-increasing tension, collapsed, both on the military and the diplomatic front, at the first application of serious pressure and capitulated at once to the Russian demands. Moreover, the predominant feeling after the settlement appears to have been not resentment at defeat but relief at the termination of an intolerable situation and thankfulness to have avoided worse evils. Here again the moderation of the Soviet Government was displayed with excellent effect....[49]

The diplomatic crisis in itself had strengthened the foreigners' position in China, by demonstrating that Manchuria, and by extension China itself, were clearly vulnerable to Western action.[50] Moreover, while the crisis had shown that the notion of a unified Chinese diplomatic response was not something that was likely to appear in the near future, the ensuing military conflict showed quite clearly the weakness of the Chinese armed forces and their inability to resist modern military *matériel* and tactics.[51]

Conventional interpretations point to a number of factors regarding the significance of the crisis. First, there was the importance of the crisis *per se*. Aside from the success, and conduct, of Soviet forces, it was pointed out that no open war had been declared and that the Kellogg Pact, which had neatly been circumvented by the Soviet authorities in launching their military incursions, remained intact.[52] Indeed, the overwhelming consensus was to the effect that the Soviet Union was in an overwhelmingly strong position. On the other hand, the crisis had sent Chinese foreign and domestic policies into disarray. It also demonstrated vividly the dichotomy between the central Chinese and Mukden governments. In this last sense, it quickly became clear that various Chinese officials had been working at cross-purposes during the conflict: Sun Fo, the local Minister of Railways, had published an article in the *North China Standard*, rallying the people, when, at the same time, Chinese ministers in Washington and Berlin were supplicating for intercession.[53] Wang, the Foreign Minister, issued conflicting statements at the time.[54] Concurrently, Chang Hsüeh-liang began to make independent proposals to the Soviet Union. By 14 November, these confused political activities began to display themselves in their true light.

On that date, Wang issued a note, via consular links, from the Central Government to Commissar Litvinov. The latter replied that Nanking's proposals were pointless, as Chang Hsüeh-liang had already accepted preliminary conditions for a peace.

And yet, despite this masterful Soviet display, within a year of this performance it was the Japanese who had assured themselves of *de facto* control of Manchuria and within two years there were already discussions in progress for the sale of the railway.[55] Notwithstanding Lampson's observations, the Soviet Union was to incur severe short- and long-term losses as a result of its intervention. Three major areas are of importance in such a reappraisal: one is the politico-strategic dimension; the second is on an economic plane; the third is a combination of these, but with specific reference to the effect of the conflict on the Russian community in Northern Manchuria. If the crisis and conflict are viewed in this light, it would have to be viewed as a very clear defeat-in-victory.

With regard to the first of these areas, it is necessary to see the Soviet military intervention and its relationship with the politico-strategic dimension in a somewhat broader context than that depicted by Carr, Tang or Lampson. The military victory was, for reasons discussed earlier, undoubtedly a success, establishing the Red Army as a force to be reckoned with in the region (and thereby in itself, of course, a reason for Japan's sense of increasing insecurity, as discussed in Chapter 7). It was on the ideological side that the intervention was profoundly wanting. The Soviet action was accompanied, as described above, by a very full propaganda campaign. Judging by the positions taken within the Soviet Communist Party's Central Committee about the methods to be employed in dealing with the Manchurian crisis, the Soviet leadership was *politically* in two minds.

Contrary to Lampson's interpretation, with its fulsome praise for Soviet decision-making, the policy emanating from Moscow was not quite as surefooted as its actions in late 1929 suggested. On 25 July 1929 Coleman, the American representative in Latvia, reported that at its most recent meeting of the Soviet Central Committee there had been a most pronounced division in its ranks. One member, Ia.E. Rudzutak, argued that China, with the aid of England and Japan, was preparing to go to war. At this point, K.I. Voroshilov, the Commissar of War,[56] considered that the peasants would rise against the Chinese Government, since Russian tactics were defensive, and therefore recommended military action. Kalinin, on the other hand, recommended a peaceful solution through the application of external pressure on China. A.P. Smirnov, P.G. Smidovich and N.P. Briukhanov, too, all spoke in favour of a peaceful resolution of the crisis: war would, they argued, upset the grain-stocking campaign and the internal situation in Russia itself. Mikoyan countered by saying that the government could, despite the waging of war, arrange grain supplies for the Army and industrial centres. Piatnitskii saw a chance for the instigation of a revolutionary uprising that might overthrow the Nationalist Government in China. He went on to reason that such an uprising was already being prepared in South China and that war in the Far East was an excellent opportunity for the sparking of revolution in China, and especially so if the Soviet Union were not an aggressor. After this debate, Stalin was reportedly 'extremely annoyed' by the speeches of Smirnov, Smidovich and Briukhanov, with the latter on the verge of being dismissed.[57] In the end, resolutions were passed recommending 'needful measures to combat Chinese rapacity', *or* the organisation of protest demonstrations and the mobilisation of all organs in Siberia.[58] The tension in the Soviet leadership over the direction that their policies should take was subsequently revealed in the tone adopted in publications by Soviet 'house' journals in articles stressing the need for stability:

> If CER is allowed, peacefully, to fulfil its role and spread its already very considerable economic influence deeper into N. Manchuria, the faster will be the development of the region, the faster its colonization and, as a consequence, the more rapid its growth as an import centre.[59]

Whether the Soviet leadership understood the possible repercussions that its action might have on the Soviet Union's long-term economic interests in the region is not clear, although the possible damage to the CER may have been considered (see below). The irony is that, along with the plea for level-headedness in the Soviet Union's public utterances is an echo of the Witte line that had been pressed by Russian settlers in the region since the late 19th century, and more often than not against the thinking of the incumbent Russian government: that, above all, the interested powers should focus on the most important element in the complex Manchurian question, its economy.

As it happened, the lines of both sides of the internal debate within the Central Committee were evident in the political dimension of the conflict. There was a strong element of *realpolitik* present, but at the same time a 'revolutionary half-life' to the intervention. Neither, however, was present in strong enough proportions or form. The revolutionary aspect of the conflict drew a fair amount of enthusiasm from the Chinese population of Northern Manchuria, as is evidenced by the soldiers crossing over to the Soviet side. However, the numbers influenced by the Soviet propaganda decrying the warlord rule in Northern Manchuria, and by the military operation itself, were insufficient to precipitate the revolutionary overturn that some members of the Soviet leadership desired and, indeed, thought likely. The result in this respect was therefore an inconclusive one. At the same time, the dominant aspect of *realpolitik* – the one to which much of the foreign praise is addressed – too was flawed. In his musings on the evolution of operational art, Isserson noted of the German penetration of

March 1918 that:

> [T]here was no one among the attackers to prolong the attack through the formed breach into the depth, so that the tactical breakthrough of the front could turn into an operational penetration and rout. All grandiose efforts of tactical organization of the penetration, all technical progress in arms, all the enormous concentration of forces and means of suppression – all these turned out to be, essentially, in vain, if tactical success was powerless to develop into operational achievement.
> *It is senseless to break down the door if there is no one to go through it.*
> But this is just what happened with the 1918 penetrations. The imperialist war did not resolve the problem of penetration: it ended without having demonstrated the ability to implement this on an operational scale.[60]

Painted on the larger canvas, the image that Isserson presents of the German failure is one that applies also to the Soviet action in Manchuria. The new rules of engagement had been adhered to by the Soviet forces, and the door had been broken down. However, Manchuria displayed one further facet of modern warfare: breaking into the enemy's territory 'through the door' had to be done for a purpose. In this case, the lunge of the operation as a whole had been into nothing for nothing more than further diplomacy. Limited gains that followed the victory could not be held secure, nor the situation on the ground in Northern Manchuria dramatically transformed. One further quote from Isserson is instructive in this respect. 'The German front', he writes, 'collapsed in 1918 not so much from without, but from within, under the influence of general economic desolation and the powerful process of the revolution of the masses, which led not only to the downfall of the front, but also to the overthrow of the monarchy'.[61] With one adjustment (the revolution of the masses that, finally, did not come to pass in Manchuria), the analysis could as easily be a mirror image for North Manchurian situation, and the Soviet Union's part in it.

In sum, the Soviet campaign showed itself to be neither an outright imperialist venture (which, in the case of the Great Powers in China, was usually launched in order to stabilise a given situation), nor did it represent revolutionary vanguardism. In the case of the latter, the care that Soviet forces had taken not to disturb the Chinese population had probably helped to create the image that their war was indeed against the 'White Chinese Generals', and not against the Chinese peasant or worker. However, while this ensured that there was no lasting sense of resentment evident in the Manchurian populace towards what might otherwise have been seen as a belligerent act, nor was there evidence of the masses of either Manchuria or China rising against their own political masters.[62]

The most telling features that emerge in this respect are its effects on the Soviet Union itself, and this takes us to the second, economic plane of the discussion. As shown in the Chapter 5, the Soviet Union had steadily, and remarkably successfully, been building up its trading position in Manchuria on the somewhat shaky foundations left by the tsarist Government, but especially by the effects of the Russian revolutions. As a result of the crisis, and notably its protracted character, the import/export figures of the region had temporarily collapsed, and the Soviet Union's economic position in Manchuria was on the verge of suffering irreversible damage. Of great importance in this respect was the fact that the resolution of the crisis, while it may have appeared a military and diplomatic coup, created unbearable pressures on the CER itself. These did not find outlet until, finally, the railway came under Japanese control in 1935.

In hindsight, the Soviet Union could not have chosen a *less* opportune moment to invade. For a start, the Sino-Soviet conflict overlapped with the start of the international economic crisis (beginning with the Wall Street Crash in late October). As a result, the effects of the crisis were compounded. The importance of this point is to be seen in two main respects: (a) the increased hardship experienced in a highly specialised economy; and (b) the drastic consequences entailed for the political sphere (and especially its Russian component).

Manchuria represented a fully dependent, near monoculture economy. While the market for soya beans, its staple export, remained steady, the area's position had been exceedingly strong: prodigious success combined with near-dizzying potential. Manchuria had, in fact, not even begun to explore the various paths of development open to it. With the agricultural base growing from strength to strength in the 1920s, outstanding harvests behind it, and export figures soaring, even the inherently conservative giant, the CER, had cause for some optimism, and, perhaps more significantly, reason to take risks with its own future well-being. At the height of the economic boom the company appeared to conclude that there would be the an extension of this success through to the end of the decade and well into the next, thereby inspiring it to invest massively in construction, reconstruction and rolling stock purchases. However, not everyone shared this unbridled enthusiasm. Some two years before the dramatic reversal in Manchuria's fortunes, Professor Gins, a distinguished Russian economist residing in Harbin, had warned the CER against rushing headlong into capital purchases of this magnitude. Voicing his misgivings in *Vestnik Man'chzhurii (Manchurian Messenger)*, he issued an oblique criticism of the railway for having invested away its liquid assets without having created a sinking fund, and, almost prophetically, pointed out the danger in the railway's not having kept a separate repository for the workers' pension fund.[63] The dangers of the former were fairly obvious, while the latter became painfully clear for the CER in the wake of the combined political and economic crises. Without liquid assets, the company would leave itself exposed in the event of a severe economic crisis; so much so that it might possibly be able to cover only its own operating needs, but most certainly would not be able to manage a sudden run on the pension fund. The catastrophe which followed, and not long after Gins's warning was published, was greater than even this commentator might have imagined.

The depression was as insidious as it was subtle in its effect on the Manchurian economy:

> On the surface nothing appeared to have changed in the commercial life. The Chinese ER still remained under the joint management of Soviet and Chinese Administration, its thousands of Russian and Chinese employees appeared to have the same purchasing capacity, import and export was at its height and yet the crisis was coming imperceptibly.[64]

The economic disturbances in America and Europe had, indeed, passed virtually unnoticed in Manchuria, the events obscured by the Sino-Soviet dispute which, as shown above, at first smouldered for months on end and then erupted into open conflict. By the time the initial shocks from the markets in Germany and England had reached Harbin, the conflict had laid the groundwork for complete collapse. The disruption of trade caused by the conflict[65] had reminded the major banks of the dangers inherent in maintaining too casual a credit policy and they acted to correct it. This correction, as so often happens under these conditions, quickly became overcorrection. The conflict also broke the delicate trade link – maintained through the years of prosperity – between centre and province: provincial buyers, for example, did not reappear after the hostilities had ceased between China and the Soviet Union,[66] while the periphery was by then already overstocked with goods and there seemed little likelihood of a sufficient volume of sales to meet maturing bills. Provincial cities such as Hailar were still suffering from the recession instigated by the conflict when the major financial tremors shook the region.[67] Finally, one of the chief areas of growth in Northern Manchuria dried up at source: resettlement in the region fell by almost half in 1929 and its decline accelerated in 1930.[68]

The final collapse of the Manchurian economies, after the growth and interweaving of the underlying weaknesses, came in a crowded sequence of events that was brief, but exceedingly intense. Following the months of retardation stemming from the Sino-Soviet conflict, the economy in Northern Manchuria for a time appeared to be returning to its previous footing: banks resumed normal operation in February 1930;[69] grain prices began to creep up; bankruptcies which had occurred in the past months, the most notable being the Siberian Company in Harbin (see Chapter 7), were at least counterbalanced by reports of potential renewed investment in the region.[70] As late as May 1930, and despite a prolonged slackness in the Harbin market, business circles remained fairly optimistic of the depressed condition of the local economy lasting no more than a few weeks, or a few months at the most (irrespective of continued import shrinkage and fluctuations in currency).[71] Their predictions seemed to have been verified when, a few weeks later, London prices for beans began to edge up. The improvement, however, was fleeting: on 16 June London prices fell to levels unheard of in the post-1910 period; with them hurtled the Manchurian grain market, closely followed by the local import/export trade.[72] The decline continued virtually unabated in the remaining months of 1930, and by early 1931 bean prices were down by 135 per cent from those of September 1929.[73] Conditions in the countryside were by then critical: wealthier farmers had begun to use up their capital stock, while for the poorer sectors calamity had already been spelt by plummeting earnings.[74]

Compounding the effect of the decrease in prices and export trade was the collapse of silver: its fall by 60 per cent brought with it an equivalent reduction in local capital, savings and the value of sales of goods made to foreigners before the collapse.[75] In other Manchurian centres the effect of the trade crisis verged on the spectacular, with the population of Manchuria Station, for instance, being halved as a result.[76] By August 1931, the price quoted in London for Manchurian beans was 20 per cent lower than that of 1908–09.[77]

Of particular importance in understanding why the Manchurian economy should have experienced such a dramatic contraction, is the role of banking in the growth and collapse of the economy. This has already been touched upon in the discussion of the patterns of the development in trade, agriculture and history in an earlier chapter. It remains, however, to make an excursus spefically on the character of banking, as this was to have a marked effect on the Russian community in the later period.

The initial position of banking in Northern Manchuria was characterised, at least in the case of foreign banks, by a lack of competition[78] and limited operations, with a representative of the HSBC noting that before 1910:

> Harbin Office had shown no interest in purely local operations unless they involved foreign exchange transactions [while]… all the imports came from Russia and with the Russian Rouble prevailing… as a currency in circulation there was no room for the ordinary commercial transactions in foreign currency.[79]

By 1910, with the sharp rise in demand for beans, the situation had altered slightly. In that year, the HSBC Annual Report stated in very optimistic terms that 'the recent phenomenal growth in the bean trade furnishes a striking illustration of the development of a hitherto unrealized resource'.[80] Such bright prospects notwithstanding, the attitude of the Bank, which had emerged as the largest source of finance for the bean trade, remained quite conservative, a trait most obvious in the person of E.M. Knox, the Bank's representative in Harbin until 1925. Knox, who had a penchant for hookrugs, often spent his time at the office making them; business, if it came after he had fixed his daily £10 000, and even if the transaction was completed before 10.00 a.m., would receive a curt 'nothing doing' from him.[81] Yet, it was observed that 'he used the exceptional position of the Harbin office as fully as it was possible to do. His quotations for bills were sometimes fanciful, but were accepted without dispute'.[82] So strong was the Bank's position by 1924 that its chief rival, the International Banking Corporation, later known as National City Bank, was rumoured to have sent a representative from New York to liquidate their Harbin branch.[83] The representative, Mr Curtis, a most perspicacious individual, discovered the further possibilities of the North Manchurian market and instead of liquidating '... started very brisk activities and very acute and sometimes unfair competition with Harbin Office. He went to such an extent that he offered a refund of 50 or 100 yen or more against desirable exchange contracts'.[84]

By then there were two major elements aiding the expansion of foreign banks' activities in the region: the onset of the second and most significant decline of Russian economic influence in the area, and the chaotic currency situation there, which, besides keeping foreign banks out of direct negotiation with the countryside, allowed a host of traditional forms of credit operations to flourish. These credit operations formed an informal network and provided for the role of the foreign banks as middlemen to the middlemen in the bean trade. The foreign banks, although they did offer cheaper credit, conducted a restrictive policy in accepting customers.[85] Moreover, the terms governing the handling of import/export payments were quite strict, involving demand drafts or telegraphic transfers on London and New York, with currencies being viewed strictly as commodities.[86] The Chinese credit operations, on the other hand, indulged in all form of credit and currency dealings, profiting in the process from rural loans, purchases and local currency fluctuations. In 1927 provincial authorities were forced to acknowledge the rampant forms of development in this area when they introduced rules for the operation of moneychangers to 'prevent speculative tendencies'.[87]

The period from 1924 to 1929 was marked by intense competition, as well as the elaboration of the bubble of prosperity, as banks vied for, and created, custom in an expanding market situation. The years 1927 to 1929 were particularly representative of vigorous financial activity as M.W. Wood, who replaced Knox in 1925, observed:

> In these three years we financed the greater part of the large soya bean export business [mostly with the East Asiatic Co.] and the National City

Bank took second place. Our purchases averaged £100000 a week throughout the year and at least once the agency was credited with having earned enough to pay the dividend.[88]

Wood, whose intention it was to raise the tempo of the Bank's activities in the region after the years of Knox's conservative attitude to local business, found that he was able to achieve a good deal of improvement, despite the continued forays by the National City Bank,[89] but refused to involve the Agency in any exports other than beans, although a share of the local import trade was undertaken.[90]

These were years of particularly acute competition for another reason: the return of Russian business interests, and specifically that of banking. The Soviet government, as has already been discussed, had shown a very strong inclination to claim a share in Manchurian growth, this being most clearly evident in its lively action to prevent the liquidation of the Russo-Asiatic Bank:

> from the beginning the opposition of the Soviet Government has been continuous and severe. They have made and it would appear are still making every effort to gain control of the Bank. Their main efforts seem to have been directed to the attempt to buy over a Mr Puteloff, who held controlling balance of shares in his hands.[91]

The controversy over the bank further revealed the nature of banking during this period, when, in 1932, Russian businessmen who had lost money through the liquidation of the bank complained to the Lytton Commission of favouritism shown by the bank to Soviet subjects, with debtors of that nationality escaping without forfeiting 50 per cent of their businesses, despite the bank's regulations containing strict provisions for this.[92] While the liquidation of the Russo-Asiatic Bank was being contested, *Dal'bank*'s activities showed a pronounced keenness. By employing distinctly Chinese methods of banking (allowing loans on the basis of personal references from well-known members of the business community rather than collateral, for instance) *Dal'bank* secured, as was noted in the last chapter, an active financial role in over half of Harbin's bean-oil refineries and bean mills by the end of 1926. Furthermore, by 1929 all the refineries and mills processing beans in the *entire region* had at some stage received its credit.[93] Between 1927 and 1928 *Dal'bank* eased its credit requirements by not tying loans to overall plans of operations (loans were therefore being granted without reservation so as to prevent delays in the despatch of consignments). As a result of such policies, *Dal'bank* came to finance virtually all large European firms involved in the bean trade, and this was done, moreover, on a regular basis.[94] As a consequence, the bank's turnover in 1927–28 was 2.5 million yen as opposed to 1.9 million yen in the previous financial year. Its active current accounts rose by a similar margin in that year.[95]

The years 1927–8 saw competition increase further with the entry of the Standard Chartered Bank to the Manchurian market,[96] and the expanded operations there of the Thrift Corporation Bank. The latter, an American bank, announced the opening of a branch in Hailar, with capital of £100 000. The new branch, as with the office in Harbin, was to be managed by the senior members of staff of the defunct Russo-Asiatic Bank. As part of its strategy, the American bank sent its officers to Hailar, where they were to visit clients of the late bank.[97]

The market slump and crash, introducing the initial phase of economic reversal to the region, rapidly revealed the gaping chasm created by this period of inter-bank competition. With the onset of the financial crisis in China proper, commercial and banking organisations there had formulated projects to counter its effects.[98] However, no such measures were conceivable in Northern Manchuria, as the credit and currency systems were too disparate to allow any immediate, formal unified action. Joint action by the banks, insofar as this existed in Northern Manchuria, came in the form of their response to the Sino-Soviet Conflict. When the crisis matured into open conflict, and *Dal'bank* ceased its operations altogether, the remaining banks adopted the informal policy of restricting or withdrawing credit, with the result that bank credit disappeared completely, thereby leaving the business community at the mercy of moneylenders and usurers. With the worsening of the financial situation at the very start of 1930, foreign banks realised that the Manchurian bean exporter was in dire straits and so intervened 'collectively' in the hope that trade might be resuscitated in the process.[99] Beyond day-to-day transactions, consolidative activity was minimal on the part of the foreign banks. In this respect, there was, for example, the instance of the Managing Director of the HSBC visiting Manchuria to discuss the formation of a central bank for the Three Eastern Provinces to stabilise or regularise the currencies in circulation there.[100] Together with the Yokohama Specie Bank, the HSBC, it should be noted, also served the function of maintaining silver quotations.[101]

Thus, when the Chinese Commercial Organisation of Harbin and Futiatien made an appeal to the Main Administration of the Three Eastern Provinces (Manchuria) in 1931, offering to circulate a new currency to the sum of $50 million, which was to be earmarked for use in grain sales only,[102] the soil was already too barren for such a measure to take root. Due to the absence of a unified currency policy and any form of check on currency emission, provincial banks were able to use unlimited issue of banknotes to manoeuvre in the grain market, and thereby partly monopolise the purchase of grain from producers.[103] By artificially boosting the prices in a buyer's market, these banks further damaged an already crippled sector of the economy. Moreover, with the shrinkage of credit in the cities, the very face of competition in the banking sector was altered: minor banks entered the fray to fill the need for credit, and in this respect began to compete with usurers; both groups issuing short-term loans at high interest rates.[104]

In 1931 Manchuria finally emerged on the path towards unification and stabilisation, but under Japanese tutelage. By the mid-1930s the local market was at last showing signs of revival, but by then the region had transformed from an essentially export-oriented zone to one with an excess of imports. In the process, banks had suffered great losses, although those that had invested heavily in local industry, amongst their number the National City Bank and *Dal'bank*, bore losses 'several times larger' than those of the more cautious institutions and, by comparison with the National City Bank's performance alone, the HSBC must be classed in the latter group. The banks that had survived the initial convulsions of the early 1930s were forced to adopt new methods of finance, including regular perusal of the books of client-companies by bank representatives; a procedure virtually unknown during the period of growth.[105] Investment policy had in some cases altered too: directors began to invest in a variety of enterprises, although principally in goldfields and railway construction.[106] The diversification was, to some extent, supplemented by the forced realisation of loans through appropriation of goods or, by default, the companies themselves. This process led to new spheres of activity for the banks and, to an extent, amelioration of their situation. Thus it is not altogether a fair appraisal when Ostrenko, of the HSBC Agency, concludes:

> It is easy to be wise in the light of subsequent events but had it been possible to foresee the approaching crisis of 1929 and the great losses suffered by Harbin Office through the failure of its clients in the years following 1929 it might be said that the old conservative policy of Mr Knox would have been more safe, more secure and in the long run more profitable to the Bank as a whole than temporary success in gaining new business.[107]

The Bank had, in the process, acquired large firms such as the Russian-owned Churin & Company, the latter with numerous branches scattered across Manchuria and interests in retail trade, agriculture and light and heavy industry. The company owned enterprises producing tobacco, sausage, paint and enamel; distilleries, vodka, vinegar; leather- and soap-works; brewery, wine cellar; tea-handling; bakery; wholesale and export department; automobile department; technical divisions with large workshops; agricultural department. Later the company purchased a timber mill and the Sungari Mill.[108] The closing years of the decade saw signs of promise appearing in these areas of investment, with Churin & Company showing a steady yield by that time.[109] Were it not for the changing political fortunes of the region, the Bank might have found itself planted that much more firmly in a region of economic potential. For the Russians who had initiated these businesses and seen them through their initial stages of development, such potential had long since slipped away.

How did this translate for the indigenous Russians specifically? Many Russian companies began to dip into their capital (and more often than not their reserves too) to weather the economic hardships. Because of the prolonged nature of the political crisis, a proportion of them were soon on the brink of bankruptcy.[110] For some of the businesses, the alternative to bankruptcy was to reduce the number of employees supported; a situation that led to an increase in unemployment figures for Russians in particular (as they were the key nationality involved in the trade of the region).[111] Wages too began to tumble, partly due to the crisis itself, and partly through the Soviet ascendancy.[112] Foreign companies, many of which were affected by the economic crisis (notably American firms), began to regard the political instability as an added liability and, therefore, were encouraged to transfer operations, leaving much of their predominantly Russian staff behind. Some major Russian capitalists joined their number, and in a few cases withdrew from trade altogether, transferring capital in the process. In the case of the latter, an interview with a Russian accountant based in Harbin at the time showed that the company he worked for just 'packed up and left' in the course of the 1929 crisis, leaving him to keep the operation going 'in some measure'. The company was not to return to Harbin.[113] Many of these companies had already been thinking about moving in the past, so the crisis simply confirmed their earlier fears and hurried them on in the process of relocation.

However, the biggest losses were arguably those associated with the CER, which, being at the core of economic activity and development in the region, suffered greatly (and doubly so). First of all, there had been the loss in carriage.[114] Secondly, activities of the railway's commercial agencies and auxiliary enterprises – the latter stunted even before the crisis took its grip – came to a complete standstill at this point.[115]

Having found itself in such a poor financial position, the CER's economic woes soon came to be translated into political friction. A major area for the interplay between the economic and the political was that of the staff dismissals that took place in the wake of the crisis and the reinstatement of Soviet officials in the CER's administration. The warnings issued by Professor Gins in 1927 returned to haunt the company after 1929/30, and in especially pointed way. With the company's financial situation already under strain as a result of the capital investment discussed above, staff dismissals became a logical step to take, but this was fraught with political complications as many of those targeted were Russian *émigrés*, and therefore suspected that they had been victimised. A similar problem arose over the issue of outstanding CER debts to Russian creditors, the majority of whom were émigrés too (see Chapter 7). In combination, these elements made up a strong and persistent political undercurrent.

When the Lytton Commission came to Harbin in 1932 to examine the situation after Japan's coup, it received a letter from CER employees dismissed after the 1929 conflict. Highlighted in the petition was the return of the Soviet 'vanquishers' to the CER administration, and the 'illegal' sackings of Russian employees.[116] '[T]housands of...poor people', the letter suggested plaintively and with simmering anger, 'do not stretch out their hands to beg...'.[117] These former employees had devoted their collected savings, it continued, to send representatives to Changchun to lobby the new Manchukuo authorities. With no response forthcoming, the former workers asked pointedly: 'Is it not an act of political vengeance, which can in no way be seen as [proper] administration of an enterprise that is [a] so-called "pure[ly] commercial [one]"'.[118] Members of the Lytton Commission were, finally, invited to visit the CER Pension Department on *Torgovye Riady*, opposite the Russian Orthodox cathedral in *Novyi Gorod*, to see the gatherings of '... hundreds, if not thousands' of these unemployed workers. 'Not a single one of these poor people', the letter concluded, 'will complain about the hospitable and good-natured Chinese people, who have given refuge to thousands of Russian people. These complaints are without a doubt against the Communists and Chinese "Generals", who are not familiar with the sense of lawfulness and equity'.[119]

Whether it was true or not, the *belief* that the Russian railwaymen were being starved and humiliated by Soviet efforts was sufficient to generate a great deal of resentment and hostility; much of it, it must be said, in a fog of confusion – no mention had been made in the letter itself, or in any popular medium, of the suspect financial methods highlighted by Gins. By intervening militarily, the Soviet Union heightened internal tensions between Russians and Chinese too. Finally, there was also the increase in tensions between Russians and Soviet citizens. The latter was most important, as the non-Soviet Russians constituted 50 per cent of the total Russian population and held important positions in municipal councils. A combination of these factors – and notably the last – led to a marked deterioration in the political mood in the conurbations.[120] Adding to the tensions (and the confusion) in the towns were the curious epiphenomena of the contests between Soviet and Chinese authorities. The Lytton Commission had also received a petition from the Ukrainian Association, whose building had been seized by Chinese authorities during one of the sustained bouts between Chinese and Soviet legality on the CER.[121]

But the dislocation and turmoil caused by the Sino-Soviet crisis in Harbin was minimal by comparison with its effect on the countryside and northern provincial centres. There, the Soviet military effort was under no orders to exercise restraint, as it had been with Chinese settlements. Indeed, a key goal of the 1929 incursion was to allow Soviet forces to systematically deal with pockets of actual, and potential, 'White' activity in the border areas roughly bound by Manchuli, Chalainor, Hailar, Bukhedu and *Trekhrech'e*.[122] Such was the efficiency of the Soviet efforts that many small Russian settlements which otherwise might have escaped the full brunt of the economic depression were sucked into the political and economic maelstrom. Most of these villages and towns were populated by peasants, many of whom were *Starovery* (Old Believers). The Soviet action targeted such villages with a ferocity that caused them to splinter, forcing nearly 10000 Russians '... to abandon their hard-earned belongings... and save their lives afresh'.[123] Their departure was much like it had been for the many thousands who had crossed the Sino-Soviet border some ten years earlier: rough-built carts filled with a few personal belongings, drawn by a horse and accompanied by whatever livestock could be controlled in the course of the difficult trek. Their departure on this occasion was clouded not only by the spectre of the Bolsheviks, but also of roaming bands of Chinese deserters and avaricious local officials who preyed on the helpless convoys as they passed through their bailiwicks.[124] 'Never', a report on the 1929 conflict concluded, 'has the absence of rights and the helplessness of Russian *émigrés* been as clearly seen as in these days'.[125] Although the Russians who fled from border settlements on or near the railway lines found their passage easier, with little if any intervention from the Chinese, their escape was in many respects no less traumatic. As one wool- and fur-dealer at Hailar recalled of the chaotic, frightening period:

> My family and I decided also to leave Hailar for Harbin. I made an arrangement with the station cashier that for a predetermined 'reward' I would receive tickets at the precise moment that the train was approaching and the police officers' backs were turned to the door leading to the platform. It was only in this way that I managed to secure passage. However, even then it was not easy to board the train, as the coaches were crammed with people. Eventually, we succeeded in entering the buffet-wagon, in which business had already ceased. It was night, and the only spot we could find to rest was on the floor, between some tables.[126]

Twelve years earlier, the same man had, with the aid of a porter, been struggling to force his way through a window of an overcrowded carriage at a Russian railway station on his way into exile.[127]

The damage to the provincial sector of Russian life in Northern Manchuria was such that an aid agency estimated total Russian losses to be over 200 killed, many hundreds injured, over 800 forcibly 'repatriated' for trial and punishment in the Soviet Union and over 3 million silver dollars in lost possessions.[128] Hundreds of families, the agency observed, were still not in a position to recover and depended entirely on whatever aid could be provided by its very limited resources.[129] Cases of cruelty and atrocities at the hands of Soviet forces, notably in the *Trekhrech'e* area, remained unaddressed.[130] Much of the infrastructure vital to the conduct of Russian economic and administrative activity in the periphery had been seized by the Chinese authorities themselves.[131]

The last factor is of particular significance, as it appears from the refugee organisations' various petitions (despite the fact that most of these point their fingers at Soviet 'pressure' as being the reason) that the local Chinese authorities in the border areas saw this as a good opportunity to gather all forms of control into their own hands.[132] The *KhkpRb* concluded grimly of the situation that had evolved in the wake of the Sino-Soviet Conflict in the following way: 'Deprived of the links with the railway and its aid, suffering from the destruction of enterprise, the absence of basic rights and the onset of anarchy, [the Russian Emigration] exhausted all hope of existence, irrespective of its loyalty to authority, love of peace and its work skills'.[133]

We have mentioned that the economic crisis and the Sino-Soviet conflict acted in concert. We have also suggested that the compound effect of these phenomena was far-reaching. It is appropriate here to consider the question of the economy and political stability.

After the 1929 crisis, it was stability that figured as the one key focus of attention in the region. Arguably, it was because of the desire for, and the pursuit of stability (rather than simply clear hegemonic or annexationist motives alone) that Japan intruded into Northern Manchuria after the 1931 crisis. Nor was it simply a Japanese pretext that lay behind the move. By 1931 there are many sectors of Northern Manchurian society that yearned for, and sought, stability. The indigenous Russians were among those. When Japanese forces reached the streets of Harbin in 1932, they were greeted by rousing *Banzais* from Russian onlookers crowding the pavements.[134]

The key to understanding this manifestation, as well as the rapid political metamorphosis of the region, lies in the intertwining of politics and the economy. To provide a foundation for analysis, a tentative theoretical framework should be devised to permit methodical investigation of the events in Northern Manchuria in the 1920s.

What, then, was an appropriate framework? Initially, this would have been to define the North Manchurian sub-economy in terms of a world economy. In this way we might appreciate the differences between the North Manchurian economy and that of China, which might in turn suggest local pressures that were likely to have shaped local political activities and tendencies. In fact, we might go so far as to 'locate' the North Manchurian economy and polity in structural terms (whether it is core, periphery or semiperiphery). This, in turn, would allow us to gauge the balance of power between the state machineries in the core areas and the periphery. As Immanuel Wallerstein argues, and the case of Northern Manchuria, it seems – at least *prima facie* – to verify:

> Political struggles of ethno-nations or segments of classes within national boundaries of course are the daily bread and butter of local politics. But their significance or consequences can only be fruitfully analysed if one spells out the implications of their organizational activity or political demands for the functioning of the world-economy.[135]

However, although this tentative approach was, on the whole, satisfactory for the analysis of politics in Northern Manchuria in the 1920s, it left one facet unclear. Employing the proposition of a world economy as a starting point would certainly explain *why* the Soviet Union was involved in the region throughout this period (even with the beginnings of Socialism in One Country – a concept which is, incidentally, to some extent undermined by this mode of analysis – the Soviet Union was active, and increasingly so, in Northern Manchurian economy). But it does not explain why the Soviet Union adopted the somewhat perplexing foreign policy that it did (as described above). The explanation, or a facet of the overall approach, is to be found in the use of the concept of 'development' as employed by Marx, Marxists and liberals alike, and as is shown by Gavin Williams in his 'Imperialism and Development: A Critique'.[136]

Strictly speaking, Williams' argument pertains to the post-world war II world, but its roots may be found in 1917 and earlier. The notion of development, says Williams, is a common term for Marxists and liberals alike. It is a recognised 'good'; a common currency of language and ideas. It is, in short, a universal yardstick.[137] Our conclusions? Not only did the Soviet Union play a role in a capitalist world economy, but it also shared a vocabulary with its rivals. The implications of this are significant and certainly help to explain the confusion associated with its role in Northern Manchuria (as trading partner; revolutionary mast-head; as a potential aid to the 'development' of the region). The absence of a critical approach to the Soviet Union's own rôle showed through in the inconsistencies that arose: the possibility of armed intervention triggering a national revolution (clearly misrepresenting class configurations, class strengths and weaknesses, the relationship of Manchuria and China); the need to protect its own interests in the capitalist world economy, but without weighing carefully the likely effects that military intervention would have on the core/periphery relationship the Soviet Union enjoyed with Northern Manchuria; the social analysis of the Manchurian polity (classic use of 'stages'), which signifies a misrepresentation of Manchuria's nature – is Manchuria feudal or primitive capitalist; is China feudal or capitalist? Both existed in the same world system, but their relationship was not altogether clear.[138] As Williams observes: 'The establishment of the USSR...provided an alternative source of capital, technology and markets, as well as political and military support for a "non-capitalist road to development" within [an] international division of labour'.[139]

Therein lies the heart of the confusion. The Soviet Union was providing an *alternative* to capitalism, while, through the terms of reference it employed, goals it set and economic engagement it undertook, at the same time being immersed in a capitalist world system.[140] The 'aid' it provided to the radical cause in Northern Manchuria (and, as is apparent from the Soviet leadership's thinking, by extension to China as a whole) was supposedly to free the area of the capitalist yoke. Instead, its own position was undermined, allowing a new core state (Japan) to assume controlling influence (the Soviet Union not being strong enough to prevent this from taking place). Having introduced 'revolutionary instability' in such a spectacular and conclusive fashion to the Northern Manchurian region, the Soviet Union withdrew and sought accommodation with the Chinese authorities, thereby acknowledging its re-immersion (or, perhaps more appropriately, *continued* immersion) in the capitalist world system. Such a contradictory approach showed itself, finally, to be a hollow one.

# 7
# Decline into Oblivion, 1930–31

The Soviet Union's victory over Chinese forces in 1929 should have come to be regarded as a major triumph. In the military sphere, it had conducted an intelligent campaign, co-ordinating ground and air strengths in an action which could not be matched by Chinese forces. The military side had been supplemented by a timely and well-staged international information effort, which succeeded in convincing the international community that the Soviet Union had responded militarily in order to stop the Chinese authorities in their attempt to evict Russian nationals from the CER and Manchuria.[1] The Soviet Union had also chosen a strategically opportune moment to launch its military action, both cutting off the Manchurian forces from receiving any support from the central government at Nanking, and, simultaneously, prevented the northern forces from contributing to the national government's own struggle with the rebel troops under General Feng Yü-hsiang and the so-called reorganisers.[2] Where the Soviet authorities failed to gain full advantage, however, was in the diplomatic end-game.

The sweeping success of Soviet forces in humbling their Chinese opponents brought with it a carthaginian peace. Chinese representatives were forced to travel to two sets of negotiations to arrive at a suitable settlement, in Khabarovsk (December 1929) and Moscow (January 1930). At the former, Tsai Yun-sheng, the Minister for Foreign Affairs at Harbin, had led a delegation which was treated as if it had been sent by 'vanquished nation;'[3] an image that in itself did much to turn the international community's sympathies away from the Soviet Union. Finally, Tsai signed an agreement which neither Mukden nor Nanking governments could bring itself to ratify. Contained in the Khabarovsk Protocol were proposals which were, in some cases, contradictory, and whose general thrust would have returned Northern Manchuria to a situation that had existed there during tsarist times.[4] Rumours began to circulate in China that the Soviet Union would nominate members of its victorious Far Eastern Red Army to positions in the CER. In the event of a deteriorating political situation on the railway line, these officers would be able to take control at a moment's notice, it was conjectured.[5]

The broader geopolitics of the region too were affected by the nature of the Soviet victory in Manchuria. In the course of the conflict, the Soviet Union had destroyed the Chinese river flotilla (based on the internal waterways of Northern Manchuria), broken up the military and expelled it from the Barga Uezd, where Chinese influence had been taking root for some years. In the process of achieving this, the Soviet Union had destroyed Chinese prestige in the eyes of the Mongols. Not only had Outer Mongolia become an allied state of the Soviet Union's and inner Mongolia come closer to the latter's orbit, but the Mongol people themselves had a vivid demonstration as to why they should remain aligned this way. In fact, a large part of the conflict had, on the Soviet side, been carried out by minority groups. Mongolian divisions had been employed, as had Koreans (based in the Russian Far East and Eastern Siberia) in the Red Army itself.[6] Such internationalism was supplemented by co-ordinated propaganda work, thereby not only employing Khabarovsk as a military headquarters, but also as a nerve-centre for demoralising the enemy: 'Evening broadcasts in Russian, Chinese, Japanese, English and Esperanto', wrote one commentator, '[had] impressed upon the Chinese the mistaken actions their political and military leaders in expressions that are unfit for publication'.[7] Furthermore, the China Press noted that the conflict had brought back into operation a notorious trio of Soviet agents: Bliukher, Borodin and Karakhan.[8]

The events of 1929 had in important ways closed a number of circles for the Soviet Union. The insecurity deriving from the Russian civil war and the need to neutralise the region[9] had been dealt with by putting into place a 'frontier of steel'.[10] For the first time since Russia's humiliation at the hands of the Japanese in 1904, the image of Russian military strength had been re-established in the region And, finally, it appeared to pave the way for the containment of the *émigré* scourge in Manchuria. These were, however, gains from a distinctly Soviet perspective. Soviet actions had also brought into sharp focus the intricate nature of politics in the region. One commentary in China went even further, describing the Sino-Soviet conflict as having '...sharpened the unfortunate Manchurian question'.[11] The writer concluded that the conflict '...put on the map the peaceful existence of the whole of the Far East, where the most diverse interests criss-cross and where everything bubbles no less than in the notorious Balkans'.[12] Other analysts in China saw the Soviet triumph in slightly narrower terms, suggesting that 'it is clear that talk of the destruction of Chinese control in Manchuria and of the possibility of a division of this territory between Red Russians and the Japanese appears to be not without foundation'.[13] Despite the seemingly contradictory images that these analyses convey (one of a multi-faceted seedbed for conflict and instability, the other a more straightforward division of power between two states), they both served to characterise the nature of Manchurian politics at this time.

A clear division of Manchuria into simple spheres of influence would have encouraged a more clear-cut relationship between the Soviet Union and Japan. Indeed, such a view is indicated by at least part of the China press, which stressed the various forms of diplomatic and political support which Japan provided the Soviet Union in the course of the crisis.[14] However, this does not fully explain how Japan could support the Soviet Union in the 1929 crisis *and* continue to advise one of its chief adversaries in the region (the young Marshal Chang Hsüeh-liang). Difficult too is the task of judging what the implications were of the Soviet Union employing Koreans in their military activities in an area where the Japanese themselves were running a major migration programme for the Koreans.[15] The potential for the spill-over of radicalism into the Korean communities in Japanese-controlled Southern Manchuria would, at least *prima facie*, seem likely. And, finally, the co-ordinated Soviet attack on Chinese forces was certain to cause internal destabilisation within the Manchurian social and political systems. Of particular concern in this last respect was what might happen to Chinese troops as a result of the total routing they suffered, rather than simply a symbolic victory. In the event, Soviet actions had led to the destruction of the Manchurian Guard and a general disorganisation of the Manchurian forces. Many of the men who fled from their ranks after the complete destruction of their divisions turned into bands of *Hunghutze*,[16] thereby adding to the internal destabilisation in Manchuria; destabilisation which, as we have seen earlier, the Japanese were not well suited, or inclined, to deal with.

The Sino-Soviet conflict had one other major result. Chang Tso-lin, the ruler of Northern Manchuria, had built up a regime that had acquired a reputation of strength both within its own borders, as well as China as a whole. His military victories, the 1927 raid on the Soviet mission at Peking and his ability to develop the status of *primus inter pares* among his fellow warlords had given him a much-respected position in East Asia.[17] After the elder Marshal's assassination in 1928, his son Chang Hsüeh-liang had inherited an administrative infrastructure and military which were quite enviable.[18] Virtually at a stroke, the Soviet offensive had demonstrated that this regime was something of a 'paper tiger', to use a later Chinese political metaphor. Chang's seemingly formidable army had been able to offer little resistance. Indeed, in most areas of engagement with Soviet forces it had simply crumpled in a most embarrassing fashion. The fact that there had been no southern forces engaged in the course of the conflict meant that the focus for the débâcle was very firmly on the Mukden authorities, and their shortcomings quite unambiguously revealed. In a region commanded by warlords, where military might remained a fundamental claim to authority and the ability to practice the enforcement of power, the display of such vulnerability was very grave indeed.

However, the situation here was further complicated by the miscalculation made by the Japanese in their southern 'fiefdom'. Despatching Chang Tso-lin himself, together with virtually the entire senior command of his government, should have had the effect of wiping the slate clean, allowing Japanese patrons to develop new and stronger relations with the regime which replaced the elder Marshal's. Instead, the Japanese were faced with an administration which was even more troublesome than the last. In this case, however, it was not only an overly ambitious Mukden leadership that had to be dealt with, but also the guerrilla-like action from increasingly nationalistic and anti-Japanese rank-and-file Chinese soldiery. Sabotage, widespread sniping from the undergrowth and terrorist activity, albeit at times inept, grew in frequency, and, indeed, spread spatially during the young Marshal's brief reign.[19] Most importantly, by 1930–31 the terrorist activities had spread to Harbin itself, where any official response to such incidents, no matter how minor these might be, could potentially bring the interests of Japanese authorities into conflict with those of their Russian counterparts.[20] The impact of this extension of violence to Harbin was made all the greater because of the increase in lawlessness amongst 'White' Russians in that city, and, although this had a direct impact only on Soviet Russians at the time, the disobedience could have extended to other foreigners too.[21]

In short, he events in 1929 spelt confusion and instability for Japanese interests in Manchuria in the same measure as they suggested themselves to be ones bringing clarity and consolidation to those of the Soviet Union. Perhaps the most worrying signs of how severe conditions would have seemed to the Japanese representatives in Southern Manchuria can be seen in the appearance of a triple threat to Japan. First, the emergence of a strong Soviet Union, seemingly employing coordinated military, economic and political measures in an assured fashion.[22] Secondly, the difficulties that the Japanese authorities had in maintaining a balanced line in Manchuria, which from some accounts appeared quite restrained in its form so as not to allow the Chinese to find cause for any escalation in their militancy.[23] Thirdly, and increasingly important in this period, was the image of the Chang Hsüeh-liang leadership as an obvious liability to Japanese interests in Manchuria.[24]

Japan's position had, as a result of Soviet military action against Chinese forces in the summer of 1929, become far more complicated for all these reasons. It had now to decide whether it should continue to view the situation in Manchuria as the clear division of authority that had existed there since it acquired the SMR after the Russo-Japanese War, or as a more complex political matrix that appeared to have undermined its own geopolitical position in the region, and suggested that this process might have taken on a logic of its own. For Japan, the exertion of the combination of economic and political pressures that *it* had employed, and could develop further still, seemed increasingly to be an appropriate way to slice through the Gordian Knot that it had been confronted with. To a degree, through the its military solution of the 1929 crisis, the Soviet Union had laid the basis for the compelling logic of such a solution.

The formulation and implementation of politico-military strategies such as those employed by the Soviet Union in 1929 mean little if they do not take into account sufficiently the nature of local relations, or the effect that these strategies may have on the latter. Thus, while the Sino-Soviet crisis and subsequent military conflict may have resulted in a decisive Soviet victory, ironically this victory also helped to show that its policies in Northern Manchuria were on the verge of bankruptcy.

With the CER, the main area of friction between Chinese authorities and the Soviet Union, Soviet rights had been restored on paper. In practice, however, these rights had quickly come to mean very little. The protracted period of crisis brought the operations of the CER to a stand-still. Given that these had in any event been sailing on an uneven keel since the start of the unofficial struggle for control over the CER in 1924, the effect of the 1929 events on its operation as a bona fide commercial organisation was nothing short of disastrous. Political and economic factors merged to make the railway appear crippled, and, by extension, the Northern Manchurian economy too. To make matters worse, Soviet military action not only undermined the railway's future, but it had also been aimed at mopping up potentially troublesome pockets of 'White' Russian political activity; pockets which were coincidentally settlements of Russian peasants who had been building up a solid rural economy in separation from the operations of the CER. In effect, the root and branch approach that the Soviet forces adopted to clear the political atmosphere in Northern Manchuria instead contributed to comprehensively undermining Russian economic activity in a region which was, in any event, poised to plunge into even deeper economic crisis as a result of other external factors (that is, the onset of the Great Depression in Manchuria).

On the surface, Soviet control of the railway's administration was re-exerted with a distinct sense of vengeance, reflecting nearly five years of frustration in its attempts to deal with the *émigré* problem that had been caught up in the relations between Moscow and Mukden. The resounding military defeat suffered by Mukden echoed in the sense of hopelessness that pervaded the ranks of the Chinese Russians working for the railway. As one Harbin commentator put it, Russian CER workers were thrown out '...by the bundleful to the whim of fate', or the possibility of a return to the Soviet Union and the prospect of another, and arguably more certain, fate.[25] As discussed in the last chapter, this treatment could be interpreted as political reprisal, or as a symptom of sharp decline in the railway's commercial fortunes. To those who lost their jobs, however, it mattered little which was the true explanation.[26]

In an important sense, the military and political events in Manchuria itself in 1929 were but a backdrop to a concerted economic squeeze being applied by the Japanese in concert with the Mukden and KMT government in China. Japanese commercial interests were pushing the Southern Manchurian economy northwards, taking advantage of the economic ossification that was taking place there.[27] This supplemented the SMR's sustained cut-throat competition with the northern line over the transport of Northern Manchurian commodities in the boom years (as discussed in Chapter 5). The combination of these factors alone had ensured that viability of the CER's commercial operations was under considerable threat. In addition to this, however, was a further dimension of Japanese influence. The politically charged nature of the CER operations, together with the large volumes commercial freight activities on its lines, now gave the Chinese authorities reason to contemplate a policy which, without the political dimension and the issue of the future control of the CER being taken into account, would have seemed bewildering: the creation of a Chinese-controlled railway system to compete with the CER. Such plans, which were both expensive and, seemingly, counterproductive would be financed by Japanese sources so long as any business the new lines generated moved southwards.[28] After 1930, this, together with search by Chinese authorities for alternative forms of transport to move Manchurian produce to Japanese-controlled lines, and notably the SMR, meant that a major shift of commercial traffic had occurred from the CER. By that time, of course, the effects of the Great Depression on the global economy had begun to bite too, thereby further worsening the CER's situation.[29] The combined effect of the political and economic factors left the Soviet Union to contemplate a situation that had become virtually untenable. It became clear too that the Japanese activities were not just aimed at the Soviet presence, but against most foreign commercial activity too.[30] Logically, such an approach made great sense. Russia, and then the Soviet Union, had done much to steer other foreign interests away from Northern Manchuria, initially through bilateral agreements reached with Chinese authorities, but later as much through the maintenance of quintessentially Russian settlements, where foreign merchants would find it difficult to penetrate with their own business activities. In this, ironically, both the Tsarist and Soviet authorities were greatly assisted by the relative closeness of the indigenous Russian population to Chinese life;[31] a situation that was never fully exploited by either. Here, the *émigré* population held an advantage that was, paradoxically, strengthened by their weakness. Part of the reason why *émigré* businesses were able to communicate with the indigenous population, and individuals were so successful in integrating into the ranks of Chinese civil authorities and, at least for a time during the Chinese civil war in the 1920s, into the Chinese military, was because they had little choice but to work closely with the Chinese. It must be remembered that Russians did not have the protection of foreign constabularies or military in China, as did the many foreigners who were shielded by extraterritoriality.[32]

But such a structural explanation does not do full justice to the other, and perhaps more important, factor: the ability of Chinese and Russian *émigré* cultures to commingle in the way that they did. Language, here, is very important, and the level achieved by many Russians in acquiring both the 'high' Chinese language and its vernacular forms (together with an all-important capacity to capture nuance and humour) was notable among the Russians of Northern Manchuria. The formal and informal levels of language employed both by the Russians and Chinese (remembering, of course, that the main form of *pidgin* used in the region was Russian) resulted in a closeness that was quite distinctive. Moreover, it also meant that in many cases the Russian traders and merchants were able to do business without the use of the comprador, being in a position to not only speak directly with their Chinese counterparts, but also to adopt many of the psychological and cultural tactics of the dominant culture. Interestingly, these abilities were evident in many areas of Manchurian life, perhaps the most noteworthy being with respect to the Russian *émigrés* who served for, or worked with, the Chinese military. A most striking example of these abilities is displayed in some of the correspondence of the 'Mad' Baron von Ungern-Sternberg with Chinese provincial authorities. The skills, careful measure of the person he was corresponding with, and the necessary – but at all times *natural* – levels of deference are all present:

> The good will which you always extended me animates me with courage to claim your attention by means of this letter.... [T]he reminiscences of the hard trials in the years of 1918, 1919 and 1920, which have always been associated with your encouragement and sympathy, shall forevermore live in my memory, and now I use them as foundation stones in the belief that you would continue extending your protection to me now. I recollect your kind invitations and mentally return to our discussions on the subject of European policy. I beg permission to remind you of my earnest assertions that no deliverance could be expected from the West, that all our chances are lodged with the East. As to western nations, the disintegration of public morals, including the young generation and the females of the tender age always struck me as appalling.[33]

Thus, even if the subject matter may seem to be something as utopian as the Eurasian empire von Ungern-Sternberg saw rising from the plains of Mongolia, the style and form of his thoughts slip comfortably into the Chinese idiom:

> It is imperative to take advantage of the turmoil, i.e., to interrupt the unprofitable struggle with the Chinese forces and exploit them for the

re-establishment of the Manchurian Khan, for in the opinion of the population he personates a great and impartial judge – a patron and defender of all tribes of the Central Empire. It is indispensable to act under the guidance and superintendence of one person who would stand at the head of the whole enterprise. Until such person be found no success can be expected. A leader is wanted. This office may be filled only by a person who commands popular support, and there could be no more suitable person to discharge those functions than General Chang Tso-lin.[34]

Curiously, even the political philosophy represented in the Baron's letters to his Chinese patrons is not far removed from that in evidence in the region as a whole at the time. Von Ungern's rejection of Western values as those in terminal decline, and his search for political regeneration through the rise of an Eastern potentate, commanding an empire that stretches to the Caspian,[35] was in his mind the basis for the restoration of order and monarchy in the Russian empire. However, his thoughts mirror – indeed anticipate – a political *raison d'être* for other powers in the region too. In a treatise entitled 'Manchukuo and a Renaissance of the Oriental Political Philosophy', Fujisawa Chikao a Japanese political philosopher, set out an elaborate defence of his country's action in Manchuria. The basis for this defence is the rejection of the modern Western ideologies, which he regarded as being unable to '…banish…social distress and chaos, which continues, with increased momentum, under modern democratic individualism'.[36] The basis for the new state was equally telling: '[t]he newly created State of Manchuria in its declaration of independence lays particular stress on the realisation of the principles of open door policy and of equal opportunity in accordance with the Ancient Way of the Sage-King'.[37]

Thus, it might be concluded that not only were the Russian *émigrés* able to employ the form and courtesies so important in Chinese social intercourse, but in some cases, even with an extreme one as von Ungern-Sternberg, their ideas were able to meld into the mainstream of political thought current in the Northeast Asian region as a whole. Their abilities in this respect were, at least potentially, more effective than those of other Westerners (including, of course, the Bolsheviks), who could offer political manners and ideologies that were based on diplomatic style and notions of democracy (both from the Right and Left) that were very clearly Western in their form and content.[38]

In some senses, therefore, *émigré* political thought and outlook in Northern Manchuria was well-placed to be assimilated into the crystallisation of Manchuria's Japanese-sponsored separateness after the declaration of the sovereign state of Manchukuo on 18 February 1932. Monarchy, the distinctiveness of the region, its symbolic importance as an image of the new Asian political path, and, for the many of the *émigrés*, the rebirth of the familiar old order were to characterise the brief emergence of a reinvigorated community whose political spirit had for so long been suppressed by Soviet and Chinese action. The somewhat unlikely patrons of this rebirth of *émigré* political values were the Japanese themselves. With the creation of Manchukuo, a major boost was given to Russian *émigré* organisations, and notably the Bureau of Emigrants, which became the *de facto* governing body of Russians in Manchuria. Its leadership came to steer the *émigré* population to increasingly familiar social and political patterns, but always, of course, under the watchful eye – and fiscal control – of the Japanese advisers to the new Manchukuo 'empire'. The Bureau acquired political weight where other earlier organisations that had been formed in Harbin, such as the Harbin Relief Committee of Russian Emigrants in North Manchuria (China), which had been so important in providing the logistic and material support to the thousands of persons displaced by the hostilities of 1929, could function only as charitable bodies.

The sublimation of the Russia created in Northern Manchuria was most vividly seen on 8 June 1941, when the head of the Bureau, General V.A. Kislitsin, in the presence of a number of 'honoured guests' (many of them Japanese, including the head of the Japanese Military Mission, General Yanagita) and hundreds of Russian *émigré* onlookers, unveiled the Monument in Honour of the Warriors against the Comintern in Harbin's cathedral square. The monument had its origins in the death of a young, little-known 'partisan' named Mikhail Natarov at the hands of Soviet forces two years earlier. His name became the symbol of the *émigrés'* 'struggle against the dark forces [of the Comintern]'.[39] A year later a similar monument 'to those who fell in the battle against the Comintern' was unveiled – again in the presence of a retinue of senior Japanese officials – at Hailar, with badges 'for assiduousness' and certificates being handed out to those involved in the raising of the edifice.[40] Japanese preoccupations with imperial propriety and Russian *émigré* aspirations for a renewal of empire for a time appeared to be perfectly intertwined. The harmony was completed on the Russian side by the perfunctory military uniforms for its officials, the banquets in the imperial Russian ballrooms of Harbin and the restoration of a semblance of military discipline and the moral codes of old.[41] The dovetailing of such like-mindedness is best depicted in a publication commemorating the formation of the 'Great Manchurian Empire'. Writing on the theme of the work of the Bureau, its author notes:

> the great assistance to the Bureau's work from government's benevolent attitude towards it, being always attentive and concerned in protecting the interests of the Russian exiles. Deprived of its homeland, the emigration has found in Manchukuo a second fatherland. Especially valuable for the Bureau and the entire emigration are the relations with the head of the Imperial Nipponese Military Mission at Harbin, General Yanagita, who in all areas shows himself to be a true friend and great protector of the Russian emigration.[42]

While one can sense in this passage some of the close, and ultimately stifling, control that the Japanese exerted on Russian *émigré* associations such as the Bureau,[43] it is difficult to escape the sentiments of something of a kindred spirit that wafts from the prose.

Although many of the associations that arose under Japanese patronage were formed after 1934,[44] they joined a large number of Russian social, religious and charity organisations that had been in existence since the 1917 Revolution.[45] Together, and under the overarching control of the Bureau of Emigrants, they formed the infrastructure of *émigré* society in Manchuria after 1931. In their shape was both the order required by the community's Japanese patrons and an image – but only an image – of a Russian empire-in-miniature. Such a symbiosis ultimately found more militant outlets in the form of Fascist organisations and an ill-fated Russian military wing of the Japanese Kwantung Army, known as the Asano Brigade.[46] As with the former Russian Empire, the *émigré* community incorporated associations of the various national minorities that were represented in Manchuria. Minorities that had previously been squeezed by the Chinese authorities were to be accommodated (and monitored) beneath the umbrella of the Bureau.[47]

The impression that this left was of a thriving community, complete in every carefully formed and preserved detail of an existence that had already begun to disappear in the Soviet Union itself. And to an extent this was indeed the case. The *émigré* organisations, educational institutions and cultural bodies maintained an association with a Russian Empire that had long gone; an association that in some respects remains to this day.[48]

But the Russian *émigré* presence, even within this narrow ambit, was to linger with conflict at its core. The years of commercial and political turmoil experienced by the Russian community in Northern Manchuria inexorably loosened its grip on the economic levers of the region. And, as if it was intended as a final, damning gift to a group that had given it so much trouble in the 15 years it had tried to establish its place in the region, the Soviet Union ensured that the CER was to remain both a source of conflict and the cause of the further undermining of the Russian community's place in the local economy. Not for the first time, the setting was one of irony. As the Japanese and Manchukuo authorities were establishing the basis for the community's life within the new Empire, the Soviet Union was, just as deliberately, working to vouchsafe its further economic decline.

The handover of the railway was carried out in a tense and forced way in late March 1935. Talks on the terms of this transfer had been both long and difficult. As early as 1931, it was clear to the Soviet Union that the CER was an immense liability to it, both in political and economic terms. Moreover, this was a liability that the Soviet Union could ill afford at a time when its economy was undergoing massive structural changes through the introduction of 'Socialism in One Country' and the First Five-Year Plan. Having launched a twin-pronged process of industrialisation and collectivization, and done so at break-neck pace,[49] the Soviet Union's capital reserves were placed under immense pressure. A very great proportion of available funds were perforce directed to the building up of the means of production. A dramatic rise in currency emission supplemented the forced increase in export of raw materials; the former having the effect of drawing the Rouble farther and farther away from trading on the international *bourse*,[50] while the latter raised international suspicions of the Soviet Union having adopted a policy of dumping.[51] The Soviet Union, through the combined effect of sheer pace of internal development and the increased alienation from the external economic environment, became more inward-looking. In this context, the logic of using Soviet capital for the further development of the Northern Manchurian economy became less compelling.[52] On the other hand, the strategic considerations of how to maintain influence in a zone buffering the Soviet Union from Japan, and also the problem of the Russian *émigré* presence on that territory remained issues of some torment for Moscow. A Soviet Foreign Ministry statement released in February 1932 responded in a tortuous way to a Japanese request to allow the transport of Japanese troops on the CER. The statement stressed that such a request was in conflict with the understandings flowing on from the Treaty of Portsmouth. On the other hand, given Japan's enhanced political position in Manchuria after 1931, the Soviet Union was hardly in a position to resist. It was therefore made clear that '[i]n giving its consent to the transport of to the stations [at Harbin, Imianpo and Heilin], the Soviet Government makes that consent conditional on the assurances of the Japanese Government that the rights and interests of the USSR in the CER will in no circumstances be infringed by the Japanese authorities and high command'.[53] But at the same time as giving way on this count, the Soviet authorities expressed concern (as, indeed, they had on many other occasions) about the possibility of further problems with the Russian *émigrés*. Karakhan, in a statement in December 1932, made clear the Soviet sense of discomfort in this respect. '[There] are tens of thousands of insurgent White guards in Manchukuo and Japan', he said, 'who are struggling against and preparing for armed struggle against the USSR. The Soviet government, however, has never demanded their surrender, and the Japanese government itself, which can hardly regard them as representatives of an independent State, has never proposed to surrender them to the USSR, apparently understanding that such questions concern the internal politics of the country in question'.[54] Thus, while facing an inexorable growth in Japanese presence and influence in Manchuria, the Soviet authorities had also to contemplate the perpetuation of the *émigré* problem; a dilemma, then, of sizeable proportions.[55]

Initial signals of the Soviet Union's wish to shed the liability of the CER were issued by the Soviet Union in 1932, although the price it was suggesting was far too high for the Manchukuo authorities to accept.[56] By the time serious negotiations began in Tokyo on 26 June 1933, Iu. Rudyi, the Soviet head of the CER, had ordered an end to any repairs to the railway and had begun the process of transporting its movable property to the Soviet Union.[57] Although these measures alone were sufficient to ensure that the CER's operations would remain troubled, the Soviet Union's most significant coup was to use sleight of hand to avoid responsibility for the massive number of debts accrued by the railway since 1917, most of these being to Russian concerns in the region itself.[58] By the time the railway was transferred to Manchukuo on 23 March 1935, the figure owed to creditors was 20 million yen.[59] However, in the course of the talks the amounts discussed from the Soviet side appeared to be far lower.[60] As the talks progressed, it became clear that the Soviet Union was doing all in its power to avoid responsibility for the outstanding debts.[61] When, finally, the agreement was reached on basis of the Soviet Union's inaccurate financial statement, it was a hurried affair settled in a flurry of activity on a Sunday. The Manchukuo representatives who were responsible for countersigning the incorrect balance sheet did so only after the intervention of the Japanese Minister of Foreign Affairs, Koki Hirota. The reason given for such a forced procedure was that a final agreement over the railway would have been in the balance had the preliminary steps not been taken quickly.[62] In fact, it appeared more as if the Soviet Union was working – successfully, as it turned out – to hide accumulated debts that would have made the amount of the final settlement even less impressive than it already was.[63]

The tactic employed by Soviet negotiators in dealing with the contentious issue of the CER creditors in effect left the problem of the amassed debts in the hands of the Manchukuo government. Recognition of this by the latter helps to explain why it had been so reluctant to sign off on the Soviet Union's balance sheet. What the Soviet Union had in the end claimed responsibility for were the *pre-9 March 1917* debts, a large proportion of which had already been settled by a former CER General Manager Ostroumoff,[64] whereas those accrued in the period 9 March 1917 to 23 March 1935 were left to the new management to look after.[65] Given that the Soviet-led CER management had, from some reports, been pursuing a policy of selective non-payment of debts for some years,[66] these debts were sizeable. After strenuous efforts on the part of these numerous creditors, whose legal actions – a considerable number of which had been in the Manchurian courts for some years – had been pursued doggedly by them, it became clear that neither the Manchukuo authorities nor Japan was interested in seeing these matters resolved.[67] Indeed, for the latter this allowed a neat side-step and, at the same time, the ability to use another means to keep Russian commercial activities in Manchuria in check. In the meantime Japan could promote its own economic presence in a relatively uncontroversial way.

The Soviet Union therefore succeeded in leaving the region with an open wound that simply refused to heal.[68] As if to add insult to injury, the transfer of authority on the CER had occurred in a military-like fashion, with Rudyi, the departing General Manager of the CER, making a speech to company workers at midday on 23 March 1935, informing them that the Soviet Union had relinquished all further controls over, and responsibilities for, the railway. At the end of his brief statement, 98 per cent of Soviet management and administrative staff stepped aside and their Manchukuo replacements took their place at their desks. This unusual form of transfer meant that the new officials were literally to continue to write the history of the CER on a new, blank page, as they had neither Russian language nor the benefit of many of the documents and records that the former employees had taken with them (including many documents covering receipt of goods and services).[69] Thus, not only was further controversy injected into the matter of the creditors, but an atmosphere of general confusion was created in the important early period of operation of the new NMR. As one observer of this curious scene noted: 'given the peaceful transition of the railway lines under the watchful gaze of Manchukuo and Japanese troops, [this] "seizure", rather than a peaceful handover, of the main administration was totally uncalled for'.[70]

The nature of the transfer of the CER, the lingering controversy over its debts to members of the Russian community in Northern Manchuria and the depths which the railway's financial problems plumbed in major part contributed to, and served as a backdrop for, the perpetuation of instability for the community into the period of the new imperium. Many parts of the small-business sector and the more sizeable operations of families such as the Skidelskys and Kovalskys had limped through the turbulent late 1920s, only to find that the 1930s were in large measure even worse. The relative political order that was to descend upon the community, and Northern Manchuria as a whole, as a result of the imposition of Japanese hegemony had for many of them come too late. The Japanese presence brought with it a steady, orderly infusion of funds for commercial development of the region, but this money was wholly earmarked for Japanese enterprises. Russian firms were still obliged to generate their own capital, or to seek funds on the limited foreign capital market at Harbin. And it was here that the Russian community's economic end-game, so to speak, was played out.

Most Russian firms, and many individual Russians, were connected with the railway either through commercial ties or direct employment. The confluence of commercial pressures, the political strife that had gripped its operations for over four years (culminating in the 1929 crisis) as well the controversial, politically-charged activities of the last Soviet managers, Ivanov and Rudyi, had ensured that it was neither in a commercial position to support these local Russians, nor in most cases a political inclination to do so. This rough passage had in the late 1920s already made its impression on the reputation and credit-worthiness of a large number of small Russian firms in Northern Manchuria.[71]

But this was at one and the same time both complemented, and to an extent perhaps even overshadowed, by the plight of the large-scale Russian business in the region. Here too the storm surrounding the CER had left its mark, and relatively early on. One of the important business families in Northern Manchuria were the Skidelskys, whose activities had gradually shifted from Siberia to Manchuria in the course of the revolution and civil war in Russia.[72] Within a few years of establishing itself there, the Skidelsky family had built up major interests in coal and timber; both important areas not only for any large-scale development of the Northern Manchurian economy, but also to the railway itself.[73] Indeed, it could well be argued that both the short-term benefit from, and long-term plans for, the exploitation of these natural resources were intimately tied to the CER. As important, however, was the family's social and political significance in the fabric of the Russian community in Northern Manchuria. The Skidelskys' mining concession (the Mulin Mining Company) was, quite rightly, seen as a model of Russian success in the region. With an area of 130 square kilometres and situated on an Eastern spur of the railway, the concession produced approximately 250 000 tons of coal per annum and supported a complete self-contained village [with a number of] Russian engineers, 6000 Chinese *coolies* [labourers] and their families.[74] There were Chinese and Russian hospitals, schools, over 100 houses for Russian employees and three barracks for the Chinese labourers.[75] As would befit such a family, the Skidelskys' home in Harbin was on Bolshoi Prospekt, the most prestigious of Harbin's thoroughfares. Inside the house was, by Skidelsky's own estimation, the finest collection of Russian paintings outside Russia.[76] The family even had a resident beggar outside their front gate.[77]

The Skidelskys were, ironically, both an illustration of the precarious state that Northern Manchuria's Russian economy showed itself to be in the wake of the Sino-Soviet dispute and conflict, and, ultimately, victims to it. Beneath the veneer of affluence and respectability, the Skidelskys, as with other substantial *émigré* Russian concerns in the region, had been floundering for some years. In part, this had been due to the overambitious development schemes that the heads of the company had initiated in Manchuria. However, given that the region's main asset, with the exception of agricultural produce (notably soya beans), was its wealth in minerals and timber, such schemes under different circumstances would have been a natural direction for companies such as the Skidelskys' to take. This, then, leaves the question of why they could not make a success of their projects, having done so well in Eastern Siberia only a few years earlier. Rarely are answers to such questions simple ones, but in the case of the Skidelskys, and an entire series of other companies both large and small (and in areas as diverse as mining and retail sales), the answer was the same: shortage of capital. It was a problem that became especially apparent, of course, after the international economic depression gripped Harbin, some two years after the Wall Street

Crash. However, the contraction of the international economy that resulted from the events in the United States was not the cause of, but rather an accelerating factor in, a process that had begun some years earlier. The Skidelskys' company history illustrates this point well.

Despite the solid performance of the Skidelsky & Successors company in Eastern Siberia, the heads of the business (and especially Solomon) were regarded with remarkable hostility by sources of foreign capital in Harbin. As early as 1922, correspondence between the HSBC's Harbin Branch and the Head Office shows considerable antipathy towards the Skidelskys' business. In the August of that year, the Head of the bank's Vladivostok Office, M.W. Wood, received a memo chastising him for having advanced 20 000 yen to the Skidelskys, employing rents and a CER pronote as a basis for the loan (the Head Office had a month earlier rejected Solomon's request for a loan because the property he wished to use as collateral was unacceptable because the bank was precluded from owning such collateral at Vladivostok): '[W]e cannot say that you were well advised to [do so].... I consider both Skidelskys unreliable, and I don't suppose they give a thought to their outstanding Rouble-Sterling and Rouble-Yen exchange contracts'.[78] In an earlier report from Harbin Branch to Head Office, the case against the Skidelskys is put even more graphically. Under the heading 'Skidelskys – *Opinion*', the Harbin Branch's Manager, Baker noted that:

> On each occasion he [Solomon Skidelsky] wasted about half an hour of our time – chiefly in trying to raise more money out of the Bank and wanting us to take undesirable security e.g. C.E.R. pronotes. These are only paid at due date when there is any cash in the till, which is nearly akin to when the moon turns green. In parenthesis, I must do the railway the justice to say that they are owed over Yen 11 million by certain Allied Governments: that I have on very good authority, but until they pay, we and other creditors of Skidelsky look like having to whistle for our money. When he called on us he said the Railway actually owed him Yen 4 Million and would shortly owe him 11 million. I have heard since, that the railway recently gave him Pronotes for about one million Yen and that he had got the Banque Industrielle de Chine, Peking, to discount them. He has been, and is now, at Peking, possibly to pay his respects to the Portuguese Minister, having recently 'arranged' to be made Portuguese Consul here, vice our Consul. But there is not even a solitary 'goose' here.[79]

The bank's relations with the Skidelskys, with their work their borrowings and returns kept under unusually close scrutiny,[80] continued in this vein for the duration of their stay in Harbin. The Skidelskys were quite colourful characters, but there is little doubt from their plans that they had in mind the creation of a bona fide commercial edifice in Northern Manchuria, and not simply hustling for money as much of the bank's internal correspondence would lead us to believe.[81] If the activities that the Skidelskys engaged in to generate capital appeared as less than dignified for a family of their stature, then it would also underline how hard it was to secure funding for large-scale projects or businesses in that environment. Equally important, moreover, is the central rôle played by the railway in the business affairs of the region, serving as the single most important point of reference in matters concerning loans, security, repayment and, at least implicitly, the raising of capital. It was, moreover, a rôle that was to increase rather than diminish in subsequent years. Emerging too, even at the early stage referred to in the bank's correspondence (although this receives very little critical discussion; the bulk being reserved for the Skidelskys), is the erratic nature of the railway's own financial processes, and a distinct impression of its being strapped for cash in its own right.[82]

As the economic crisis bit deeper into the Northern Manchurian heartland, so too it spilled over into the politics of the region, dragging a family such as the Skidelskys – which might in other settings been seen as a pillar of society – into the grubby politics of the street. Perhaps the most squalid example of this was the ill-will, controversy and sheer desperation generated by the liquidation of the Russo-Asiatic Bank in 1926.[83] Rather than searching for the broader reasons for the collapse of the bank, its aggrieved clients singled out the Skidelskys as a prime example of unseemly favouritism exercised in its liquidation. Pointed to was the Skidelskys' Soviet passport status, which gave them, apparently, an advantage in concluding unsecured loans of 'several million Yen' with the bank. Painting a dismal picture of the family's business prowess, the petitioners depicted the Skidelsky brothers as 'hopeless debtors', whose modest property holdings had already been mortgaged to the hilt, and whose forest concessions had been almost entirely exhausted.[84] And yet the same 'hopeless debtors' had, the petition argued, been in collusion with the Chinese authorities (with whom, the signatories asserted, the Skidelskys shared ill-gotten gains), and with 'criminal leaders' of the Jewish National Bank, the Jewish Commercial Bank, the Mutual Credit Bank and the Soviet *Dal'bank*.[85] They went on by suggesting that Solomon Skidelsky had used his status as Portuguese Consul to 'press' Chinese and foreigners alike, and the brothers' settlement with the bank was covered by an agreement that, the petitioners concluded in their barely literate English, '…was written for the purpose of making out the Skidelskys as the owners of money belonging to others, and to snatch off part of this money belonging to others, and to snatch off part of this money for the benefit of the Chinese'.[86] The document had spun together every possible sordid political strand into the final, bitter fabric of an explanation of why they themselves had been left without money. At the centre of this political phantasmagoria were the Skidelskys.[87]

Russian-owned companies with less controversial images to contend with nonetheless found themselves slipping steadily into similar patterns of financial difficulty and, ultimately, decline. Ironically, Churin's (the prestigious Harbin Department Store that was to display the Skidelskys' sumptuous art collection later in the 1930s) too found it difficult to secure capital to keep its highly diversified business going.[88] Lopato, the old, well-regarded Russian tobacco company went the same way, being bought out by the BAT Company.[89]

From the records of the HSBC alone, it is clear that extreme scepticism had set in regarding Russian businessmen and their companies in Northern Manchuria. But without Soviet, Japanese, Chinese or local capital being made available to them, it was only the foreign banks that could provide a lifeline to these after the local economy had ground to a near standstill. Ironically, among the businesses that the HSBC had backed almost unreservedly was the Siberian Co., a Danish-based company which had been a leading buyer of soya beans. Its collapse, through the very malpractices that the bank had scrutinised and rejected applications of Russian companies for, led to an even sharper decline in local business conditions and the withdrawal of a number of suppliers of capital from the Harbin money market.[90] And yet the exceedingly cautious outlook that had come to characterise the foreign lenders' views of Russian commerce in the region was to largely remain, as if shaped by the early commentary such as that produced by the HSBC about the Skidelskys. In a sense, the fate of Russian commercial activity, and indeed the Russian community as a whole, in Manchuria came to hinge on views such as that expressed by HSBC's Head Office about the manager of the Russo-Asiatic Bank's Pristan' branch: 'Mr Blacher', it wrote, 'has no conception of what "running straight" means.... [You] should endeavour to watch [the Russo-Asiatic's] manoeuvres as closely as possible'.[91] Deprived of a viable business environment, Russian businessmen and merchants had found it more and more difficult to 'run straight', and, hardly surprisingly, found themselves under ever-increasing examination. Under the Japanese-backed Manchukuo government, Russian businesses, personalities and, indeed life as a whole, became subject to even more acute scrutiny. Together with the fears instilled of the 'imminent invasion' by the Soviet Union, the atmosphere became one of comprehensive control and, finally, something of a spiritual extinction for the Russians and their business circles.[92] Ironically, the peace and stability that the early Russian traders and merchants had yearned for had at last appeared in their region, but their dreams of a vital, and permanent, Russian economic presence were most decidedly at an end, replaced by the twin processes of economic internationalisation and political subservience to Japan. Until its forces returned to the region after the defeat there of Japanese forces in World War II, at an end too was any significant rôle for the Soviet Union in either the polity or economy of Northern Manchuria.

# 8
# Manchuria and the Geopolitics of Myth

In examining the Russian presence in Northern Manchuria, and focusing as we have on the period 1924–31, the latter shows itself to have been one of great importance to our appreciation of both the region itself, and the Soviet outlook in Northeast Asia as a whole. In this respect, particular attention has been paid to the crisis of 1929, which brought with it significant political, military and economic dimensions.

The underlying argument suggests that the existing approaches to the study of Northern Manchuria failed to recognise the considerable importance of the crisis both to the political relations in the region, and to its political economy. It has been shown that in order to appreciate this fully, particular attention must be paid to the confluence of political and economic crises, as the combination of these constituted a key factor in undermining the rationale for the Soviet and Russian *émigré* presence alike.

However, a full understanding of the importance of this period cannot be arrived at without the examination of a number of other contiguous areas of study, each of which contributes to the nature of the crisis itself and to the resilience (or rather the lack of it) of the Russian 'colony' in Northern Manchuria. The historical, political and economic character of the region in which the Russian settlement established itself is one that exhibits the effects of imperial outstretch, or overstretch; generating ambiguities which were to ultimately find negative political forms. The Russian community in Northern Manchuria had, in this respect, reflected quasi-autonomy deriving from physical distance. In combination with this, there was a steady adherence to the founding principles of an outpost whose focus was to have been, above all, commerce and industry; principles laid down by Witte in the creation of a notion of a 'bridge of steel' spanning the Russian East.

The independent outlook manifested itself frequently, and after 1917 framed the curious elaboration of relations between centre and periphery in Russian/Soviet politics. With this came new political perspectives too, and especially those connected with the painful lessons of the Russian Civil War. The impact of the latter had the twin effect of politicising the

Russian community beyond levels previously experienced, and of crystallising the new Soviet state's concerns regarding territorial integrity and common security in the region. For the Soviet Union the need to contain, and ideally extinguish, the elements of Russian society in opposition to it in Northern Manchuria became impossibly intertwined with economic exigencies, notably the need to maintain control of the CER and establishing solid trading patterns. This, in turn, produced a political pragmatism that came to be very much at odds with the revolutionary/liberationist ideology espoused for (and in) China proper, as evidence by the work of the Soviet advisers. This came to represent, it has been argued, a paradox of Soviet policy in China as a whole during the period in question. Furthermore, this paradox heightened the political turbulence in Northern Manchuria itself; a turbulence which was eventually to create major dysfunction in its economy. In tracing this, attention has also been paid to the nature of the economy, investment patterns and how the political factors influenced these, and did so ultimately at the expense of indigenous Russian commercial community. With the steep decline in Russian influence in the region, so rose the logic of early Japanese intervention there, confirming the bankruptcy of the Soviet presence and creating, for a time, a fragile (and ultimately illusory) image of a Russian *émigré* imperium.

While such an image of empire was not, of course, reflective of their true power, the novelty of this 'last hurrah' from the Russian *émigrés* was nonetheless of some importance in its contribution to the political topography of the Northeast Asian region during the interwar period. The *émigrés'* claim was only one of a number that were evident in the Northeast Asian region during these years, with the major players there (China, the Soviet Union and Japan), all playing out what can best be described as the geopolitics of myth; resonances of, and allusions to, empires past, present and to come.[1]

Russia's expansion eastwards had in the early period been shaped by economic and political needs, but there was also an element present of *oeuvre civilisatrice*.[2] The extension of Russia's own heartland into Northeast Asia had already been brought to some prominence at the turn of the twentieth century, when the 'geographical pivot' of history, to use Halford Mackinder's concept, shifted from sea power to land power, with people and machinery coming to be more cheaply and efficiently moved by railway than by sea.[3] Russia, in this sense, played a key role in reshaping the 'heartland' of Northeast Asia. Its expansion into Siberia, and the construction of an ambitious railway system to do so, vivified the logic of extending Russia beyond its traditional borders,[4] and it was on the fragile basis of this logic that the *émigré* community's appeal for recognition of its claims to legitimacy ultimately rested.

This territorial and political expansion on Russia's part had, however, been viewed quite differently in other quarters, notably by Japan, whose fears regarding Russian motives had helped to precipitate the Russo-Japanese War,[5] and largely shaped subsequent relations between the two states. On China's part, the unfolding of this political pattern encouraged the formal opening up, and beyond that a forced pace of colonization, of Manchuria between the late nineteenth and early twentieth centuries. As discussed in Chapter 1, the Chinese Empire had ceded a limited amount of land to Russia and, through the treaties of 1858 and 1860, governing the Amur and Ussuri Rivers respectively, 'firmed' the land borders between the two states.[6] China's method of retaining control of Manchuria had been first and foremost to populate it with *Han* Chinese; a strategy which had achieved considerable success. Nonetheless, the political cohabitation in Manchuria remained an unhappy one, with guises of extraterritoriality, colonization being in evidence, but at the same time no formal annexation of the area having taken place, leaving it in a state of limbo. The problem of reading Japan's aspirations complicated the picture further.

Japan's acquiring a 'share' of Manchuria through its victory in the Russo-Japanese war changed the overall balance of power in the region considerably (and favourably) for it, but it left the issue of economic dominance unresolved, with neither the colonial powers (Japan and Russia) nor China itself able to take sufficient control of the economy. The complex crisscrossings and patterns of power in Northeast Asia in an important sense therefore differ from those present in South and West Asia, where Russia and Britain had been engaged in the 'Great Game;' regions where the lines of geopolitical influence and division were far more clear-cut than they were in Northeast Asia.[7]

It might be observed, then, that the notion of the 'Great Game' has coloured the study of Northeast Asia in the modern period, imparting on the region an orthodox interpretation of its political make-up, represented mainly in terms of 'spheres of influence', as well as negotiated divisions of control of territory, politically skewed settlement patterns, and, ultimately, a distorted understanding of the core nature of politics there. As important, however, is the fact that the 'Great Game' as a concept has largely excluded the unique historical political forms and shapes of the Northeast Asian region; centuries-old traditions in political and military organisation, in effect, being eclipsed by lines of interpretation that are centred on the Western notion of state, and the expression of interests in an almost exclusively Europocentric form.[8]

In re-interpreting the geopolitics of the region, it is important to recognise and incorporate the resonances of memories and histories of earlier empires there. These were, arguably, far more free-flowing than is allowed for by Western-based discussions of 'spheres of influence,' and the political logic that is implicit to these. An alternative perspective might be one that is based on an appreciation of political logic, form and imagination *other* than that locked into one of a Western statist interpretation. Evidence of such alternative perspectives was especially prominent in the Manchuria of the interwar period.

Perhaps the most important point to note in this respect is that images of politics in Northeast Asia, and especially its Manchurian component, are not only informed by the colonial edifices created by the major powers, but also by the place of nomadism as an underlying influence, and the nomads' concepts of empire-building an important point of reference.[9] The primacy of a highly mobile military is incorporated in this, as is the relationship between nomadism and settlement, in which the creation of 'states' and 'empires' was of a more fluid form than experienced in the state system generated by Europe after the Treaty of Westphalia. In Inner Asia, their formation was an exercise in exploiting the wealth of dispersed settlements, thereby creating periods of political linkage and continuity for them. Such an image of empire, founded upon the notion of the extraction of economic benefit from settled areas by highly mobile forces, stood in stark contrast to Western perspectives of growth, reinforcement and, above all, the apparent *permanence* of empire.[10]

Ancient notions, images and methods of empire-building were revived in the interwar period, over a considerable geographical spread and in a number of intriguing forms. In Manchuria, these ranged from audacious plans for a Eurasian Empire mooted by Baron von Ungern-Sternberg, to the activities of local bandits, the *Hunghutze*, who effectively controlled large portions Northeastern China, claiming via their semi-formal 'empire' a living and booty from the isolated settlements.

The fluidity that resulted from these political forms encouraged, it could be argued, the appearance of broader, more exotic ideologies of empire, and these for a time competed as rival world views on this ancient field of contest. The suggestion here is that a number of proto-empires had actually emerged in this period, perhaps providing not entirely tangible forms, but at least, as in the case of the one proposed by von Ungern-Sternberg, an intriguing glimpse of themselves.

What was the impetus for these political manifestations? At the heart of any re-interpretation of the inter-war period in Northeast Asia , and the Russian contribution to it, is the proposition that what one sees in the region as a whole at this time is the interplay of three elemental aspects of political and economic change that gripped the region in the first half of the twentieth century. This interplay made existing, state-focussed lines of political control less clear-cut, and allowed for the re-emergence of earlier, more primal understandings both of politics and empire.

China underwent forced division and fragmentation, which showed itself successively in the aftershocks of revolution (1911) and a prolonged, debilitating civil war (beginning more formally in 1925, but with opening disruptions from as early as 1920, and arguably going on until 1949). In many respects, of course, China served as a core for forces of destabilisation, and these resonated on the periphery of the 'Middle Kingdom.' Russia too was wracked by revolution, with a disruptive preamble that began at the turn of the century (1905), took fiercer forms in 1917, and culminated in its own destructive civil war of 1918–24. And, finally, there was Japan's rapid industrialisation together with the pressure of political restructuring; the confluence which in itself constitutes something of a revolution, but is rarely recognised as such. The force of the impact of a highly compressed process of westernistic industrialisation, as well as the rapid introduction of Japan to the sharp changes of global commercial and trading processes, shaped considerably the Japanese political outlook. In combination, this period represented the tail end of a root-and-branch political transformation that was the Meiji Restoration.[11]

The sum of these broad politico-economic upheavals in this period gave rise to a number of features for the region. First, there was a *de facto* 'loosening' of the peripheries of at least two of the existing empires. Russia, through its temporary loss of control of Eastern Siberia and Russian Far East during the Civil War and Allied Intervention, found itself in a situation in which it became organically intertwined with some of its neighbouring states. China, through the fracturing that occurred as a result of the rise of warlordism, and the appearance of a number of ideologies on its northern perimeter, experienced something similar. Secondly, there was, in effect, the imposition of the notion of a periphery on the island state of Japan, both in terms of the barriers to further economic expansion, and the rude reminders of strategic threats (many of these perhaps more a perception than actual) to its own borders.[12]

Through the changes and political developments, the peripheries of all three states in this period were perceived to have begun to overlap, instigating confusion, disembodiment and protracted political instability. Efforts to divide Manchuria into spheres of control served as a prime example of this. The formal arrangements arrived at between China, Russia and Japan functioned to some degree in theory perhaps, but certainly did not in practical political or economic terms. There existed not only high degrees of mistrust between the individual players, but there also appeared economic inefficiencies which prevented each party from deriving full benefit from what was otherwise one of the potentially richest regions in China.[13]

In addition to the broader lines of distrust and confrontation, there were also complex tensions and conflicts present on a number of other plains. First, there were those between Chinese Republicans and local warlords, as well as 'unholy' alliances between Republicans and warlords against Soviet Russian influence.[14] Moreover, the Soviet Russians themselves were in conflict with the Russian *émigrés*, or in their parlance the so-called 'White Guardists.' And, as has been seen, the Japanese too from time to time had to counter loosely-formed alliances on the ground in Manchuria. But even within its own political system, Japan had its own political divisions to contend with, notably between moderates and militarists, with the latter both ensconced in, and focussing on, Manchuria, using this international trouble spot as a form of leverage to destabilise the political situation in Japan itself.[15] And, finally, the *Hunghutze* arrayed themselves against virtually the entire spectrum of powers with interests in Manchuria. In describing this dense weave of politics, one must also observe that this was a relatively protracted 'game', but, unlike the situation in South and West Asia, with few tangible boundaries or comprehensible rules to effectively guide any of the 'players'.

With the failure (and indeed the apparent demise) of the politics of pragmatism, greater attention came to be focussed on more exotic forms of ideology, with competing interests becoming embodied in the latter. Particularly pronounced in this respect were Japan's considerations of its own 'limits of empire.' A consensus was becoming apparent regarding the need for territorial expansion, but in what direction should this be, and what forms might it take? The debate which emerged was essentially one between the civilian authorities and the militarists, with the latter gradually gaining the upper hand in the course of the dialogue.[16] The militarists themselves were divided on the issue of whether or not to expand into China, which is why the evocation of a higher 'authority' (a teleological appeal of finding national greatness in a Japanese-centred Asia) came to be of significance.

Similarly, in the case of the spread of Russian-inspired revolutionary 'disease' (Communism) in the periphery, with, for example, the rapid toppling of the Mongolian monarchy, and the establishment of 'progressive' politics in that state.[17] At the same time as these 'progressive' forces of Bolshevism made themselves felt on some fronts in these 'frontier' territories, there appeared threats to it on others: the counter-revolutionary activity conducted by a fringe group of Russians, as well as other political forms, none of which was entirely distinct, in the Russian Far East. These manifestations were a shade too independent for Moscow's liking and they brought with them the fear that the splinter bodies of authorities might ultimately find accommodation with Japan.[18]

Central Asia too was a problem for the new Soviet state. This was especially so between 1917 and 1921, a period replete with botched attempts at seizing power, and the failure of the Bolsheviks to exert either authority or influence. In March 1918, for example, the Kokand government sought to create the Farghana Khanate; an attempt which immediately led to the rise of Basmachi guerilla resistance to the perceived Bolshevization of Central Asia.[19] In addition to the lines of Russian opposition to the Bolsheviks, therefore, the latter also had to deal with failed attempts at autonomy and independence in the Muslim areas, resulting in a sense of chronic instability.

What we see emerge from this general turbulence is a broad pattern of responses, and perhaps the politics of re-conceptualisation, taking place.

Taken together, it is clear that they provide competing claims to the control – or rather the *shaping* – of empire. Some of these stem from an underlying ideological tendency to *formal* empire and territorial demarcation; others to appeals to imagined forms of ideological and political expansion. The USSR, despite its early experimentation with the export of liberation and socialism, gradually shifted to a more straightforward, conventional 'hardening' of its border areas, thereby reversing the attempts in the early years of revolutionary euphoria to blur the lines between ideology and the practise of international relations, as these spilt over into adjacent states.[20] This process was most clearly demonstrated through its gradual return to the notion of an extension of its sphere of activity to re-incorporate an economic catchment area through the reaffirmation of its railway interests in Eastern Siberia and Manchuria, and the pursuit of strategies of trade and commerce that were a far cry from the professed idealism.[21]

China too, through its efforts to tame the northern border areas and bring warlordism under control, was attempting to formalise its previous shape of empire. In this the central Chinese government was trying to bring a variety of warlords to heel, but with little success, and, as has been shown, there were instances of direct contradiction, and even negation, of policy. In the midst of this political muddle it, like the local authorities, had to deal with the other 'empire-builders', the *Hunghutze*.

The warlords themselves controlled distinct epicentres of power, and actively competed in emulating older forms of political control and broadening their political sway. This resulted in a palpable ebb and flow of power through the Chinese mainland, and although this could be written off exclusively to an often brutal Chinese civil war, the forms that the political and military struggle took lent themselves more to the older understandings of military dominance employed in the effort to capture and shape 'empire.' The use of Russian and other foreign mercenaries by the warlords reinforced this point, with Russian officers and soldiers often incorporated into forces which resembled the free-flowing armies that dominated the core region at earlier points in history.

Japan, in its efforts to build up its own economic and political stock in Manchuria, also employed Russians, exerting both political influence and steadily squeezing out Soviet economic presence in the region via intense trade competition. It should be noted too that while it is peripheral to the present study of the Russian presence, Korea too became very much a part of the flow of politics on the broader 'chessboard' in this period, both through the Japan's further exertion of political and cultural dominance of that state, as well as through the forced spread of the Korean people into the broader areas of its 'sphere of influence'.[22]

Such a political context was sufficient to ensure that the situation in the Northeast Asian region remained fluid, but there were, in addition, other factors which contributed to this condition, these being the representations of rarified ideologies which are more to do with myths and rationale for empire, rather than simply the elaboration of power politics.[23]

China, given its politically parlous state during this period, was perhaps the most unlikely to achieve a return to the authority or might of a 'Middle Kingdom' in a region which it had traditionally identified with its own empire. But such notions were nonetheless to some degree evident in its governmental policies, and, more notably, strongly shaped the outlook of its central government.[24]

Japan too, with its increasingly modernist character, began to express an outlook that suggested its own somewhat idiosyncratic landscape of regional power and empire. As mentioned earlier, this started through the ambiguous probings near the centre of the region (Eastern Siberia, the Russian Far East and Manchuria), but eventually became something much grander, taking in Asia as a whole. Japanese activity in Manchuria is instructive in that we can see quite clearly the conversion of outlook from vague explorations, through tentative rationalisations and, finally, to the conclusions that Japan had a claim to the sovereignty of what had historically been Chinese territory. The transformation came, it is evident, through the application of peculiar slants of reasoning, which, in turn, added to the logic of expanding the Japanese state into a broader context still:

> We must clearly realise that there is besides a higher plane of what might be conceived of as *supra-reactionary* political regime, which cannot be made arbitrarily, but which has grown spontaneously out of the protoplasm of a family; only in such a political structure, metaphysical hierarchy is *a priori* established between the sovereign, as legitimate performer of the Universal Law, and his faithful subjects. This is a sketchy elucidation of the intrinsic nature of the Japanese Family Monarchy which, towers high above the duality of democracy and autocracy. We shall now understand the reason why in Japan democracy became aware of its proper limits, on the one hand and on the other hand why dictatorship of any kind whatsoever can not win the hearty support of our people.[25]

As discussed in Chapter 7, such convoluted reasoning was used by Japan to lay claim to Manchuria (or Manchukuo), but it also represented an embryonic manifesto for a far grander empire; a manifesto in which the 'Japanese way' provides a rationale for Japan to occupy the 'heartland' within the region, but also the philosophical underpinnings for a much wider expansionism that quite naturally followed on from this.

In a later exposition, indeed, a Japanese nationalist such as Fujisawa was able to present a more distinct, and far more ambitious, vision than had been associated with Manchuria: 'Nippon's national flag is an ensign of "red heart", or fiery sincerity. It alludes to the heavenly mission of Japan to tranquillize the whole world.'[26] Such reasoning readily provided for broader interpretation, and still more 'practical' prospective extensions of Japanese power. Such outlook finally allowed for the conclusion that '[t]he doctrine of "Asia for the Asiatics" is based on the supreme principle that Asia must be safeguarded and maintained by Asiatics'.[27]

What was evolving here, and was spurred on by the political instability of the 'heartland,' very much encouraged the natural flow of such 'logic', quite clearly being that of a Japan-centred notion of Pan-Asianism; a doctrine that would eventually manifest itself broadly as the Greater East Asian Co-prosperity Sphere,[28] but in its early stages seemed to reside largely in the twists and turns to achieve philosophical authority over the Manchuria-based heartland.

However, Japan was elaborating grand visions which in their philosophical essence were quite close to those put forward by others before them. In the case of Russia, Prince Esper Esperevich Ukhtomskii had in the late nineteenth century expressed similar ideas as these, finding their home at the core of the outlook of the *Vostochniki* (Easterners).[29] This group had, through their own newspapers, pamphlets, as well as articles in European journals, put forward the view that Russia would achieve its empire in the East through '... secret powers of emotional sympathy...' with the Eastern races.[30] By the turn of the century, this had become a fully fledged ideology, perhaps best summed up in Ukhtomskii's own words:

> Asia – we have always belonged to it. We have lived its life and felt its interests. Through us the Orient has gradually arrived at consciousness of itself, at a superior life.... We have nothing to conquer. All these peoples of various races feel themselves drawn to us, and are ours, by blood, by tradition, and by ideas. We simply approach them more closely. This great and mysterious Orient is ready to become ours.[31]

Cultural identification such as this came to be the core of the political outlook for all the main players in the region during the interwar years. Ironically, Soviet Russia proved to be the weakest link in this politico-cultural and geostrategic competition, having for all practical purposes jettisoned its 'higher ideals' of socialist internationalism in favour of the carving out of formal borders and the *Realpolitik* of concluding treaties to vouchsafe these.[32] The broader Russian visions of empire were, instead, picked up, and forwarded, by the Russian *émigré* political fringe groups, maintaining images of empire that evolved within a political environment dictated initially by Chinese central and warlord governments, and then later under Japanese tutelage.[33]

The Russian fringe's visions of empirium were interesting because they contained an 'orthodox' view of a quintessentially pre-revolutionary Russian community which had evolved, and would continue to evolve, within a more stable, sheltering external political environment; as it happened, first under Chinese suzerainty, and then under the somewhat harsher Japanese political patronage and control. At the heart of the Russian *émigrés'* outlook were not only claims of a long association with the locality (tracing these to Ivan the Terrible's reign, and the first appearance of Russians on the River Amur), but also their status as a core for the preservation of non-Bolshevik Russia, and thereby maintaining the uninterrupted lineage of Russian language, culture, and forms of politics from the 1700s, through to the 1930s, and, in principle, well beyond. The publication of *The Great Manchurian Empire* (discussed in Chapter 7) brought with it the echoes of the heritage of the *Vostochniki*, but expressing a political perspective that was distorted by exigency and pragmatism. While this was a Japanese-sponsored publication (with the nominal heads of the 'committee' responsible for it publication being Japanese militarists M. Niomura and R. Kato), the imagination which fills its pages is an entirely Russian one, and the image of the continuity, indeed the further flourishing, of the Russian–Manchurian empire (but not, it should be noted, Manchukuo, which appears only as a protective 'shell' within which the Russian imperial imagination is exercised, rather than serving as the work's inspiration) is entirely consistent with the way in which many Russians in China saw their role. And from within this core Russian *émigré* community came the other splinter groups discussed in earlier chapters; groups which saw the 'empire' in somewhat different, more exotic, and often more violent, moulds. Within these were the fantastic imaginings of Baron R.F. Ungern-Sternberg, a 'visionary' whose political ambitions, as we have seen in Chapter 2, were nothing short of audacious. Suffice it to say here that Ungern, who roamed the plains of Manchuria and Mongolia with a band of cavalrymen, in a fundamental sense drew inspiration from the true core of the history of the region. In essence, his was political form based on unhindered horse-borne warfare and nomadic imposition on settlements. The 'Eurasian empire' he envisioned spanned East and West and represented a political core that was close to the Russian-Inner Asian 'heartland.' Indeed, in many respects this delusional image of empire mirrored that of the *Vostochniki*, whose proposition of a Russian-led empire in the East was, as we have seen earlier, also based on a mystical core that linked Russian 'spirit' with that of the Eastern peoples.

Von Ungern-Sternberg in larger-than-life form, but arguably the other major players in the region in a considerably less phantasmagorical form, recognised one key aspect of the Northeast Asia during the interwar years: the racial and cultural 'melting-pot' that was seemingly there to be used in the building up of empire. This was a characteristic noted by a number of visitors to the region, but is perhaps best depicted by an American Senator, Albert J. Beveridge, after his visit to Manchuria at the turn of the twentieth century:

> And you are struck by the fact (nay, if you be Anglo-Saxon, you are startled by it) that all of this mingled motley of humanity get along in

perfect harmony. The bronzed Korean, the queued Chinaman, and the blue-eyed, yellow-haired Russian soldier arrange themselves on an open flat-car in a human mosaic of mutual agreeableness. There is no race prejudice here! Superior to all the world, as the Russian believes himself, he shows no offensive manner towards the other races with which he so picturesquely mingles. It is a thing that you must have noticed up in Siberia, where the Russian peasant is also coming into contact with semi-oriental peoples. But, with the blood of racial bigotry coursing through your veins, here this social fusion startles you. It is a strange page suddenly opened before you. And it is a page you will read again and again every day as long as you are in Manchuria. And from a reading of it a lesson may be learned, and part of Russia's secret of dominion revealed.[34]

The 'strange pages' were those that the main players read and studied, producing competing visions of what was, to a degree at least, already in place: a 'heartland' of empire, with a character that was already quite distinctive, but geographically largely undefined. The question was, how was it to be given shape and intellectual form?

Each of these visions of empire was based on regional political continuities and histories. Each, in effect, vied for dominance of a core *Eurasian* territory, while simultaneously having to accommodate or absorb the sharp discontinuities present there. And, although the physical form was quite different in the case of each of the contending parties, it was the presence of these rival visions of empire that provided a fascinating, kaleidoscopic interplay of 'what was', 'what might have been' and 'what might be'. In a sense, therefore, it was the visions of empires past, present and future which provided the political dynamic for the region. Through the logical exposition of, and the acting upon, these competing visions of empire emerged the geopolitics of the interwar period. These were ideologies interlaced with power politics, together forming strategic perspectives on mythical empires.

# Appendix

To the Commission of Enquiry of the
League of Nations.

### SUMMARY OF PETITION

from the depositors of the Russo-Asiatic Bank in Harbin.

The French Government, knowing that in China one cannot entrust European property to the Chinese authorities, undertook the duties of protectorship over the Russo-Asiatic Bank in Harbin, granting to same the rights of a French establishment in China, – the rights of extraterritoriality. –

Having confidence in the French Government, not admitting of any deceit, a number of Europeans of Harbin deposited at this Bank all their hard-earned lifelong savings. The Chinese authorities, from the name of their establishments and enterprises, likewise, preferred to keep their reserves in a Bank which was under French protectorship. On the 26–28 of September 1926 by the decision of the Paris Seine Commercial Court, the Bank was declared to be in voluntary liquidation.

The Bank's sure and verified Assets were: about 11 million Yen; its Liabilities $4\frac{1}{2}$ million Yen. The French Consul in Harbin used to issue directions regarding the Bank at the outset of its liquidation. The Chinese Peking Government declared that it takes the Bank into its own "Government's" liquidation. The persons who formed the body of the Government of France, understanding the intention of the Chinese to plunder the property of the Bank in accordance with the general system of disposing of the money and property of foreigners, – did not wish to insist upon its being inadmissible that the Bank should be seized by the Chinese, – did not wish to do so upon the pretext that this could possibly lessen the friendly relations with the Chinese temporary leaders, i.e. – they decided to purchase friendship for the money savings belonging to several thousand different Europeans and which had been entrusted to the French establishment in Harbin. The French agent at Peking, who held the post of Assistant of the Chief Liquidator, turned a blind eye upon the misdeeds committed by the Chinese, receiving for doing so big sums of money under the aspect of salary – this out of the savings of the depositors, savings that had been entrusted to the French authorities and over the loss of which bitter tears were wept. Another French agent took out of the Bank in Harbin the sum of above 6.000 Yen, as his own money in total, being aware that to other creditors nothing had been paid or there had been given out but small amounts of their money.

In result of the above occurencies [sic] and of the seizure of the Bank by the Chinese, the latter took out in first instance all their deposits in full amounts – unproportionally. [sic] The Chinese authorities secretly sold the real estates of the Bank in liquidation which represented a great value – to Chinese Banks, of those in which these authorities are masters and shareholders – for a price by ten times lower than their real cost – with a less of several hundred thousand Yen. They gave back to the "Councillor" of the liquidation of the Bank – to the chinaman Mr. Lutai – 6 houses free, without exacting the indebtedness of 300.000 Yen, which were fictitiously written out in the name of Mr. Bren. The Harbin Government ordered the release of the arrest laid upon the money of the debtor Mr. Kovalsky in the sum of 400.000 Gold Roubles. And now for covering the indebtedness of 700.000 Yen – Mr. Kovalsky has no money at all – everything is concealed. They returned to the debtors mortgage deeds on property of full value – for 1/5 part of the payments of debts, thus bringing big losses. They concluded other criminal affairs with debtors, bringing a loss of several hundred thousand Yen. A covetous "unmindfulness" has been exhibited in regard to the indebtedness of the Chinese Eastern Railway in favour of the depositors in the sum of 484.000 Silver Dollars. The Liabilities of the Bank have been unjustly decreased by 1.300.000 Yen, – in the form of cheating and falsely counting the currency in "monetary" marks.

Instead of a normally conducted, a full and favourable liquidation of the Bank in a period of 6 months, with an expenditure of 20–25 thousand Yen, the liquidation has been deceit fully dragged on for the length of nearly 6 years, and alongside with other misdeeds, – there have been expended, in the form of salaries, – above 700.000 Yen, plus 30% of cost or quarters in the buildings of the Bank.

They have upheld and have continued the big criminality – a "Panama". For the money belonging to the depositors, in the sum of several million Yen, were organized the Mulin Colliery and Railway enterprises. The income must be divided into two parts; between the Chinese Treasury and the financier. In accordance with the status and regulations of the Bank and with general regulations, the Bank cannot have a debtor for a sum above 10.000 Yen, – without a security. It was required: to place at the Bank 50% of the shares of the Mulin enterprises (as it had been done with the "Sungari Mills Company"). However the criminal collaboration of the directors and the ex-directors of the Bank – with the Soviet subjects are Skidelskis, put down the Skidelskis as debtors of the Bank and without any security for the entire sum of several million Yen, placed by the Bank into the Mulin enterprises. The noting down of the Skidelskis as debtors to the Bank for the money which had been spent for the organizing of the Mulin enterprises, was done quite consciously – and was clearly an act of theft.

This criminal act resulted in the unlawful noting down the Skidelskis as participants in the Mulin enterprises. In accordance with the laws of all governments it is inadmissible that stolen property or money should be given into the possession of the thieves. The Chinese authorities, with covetous aims, let the Skidelskis be considered as the fictitious participants in the Mulin enterprises.

For the full satisfaction of the claims of 2 thousand depositors with a compensation for the cheating and false making up of accounts, and for their getting lawful persentage [sic] (interest) – should now be required million Yen. The property of the Bank on hand – is of 300.000 Yen. There is small hope of getting the money from any other sources. The only real resources lie in the Mulin enterprises.

Earnest petition: to grant assistance for saving people from disaster to help in returning to unfortunate and ruined people their means of existence.

For effecting this it is necessary that the orders should be issued as follows:

1. That the Russo-Asiatic Bank in Harbin, which is under the protectorship of France and which was declared by the Paris Court of Justice to be in voluntary liquidation, – should be taken back from the Chinese, who had seized the Bank and should be returned to the depositors themselves under the control of the French authorities, in the person of the French Court liquidators or in the person of the French Consul at Harbin.
2. That Messrs. Skidelskis, should be undeferringly [sic] set aside, and forever, from the Mulin enterprises, wherein they were quite unlawfully enlisted.
3. That the Bank should, without delay, be re-established in its lawful participation in the Mulin enterprises, as the real and only financier – undertaken of same.
4. That there should be effected, absolutely with the participation of the French authorities, and the depositors of the Bank, a most careful and impartial investigation of all actions regarding affairs of the Bank for the purpose that all unlawful acts should be anulled [sic] and that the persons, who had committed those misdeeds, should be made to answer by the law.
5. That measures should be undertaken instantly for the guarding of the property and of the documents of the Bank.

S. O. S.

Signed: Depositors and Representatives of the Depositors.

[Mr. Krougloff and others, 14 May 1932]

# Notes

## Introduction

1. M. Beloff, *The Foreign Policy of Soviet Russia, 1929–1941*, Vols I & II, London, 1947, 1949 (especially vol. I, pp.70–88); P.S.H. Tang, *Russian and Soviet Policy in Manchuria and Outer Mongolia, 1911–1931*, Durham, 1959. See also: D.J. Dallin, *Soviet Russia and the Far East*, New Haven, 1948; H.L. Kingman, *Effects of Chinese Nationalism upon Manchurian Railway Development, 1925–1931*, Berkeley, 1932; G.A. Lensen, *The Damned Inheritance: The Soviet Union and the Manchurian Crises, 1924–1935*, Tallahassee, 1974; S. Smith, *The Manchurian Crisis, 1931–1932; A Tragedy in International Relations*, New York, 1948; C. Thorne, *The Limits of Foreign Policy: The West, the League and the Far Eastern Crisis of 1931–1933*, London, 1972.
2. S. Eddy, *The World's Danger Zone*, New York, 1932, p.67. Other writers from the period reinforced this view. The more important of these are: G.E. Sokolsky, *The Tinder Box of Asia*, New York, 1933; T.P. Etherton and H.H. Tiltman, *Manchuria, the Cockpit of Asia*, New York, 1932; R.S. Pickens, *Storm Clouds over Asia*, New York, 1934; O. Lattimore, *Manchuria, Cradle of Conflict*, New York, 1932. More recent scholarship which reinforces such a thesis (and virtually ignores the 1929 conflict) can be found, for example, in C.J. Bartlett, *The Global Conflict: The International Rivalry of the Great Powers, 1880–1990*, London, 1995. Remarkably, perhaps the most detailed recent study of the Manchurian problem, Louise Young's *Japan's Total Empire: Manchuria and the Culture of Wartime Imperialism*, Berkeley & London, 1998, continues this approach to the Manchurian problem by providing a most admirable level of detail about the transformation of Manchuria into Manchukuo, but, curiously, devotes no attention to the 1929 conflict.
3. 1931 was described as such by historian A.J. Toynbee, cited in J.T. Pratt, *War and Politics in China*, London, 1943, p.216.

## 1 The Birth of Politics in Exile

1. Peter S.H., *Tang Russian Policy in Manchuria and Outer Mongolia, 1911–1917*, Durham, 1959, pp.10–11.
2. E.G. Ravenstein, *The Russians on the Amur*, London, 1861, p.3.
3. The *Nuchens, Sushens, Ilous* and *Mohos* (the Manchus were directly related to the first – named and descended from the others). (Ibid.)
4. Ibid.
5. Li Chi, 'Manchuria in History', *Chinese Social and Political Science Review*, Peiping, 1932, vol. 16, pp.251–2.
6. For an account, see J.K. Fairbank *et al.*, *East Asia: Tradition and Transformation*, London, 1973, p.216 *et seq*.
7. M. Mancall, *China at the Center: 300 Years of Foreign Policy*, New York, 1984, pp.17–18 (Nepal, Burma, Korea, Annam and the Liuchu Islands were all vassal states at this time).
8. Owen Lattimore, *Manchuria: Cradle of Conflict*, New York, 1932, p.38.
9. Ibid. p.46.

10. Ibid.
11. Ibid, p.44.
12. Tang, op cit., pp.15–16.
13. Cited in Tang, p.16.
14. H.P. Bix, 'Japanese Imperialism and the Manchurian Economy', *China Quarterly*, 1972, vol. 51, p.246.
15. Tang, op. cit., p.17.
16. Ibid.
17. Bix, op. cit., p.426.
18. Ibid. By the Treaty of Aigun of 1858, Russia came to control the left bank of the Amur from the River Argun' to the Pacific Ocean. Two years later, under the terms of the Treaty of Peking, Russia's rights to the Ussuri region were formally recognised by China. By this stage, the overall area under Russian control had grown to 855 600 square miles. (I.A. Iakushev 'Amur ili reka chernogo drakona', 1931(?), p.3, Gosudarstvennyi arkhiv Rossiiskoi Federatsii [GARF], Fond 5869, No.1, Khr. no. 32.)
19. Bix, op. cit., p.426.
20. Ibid.
21. Chang Tso-lin finally formally emerged entered the political arena after having sided with the Japanese during the Russo-Japanese War. Because of this, the Japanese gave him the governorship of his native Fengtien Province. In the spring of 1922 he declared Manchuria an autonomous state. (See V. Vilenskii-Sibiriakov, *Chzhan-tszo-lin: Man'chzhurskaia problema*, Moscow, 1925, pp.42–4. For a full account of Chang's rise to power, see G. McCormack, *Chang Tso-lin in Northeast China, 1911–1928*, Palo Alto, 1977.)
22. Chinese Academy of Science, *A History of the People's Revolutionary Movement in the Northeast in Modern Times*, Changchun, 1960, p.263.
23. Bix, op. cit., p.426.
24. These expeditions were 1643–46 and 1649–53 respectively. Ravenstein writes of the size of these early forays: 'In all, 532 Russians had left Siberia for the Amur at one time or another under Khabarov's command'. (Ravenstein, op. cit., p.25.) Their success, however, was far in excess of the numbers involved. Iakushev, for example, describes Poiarkov as a Russian 'conquistador' who won for Russia territory far in excess of that conquered by Pizarro for Spain in the Americas in the first half of the 16th century. (Iakushev, op. cit., p.2.)
25. Ravenstein, op. cit., p.13. See also Iakushev's description of Khabarov's 'cruel seizure' of the Amur basin (op. cit., p.2).
26. Ibid., p.8.
27. Tang, op. cit., pp.20–1. The treaty is regarded by G. Vernadsky in his *Political and Diplomatic History of Russia* (Boston, 1936) as 'a complete failure for Moscow diplomacy.' (p.222). The treaty, nevertheless, gave Russia the right of tariff-free trade with China.
28. Ravenstein, op. cit., p.71.
29. Vernadsky, op. cit., p.240.
30. Tang, op. cit., pp.28–9. These advances came as a result of Muraviev's second expedition, which began in 1854.
31. D.J. Dallin, *The Rise of Russia in Asia*, London, 1950, p.24.
32. Tang, op. cit., p.24. The purpose of the programme was to convert peasants registered at Nerchinsk into Cossacks. From a total population of 29 000 males, Muraviev intended to form 12 battalions of 1000 men each. This was approved by Nicholas I on 27 April 1851. (Ibid.)

33. For details of this, and a discussion of the contentious phrasing, see R.K.I. Quested, *The Expansion of Russia in East Asia, 1857–1860*, Kuala Lumpur, 1968, p.146 *et seq.*
34. Cited in Tang, op. cit., p.32. Muraviev's own glory, however, was quite short-lived. In early 1861 he went into retirement after his project for the division of Eastern Siberia into two Governor-Generalships was rejected by the central government. (I.I. Lin'kov *et al.*, *Deiateli Rossii XIX – nachala XX v.: Biograficheskii spravochnik*, Moscow, 1995, p.121.)
35. Iakushev, op. cit., p.3.
36. Ravenstein, op. cit., pp.153–4.
37. Derived through the conversion programme for the Nerchinsk peasantry. (see above, note 32.)
38. In describing the lot of these settlers, Dallin cites the Russian explorer Nikolai Przhevalsky: 'These settlers look upon the new region with animosity and consider themselves deportees. One hears bitter complaints about the hardships, and sad reminiscences of former habitations'. (Dallin, op. cit., p.24.)
39. Soviet historians went so far as to describe Badmaev as a '*pridvornyi aferist*'. (*Krasnyi Arkhiv*, Moscow, 1932, No.52, p.40.) For a concise depiction of the context within which Badmaev was working, see D. Geyer, *Russian Imperialism: The Interaction of Domestic and Foreign Policy, 1860–1914*, Leamington Spa, 1987, pp.187–91.
40. These close relations were as much a tactical expedient as a representation of increasing warmth between China and Russia (a useful depiction of this can be found in P.H. Clyde and B.F. Beers, *The Far East: A History of Western Impacts and Eastern Responses, 1830–1975*, New Jersey, 1975, pp.210–11).
41. Tang, for example, sees Witte as having realised 'the political and strategic significance of the Trans-Siberian Railway as an interrelated part of his larger policy in Asia.' (Tang, op. cit., p.36.) A fuller discussion of Witte's ideas on this subject appears below.
42. A note dated 25 March 1895, in *Krasnyi Arkhiv*, 1932, No.52, p.40.
43. S.Iu. Witte, *Vospominaniia*, Moscow, 1960, Vol. 2, pp.44–5.
44. G. & S. Stokes, *The Extreme East: A Modern History*, Hong Kong, 1964, p.215.
45. Ibid.
46. The Russo-Chinese Bank was Russian-controlled, but with a high level of French investment. See R.K.I. Quested, *The Russo-Chinese Bank*, Birmingham, 1977 (especially pp.3–31).
47. Cited in *Krasnyi Arkhiv*, 1932, No.52, p.45.
48. Witte, op. cit., p.55.
49. Cited in K.S. Weigh, *Russo-Chinese Diplomacy*, Shanghai, 1928, p.252. By this clause, China had thereby '…abandoned all rights of jurisdiction in her own territory, and, therefore, all people whether they be Chinese or Russian or foreign residents within the railway area, had to be under Russian laws'. (Ibid.)
50. From a telegram, dated 21 May 1899, sent by the Russian representative at the talks between Russia and Britain. *Krasnyi Arkhiv*, 1932, vol. 25, p.128.
51. See Tang, op. cit., pp.50–1.
52. Witte, op. cit., p.180.
53. Ibid.
54. Ibid. The Witte account of Kuropatkin's enthusiasm to seize the whole of Manchuria is, of course, highly coloured by his eagerness to depict himself as being the one with a deep sense of political wisdom. An important forthcoming book by David Schimmelpenninck van der Oye, provides a fascinating depiction the misgivings that Kuropatkin felt about taking more of Manchuria. As a quote from a memorandum dated 14 March 1900 indicates, the general feared that

such a step would not only jeopardise friendly relations with China, but also the spill-over effect of having '...Manchuria's huge population within [Russian] borders...' would be too great a threat to Russia. See *Toward the Rising Sun: Russian Ideologies of Empire on the Path to War with Japan*, DeKalb, Il., 2001, ch. 5. (I would like to thank Professor Schimmelpenninck van der Oye for very kindly allowing me access to his manuscript ahead of publication). However, as developments in Manchuria in the post-Russo-Japanese War, the retention of the northern part of Manchuria as a sphere of Russian influence was a deeply flawed proposition, as the economic catchment area that Russia had as a result of the formal division was insufficient to sustain either a profitable railway operation, or a viable sphere of activity for Russian commerce. The idea of maintaining economic control of only part of Manchuria (and, by implication, of course, only part of the 'huge [Chinese] population' within the Russian sphere) was therefore a flawed one, regardless of Kuropatkin's strategic thinking and fears.

55. Mo Shen, *Japan in Manchuria (An Analytical Study of Treaties)*, Manila, 1960, p.87.
56. Witte, op. cit., p.180. (Northern Manchuria refers to Russia's resultant sphere of influence, that is the provinces of Heilungkiang and Kirin – see Map 1.)
57. Ibid.
58. Ibid.
59. T.E. Polner, *Obshchezemskaia Organizatsiia na Dal'nem Vostoke, Tom II*, Moscow, 1908, p.86.
60. Ibid., p.90.
61. *The China Weekly Review* (formerly *Millard's Review*), Shanghai, 23 October 1920.
62. Ibid.
63. Ibid. (Refers to local Harbin dollars.)
64. Weigh, op. cit., p.218. The extent to which this localised power was to be felt is perhaps best demonstrated by the fact that when the Revolution of February 1917 occurred on the streets of Petrograd, news of its outbreak was suppressed by the railway authorities until it finally leaked out a month after the event. Even then it required the formation of a Republican Executive Committee by the authority of the First Provisional Government to reduce the power of the then Manager of the CER, General Khorvat. (Ibid.)
65. *Vestnik Azii*, Harbin, No.3, 1910, pp.22–3.
66. In Shanghai, for example, the following taxes were collected by the local municipal administration: 1 per cent of the annual income derived from property; 1/20 per cent of the value of the property itself; customs duties not more than 1/10 per cent of the value of goods. In Harbin, by contrast, all customs duties were collected by the CER, thereby giving it another area of considerable fiscal influence. (*Vestnik Azii*, No.3, 1910, p.26.)
67. Ibid.
68. Ibid., p.43. Although there is no evidence to demonstrate it, one must wonder if the Chinese recognised that equality in an administration without real power was really very similar to being without a voice in the administration of the treaty ports in China proper.
69. Cited in Weigh, op. cit., p.251.
70. Amounting to approximately 300 000 acres.
71. For a vivid depiction of Harbin's pre-history and early development, see D. Wolff, *To the Harbin Station: The Liberal Alternative in Russian Manchuria*, Stanford, 1999, pp.14–48.
72. *Far Eastern Review*, May 1909, p.424.
73. Polner, op. cit., p.88.

74. Polner cites the combined percentage for non-railway employees as 35.5 per cent of the total working population. (Ibid.)
75. Ibid.
76. Ibid.
77. Ibid. (1 *verst* = 3500 ft, or approx. 1 kilometre)
78. Ibid.
79. Ibid., pp.87–8.
80. Ibid., p.90.
81. Ibid.
82. The transformation had been helped by two factors: (i) the CER's Construction Division having applied itself to the planning of the Pristan' area, dividing it into districts and providing the guidance for the construction roads and utilities; (ii) Harbin's municipal administration having finalised the zoning of areas under construction, thereby putting to an end the erection of improvised accommodation for business and residence alike. Heads of businesses also recognised the value of the river as an economic 'artery', and therefore moved their main offices to the district. (M. Tairov, 'Pristan' I novyi gorod', *Politekhnik*, No.6, 1974, pp.37–8.)
83. A. Vespa, *Secret Agent for Japan: A Handbook to Japanese Imperialism*, London, 1938, p.190 *passim*.
84. Polner, op. cit., p.88.
85. Ibid., p.89.
86. Ibid.
87. Weigh, op. cit., p.217.
88. Polner, op. cit., p.89.
89. *Vestnik Azii*, No.1, July 1909, p.102. The experience here, as elsewhere in Northern Manchuria, was one where local enterprise required a long period of subsidy and support in order to establish itself; support which was rarely forthcoming from either the railway or the Russian government itself (see Chapter 5 for a detailed discussion).
90. Ibid., p.103.
91. Exports of the native grains by this period had, according to CER statistics, reached about 100 000 *poods* (1 *pood* = 36 lb. or 16.33 kilograms). (Ibid., p.104.)
92. Ibid. See also Bix, op. cit., p.433. The latter explains that before the war, Japan had been in economic equilibrium with Russia in Northern Manchuria.
93. Ibid., p.420.
94. *Vpered*, 14 January 1905.
95. I. Spector, *The First Russian Revolution: Its Impact on Asia*, New Jersey, 1962, p.77. For a more detailed reading of the 1905 events in Manchuria, see R.K.I. Quested, *'Matey' Imperialists? The Tsarist Russians in Manchuria, 1895–1917*, Hong Kong, 1982, pp.139–54.
96. Spector, op. cit., p.78.
97. Soviet historian M. Betoshkin established that there were about 3500 Bolsheviks operating among Russian troops in Manchuria, with agitators dispatched from the party's centre for Siberian operations at Chita. (Ibid., p.78.) It is quite likely that Linevich was confusing the more vigorous political activities within his own ranks with the relatively benign response of the civilian population to the events in St Petersburg. After all, if Soviet sources, or Linevich's own impressionistic assessment, are correct regarding Bolshevik presence in Manchuria in 1905, it alone would have made up nearly a quarter of Harbin's Russian settlement! (It should be noted that such claims regarding the Bolsheviks' political activity amongst Russian troops was something of a standard approach in Soviet scholarship.)

98. *Vestnik Azii*, No.3, January 1910, p.7.
99. Ibid., p.5.
100. P.N. Patrikeeff, Interview, Sydney, September 1975.
101. A. Balawyder 'Russian Refugees from Constantinople and Harbin, Manchuria enter Canada (1923–26)', *Canadian Slavonic Papers*, vol. 14, 1972, p.25.
102. Lattimore, op. cit., p.247.
103. This is depicted in the two-volume memoirs of I.I. Serebrennikov (*Moi vospominaniia*, Vols I & II, Tientsin: 1937 & 1940), based on his life in Siberia, Manchuria and China in the period 1917–24. On a visit to Harbin in 1921, he notes with a certain amount of resignation that the city '...was, on the whole, the same: the same conversations, rumours, expectations'. (*Moi vospominaniia*, Tom II, p.114.)
104. Resettlement for many of those who entered Harbin consisted of life in immigrant barracks; a similar bleak environment to that endured by the Shantung workers entering the the city. (See G.W. Gorman, *Two Millions to Manchuria*, Shanghai, 1929[?], pp.33–5.)
105. Recognised in its foetal form by Rosemary Quested in her seminal work on Russians in Manchuria, *'Matey' Imperialists?*, op. cit., pp.155–9.
106. Quested cites a figure of 479.6 million roubles having been spent on schemes in Manchuria up to 1903. (Ibid., p.155). Nikolai N. Liubimov, in his *Ekonomicheskie problemy Dal'nego Vostoka (Vostochnaia Kitaiskaia zheleznaia doroga)*, Moscow, 1925, suggests that, inclusive of interest charges, over 400 million roubles were spent on the railway alone (p.7). By January 1907 this figure had risen to over 750 million roubles. (Ibid.). By the late 1920s the figure had reached 1044 million roubles (representing nearly 40 per cent of the foreign investment in railways in China as a whole). (M. Fritsendorf, *Severnaia Man'chzhuriia: ocherki ekonomicheskoi geografii*, Khabarovsk, 1929 p.157.)
107. Mark Mancall, 'The Kiakhta Trade', in C.D. Cowan (ed.), *The Economic Development of China and Japan*, London, 1964, p.23. Mancall reminds us that the Treaty of Nerchinsk (1689), the first signed by China with a non-Asian power, may be regarded as being favourable to the Chinese because it forced the Russians to leave the Amur river basin area. Similarly, the Kiakhta Treaty, and the style of trade that it institutionalised (which Mancall contrasts with the Canton – or Treaty Port – system), may be seen as the Chinese response to increased pressure from Russian traders in the border region, with the object to limit severely rather than to encourage trade with Russia. In this document too China was technically at an advantage as nothing was said of Chinese traders entering Siberia. (See 'Sino-Russian Trade', *The Chinese Economic Monthly*, vol. III, no. 6 (June 1926), pp.232–6.
108. Mancall, op. cit., p.48.
109. A tentative conclusion (and especially for the period up to 1905) offered in Quested, op. cit., pp.330–1.
110. This might be translated as slovenly or disorderly.
111. See, for instance: 'Sino-Russian Trade', *The Chinese Economic Monthly*, vol. III, no.6 (June 1926) pp.232–6; A.E. Gerasimov, *Kitaiskie nalogi v severnoi Man'chzhurii*, Harbin, 1923.
112. Mancall, op. cit., p.23.
113. Gerasimov, op. cit., p.102.
114. A.E. Gerasimov, 'Ocherki ekonomicheskogo sostoianiia rainov verkhovev r. Sungari', *Vestnik Man'chzhurii [VM]*, 1929, no. 10, p.55.

115. Ministerstvo Torgovli I Promyshlennosti. Otdel Torgovli, *Po voprosu o polozhenii Russkoi torgovli I promyshlenosti v Man'chzhurii*, Petrograd(?), 1914, pp.20–1.
116. *O polozhenii Russkoi torgovli I promyshlenosti v Man'chzhurii*. Zapiski Kharbinskogo Birzhevogo Komiteta, Harbin, 1913, pp. 8–9, 13.
117. Ministerstvo Torgovli, *Po voprosu*, op. cit. pp.1–3.
118. Cited in B.H. Sumner, 'Tsardom and Imperialism in the Far East and the Middle East, 1880–1914' (Raleigh Lecture on History), *Proceedings of the British Academy*, vol. XXVII (1940), p.14.
119. Ibid. pp.19–21.
120. Best summed up in the new Minister of the Interior Plehve's statement of 7 May 1903 to the special council: 'Russia has been made by bayonets not diplomacy... and we must decide the questions at issue with China and Japan with bayonets and not with diplomatic pens'. Cited in ibid., p.14.
121. Ministerstvo Torgovli, *Po voprosu*, op. cit., p.28.
122. Just how sharp the margins were can be seen from the examples of October 1912, when the CER tariff was 1.5 kopeks per pood higher than that of the SMR. Despite a good harvest, which should have increased traffic in soya beans by 3.4 million poods, the difference in tariff resulted in a reduction of 670 000 poods. Ibid., p.37.
123. Ibid., p.34.
124. *O Polozhenii*, op. cit., p.9. The document refers specifically to Witte and snipes at the changing attitude of the CER.
125. Ibid. p.8.
126. Sumner, op. cit., p.12.
127. See, for example, Byvshii Churinets, 'Torgovye I kommercheskiie predpriiatiia', *Kharbinskaia Starina* (1936 issue), reprinted in *Politekhnik*, No.10, 1979, pp.221–3, for a sketch of the scope of these activities.
128. See Chapters 5 and 6.
129. Ibid.
130. Gerasimov, *Kitaiskie Nalogi*, op. cit. pp.21–2.
131. Ibid. p.24.
132. Ibid. p.22.
133. Ibid. pp.19–20.
134. Ministers tvo Torgovli, *Po voprosu*, op. cit., p.52.
135. Marakueff, Aleksandr V., *Foreign Trade of China and its Place in World Trade*, Harbin, 1927, pp. 64, 66.
136. Ministers tvo Torgovli, *Po voprosu*, op. cit. p.43 (figure refers to Harbin).
137. *O Polozhenii*, op. cit. pp.14–15.
138. In 1913 the interest rate (including brokerage) was about 18 per cent. Fixed assets, on the other hand, had a return of 15 to 20 per cent gross. (Ibid. pp. 6–7.)
139. Gerasimov, *Kitaiskie nalogi*, op. cit. pp.19–20.
140. Baykov, Alexander M., *Soviet Foreign Trade*, Princeton, 1946, pp. 4–6.
141. Dairen's share of the import market had grown from 68 per cent (before WWI) to 92.5 per cent (in 1920). A.A. Neopihanoff 'The Development of North Manchuria', *Chinese Economic Journal*, Vol. II, no. 3 (March 1928), pp.264–5.
142. 'Flour Market in North Manchuria', *Chinese Economic Bulletin*, Vol. XI, No.33 (1927), pp.16–18. When demand made itself felt in Siberia, prices for wheat from the Heiho region would shoot from $0.70–1.00 to $2.00 per pood. This was to have a serious (and chronic) effect on Chinese flour mills in Heiho. Competition between the main mills was cutthroat, upping the purchase price

of grain and forcing down the price of flour when it went to market (frequently the wheat was purchased from farmers at $1.50–1.80 and sold as flour at little less than $2.00 per pood).
143. Russian flour milling, which was hardest hit by the closure, took the lead in this by constructing warehouses on the Chinese bank of the Amur to allow transport of flour to Russian soil as contraband (or as baked bread). (Ministerstvo Torgovli, *Po voprosu*, op. cit., p.40.)
144. Hongkong & Shanghai Banking Corporation Archives [HSBC] S/O Files, vol. 90, Minter to Wood, 22 November 1924.
145. HSBC closed its office finally on 30 September 1925. The territory was starved of financial services, reflected in a bank officer's comment in late 1924 that 'The officials at present are ready to do practically anything to get us to stay in Vladivostock [*sic*] and would no doubt like us to launch out in all directions. If we could be certain that we should not be subject to expulsion from the country at probably only a moment's notice we might take up some of the attractive line of business offering'. (Ibid.)
146. In January 1924 the manager of the Ussuri Railway informed the manager of HSBC, Harbin Branch, that he knew 'positively that any interference with the Bank in Vladivostok is made by the local authorities without sanction from headquarters'. (HSBC S/O, Vol. 90, Knox to Baker, 1 January 1924.)

# 2 The Soviet Union, Northern Manchuria and the Civil War

1. See, for example, Quested's account of 1917 and Harbin in her *'Matey' Imperialists*, op. cit., pp.309–24; F. Patrikeeff, 'Revolution in Northern China' in H. Shukman (ed.), *The Blackwell Encyclopedia of the Russian Revolution*, Oxford, 1994, pp.266–7. A recent work by J.J. Stephan, employing, *inter alia*, the work of J.A. White (*The Siberian Intervention*, Princeton, 1950), Quested (*'Matey' Imperialists*) and P.M. Nikiforov's (*Zapiski prem'era DVR*, Moscow, 1974) concludes simply that '...an attempt to seize control in Harbin wilted under the barrels of Chinese guns'. (*The Russian Far East: A History*, Stanford, 1994, p.114.)
2. Patrikeeff, op. cit., p.266.
3. The radicalism that was demonstrated by Harbin, especially in the decade or so before the 1917 revolutions, was considerable in the regional context, although, of course, the numbers involved were very small when viewed from the perspective of Russia as a whole. In 1907, for example, the Vladivostok RSDRP Committee, which fashioned itself into a Far Eastern 'centre', held a conference at Nikol'sk-Ussuriisk. The meeting was attended by 16 delegates, representing a membership of some 300 members. While the numbers here are very small, it is nonetheless interesting to note that one third of this membership was in Harbin (Stephan, op. cit., p.106). Demonstrations were a common sight on the main thoroughfares of Harbin throughout the revolutionary period. And, again, while small in size, they were marked by considerable enthusiasm and the waving of resplendent banners. F.A. Fuhrman, an engineer with the American interventionist forces in the Russian Far East, who was in Harbin for May Day 1918, recorded some of the scenes of vigorous demonstrations by a cross-section of local labour and political organisations in a collection of photographs. (F.A. Fuhrman Collection, Hoover Institution Archives [HIA], Envelope A.)

4. In the English language: J.F.N. Bradley, *Civil War in Russia, 1917–1920*, London, 1975; W.H. Chamberlin, *The Russian Revolution: 1917–1921*, New York, 1965; D. Footman, *Civil War in Russia*, London, 1961. In Russian there are: N.N. Azovtsev *et al.*, *Istoriia grazhdanskoi voiny*, Moscow, 1938–1960; L.M. Spirin, *Klassy I partii v grazhdanskoi voine v Rossii*, Moscow, 1968.
5. A more significant recent contribution has been by Evan Mawdsley, *The Russian Civil War*, London, 1987. Other work of note has been in the form of essays by A.P. Allison, 'Siberian Regionalism in Revolution and Civil War', *Siberica*, 1 (1): 78–97; J. Channon, 'Siberia in Revolution and Civil War' in A. Wood (ed. & introduction), *The History of Siberia: From Russian Conquest to Revolution*, London, 1991; J. Erickson, 'Military and Strategic Factors' in Wood (ed.), *Siberia: Problems and Prospects for Regional Development*, London, 1987; N.G.O. Pereira, 'White Power during the Civil War in Siberia (1918–1920): Dilemmas of Kolchak's "War Anti-Communism"', *Canadian Slavonic Papers*, 29 (1): 45–62; Pereira, 'Regional Consciousness in Siberia Before and After October 1917', *Canadian Slavonic Papers*, 30 (1): 113–33; F. Patrikeeff, 'Revolution in Siberia' in H. Shukman (ed.), *The Blackwell Encyclopedia of the Russian Revolution*, op. cit., pp.259–63; Stephan, op. cit., pp.117–55; J. Forsyth, *A History of the Peoples of Siberia: Russia's North Asian Colony, 1581–1990*, Cambridge, 1992, pp.229–39. Russian language sources include: N.N. Azovtsev, *Grazhdanskaia voina v SSSR*, Moscow, 1980–86; P.A. Golub, *Revoliutsiia zashchishchaetsia: Opyt zashchity revoliutsionnykh zavoevanii Velikogo Oktiabria, 1917–1920*, Moscow, 1982; Iu. I. Korablev *et al.* (eds), *Zashchita Velikogo Oktiabria*, Moscow, 1982.
6. A. Wood, 'From Conquest to Revolution: The Historical Dimension', in Wood (ed.), *Siberia: Problems and Prospects*, op. cit., p.53.
7. Channon, op. cit., pp.159–60. Indeed, the primary engine of imperial outstretch into Manchuria (discussed in Chapter 1) appears to have been the same enthusiasm for 'new free lands, gold and furs'. (I.A. Iakushev 'Amur ili reka chernogo drakona' GARF, Fond 5869, No.1, Khr. 32, p.2.)
8. Channon, op. cit., p.160.
9. Channon observes that if Siberia were to have gone its own way, internal customs barriers could be dispensed with, thereby providing Siberia with added economic advantage. Separation from Russia would also encourage the growth of regional self-consciousness. Ibid., p.161.
10. Ibid., p.163. This figure should, however, be qualified by their much better result in the Far East total, which was 25 per cent of the total vote. (Stephan, op. cit., p.114.) Within the latter, the Bolsheviks were, predictably, especially successful in the conurbations (49 per cent of the vote in Vladivostok, 40 per cent in Nikol'sk-Usuriisk and 19 per cent in Blagoveshchensk and Nikolaevsk.). Interestingly, the Bolsheviks were also able to garner 46 per cent of the vote in Harbin too. (Ibid.)
11. Channon, op. cit., p.161.
12. Ibid. Stephan confirms such an analysis, citing Lenin's view of the poor showing of the Bolsheviks in the elections to the Constituent Assembly being the result of the *sytost'* ('satiety') of the Siberian peasantry. (Stephan, op. cit., p.114.)
13. J. Smele in his introduction to D. Collins and J. Smele (eds), *Kolchak I Sibir* (New York: 1988) estimates that there were at least 19 separate governments in Siberia when the Bolsheviks lost their power there. (p.ix.)
14. Mawdsley, op. cit., p.313. The same point may be made about much of the Western material on the Civil War in Siberia too.

15. A.S. Whiting, in his *Siberian Development and East Asia: Threat or Promise?* (Stanford, 1981, p.14), suggests that we should see 'East Asian Siberia' (comprising of Irkutsk, Buriatia, Yakutia, Chita and Amur, Magadan, Kamchatka, Sakhalin areas, together with the Khabarovsk and Maritime *kraia*) as a separate and distinct region, linked historically with the triangular relationship between China, Japan and Korea. Such a perspective is further developed by Stephan in his work on the Russian Far East as a cohesive, and coherent, political and economic entity. (op. cit., pp.53–61, 81–106.)
16. Channon, op. cit., pp.163–75.
17. Von Ungern-Sternberg was captured, tried and executed soon after the final defeat of his forces. In the case of Semenov, this year marked only his last military engagement on Russian soil. He, like so many of the other 'fringe' actors on the White side in the Siberian/Russian Far Eastern theatre, found sanctuary in bordering territories (see note 24 below).
18. Channon, op. cit., p.176. Mawdsley in his work also tends to depict power relations with a broad sweep: '…from the Volga to the Pacific', op. cit. p.104.
19. For a short biography, see Patrikeeff in Shukman, op. cit., p.326.
20. See, for example, Mawdsley's account of Semenov, op. cit., pp.233–4; David Footman 'Ataman Semenov', St Antony's Papers on Soviet Affairs, Oxford, 1955.
21. Such an image is reinforced by Soviet and post-Soviet historiography on the subject. A 1993 biographical dictionary of political personalities in the Russia of 1917 provides a full entry only for Dutov, while of the others only Khorvat and Semenov are mentioned, and even then only in passing. (A.S. Velidov *et al.* [eds] *Politicheskie deiateli Rossii 1917: bibliograficheskii slovar'*, Moscow, 1993.) A 1995 biographical dictionary of government officials of pre-revolutionary Russia makes no mention of General Khorvat at all, and this despite the fact that he occupied the senior position in administering what was a most expensive Russian venture in the Far East, the CER. (Lin'kov *et al.*, op. cit.)
22. W. Klemm, in his foreword to Khorvat's memoirs, encapsulates this initial image of the man and his ambitions splendidly by recalling a description of the General as '[a] king of fairytales'. (HIA, D.L. Khorvat Collection, Box 1, Folder 1.) A similar comic edge was provided for his 'kingdom', which a visiting Grand Duke described as 'Happy Khorvatia'. ('Konchina Gen. D.L. Khorvata' *Luch Azii* 1938, Nos 33–5, p.21.)
23. A.A. Purin to I.A. Iakushev, 20.11.29, *Vol'naia Sibir files*, GARF, Fond 5869 Op.1 Khr.90.
24. After he, quite literally, fell into the hands of the Red Army on 21 August 1921 (see Footnote 30, below), von Ungern-Sternberg was questioned at length by Soviet authorities. In the course of this interrogation, he stated how little he feared the Red Army infantry divisions that had been sent out to defeat him: 'I was tied to nothing, and with my entire mass of cavalry could do battle in any direction and at any time', he said. It always seemed curious to him, he added, that the Red Army strategists had consistently employed the strategy of encircling and defeating him with divisions of infantry, when the latter were so ill-equipped to function on the difficult Inner Asian terrain. ('Dopros voennoplennogo nachal'nika Aziatskoi konnoi divizii generala barona Ungerna', in L. Iuzefovich, *Samoderzhets pustyni: fenomen sud'by barona R.F. Ungern-Shternberga*, Moscow, 1993, pp.235–6.)
25. Channon, op. cit., p.176. The hardening of territorial boundaries was made all the more appropriate by the discovery by Soviet authorities that von Ungern-Sternberg's ideas of a Eurasian Empire included the probability of his forces

moving into Tibet; a plan that was flagged by von Ungern-Sternberg at the end of his interrogation. (Iuzefovich, op. cit., n.13, p.239.)
26. Draft article for *Vol'naia Sibir*, nd, GARF, Fond 6869, Op. 1 Khr. 22.
27. Ibid. The Japanese Command displayed considerable loyalty to Semenov. In the summer of 1920, the FER authorities conducted talks with Japanese forces regarding the supply of essential provisions to the latter. The FER government agreed to Japanese demands, but in return called for the breaking of relations between Japanese troops and Semenov. The Japanese refused this, with the result being a stalemate between the two sides.
28. These included: the Omsk-Cheliabinsk partisan division under General Belov; General Bakich's division in the Lake Zaisan area; Ataman Kaigorodov's force in Mongolia; Ataman Kazantsev's division at Uriankhai; nominal control over von Ungern-Sternberg's and Kazagrandi's forces in Mongolia; Peraulov's division to the north of Verkhneudinsk; General Matsievskii's forces in the Hailar area; *Polkovnik* Glavkov's Separate Manchurian Division as well as some cavalry and volunteer divisions farther to the West. (A. Markov, *Encyclopedia of the White Movement*, Vol. I, n.p., n.d., HIA, A. Markov Collection, Box 1, p.615.)
29. Ataman Semenov's own forces numbered 7000–8000, while those of von Ungern-Sternberg were in the order of 2000 men (the latter's last clash involved only about 1000). By comparison, Japanese interventionist forces alone numbered 73 000. (I am grateful to Stephen Cooper for having alerted me to this point through discussion.)
30. Annenkov, for example, finally retreated into Sinkiang, and from there found his way into central China, where, in 1925, he became involved in the Chinese Civil War. It was only in 1926 that the Soviet authorities were able to finally have him returned to Soviet territory. He was tried and executed in 1927 (for an account of Annenkov's activities during the Civil War, see B. Gurevich's notes in *Problemy Dal'nego Vostoka*, No. 63, 1990, pp.72–8). Semenov managed to evade Soviet hands until 1946 – after the defeat of the Japan – when Soviet authorities sent a special parachute group to seize him. (Markov, op. cit., p.614a.) In the case of von Ungern-Sternberg, his end came quite by chance, when, on the way to an evening visit to some machine-gun emplacements, he was captured by Mongols, who then took him mistakenly into Red Army-controlled territory – as von Ungern-Sternberg himself observed and warned his captors of – and into the hands of astounded Soviet soldiers. (Iuzefovich, p.234.; see also footnote 24 above for the problems that the Red Army faced in defeating the Baron.)
31. His rock-solid faith in these led von Ungern-Sternberg, for instance, to write them into his Order No.15, issued at Urga in May 1921 (Iuzefovich, op. cit., p.235; for the text of the Order, see ibid. pp.230–3.)
32. For Annenkov's methods, see Chapter 4. Von Ungern-Sternberg, during his questioning by Soviet authorities, responded to the issue of his cruelty to members of his own force by saying that he was 'cruel only to bad officers and men', adding that, 'I am a supporter of the discipline of the rod, as were Frederick the Great and Nicholas I'. (Iuzefovich, op. cit., p.236.)
33. In the epilogue to his study of von Ungern-Sternberg, Iuzefovich mentions how he 'with his very own eyes saw, even held in his hands, a tea cup from which [von Ungern-Sternberg] *perhaps* drank'. (The cup was part of a set owned by a woman whom the Baron had known from Reval [Tallin] and had visited on numerous occasions in Harbin). Ibid., p.221 (my emphasis).
34. Mawdsley, op. cit., p.233.

35. Semenov and von Ungern-Sternberg both had agents working for them at various locations in China, both protecting and furthering their principals' interests and gathering intelligence from a wide range of sources. Von Ungern-Sternberg, in spite of his isolated fiefdom, was, moreover, able to maintain close contact with Harbin and Peking via his own long-range radio station ('A Letter of Baron Ungern to His Agents in Peking', Urga, 20 May 1920, in *Letters Captured from Baron Ungern in Mongolia [Reprinted from Pekin and Tientsin Times]* Washington, 1921, p.8, HIA, R.F. Ungern-Shternberg Collection, Folder XX534-10. V.)
36. In 1921 Semenov was only 31 years old, while von Ungern-Sternberg was just four years older. Annenkov completed his military training in 1908, and therefore was about the same age. The oldest of the group was Khorvat, who was born in 1858.
37. Semenov received steady material support from Japan. Von Ungern-Sternberg was able to feed his troops with meat from his own herd of cattle (requisitioned from *Tsentrosoiuz*), while his personal finances included 150 000 roubles in gold. (Iuzefovich, op. cit., p.238.)
38. The menace of this echoed in Annenkov's final defiant words before his execution in 1927: 'You [referring to his Bolshevik accusers] will yet meet in battle with my partisans'. (Markov, op. cit., p.18.)
39. Some of these concerns informed the Soviet responses to the activities of the various White leaders who based themselves in Manchuria, Mongolia and China proper, and the attention the latter paid to turning the allegiance of the Eastern Siberian and the Russian Far Eastern peasantry to the White cause (see, for example, Serebrennikov's account of his meetings with General Pepeliaev in Harbin in 1921, in the course of which he learned of the sustained Soviet efforts to convince the General to switch sides [I.I. Serebrennikov, *Moi vospominaniia*, Tom II, Tientsin: 1940, pp.32–4]).
40. For a detailed account of these permutations, see John Erickson, 'Military and Strategic Factors' in Wood (ed.), *Siberia: Problems and Prospects*, op. cit., pp.173–6).
41. Ibid., p.176.
42. For a discussion and exploration of the significance of these raids, see Chapters 3 and 6.
43. This is apparent in a number of respects. In a radio message from L. Karakhan, the Soviet Ambassador to China, to Moscow (intercepted in Paris in the mid-1920s), he outlined 'the impudence of the Whites' being explained by the current situation in China and '...their proximity to new adventurism against the Soviet Union'. Continuing this line of thought, Karakhan warned of Ataman Semenov and Generals Glebov and Diterichs having '...a series of talks' with local authorities, adding that Semenov was 'a close friend of Chang Tso-lin's'. 'I recommend', Karakhan concluded, 'immediate representations [to Chinese authorities] and the resolution of the question of the liquidation of White camps in Manchuria, Korea and Shanghai'. ('Radio-donesenie Karakhana', *Vecherniaia Zaria*, n.d. [1926?] in HIA, L.V. Golitsyna Collection, Box 2, Packet 8.) The continuity of this preoccupation is evident in the fact that among the demands placed before Chinese authorities in the wake of the 1929 Sino-Soviet conflict (see Chapter 6) was 'the disarming of White Guard detachments and the deportation from Manchuria of their organizers' (cited in H.L. Kingman, *Effects of Chinese Nationalism upon Manchurian Railway Developments, 1925–1931*, Berkeley, 1932, p.85.)
44. Following the October Revolution, the ownership of the Chinese Eastern Railway was a matter for protracted negotiation between Chinese and Russian

governments. In 1924 a formula was reached between the two governments, whereby the CER was placed under joint-control and management.
45. Erickson, op. cit., p.176. Bliukher first saw action in the region in 1918. In 1921 he was sent to the Far East to act as the Commander-in-Chief of the National Revolutionary Army and the War Minister of the Far Eastern Republic.
46. The Sino-Soviet conflict resulted in a rash of analyses in the international press, most of these depicting the Soviet Union's decisive victory as being a signal of the emergence of a strong, perhaps even monolithic, Soviet state. Despite the fact that sympathies of many of the imperialist states lay with the Soviet Union during the dispute and early part of the conflict (*The Weekly Review*, in an article entitled 'Who is Responsible for the Break?' [25.1.30], for example, noted of the Sino-Soviet dispute/conflict that it was in the foreign powers' interests to take the Russian position regarding China's seizure of the CER and to wish that Soviet Russia would 'teach China a lesson'. The article further argued that many of these states hoped that if full war were declared, this might lead to the complete defeat of China and political changes in Russia itself, placing the latter among the ranks of imperialist powers once again), these quickly turned to suspicion of Soviet motives and attitudes (an interesting account of the American disenchantment with the Soviet Union's conduct can be found in *Statia KVzhd [O Kitaiskoi Vostochnoi zheleznoi doroge]*, an article by *Oblastnik*, citing an excerpt from a report from the [*South China*] *Morning Post*'s correspondent in Washington. n.d., GARF, Fond 5869, No. 1, Khr. No. 9).
47. One can see quite clearly this sense of frustration in the confluence of the following: on 11 April 1918, Bolshevik Commissar Chicherin sent a note to Chinese authorities, demanding that dealings with Tsarist consular representatives in the Far East should cease. Three days later, General Khorvat, Kudashev (the former Russian Ambassador to China), the financier Putilov and representatives of the Entente meet to discuss the question of armed struggle with the Bolsheviks. On the same day, Semenov captures the town of *Borzaia*. GARF, Fond 5869 No.1 Khr.22.
48. The commander of American interventionist forces, General William S. Graves, sums up well the political web that the Soviet Government found itself in its relations with the White forces, Japan and China during the Civil War, when he describes the nature of Atamans Kalmykov and Semenov: 'He [Kalmykov] was the worst scoundrel I ever saw or ever heard of and seriously doubt, if one should go entirely through the Standard Dictionary, looking for words descriptive of crime, if a crime could be found that Kalmikoff [sic] had not committed. He was armed and financed by Japan, in their efforts "to help the Russian people." I say this advisedly, because I have evidence that would satisfy any open-minded person. Kalmikoff murdered with his own hands, where Semeonoff [sic] ordered others to kill, and therein lies the difference between Kalmikoff and Semeonoff. To use a Russian expression, Kalmikoff was "liquidated" [killed] by the Chinese when he was driven out of Siberia and tried to take refuge in China. Semeonoff was later driven out of Siberia and took refuge in Japan where he still lives'. W.S. Graves, *America's Siberian Adventure, 1918–1920*, New York, 1941, pp.90–1. It should be noted that while Kalmykov was unlucky in his attempt to gain sanctuary in China, other White leaders (many, such as Annenkov, equally reviled) were successful.
49. See N.M. Pegov, *Dalekoe-blizkoe: vospominaniia*, Moscow, 1982, pp.110–13. Such suspicions were no doubt fuelled by accounts of Japanese involvement in plans

148  *Notes*

to destabilise the Soviet state. A Russian living in Harbin remembers coming across a Japanese study on a plan to assassinate Stalin. On the initiative of either Japanese Army Intelligence or the South Manchurian Railway Research Bureau (or both), he recalled of the piece, a party of ten *émigrés* was sent by ship from Manchuria to Turkey, from where the assassins crossed the border to Stalin's summer residence on the Black Sea coast. The plan had been hatched from the information gathered from the interrogation of a senior Soviet official who had defected and crossed the border into Manchuria, where he was promptly arrested and questioned. The failure of this fantastic scheme was due to a double agent being in the midst of the group, with Stalin having left the resort by the time they arrived. The failed assassins were arrested. One of the members of the SMR/Army Intelligence group responsible for the plot became a member of the Upper House of the Japanese Diet (V.G. Savchik, Interview, Sydney, 14 February 1981). D.M. Volkogonov, in his *Trotsky: politicheskii portret*, Moscow, 1992, suggests that the senior official concerned was Genrikh Samoilovich Liushkov, the head of the NKVD for the Far Eastern region, who, in June 1938, slipped across the border when he learned of his probable arrest for 'not having dealt with Bliukher'. (Volkogonov, pp.196–7; see Chapter 3 for details of Bliukher) The Japanese work referred to is almost certainly *Plans to Assassinate Stalin* by E. Hiyama.

50. Erickson, op. cit. p.177.
51. See Chapter 3.
52. See Chapter 3.
53. See Chapters 3 and 6.
54. By 1930, this unease reached the level of bewilderment and something approaching panic. The *Japan Advertiser* of 10 April 1930 published an article entitled *The Proletarian Movement*, discussing the labour movement within its own borders and its relationship with Marxism/socialism. The article reasoned that if the proletarian party opposed, or acted against, the 'lazy wealthy', then this line would secure 'enormous support from the Japanese, because the latter do not lean towards the idea of existence without work'. The article continued to say that 'The Japanese do not concur with the extravagance of the capitalist West, nor with the decadent Chinese; rich men who pride themselves on their long nails'. The advice of the Japanese press 'as a whole' to proletarian parties was to take the example of the British Labour Party, which 'does not struggle for class conflict and rejects Marxism'. The *Japan Advertiser* concluded with the earthy suggestion that these parties should 'get their heads down (to their work)'. If they upheld 'the principle of labour', it continued, '[they would] undoubtedly find support in society'. (Taken from GARF, Fond 5878, No.2, Khr. No.173.)

# 3  Liberation and Exile

1. For a discussion of this term, see Chapter 7, note 32.
2. Weigh, op. cit., p.259.
3. P.P. Balakshin, *Final v Kitaii*, Munich, 1958, vol. 1, p.108.
4. Ibid. Among other actions taken by Prince Kudashev, the Russian Ambassador, was the signing of an agreement that permitted China to defer payments of the Boxer Indemnity for a period of five years; an action that was to add to the CER's financial woes. (See Chapters 5 and 6 for further discussion of the CER's financial situation in this period.)

5. This anomaly was politically something of an open wound for the Soviet Union, and particularly so when, in 1924, it had formally taken over Russia's place in the administration of the CER and gained control of Tsarist property.
6. Cited in D.J. Dallin, *The Rise of Russia in Asia*, New Haven, 1949, p.155.
7. J. Stalin, *Marxism and the National and Colonial Question*, London, 1936, p.19.
8. V.V. Vishniakova-Akimova, *Dva goda v vosstavshem Kitae, 1925–27: vospominaniia*, Moscow, 1965 (see below, p.90)
9. A similar view is expressed by Earl Swisher of the Chinese situation specifically: '[t]he most striking thing about Chinese or more particularly about Cantonese politics is the utter impossibility for a foreigner to see how they can ever be in the state they are'. (K.W. Rea (ed.), *Canton in Revolution: The Collected Papers of Earl Swisher, 1925–1928*, Boulder, 1977, pp.5–6.)
10. Balawyder, op. cit., p.24.
11. Ironically, similar disdain was held by many well-to-do Harbin Russians for the foreigners resident in their city, the latter being regarded as nothing more than 'traders...and therefore to be held off snobbishly'. (Margaret Freeman, Interview, Boston, 23 May 1979.)
12. I.I. Serebrennikov, who served briefly as the Supply Minister with the Provisional Government of Autonomous Siberia, found his way to Harbin in March 1920. Having deposited all their worldly goods with the Left Luggage Office at Harbin Station, he and his wife set out to look for accommodation in a city that neither had known or visited before. Between them, the Serebrennikovs had 10 000 Siberian roubles and 500 *Romanovskie Kreditki*; the equivalent of just 40 yen. At the time, they observed, the rent for a room in central Harbin was 150–200 yen per month, while in areas farther away from the centre it dropped to 75–80 Yen. (*Moi Vospominaniia*, Tom II, Tientsin, 1940, pp.19–20.) Because of his skills and former status, Serebrennikov managed to very quickly find both housing and work. (Ibid., pp.21–25.) Most refugees, of course, were not as lucky, although their arrival would have been similar to that of the Serebrennikovs. As one resident of Harbin put it, with the constant unemployment experienced in the city, and the willingness of the Chinese to work for very low wages, many refugees found themselves either without work or competing for jobs which paid three Harbin dollars per month or less (Savchik, Interview, February 1981. The respondent's own sister was in such a position in the early 1920s, working as a sales assistant in a Harbin shop.)
13. One former White soldier with Ataman Annenkov's forces was described as having built up his initial wherewithal from winning his fellow soldiers' and officers' rifles and revolvers in running poker schools. He would then sell this 'booty' on the open market in Mongolia and China. (Patrikeeff, Interview, June 1986.)
14. Of those formally registered with Harbin refugee agencies, numbering 16 000 in all (see below), 9989 (or well over two-thirds of those capable of working) were from a land-owning/rural worker background, 2234 were skilled workers (blacksmiths, carpenters, railway workers etc.), nearly 300 were engineers and 64 were physicians and veterinary surgeons. The remaining 1118 came from a variety of other professions and trades (including topography, banking, teaching, telegraphy, etc.). Details taken from Memorandum, 31 January 1924, from V. Golitzin (the Commissioner of the Russian Red Cross at Harbin) and Robert P. MacGrath (Executive Secretary of the Russian Refugee Relief Society of America Inc., New York City) to W.J. Egan, the Deputy Minister of Immigration and Colonization, Ottawa, Canada. HIA, L.V. Golitsyna Collection, Box 2, Folder 2.

15. Canadian officials were exceedingly cautious in their dealings with the Russian refugees in Manchuria. Of a total of 1500 individuals (i.e. 400 families) who were registered with the Russian Red Cross at Harbin (a total of 16 000 were on their books at the time), and had enough money for the passage and $US200 per family for resettlement expenses, Canada was willing to accept only 750, and even then only those with savings amounting to $400 per family and bonds from the Russian Relief Society of America, Inc. '...to take care of any of the Russians whom we might permit to enter from Manchuria, should they become public charges...'. (Letter, dated 7 February 1924, from W.J. Egan, the Deputy Minister of Immigration and Colonization, Ottawa to Prince V. Golitzin [the Commissioner of the Russian Red Cross at Harbin] Canada. HIA, L.V. Golitsyna Collection, Box 2, Folder 2.) A telegram (undated, but a copy received on 31 January 1924) sent by the Canadian Immigration and Colonization Office to refugee officials at Geneva contains a suggestion why Canada should have taken such a strict line: the country could not admit additional refugees at that time, the telegram advises, because '...many of these [were] already here unemployed owing [to their] refusal to accept work available'. (Immigration, Ottawa to Fridtjof Nansen, Geneva [n.d.], HIA, L.V. Golitsyna Collection, Box 2, Folder 2.)
16. Memorandum, 31 January 1924, from Golitzin and MacGrath to Egan, op. cit. (See also above, note 14, for detailed breakdown of those who registered with refugee organisations in Harbin.)
17. Patrikeeff, Interview, September 1975.
18. The majority of these were in the Hsingan range and along the Upper Amur, with a few villages being established near the Ussuri frontier too. (Lattimore, op. cit. p.248.)
19. Such taxes included both formal and informal categories. Taxes were levied on the peasants' land that was under cultivation, livestock, timber (both for construction purposes and fuel), and sheering of their own sheep. In addition, there were local military taxes (for 1927 this amounted to 15–30 local dollars per member of the household for in the *Trekhrech'e* area, for example) and levies on land being used for construction purposes. In the category of 'unofficial' levies imposed on Russian peasants were items such as the supply of the peasants' sheep, firewood and hay to the local police, as well as services provided to police officers and their families (including repairs to the latter's housing and the transportation of police goods; all carried out free-of-charge). Petition from Head of *Trekhrech'e* Refugees to the Head of League of Nations Commission of Enquiry, 16 May 1932, pp.4–5, HIA, Pastuhov Collection, Box no.52.
20. Patrikeeff, Interview, September 1975. (The dairy activities there were held in such high regard, in fact, that by 1924 the Russian firm of Vorontsov Brothers, whose main business interests were in Hailar, had founded a butter-manufacturing industry there. The firm obtained milk locally through a barter trade, with manufactured goods being sent from Hailar. [Ibid.])
21. The *Starovery* were, in fact, amongst the last Russians to leave China after the 1949 revolution. Most of their number emigrated to agrarian areas in the United States, Canada and Australia.
22. Although the village is typical of those described, it escaped the Soviet military onslaught because of its remoteness, being at least a full two days of travel away from the railway line and then a further day or two by train before reaching any major station. The journey included the crossing of *Ozero*, as there was no land link with it due to the hilly terrain surrounding the shores of the lake. (A. Malakhoff, Interview, Oxford, 18–19 September 1981.)

23. Ibid. The respondent's family was one of the smallest, with only four children (three brothers and herself, with a number of siblings stillborn). A proportion of the families there had as many ten children.
24. Ibid. (This 'dilution' was a way for the Communist Chinese authorities to reclaim sovereignty over an otherwise purely Russian settlement.)
25. Malakhoff, Interview, Oxford, 18–19 September 1981
26. *Vestnik Azii*, No.2, October 1909, p.55.
27. Patrikeeff, Interview, September 1975.
28. Manchuria was known as the 'country of forests', although the industry itself was based in two main areas, roughly along the Eastern and Western Lines of the CER. (B.K. 'Lesnaia promyshlennost', 1900–1932 gg'. in *Politekhnik*, Sydney, No.10, 1979, p.258.) The Skidelskys and the CER Land Department's own concessions were located in the Eastern region, while those Kovalskys and Shevchenko (later to become a Japanese-Chinese conglomerete) were in the Western region. The Vorontsovs had concessions in both regions, with their Chol'sk Concession being the richest of all. The Vorontsov family continued to occupy a most important position in the industry because larch (a genus that was 'unrivalled' in making railway sleepers, piles, telegraph poles and mine supports) was to be found almost wholly in the Western region. (Ibid., p.259.) See also V.I. Surin, *Lesnoe delo v Man'chzhurii*, Harbin, 1930.
29. During the spring thaw, when rivers could once again be used for the transport of timber, it was not uncommon for employees to work in excess of 14–15 hours a day. (Patrikeeff, Interview, September 1975.)
30. Ibid.
31. *Rubezh*, Harbin, March 1936, p.17. The publication estimated that there were over 3000 professional hunters along the northwestern line of the CER. (Their presence, it should be noted, meant too that, at least in the eyes of Soviet government, there were at least 3000 well-armed, well-trained *émigrés* within striking distance of the Soviet–Manchurian borders. This detail, it would appear, had not escaped the attention of the Soviet military when it launched its action in Manchuria in 1929 and began to round up what *émigré* officials regarded as simple peasants, but Soviet authorities argued were White Guards [See Chapter 6].)
32. Memorandum from Golitzin and MacGrath to Egan, op. cit.; see also Balawyder, op. cit., p.25.
33. Ibid.
34. Balawyder, op. cit., p.25.
35. Ibid.
36. Ibid.
37. The UK Consul-General at Manila, in correspondence with the Australian government in 1924, reported that only 'several hundreds' of the Russians from China were admitted to the United States and that the 'quota was now full'. (AA ACT A458/1, C156/3; Immigration – Russians, UK Consul-General Manila to Aus. G.-G., 3 October 1924.) The Australian government was similarly cautious at this time. Among the conditions for entry of Russians were their being demonstrably '… anti-Bolshevist in [their] sympathies'. (AA ACT A458/1, C156/3; Home and Territories Department, 8 December 1924.)
38. Vespa estimated that it was under 10 per cent of the original influx. (Vespa, op. cit., p.9.)
39. Observed by Vishniakova-Akimova, op. cit., p.113.
40. See Vishniakova-Akimova's representation of this (ibid., pp.113–14).

41. The Harbin journal *Rubezh* (No.12, 1936, p.9.) described these recruits in the following way: 'The Russian Division displayed itself in an exemplary light, and, with through tireless efforts of the officers and their zealous execution of duties, there is now in Shanghai a Russian regiment which constitutes an integral part of the Shanghai Volunteer Corps'. See also V.D. Zhiganov's work on the Corps (*Russkie v Shankhae*, Shanghai, 1936, pp.223–34). Such laudatory accounts are balanced by Shanghai's police records, which showed that '... a large percentage of reported crimes involve [Russians]'. (W.C. Johnstone, *The Shanghai Problem*, Stanford, 1937, p.109.)
42. Vishniakova-Akimova writes of a refugee named Poroshin, who arrived in Canton and there secured a position with the Intelligence Division of the Soviet South China Mission, in whose employ he remained until its forced closure in 1927, after which he accompanied members of the Mission to Moscow. However, his stay in Moscow was brief (living conditions there, Vishniakova-Akimova writes, were too difficult for him), as was a spell in the Russian Far East, where Poroshin sought work. He eventually returned to Harbin. (Op. cit., pp.212–13.)
43. Vishniakova-Akimova, op. cit., p.114. Marshal Chang controlled Shantung Province in the 1920s. The warlord employed over 2000 *émigrés* in his army. (Chang Fu-yun, Interview, San Francisco, July 1979.)
44. See Balakshin, for example, in his description of 'partisan strike units' operating across the border in the Maritime, Zabaikal and Zaamur Provinces; activities tolerated by the Chinese authorities. (Op. cit., pp.116–17.)
45. The raid on the Canton Consulate occurred seventeen days earlier and marked Chang Kai-shek's about-turn on his communist 'allies'. Two years later, a similar raid on Soviet consular premises took place at Harbin (See Chapter 6.)
46. C. Martin Wilbur & J. Lien-ying How (eds), *Documents on Communism, Nationalism, and Soviet Advisers in China, 1918–27*, New York, 1972, pp.16–17.
47. Ibid., pp.18–19.
48. The Ankuochün was the Army of National Pacification, the Gendarmes of the 3rd and 4th Regiments of which, along with uniformed and plain-clothes detectives from the Peking Metropolitan Police Headquarters, played a major rôle in the raid at Peking. (Ibid., p.473.)
49. Cited in Wilbur & How, op. cit., p.473.
50. In one of the captured documents, Jen Te-chiang, the chief of the Soviet advisory group attached to Marshal Feng Yü-hsiang, wrote to the Soviet Minister of War, Frunze, saying that he had '... started efforts to bring about conflict between Fang Yu-hsiang and Chang [Tso-lin] of Mukden. A victory for Chang would mean a victory for the conservatives and imperialists [Japan in particular], and would be dangerous for the Soviet Union'. (Ibid., p.336.)
51. Vishniakova-Akimova, op. cit., p.97. She notes with barely concealed horror the summary execution of the editors of the newspaper *Ch'en Pao* for 'sympathy' for the Soviet Union.
52. By accepting this ruling, the Communists were thereby forbidden from occupying more than a third of the places in the Kuomintang.
53. O.M. Green, *The Story of China's Revolution*, London: n.d. [probably 1938], p.105.
54. For a full, and still unmatched, account of this period, see H. Isaacs, *The Tragedy of the Chinese Revolution*, 2nd rev. edn, Stanford, 1961.
55. The Nanchang slaughter was prompted by the Communist leader Ho Lung '... rai[sing] the flag of revolt ...' in that city against the Kuomintang on 1 August,

while in Canton a last-ditch attempt [led by the Soviet consul in the Southern capital] at the '...communiz[ation] of the South...' resulted in the short-lived capture of the city on 11 December. Three days later there followed '... an appalling massacre of Communists' in that city as right-wing Kuomintang Generals Chang Fa-kuei and Chen Kung-po re-captured the city. (Green, op. cit., p.107.)

56. Executive Committee of the Communist International, Seventh Plenary Session, Moscow, November 1926.
57. Trotsky maintained to the very end that the CCP should have remained purely a workers' party, with a clear-cut programme of revolutionary socialism and strenuously opposing any merger with capitalist, bourgeois, or even obscure populist movements. (Shortly after the Canton rising, and barely a few weeks before his own deportation, Trotsky entered into correspondence with Preobrazhensky and Radek regarding the 'lessons' of the Chinese debacle. In his letters he stressed that the Chinese events had shown anew that '...any contemporary revolution which did not find its consummation in a socialist upheaval was bound to suffer defeat even as a bourgeois revolution'. I. Deutscher, *Prophet Unarmed: Trotsky, 1921–1929*, London, 1959, pp.423–24.)
58. His imposing physical stature was complemented by a presence that was larger than life. In an interview with the *North China Daily News* in January 1927, Borodin was asked to sum up the situation in China. 'The dykes have been cut and the water has begun to rush through' he responded to the journalist; '...uttered', the latter wrote, 'with a sweeping movement of his expressive hands...'. ('China in Chaos', *North China Daily News*, April 1927.)
59. Vishniakova-Akimova, op. cit., pp.371–2.
60. For a representation of such a line of argument, see C. Brandt, *Stalin's Failure in China, 1924–1927*, Cambridge, Mass.: 1958, pp.102–18, *passim*.
61. Vishniakova-Akimova, who had contact with all three, writes reverentially of the trio. Of Bliukher, she says: 'He carried himself wonderfully. He held his head high, which gave him a slightly haughty look. His hair was dark blonde and thick'. (Op. cit., p.252.) Her description of Borodin was that of an '...old Bolshevik-member of the underground. Everyone invariably approached him with respect. He gazed upon those he spoke to quietly, attentively, with interest, faintly smiling from under a thick moustache that resembled those worn by Russian workers in prerevolutionary times'. (Ibid., p.175.) Similarly, the way she viewed Karakhan was of busy, popular man who refused to be bound by his status as Soviet Ambassador and could as readily be heard presenting lectures at Peking University as conducting his diplomatic activities. 'He wore', she writes, 'a moustache, beard, was not very tall and of a fragile build. His look was fiery, direct, very firm'. (Ibid., pp.48–9.)
62. Jacobs in his work describes how he was regarded as '...mastermind of the Chinese Revolution...'. (D.N. Jacobs, *Borodin: Stalin's Man in China*, Cambridge Mass.: 1981, p.291.)
63. Karakhan had come to Peking to continue Sino-Soviet negotiations of 1922/23 which Adolf Ioffe had failed to bring to a successful completion. He became Ambassador upon the conclusion of the Sino-Soviet Treaty; a status recognised by China on 31 May 1924.
64. See, for example, the depiction of Borodin and Bliukher in the work of Sir John Pratt (a former British Consul-General to China, and in the years 1925–38 Adviser to the British government on Far Eastern Affairs). In his *War and Politics*

*in China* (London, 1943), Pratt concludes that '[t]he political and military reorganization effected by these two men enabled the Nationalist Party – the Kuomintang – rapidly to extend its control over the whole of China'. (p.196.)
65. 'On the Restoration of Soviet Influence in Northern Manchuria', *China Weekly Review*, Shanghai, No.6 (11 January 1930). From Russian translation, GARF, Fond 5878, No.2, Khr.173.
66. Ibid.
67. Ibid.
68. A.S. Whiting, *Soviet Policies in China, 1917–1924*, Stanford, 1968, p.248.
69. Red International of Trade Unions.
70. People's Commissariat of Foreign Affairs.
71. Whiting, op. cit., p.248.
72. Ibid. (My emphasis.)
73. Bruce A. Elleman, *Diplomacy and Deception: The Secret History of Sino-Soviet Relations, 1917–1927*, New York & London, 1997, p.136.
74. Ibid., pp.136–7.
75. But even then, given the strength of the rival loci of power that appeared (and established themselves) on the peripheries of China, one has to ask the question of how much in control were the central authorities in playing out this deception? (For a most useful, concise survey of the warlords, see David Bonavia's, *China's Warlords*, Hong Kong, 1995; for deeper analysis of the warlord period, and its characteristics, see Lucian W. Pye, *Warlord Politics: Conflict and Coalition in the Modernization of Republican China*, New York, 1971 and Ch'i Hsi-Sheng, *Warlord Politics in China, 1916–1928*, Stanford, 1976.)
76. A more differentiated perspective is suggested by some of the Chinese political personalities themselves. Eugene Chen – the Republican Foreign Minister and a friend of Borodin's – saw the situation as a precarious one for the Soviet presence, with only Borodin singled out for particular attention, and even then only for his brief, and fragile, role as a mediator between the various factions in the Chinese body politic. He achieved this, Chen observed in a qualified way, because '[i]n his years in China he has been able to get a glimpse into the mind of the Chinese – just a glimpse, because every province in China produces a different kind of man'. (P. Chen, *China Called Me: My Life Inside the Chinese Revolution* New York, 1979, p.117; for an image of Borodin that is quite at variance to that of the superhuman often portrayed, see pp.112–16) Just how tenuous a place Borodin and his fellow advisers occupied is revealed by the fact that the point at which Pratt and others (see above, note 63) would suggest was the zenith of their power and influence was also the time when warlords such as Feng Yü-hsiang and Chang Tso-lin were demonstrating that China was far from political unity. In an interview published on 1 May 1926 (itself a date of considerable irony, being the hallowed May Day), Chang observed that '...my sole object in this war [i.e. with the forces of Southern China and those of Feng] is to eradicate Bolshevism from China'. (In *The Hankow Herald*.)
77. Reported from a Moscow dispatch in *Osaka Mainichi*, 5 February, 1926. (Cited in *The Peking Leader*, 19 February 1926.)
78. K. Griunval'd, 'Pribuzhdenie Kitaia', n.d. (1925?) GARF, Fond 5878, Kh. No.84, p.22.
79. Ibid.
80. Ibid., p.23.
81. Green, op. cit., p.71.

82. Capt E. Pick 'China in the Grip of the Reds', *North-China Daily News and Herald Ltd*, Shanghai, August 1927 (HIA, Jay C. Huston Collection, Box 1, Packet 2, Folder 4), p.22. In its generality, Pick's account rings true in some respects, but, given the date of publication, probably was guided by the documents seized in the Peking and Canton raids themselves. Of particular interest, in terms of the distortions in this 'insider's' report, is the inclusion of Eugene Chen, who may have been quite close to Borodin (indeed, Chen's sons accompanied Borodin and his wife on their epic escape through Mongolia in 1927), but there is little indication of his having been a simple Moscow 'operative' (Indeed, his career after the departure of the Soviet advisers suggests a totally different picture, given that Chen remained with the KMT Government headed by Chiang Kai-shek until his split with the latter [in December 1931] over his 'passive' policy towards Japan after it had seized Manchuria [Interview with Mr Robert Haas, Lytton Commission, Shanghai 25 March 1932. HIA, V.D. Pastuhov Collection, Box 24]. See also the memoirs of Percy Chen, op. cit. *passim*.). Equally so is the notion that the consulates were intimately linked and instrumental in passing on information to their 'centre'. And, finally, the withholding of Moscow's commentary on Chinese political personalities seems to be a distortion of information gathered from the Canton consulate. (Green, op. cit., p.106, writes of '[m]any wounding comments *by Russians in Canton* on their Chinese friends were also revealed [in the raid], the Chinese generals in particular being described as entirely ignorant of the arts of war and in other respects wanting in ability'. [My emphasis])
83. Pick, op. cit., p.22.
84. Ibid. Ironically, Moscow is given such a pervasive and instrumental rôle by Pick that it can predict even its own downfall: '[The next day they received the]... depressing message advising us for the first time of the precariousness of our situation'. (Ibid.)
85. *The China Advertiser*, Tientsin, 21 September 1923 (as cited in the *Central China Post*). HIA, Huston Collection, Box 1, Packet 2, Folder 4.
86. The foreign press's depiction of the Bolshevik 'machine' in China reached a peak by the late 1920s, with the appearance of Bolshevik tentacles reported as far away as Singapore (*The South China Morning Post*, a China Coast newspaper at Hong Kong, in an article dated 7 March 1928, and entitled 'Red Singapore', reported that police there had made a 'big haul' of Communist documents [Jay C. Huston Collection, Hoover Institution Archives, Box 1, Packet 2, Folder 1]). A year earlier, Hankow was seized by a series of strikes. During one of these – a bank strike in late March – a notice was taken from *The Hankow Herald* and affixed to the door of one of the Hankow banks. Aside from the banks' actions, the notice righteously asked: 'Servants of the foreigners will be ordered to quit. Why is this being done? **ASK M. BORODIN!! He knows**. (University of Warwick, Modern Records Centre. Original emphasis.)
87. See, for example, Swisher, op. cit., p.6; Chen, op. cit., *passim*. Something of the claustrophobic, and treacherous, political climate in China is well portrayed in A. Malraux's *The Conquerors* (for Canton specifically) London: 1983 and *Man's Estate* London: 1968. See also Chen, op. cit., p.107.
88. Vishniakova-Akimova, op. cit., p.167. Contemporary accounts of the treatment meted out to Soviet consular officials show some sympathy to the latter. Knight Biggerstaff, in his study on the raid on the Soviet Embassy in Peking in April 1927, sheds light on their plight in Peking and other locations throughout

China by suggesting that '[a]s the situation was actually worked out, the Chinese government opened itself to criticism for violations of International Law almost as flagrant as those which it showed the Soviet government to be guilty of'. ('The Diplomatic aspects of the Raid on the Soviet Embassy in Pekin by Chinese Police and Troops, April 6 1927', Harvard: January 1928, p.20. HIA, S.K. Hornbeck Collection, Box 101.)

89. Aside from the regular forms of tracking carried out by the intelligence services, foreign diplomatic representatives and the Chinese authorities themselves, curious hybrid organisations such as the Chinese Maritime Customs service (run by British officers, and in places with White Russian employees too, but working in more junior positions) also provided intelligence reports on movements of Soviet officials, and, indeed, political reports too. In the border town of Manchuli in Manchuria, the Customs' officer-in-charge was J. Gibbes, an Englishman who had been the tutor to the last Tsarevich and, after China, became a Russian Orthodox priest in Oxford. His logs for the period show a detailed record of movement *inter alia* of all Soviet officials crossing the border at Manchuli, where they had come from (including transit points such as Harbin) and where they were travelling on to. (J. Gibbes Papers, Oxford; G. Gibbes, Interview, Oxford, September/October 1980). Less conventional forms included the detective methods adopted by journalists seeking to establish the number of consular staff in given Soviet consulates. After rumours had appeared in Peking hotels and clubs to the effect that the Soviet embassy there housed personnel of '... more than a thousand Reds', Ariel L. Varges, the Far Eastern correspondent for *International News* of New York, suggested that this figure was much exaggerated, and that there were only 125 'reds' in the embassy. His figures were based on an interview with a baker from whom embassy staff ordered their daily bread (he learned that the 'Red bread supply' was constant at between 100–125 loaves per day. 'Inasmuch as the Russian is a heavy bread consumer', Varges argued, 'one may accept the bread supply being allotted to one Red per day'. This figure was cross-referenced with the testimony of a local cinema operator who projected films at the 'Red Mission', and who estimated that attendance was usually '... 120 persons excluding Chinese servants'! (*The Hankow Herald*, 26 March 1926, in HIA, Huston Collection, Box 3, Packet 3, Folder 3.)

90. *China Advertiser*, Tientsin, 21 September 1923. (HIA, Huston Collection, Box 1, Packet 2, Folder 4.)

91. The advisers' business often involved crossing borders into temporarily – and at times chronically – hostile areas of China, encountering border officials and local political peculiarities which could, from time to time (and unpredictably) delay their progress. Given the relatively small numbers of people involved, the process was exhausting too. Chinese authorities had imposed a limit of 10 staff members on each consulate when relations had been established between the two states in 1924. By 1926, Soviet negotiators at an informal Sino-Soviet Conference were pressing Chinese authorities to lift this restriction, ostensibly to allow the expansion of Soviet trade bureaux housed in the consulates – a detail which itself was objected to by Chinese officials. (*The Hankow Herald*, 9 February 1926 in HIA, Huston Collection, Box 3, Packet 3.)

92. *Central China Post*, 27 February 1926 (HIA, Huston Collection, Box 3, Packet 2)

93. Pick, op. cit., p.26.

94. Naum (Leonid) Eitingon later went on to become an accomplice of R. Zorge in Shanghai and was a mastermind of Trotsky's assassination in Mexico (for details see Volkogonov, *Trotsky*, op. cit., p.330).

95. Pick, op. cit., p.26.
96. 'China in Chaos', *North China Daily News*, January–April 1927.
97. 'Red Sympathizer Disgusted' (Shanghai, 31 December 1926), cited in *North China Daily News*, April 1927.
98. 'Borodin the Boss' (Mukden, 6 February 1927), cited in *North China Daily News*, April 1927.
99. Ibid.
100. 'Borodin and his Tools Preach Hate' (Hankow, 21 December 1926), cited in *North China Daily News*, April 1927.
101. Hassis's father was a teacher at a Jewish school. His education consisted of seven years in a school of commerce, and a further two years in the Soviet Military Academy after the Revolution. He joined the revolutionary movement in 1915 and in the following year entered the Tsarist army as a private. From 1917 to 1922 Hassis served as a Political Commissar in the Red Army in the Volga region and Turkestan. In 1924 he graduated from the Far Eastern Department of the Soviet Military Academy. (Taken from an autobiographical note contained in a report discussing his case at a Communist Party meeting in Shanghai, n.d. [HIA, Huston Collection, Box 1, Packet 1].)
102. HIA, Huston Collection, Box 1, Packet 1.
103. Green, op. cit., p.71.
104. Ibid.
105. A relationship not improved by Borodin's frankness in his views of Chiang's stature as a Chinese leader. '[Chiang] is too small', Borodin once remarked, 'to cope with his formidable problem and his entourage pursue their own personal aims'. (Reported in *South China Morning Post*, 7 March 1928.)
106. Understandably, this difference in approach earned Moscow's displeasure for Borodin; displeasure which became particularly noticeable some months before Borodin was dislodged by Chiang. The removal of Borodin and the other advisers confirmed, in Moscow's view, that he had '... made a mess of things'. (Green, op. cit., p.71.) Interestingly, while Borodin's approach made a great deal of sense in terms of Chinese culture and the specific conditions in the country he worked in, Moscow's insistence on a more forceful pace was in keeping with the fragile state of many of its operatives in China (such as the hapless Hassis discussed above).
107. I am grateful to Michael Yahuda for this perspective on a 'united front' (presented at the Huang Hsing Foundation Lecture in Asian Studies, St Antony's College, Oxford, 7 November 1995).
108. 'Borodin and his Tools Preach Hate' (Hankow, 21 December 1926) cited in *North China Daily News*, April 1927.
109. Ibid.
110. 'Comrade Borodin Talks: A Flamboyant Statement' (Hankow, 20 January 1927) cited in *North China Daily News*, April 1927.
111. Not for the first time, Japan played a very discreet hand in this; reminiscent, indeed, of its response – or lack of it – to the events preceding the Russo-Japanese War. Captain F. Brinkley, *The Times* correspondent in Japan, reported the following in the wake of the treaty of peace in September 1905: 'When a prominent journal of St. Petersburg enunciated the doctrine that extermination, as one exterminates noxious vermin, was the only appropriate manner of dealing with Russia's present foes, an outburst of indignation might have been expected in Japan. There was nothing of the kind. The atrocious doctrine elicited only passing reference'.

112. 'Comrade Borodin Talks ...', op. cit.
113. These men are often described as 'Communists' by *émigré* sources, but emerge from these as grey political actors rather than the rhetorically inclined senior Soviet operatives that we associate with China proper. (See, for example, A.W. Serapinin's description of A.N. Ivanov, who took over the management in September 1924, and A.I. Emshanov, who took over from him in April 1926, in 'Kak iuzhno-Man'chzhurskaia zheleznaia doroga rasplachivaetsia s kreditorami byvshei Kitaiskoi Vostochnoi zheleznoi dorogi' GARF, Fond 6845, No.1, Khr. no.226, p.3.) Moreover, there is some evidence of a strong dissonance between Soviet officials with the CER and Soviet diplomats (*Peking Leader* of 25 April 1926, in reporting Ivanov's resignation '... on the grounds of overwork ...,' suggested that his replacement by Emshanov '... indicates the termination of the powerful influence hitherto exerted by Comrades Karakhan and Grandt [the Soviet Consul at Harbin] in the affairs of the CER'. The article also describes differences between local Soviet officials and those at Canton and Peking.)
114. This is a difficult area to speak conclusively on, of course, given the highly charged emotions associated with it. However, one must observe two important factors contributing to such a conclusion: (a) the very poorly developed network of Chinese Communist Party activities in Manchuria. Despite the existence of some Japanese-generated material on this subject, this appeared in the wake of Japan's seizure of Manchuria in 1931, and may therefore to be regarded as more a defence of that action than a detached appraisal. (See, for example, 'Conversation with Col. Komatsubara, Chief of Harbin Special District, Harbin, 16 May 1932', and 'Activities of Communists in Heilungchiang Province', HIA, Pastuhov Collection, Box 24.) More balanced accounts, insofar as they exist, play down the role of the CCP there (see, for instance, M.Y.L. Luk, *The Origins of Chinese Bolshevism: An Ideology in the Making, 1920–1928*, Hong Kong, 1990, which suggests that there was virtually no activity at this time. The China Coast press, despite strenuous attempts to depict Communist subversion in the region, provide little evidence to support this. A typical example of the newspapers' efforts include a bizarre account in the *Hankow Herald* [1 May 1926] of the seizure of a Soviet steamer by a Mukden war vessel: the steamer, which came from Vladivostok, was supposedly carrying three million rounds of ammunition and 60 000 rifles and machine guns, although the authorities found nothing on board. The explanation given was that the ship had *returned* to Vladivostok before the interception as '... she had become frightening or something ...'); (b) the numerous accounts offered by the Chinese and *émigré* circles of Communist bands active in Northern Manchuria during the Sino-Soviet Conflict of 1929 are, equally, very thin, providing little – if any – evidence of a linkage of the Manchurian and Chinese political theatres (The Pastuhov Collection, HIA, Box 27, contains a file on Soviet 'agents' captured by Chinese authorities in the course of the Sino-Soviet Conflict in 1929. The photographs show a predominantly very young, motley group of people, none of whose names appear in contemporary accounts – such as Vishniakova-Akimova's, op. cit. – of Soviet activities in China proper.)
115. The raid, while it was carried out efficiently, was not a propaganda coup. *Kung Pao*, in an article entitled 'What was found during the raid' on 13 June 1929, stated with some gravity that 42 documents were listed. 'Among them', the article continued, 'there are documents pertaining to Feng [Yü-hsiang]'s work with the USSR, preparatory steps for terror etc'. The documents could be

divided into three parts: (i) various documents and correspondence (11 items in all), including 'a list of collaborators and agents who received money from the Consulate', with 'an annexed report of 78 pages'; (ii) 'Revolutionary books (147 pieces)'; (iii) Japanese diplomatic postage stamps '...intended to lend correspondence diplomatic immunity and a forged seal of the American consulate'. (HIA, Huston Collection, Box 3, Packet 2, Folder 2.) For a detailed, albeit highly coloured, discussion of the seized documents see *The Sino-Russian Crisis: The Actual Facts Brought to Light*, Nanking, 1929, Appendix 8.
116. See, for example, Serapinin, op. cit., p.3. According to a petition lodged by sacked CER employees with the Lytton Commission of Enquiry in 1932, they conducted a vigorous campaign to have their situation settled. The former employees (who the petition claimed were owed over 20 000 000 Gold Roubles) were, they said, treated 'not like creditors of the railway, but as pitiful beggars ...,' receiving only 100 roubles of their own savings every 3–4 months. (S.A. Poperek, 'To the Inquiry Committee of the League of Nations from the Delegation of discharged employees of the CER', 9 May 1932, HIA, Pastuhov Collection, Box 3.) The agitation served both as an irritant to the Chinese authorities, and cause for them to represent the Soviet management of the railway as being politically driven.
117. Jacobs, op. cit., p.287.
118. Ibid.
119. Whiting, op. cit., pp.246–7.
120. G. Gibbes, Interview, 12 September 1980.
121. As Gibbes observed, his gait suggested that he was *still* in chains, walking with a 'slow shuffle rather than a firm step'! (Ibid.)
122. At times these commercial activities brought with them curious – if not bizarre – developments. Gibbes recounts one such transaction, with 40 000 pelts that had been seized at the border by the Soviet Customs, having been put up for sale. A foreign buyer agreed to buy these, but would do so not in US Dollars (as the Soviet authorities wished), but in roubles. As a consequence, Geitsman had to use his friendship with Gibbes (a friendship which had developed since they first met, with the Consul having gently alluded to the fact that he had 'walked in irons' at the instigation of Gibbes's former employer) for the buyer to bring two Russian trunks full of roubles from Shanghai. 'To avoid difficulties, and to "lessen Customs formalities" [Gibbes] was asked to take charge of, and transport, the money'. He did so, using a special Chinese passport in order to bring the money. 'He [was] not questioned or bothered by Customs, nor [were] the trunks even opened!' (Gibbes, Interview, 12 September 1980.)
123. Report of 3 June 1927, by Assistant in charge of sub-port, J. Gibbes, Manchouli.
124. G. Gibbes reported that Geitsman, probably through his friendship with Gibbes's foster father, J. Gibbes (who was closely associated with Russian refugees), became involved in aiding the Russian refugee effort, especially in the *Trekhrech'e* area. Gibbes Senior suspected that these efforts, together with the 'drinking of his cocktails', contributed to his removal and eventual arrest. (Report of 5 July 1927, by Assistant in charge of sub-port, J. Gibbes, Manchouli.)
125. Report of 3 June 1927, by Assistant in charge of sub-port, J. Gibbes, Manchouli. Geitsman was arrested in Irkutsk, where he went a month after leaving Manchuli, charged principally with consorting with the 'whites'. He was transferred to Chita, where he eventually committed suicide. (Gibbes, Interview, 12 September 1980.)

160  *Notes*

126. Report of 3 June 1927, by Assistant in charge of sub-port, J. Gibbes, Manchouli.
127. Ibid.
128. Ibid.
129. Gibbes notes in a report from early 1925 that in Hailar, for example, the publication of the Karakhan Note resulted in '[The Soviet] traveller there ... ha[ving] become much more aggressive'. But this also led to Soviet diplomatic couriers having to '... be furnished with a guard of two persons to accompany them to [their] destination'. (Report of 4 July 1925, by Assistant in charge of sub-port, J. Gibbes, Hailar.)
130. When the Soviet Government assumed its place in the administration of the CER, one of its first actions was to declare that no stateless person (few other than Russian *émigrés* would have fallen into this category) could remain in the employ of the railway. The Mukden authorities countered this by issuing, without interviews or other formalities, approximately 3000 passports to individuals whose employment was to be terminated, leaving them in their positions as Chinese nationals. (Patrikeeff, Interview, September 1975) Such defence of *émigré* rights, however, tended to be episodic. (See, for instance, Chapter 7 for an account of Mukden's responses to claims from Russian business against the CER.)
131. Report, May 1925, by Assistant in charge of sub-port, J. Gibbes, Manchouli. Gibbes adds, with the air of the long-suffering, that: '[f]unerals, of which there have been two, are naturally less demonstrative out of consideration for the feelings of the principal actors, the chief differences being the substitution of a red star for a cross at the head of the procession and speeches for blessings. The inevitable band continues to play but, as formerly, some well known funeral march is selected and the "International", on this occasion at least, is laid to rest with the departed'. (Ibid.)
132. Lashevich, born in Odessa in 1884, was initiated into radical politics while still at school. In late 1901 he became a member of the Iskra tendency of the Russian Social-Democratic Labour Party. He later joined the Bolshevik faction. His career as a revolutionary brought frequent arrests and exile in Vologda province and Narym (in Western Siberia). During the First World War he was conscripted and twice wounded in combat. At the time of the February Revolution he was in Petrograd, where he worked with the Soviet of Workers' and Sailors' Deputies and later was appointed to the city's Revolutionary Military Council. (F. Patrikeeff, 'Lashevich, Mikhail Mikhailovich' in H. Shukman (ed.), *The Blackwell Encyclopedia of the Russian Revolution*, Oxford, 1994, p.339.)
133. Lashevich, a member of the Central Committee since 1923, was demoted to candidate member in 1925 and removed altogether in 1926 (for his participation at an opposition meeting held in a wood outside Moscow). [F. Patrikeeff, op. cit., p.339.] Curiously, he was expelled from the Communist Party by the 15th Congress of the VKP(b) in 1927 – while he was at the head of the CER – for his links with the Trotskyite Opposition, with membership being restored the following year (A.S. Velidov *et al.*, *Politicheskiiie deiateli Rossii 1917: bibliograficheskii slovar'*, Moscow, 1993, p.178.)
134. Mr 'Katai', Interview, Hong Kong, 8 January 1981.
135. Ibid.
136. Such an interpretation is argued at length, and quite persuasively so, by the *China Weekly Review*, Shanghai, 11 January 1930, No.6. (An abridged, translated version, from which the quote is taken, is to be found in GARF, Fond 5878, Khr. 173.)

## 4 Politics on the Ground

1. A mixed Sino-Soviet administration existed for the CER at the time. The resumption of Russian (i.e. Soviet) participation in the railway was based on an agreement that the administration be divided evenly between Chinese and Soviet interests. Thus, the President, for example, was to be Chinese, while his Vice-President was to be a Soviet citizen. The Board of Directors too was to be split evenly between the two sides. (S. Hsü, *China and Her Political Entity: A Study of China's Foreign Relations with Reference to Korea, Manchuria and Mongolia*, New York, 1926, pp.422–4.) Also written into the agreement was that the General Manager, whose institutional rôle was of key importance (as his subsequent, deeply unpopular, actions against the *émigré* Russians very clearly demonstrated), was to be a Russian. (For an analysis of the General Manager's importance, see Tsao Lien-en, *The CER: An Analytical Study*, Shanghai, 1930, p.20.)
2. This point can be seen reflected in the fact that the Soviet Union introduced an elaborate range of passports, ranging from a full Soviet passport to a single-exit document which many Russian refugees took up and used to leave China. The latter allowed no right of residence in the Soviet Union itself. Thus, the Soviet Union could work flexibly in buffering itself from suspect 'citizens' in Northern Manchuria. (M. Freeman, Interview, Boston, May 1979.)
3. Chang Tso-lin's swift offer of Chinese papers to all stateless Russian employees of the CER checked this attempt at an administrative *chistka* [purge]. (See Chapter 3 for details.) Ironically, it too was a legally proper measure used as a counter to the Soviet Union's own political machinations using CER statutes.
4. Patrikeeff, Interview, September 1975.
5. Ibid.
6. See, for example, A.W. Serapinin, 'Kak Iuzhno-Man'chzhurskaia zheleznaia doroga rasplachivaetsia s kreditorami byvsh. Kitaiskoi Vostochnoi zhel. dorogi', p.2, GARF, Fond 6845, No.1, Khr. No.226.
7. Ibid., p.2.
8. Ibid.
9. Ibid., p.3.
10. Ibid.
11. This short-sighted approach, regularly highlighted by the Harbin press between 1924 and the early 1930s, was to be particularly embarrassing to the Soviet side when, in June 1933, it came time to discuss the transfer of the CER to Manchukuo (but in reality Japanese) control. The amounts outstanding were so considerable by then that it required much political manoeuvring and, finally, bludgeoning to avoid dealing with this messy problem. (Refer to Chapter 7 for a detailed examination of this question.)
12. For details of the blossoming of Soviet commercial and trade activities in Northern Manchuria, refer to Chapter 5; for an example of implications of accommodating parts of the Soviet Consular Corps, see Chapter 3.
13. A.P. Zanozin, Interview, Sydney, 28 January 1981.
14. Ibid.
15. Ibid.
16. Ibid.
17. Ibid. The lot of Annenkov's men was made all the more difficult because of the 'very hostile response' they received from the residents of Vladivostok, who '... preferred to sell foodstuffs to Red partisans than to Annenkov'. Zanozin

remembered hearing that the reason most often given for such attitudes was: 'You want to give us the old regime.' 'I had no reply to this,' observed Zanozin, ' what reply could there be? They were correct.' (Zanozin, Interview, Sydney, 12 March 1981.)
18. One incident alone explained why there could be some serious contemplation of changing sides. Annenkov was a misogynist who would not allow a single woman into his force (either as an active combatant or family member). Many of the brigades under his command would, as a result of this, be accompanied by a 'tail' of families following the troops. An officer from one such brigade, which had crossed into China in the Spring of 1920 and had set up camp there, approached Annenkov for permission for his family (based some distance away from the soldiers) to pass through their camp on the way to the safety of the interior of China. Annenkov, surprisingly, agreed. However, while the small group of dependants passed through the camp, a number of drunken soldiers raped the women (including an eight-year-old girl). Zanozin recounted the rest of the episode with a lingering horror: 'They were not sufficiently drunk to leave it at that. Having realised what they had done, the soldiers and officers [possibly as many as 20 in all] slaughtered the group, including the officer who had made the request to pass through the camp. To dispose of the bodies, the carnage assumed the form of dismemberment, with the parts of the bodies scattered in the woods for the wild animals to consume. The animals, as it happened, did not devour the bodies. After a few days, Annenkov sent out search parties to look for the missing officer. One such party came across a finger, and then proceeded to all that remained of the bodies. The four officers who had not escaped into the hills from the site of the slaughter were arrested and condemned to death for the crime. The execution itself was very gory, the men being chopped to death with sabres. Some time later, two of those who had fled were found hiding in the surrounding hills. Quite likely because they were good soldiers, Annenkov allowed them to escape.' (Zanozin, Interview, 28 January 1981.)
19. Zanozin himself, late in life (after he had moved to Sydney, Australia), came to quietly embrace his forsaken homeland, wearing Soviet badges and moving his membership from the monarchist Russian Club in Strathfield to the rival pro-Soviet Club in Lidcombe. His change of 'allegiance', which he wore with the ease of someone who, after many years of feeling obliged to maintain a strong political line, had successfully reassembled his memories to match the dictates of his conscience, did not sit well with his fellow *émigré*, who distanced themselves accordingly.
20. Margerita Swan. (Interview, London, August 1981.)
21. This was a very important institution – effectively a university in its own right – in Northern Manchuria, educating the elite of Russian students in areas other than the technical/mechanical/scientific specialisms offered by the highly respected *Kharbinskii Politekhnicheskoi Institut* (the Harbin Polytechnical Institute). [Ibid.]
22. Ustrialov, according to one of his students, had discussed the notion of the state with reference to the Chinese writings on the subject. 'Much later a generally accepted definition emerged from Europe, containing three points in its frame of reference: national boundaries, group/collective identity and national military consolidation. This abstraction, however, has long been represented in the Chinese character for this idea: a rectangle containing the *rot* (mouth) and *pika* (spear). Such research formed part of the discourse at the *Iuridicheskii Fakul'tet*.' (Swan, Interview, August 1981.)

23. The separatism took the form of a government, at the centre of which was a 'business cabinet enjoying the confidence of various social and political groups of the population'. The cabinet's aims were: 'the abrogation of decrees issued by the Bolsheviks; the restoration of the courts of law and administrative institutions, as well as of municipalities and *zemstvos*; the equality of all citizens before the law and preservation of civil liberties; 'Manhood suffrage'; the restoration to their full measure of all treaties and political and financial obligations with allied and neutral powers; the regeneration of the army on principles of strict discipline and its non-interference in politics; the restoration of the right of property; the solution of the agrarian problem by the Constituent Assembly; the restoration of industry and communications, and the abolition of socialisation, nationalisation and anarcho-syndicalisation of commercial and industrial enterprises, [as well as] the satisfaction of the needs of workers; the promotion of public instruction; religious liberty; the recognition of Siberia's and other individual provinces' right to autonomy, provided the unity of Russia be maintained.' (D.L. Khorvat, *Memoirs* [draft], ch. XII, pp.3–4, HIA, D.L. Khorvat Collection, Box 1, File/m.s. 1). For examples of Ustrialov's work, see his 'Rossiia na Dal'nem Vostoke' *VM*, 1925, Nos 1–2; for his controversial standing in Harbin society, see 'Ustrialov – neprimirimyi klassovyi vrag: eshche o vystuplenii Zinov'eva protiv Ustrialova' (*Rupor*, No.1410) and other articles on the subject in HIA, Golitsyna Collection, Box 2, Packet 8.
24. The closeness that some Russians felt to Chinese life was not, of course, limited to those living in Harbin. Many of those who lived in cities such as Tientsin, Shanghai and Peking had in the course of their time there absorbed the Chinese language (I use 'absorbed' purposely, as it indicates not only learning by rote, but also the gathering of many of the associated cultural traits and nuances; aspects which could only be acquired through close interaction with the Chinese, but on the basis of perceived equality). Due in large part to the ironies of history, few nationals other than the Russians were at one with the Chinese language of home and street and developed an understanding of Chinese culture and history. Some too had been imbued with elements of socialist morality, and a sympathy for the Soviet Union. But few of those encountered from the other Russian 'colonies' in China bear the marks of a political education quite like that of Mrs Swan and her contemporaries. In large part, this is almost certainly for the simple reason that nowhere in China was there such a broad commingling of Soviet and *émigré* lives and ideas as there was in Harbin, and to some extent in the rest of Northern Manchuria too.
25. I.I. Serebrennikov, *Moi Vospominaniia Tom II*, Tientsin, 1940, p.57.
26. Ibid., p.58.
27. Ibid.
28. Ibid., pp.15–16.
29. Ibid., p.59.
30. Such 'diversions' in many cases acted in counterproductive ways, and especially so when refugees tried to secure exit visas to third-party countries, as the immigration authorities of the latter would have to sift through outright denunciations, black marks and indications of suspect political behaviour and/or affiliation. Given that in these years most of the recipient countries were unlikely to take large numbers of refugees in any case – having been flooded with applications (many from Russians) from other locations – such reports often provided *prima facie* reason to delay or simply reject the applications. As was noted in the last chapter, Harbin Russians, through the reputation of unruly

and dilettante behaviour that they rightly or wrongly developed, became a very difficult group to recommend as migrants to third-party countries. Indeed, so ingrained was the awareness of denunciation-as-political-weapon that this was at times used even when, many years later the Chinese Revolution of 1949 began to displace them, Russian refugees would be waiting in a transit point such as Hong Kong. Refugee organisations functioning there (such as the United Nations' International Refugee Organisation [IRO]) would have to deal with a steady stream of cases where the applicants had been black-balled on the basis of 'supplementary information' lodged in Hong Kong itself. It is impossible to quantify this, of course, but through the recollections of case-workers there, Harbinites tended to be those of the China Russians whose visas were delayed most in this way (United Nations Refugee Organisation, Hong Kong office, Interview with case workers, 15 December 1987).
31. Serebrennikov, *Moi Vospominaniia Tom II*, op. cit., p.127.
32. Ibid.
33. Ibid., pp.59–60.
34. Ibid., p.84.
35. When Serebrennikov moved to Peking, he and his wife stayed at the Russian Spiritual Mission (which he considered did more to help refugees than the Russian Embassy [*Moi Vospominaniia Tom II*, pp.77–8]), where he came into contact with N.A. Mitarevskii, who wanted to create an anti-Bolshevik Information Bureau in Peking. The link here nearly caused Serebrennikov some embarrassment as Mitarevskii had approached both Khorvat and a shadowy man named General Khreshchatitskii, who was Ataman Semenov's representative in Peking, in his fund-raising efforts. Shortly after Serebrennikov and Mitarevskii met, both the latter and Khreshchatitskii were arrested by Chinese authorities; the reason for the arrests and the charges that were likely to be brought against the two men remaining unknown. Serebrennikov guessed that the Chinese authorities acted because of von Ungern-Sternberg's capture of Urga in Mongolia and the resultant pressure applied on the authorities by the Soviet mission. (Ibid., pp.85–91.) Serebrennikov noticed too that *Journal de Pekin* had accused the Russian Spiritual Mission of sheltering Ungernites and harbouring both *émigrés* and guns (p.87); something that made him even more cautious than he had been already been with regard to being linked with *émigré* politics. For a history of the spiritual side of the mission's activities, see the series of articles by McGain 'The Russian Orthodox Mission in China (As Retold from Russian Sources)' in *Collectanea Commissionis Synodalis*.
36. The General was apparently offered the opportunity to stay on as a 'commissar' under the new order, but refused. Such an offer can possibly be explained by the Soviet Union wishing to thoroughly humiliate him. Alternatively, this may have been an attempt to politically neutralise Khorvat himself, as well as any following he had, by co-opting an individual whose very appearance might otherwise suggest that he was, and could be, nothing other than a member of the old political order. Certainly, given the seemingly serious way he had been treated in the course of a trip to the United States, the strategy of co-optation would have, at least on paper, appeared to be a logical one. (See Chapter 2)
37. Because of the Harbin Soviet Consulate's reticence (see Chapter 3), pro-Soviet Russians would have had to rely on the very same forms of press as the *émigrés* in forming their political lines, drawing them into even closer proximity and antagonism with the latter. Therefore, the lack of a more balanced middle political line became all the more noticeable by its absence.

38. Serebrennikov is too tactful in his memoirs to be quite so forthright in his descriptions of Harbin during the time he resided there, or on occasions subsequently visited the city. However, his views are nonetheless telling. He never fails to reflect on finding in the course of his visits to Harbin that it was 'still in the grips of rumour'. Moreover, the reason for his early disquiet in contemplating making his home there (which, briefly, he considered in 1920) was made up of a complex of reasons, but quite allegorically depicted in a description of his attempts to find a specific scholarly work on the railway and its activities in Manchuria; a study sponsored by the CER itself. The author of this work, he wrote, was from Harbin. The publisher too was from that city. And yet no library, or the CER, had a copy of it. Eventually, the book had to come, on loan from the author himself, who by that time was residing in Peking. The implications were clear: Harbin had little interest in its own history, or that of its locality. Short of saying it, Serebrennikov's views seem to suggest that as a social entity it was *nekul'turnaia* (uncultured); a most damning of criticisms in the Russian idiom. At the end of his memoirs, he puts his views forward most vividly by writing: 'On the whole, Manchuria did not appeal to me. It was bare, empty – neither trees nor shrubs. Seemingly neither city nor village, on the streets it was noisy, but somehow not comfortable. Everything was strange and foreign to us: in the stores were Russian traders, Russian language was spoken, but somehow none of it smelled of a Russian soul. ... It came to me suddenly that life in Harbin would be the same: commerce, speculation and not one friendly or familiar face – and for a moment I became very sad.' (Ibid., p.249.)

39. Irene Eder writes that whereas '[t]he Chinese did not distinguish between foreigner and Jew ... White Russians, especially in Harbin, incited anti-Semitic acts'. ('Passage through China', *The Jerusalem Post, International Edition*, Week ending 5 July 1986, p.16.) By the early 1920s, the Jewish community in Harbin was over 13,000 in number, most of these being Russian Jews (making the community, if one were to separate it from the Russian, one of the largest foreign presences, after the latter, in Manchuria). The size, and strength in the organization of the Jewish community, allowed it to actively resist the occasional violence that was fomented. (Ibid.) Interestingly, Eder concludes of their presence here, as well as in China as a whole, that '... except for some cherished memories, China left no imprint on Jewish life and the Jews left no mark on Chinese history'. (Ibid.)

40. Boris Bresler 'Harbin Jewish Community (1898–1958): Politics, Prosperity, Adversity', unpublished paper presented at the Symposium on Jewish Diasporas in China: Comparative and Historical Perspectives, John K. Fairbank Center for East Asian Research, Harvard University, 16–18 August 1992, p.10.)

41. Ibid. (While Bresler is persuasive here in his depiction of the political situation present in the city, Harbin's Komsomol organisation went under the name of *Otmol'tsy*.)

42. In early 1921 news spread around Manchuria of an uprising against Chang Tso-lin on the Eastern Line of the CER, and, characteristically, the rumour was that this might extend to all settlements and, finally, possibly the seizure of Harbin itself by rebel troops. At the same time, General Pepeliaev, an important figure in the Russian civil war, was 'exceedingly busy' in making his own plans to advance into the Iakutia Oblast. At the time, he was 'fully convinced' of the veracity of information coming from there concerning the anti-Bolshevik sentiments of the masses in that oblast'. The excitement was compounded by the fact that on 2–4 May 1921 Chang Tso-lin's foes actually advanced on Harbin, forcing the Marshal's men to retreat to as far as the Peking Gates on the periphery

of the city. 'Harbin by evening was [at that juncture]', reported Serebrennikov, 'enveloped in a terrible silence and emptiness: neither cars nor pedestrians were to be seen, only military patrols and the occasional light from a rickshaw.' (Serebrennikov, op. cit., pp.161–2.)
43. For a vivid depiction of 'White' Russians in Shanghai and their existence on the margins of that society, see J. Pal, *Shanghai Saga*, London, 1962, pp.84–96. For Russians' ability to work with Chinese bandits in Manchuria, see below.
44. As Joanna Waley-Cohen puts it in her *The Sextants of Beijing: Global Currents in Chinese History* (New York & London: 1999): '... a significant percentage of the [Kuomintang's] revenues and police support came from Shanghai vice in its various manifestations.' (p.230) The Chung Wo Tong (a Hong Kong triad society) was established in about 1890 to carry out political work for and on behalf of Sun Yat-sen and his Republican Party. (W.P. Morgan, *Triad Societies in Hong Kong*, Hong Kong, 1960, p.25.)
45. Before the Russians arrived in the region, the *Hunghutze* had already settled into a firm patterns of life and work there. These included villages populated exclusively by *Hunghutze* and working relations with special insurance companies which concluded agreements with the bandits, who, for a certain sum, guaranteed immunity for the insured traders and their caravans. After the Russian troops began to pursue them, the *Hunghutze* broadened their activities as they were forced into the remotest, unpopulated parts of the region. (Footnote prepared by E. Varneck for Khorvat, op. cit., ch. 11, p.2, 188. HIA, D.L. Khorvat Collection, Box 1, Folder 4.) For a study of the *Hunghutze* see M. Mancall & G. Jidikoff, 'The Hung Hu-tzu of Northeast China' in J. Chesneaux (ed.), *Popular Movements and Secret Societies in China, 1840–1950*, Stanford, 1972, pp.125–34.
46. For a survey of the banditry problem in Manchuria, see the Washington Japanese Embassy's *The Present Condition of China with Reference to Circumstances Affecting International Relations and Good Understanding between Nations upon which Peace Depends–Document A*, rev. ed, Washington, 1932, ch. XII. One study of Manchuria (also published in 1932) estimated that there were more than 150 bands 'known and located' in Manchuria. The largest of these was reported as commandeering 1500 Chinese and 300 Russians. (H. Akagi, *Understanding Manchuria: A Handbook of Facts*, 3rd ed, rev., New York, 1932, p.57.)
47. Zanozin, Interview, 28 January 1981.
48. Ibid.
49. Mr 'Katai', Interview, Hong Kong, 8 January 1981.
50. The following incident, recalled by the same commercial buyer, reveals the depths and nuances of this relationship: ' "Valentin" [an official in the Police Force at Harbin], another friend and I went fishing along the Sungari at his insistence. I warned him of the danger in moving beyond 3 *versts* outside of Harbin, but "Valentin" dismissed the warning without giving any explanation. We continued to move further up the river [beyond the 3 *verst* limit] and, sure enough, a bandit appeared on the shore, signalling for us to weigh anchor and move the boat to where he stood. We did as we were instructed. "Valentin" was smiling and in a state of calm, whilst my other companion and I were extremely tense, not having encountered bandits at first hand before. The bandits [the one on the shore had been joined by others by this time] instructed us to leave the boat where it was and to follow them. They gave two out of the three of us some very rough treatment, which we were tempted to return in kind. However, we quickly thought better of it. We arrived in a clearing, where a large number of *Hunghutze*

were camped. They asked us why we had entered this area, and whether it wasn't for the purposes of spying on them. After a few more questions, they left us in peace for some time. Then, suddenly, the entire camp rose to its feet, to show respect to [as I later found out] *Vasia Kariavyi* [Vasia the Pockmarked], the local *Hunghutze* chief [who reportedly possessed a number of machine guns and an assortment of other weapons besides]. He walked over to us and asked similar questions to those posed earlier. A few moments later, he smiled, patted "Valentin" on the shoulder and invited us to eat with them. A lavish spread was laid out, and the meal ended with cigars being offered to us! After a little more conversation, we were allowed to leave the camp, reclaim our boat and carry on up the river. After we were underway, "Valentin" explained to us the reason why he had seemed so calm when we were spotted, and why he knew no harm would come to us [indeed, I remembered how, as *Vasia* had entered the camp area, "Valentin" had barked – in Russian! – at one of the bandits who had treated him a little too roughly]. Some time years before, he explained, he had strayed past the 3 *verst* limit and had been captured by the bandits. He had been very badly beaten on that occasion and intensively interrogated. Finally, when the bandits were satisfied that he posed no danger to them, and that he might be usefully incorporated into a "partnership of understanding," they released him, providing a little slip of paper with nothing on it except *Vasia's* seal. This allowed safe passage for over 40 *verst's* outside of Harbin. Eventually, "Valentin" had been issued with an official ribbon to replace his slip of paper, and it was this ribbon [which he now showed us] that the bandits had seen when we sailed our boat to shore. (Zanozin, Interview, 28 January 1981. The respondent noted that the *Hunghutze* had, in fact, gone even further than giving the intrepid fishermen a meal and safe passage. They had provided freshly-caught fish too! In return, the police officer, as he revealed many months later, had been instructed by the bandit chief to leave a few sacks of grain on one of the piers in the *Modiagou* area for later collection. The consequences of not doing this, he explained, would have been very serious. He added that the 'pass' he had been given by *Vasia* had enabled him to travel through a large number of 'protectorates', all of which accepted this sign quite readily.)'
51. For discussion of this, see Chapter 7.
52. By 1932, the Japanese presence in Manchuria as a whole had grown to a little under 250 000. (Akagi, op. cit., p.63.)
53. Japan did this in two ways. First and foremost was the system of attaching Japanese military intelligence China experts as advisers to various Chinese warlords (a Lieutenant General Banzai Toshihachirō, for instance, served as military adviser to Yuan Shih-k'ai at Peking, sending on his intelligence to Tokyo under the code name of *Banzai Kikan*). The second, which began in 1926, was the assigning of a propaganda function to the *Tokumu Kikan* (translated as Army Special Service Organisation, Special Service Agency or Special Intelligence Agency) in both Harbin and Mukden. Thus, the gatherers of information were from then on to carry out the secret publication and distribution of pro-Japanese literature and posters, as well as exerting influence over Chinese- and Russian-language press in Manchuria. (R.J. Lustig, '*Tokumu Kikan*: Intelligence Service of the Japanese Army, 1900–1945' n.p., Washington and Souteast Regional Seminar on Japan, February 1979, pp.4–6.) The intelligence network of *Tokuma Kikan* had as early as 1919 extended throughout the spheres of Russian control/influence in the region, with centres at Harbin, Blagoveshchensk,

Manchuli, Khabarovsk, Nikolaevsk and Chita. (Ibid., p.5.) The Siberian *Tokuma Kikan* withdrew with the expeditionary force in 1922, with the Manchurian operations continuing as before. (Ibid., p.6.)
54. As a transportation hub, Harbin was of considerable importance in this process. In addition to the *Tokuma Kikan*, the patriotic *Kokuryūkai* Society (the Amur, or 'Black Dragon', society) was operating in the settlement from the late 1890s, as well as the 'research departments' of a variety of Japanese private companies and organizations. (Ibid., pp.3–4.)
55. See, for example, *Zaiman Hakkei Rojin no Kazakku*, *Nōgyō*, Tokyo, 1936(?) This is an exhaustive study of Cossack settlement in the depths of Northern Manchuria, providing detailed information on its social, economic and political make-up, including (on p.26) a pictorial analysis of the individual farms (displaying family, grazing, cultivated and forest areas on the property).
56. *Daikan'en no Kaibō*, Mukden: 1941(?), is a study of prostitution at some of the inns of the Futiatien area of Harbin. The painstaking survey there included the role of local magistrates in selling their services in transporting dead bodies away from these dens, a breakdown of the origins of the innkeepers, and even tables for 'marginal' people visiting these establishments (offspring of village idiots, coolies, petty merchants, policemen and criminals appearing in these). [pp.8–9.]
57. A refugee who worked in Harbin for much of his adult life referred to his surprise at seeing a Japanese barber who, having been greeted by him for more years than he could remember, was walking down a city street, dressed in a senior military intelligence officer's uniform after Japan had formally taken control of Northern Manchuria. (Mr 'Katai', Interview, January 1981.)
58. The *Hunghutze* problem is a case in point. The Japanese were never able to deal with the bandit groups, whose otherwise suspect morality was quite firm when it came to their anti-Japanese views. Even after the Japanese took full control of Northern Manchuria in late 1931, their intelligence network was not able to penetrate *Hunghutze* organizations, nor their military in a position to crush the bandit groups. Whereas some Russians, as we have seen, were able to venture beyond the notional 3 *verst* limits, Japanese – including their military – found it hard to move anywhere beyond the settlements and, in the region from Hailun to Sakhalian, beyond the property demarcations of the CER itself. (Mr 'Katai', Interview, January 1981.) Japanese suspicious regarding the connections between Russians and the *Hunghutze* would have been heightened by articles such as that appearing in the popular Harbin newspaper *Rupor* (The Megaphone), which described how a Russian priest, his wife and two children were aided by *Hunghutze* in fleeing from *Primor'e* to Harbin. A number of the bandits, the priest reported, 'acquitted themselves well in Russian' in escorting them to the township of *Sanchagou*, from where they made their way to a railway station. Furthermore, the family, had been provided with directions to Harbin and a reassurance of safety beyond the Soviet border after having crossed into China. (No. 98, n.d. [1930?], in GARF, Fond 5878, No.2, Khr. 173.) Ironically, one of the reasons why Japanese authorities distrusted the Old Believer settlements – especially those of the Mudanzian-Pogranichnaia area, where between 1937 and 1938 Japanese authorities demanded the surrender of all firearms – was precisely because the latter were seen as '...being able to handle the *Hunghutze*.' (Mr 'Katai', Interview, January 1981.)

59. The fears generated through Chang Tso-lin with Chiang Kai-shek finding common political ground is evidenced by an interview with General Araki (the Japanese Minister of War), conducted by a member of the Lytton Commission of Enquiry in 1932: '...if you look into the record of General Chiang Kai-shek himself,' Araki observed, 'you will find that for all the support and material help he has received from the Japanese, he has evinced no trace of good will toward Japan. Once he courted Russian favour, and conducted with Russian aid his successful northern expedition, only to find himself later obliged to abandon Kwantung, Kiangsu, and other southern provinces to the Reds'. (From 'Conversation with General Araki, Minister of War, at his Official Residence, Tokyo, 5 March 1932, at 10 a.m.' HIA, Pastuhov Collection, Box 29, Folder 3, pp.9–10.)
60. Interestingly, such an attitude was reinforced by other powers, notably the United States. In the wake of the Russo-Japanese War, President Roosevelt urged Japan, as the only Asian exponent of '...principles and methods of Western civilization...,' to follow America's lead by proclaiming an Asian 'Monroe Doctrine'. The advice was accompanied by Roosevelt's willingness to provide support for Japan's reconstruction of the South Manchurian Railway in the effort to ensure Japanese economic control of the area (Kaneko, 'A Japanese Monroe Doctrine', *Contemporary Japan*, vol. 1, Pt 2, pp.176, 182. I am grateful to Katrina Savvides for the unearthing of this point) – see also T. Dennett, *Roosevelt and the Russo-Japanese War*, Washington, 1924, pp.129–30. This evolving notion of Manchuria's separateness was further reflected in Japan's consistently heavy investment in the region. A memorandum produced by Japan shortly after the founding of the State of Manchukuo in February 1932, and setting out a reasoned defence of Japan's own position, argued that at the time of the Russo-Japanese War it had '...considered Manchuria as a land to which she could send her emigrants...' but that this had been a failure (*Memorandum on the Plans for the Solution of the Manchurian Problem*, n.p., n.d. [1932?], Columbia University Library, p.2). Notions of full-scale colonization had then, the memorandum suggests, been replaced by massive investment (1.4 billion yen of Japan's total foreign investment of 2 billion yen was devoted to its interests in Manchuria. (Ibid.).
61. Volgin, '*Drama Kitaia*', *Pis'mo iz Kharbina*, handwritten *ms.*, to the Editors of newspaper *Dni*, n.d. (1928), GARF, Fond 5, Khr.53, p.1.
62. Ibid., pp.12–13.
63. Ibid., p.13.
64. Ibid.
65. Ibid., pp.13–14. (Volgin's analysis is a remarkably prescient account of Japan's decision to intervene even more forcefully in Manchuria's affairs in 1931.)
66. The closeness of the relationship was to be fully revealed at the time that the Young Marshal was summarily removed from his position by his Japanese backers. A message from General S. Honjo (Commander of the Kwantung Army, and an adviser to the later Marshal Chang Tso-lin) was brought to Change Hsüeh-liang by the latter's 'old follower' (and adviser) Lieutenant Colonel Nagatsu. In respectfully, but nonetheless brutally, phrased prose, Hondo wrote that Nagatsu '...as his [Honjo's] representative [wishes] to convey heartily to you his convictions in the last farewell as follows.... At present it must be admitted that the returning to Mukden of your Excellency, with party is not welcomed either by the Japanese in Manchuria or the Chinese people who have a personal grudge

against you because they have been oppressed, or by other foreigners. Furthermore, your presence has no important bearing on the peace of Manchuria, nor is it advantageous to the people of the Northeastern provinces. In consideration of his friendly relations with you for years I cannot help transmitting these words to you with pains'. (HIA, Pastuhov Collection, Box 24, Folder 4.)

## 5  An Economy on the Brink

1. Li Ao, *Hu Shi yanjiu*, p.226. (Cited in M.Y.L. Luk, *The Origins of Chinese Bolshevism: An Ideology in the Making, 1920–1928*, Hong Kong, 1990, p.197.)
2. In the 1860s and 1870s, Peking finally renounced all measures of control of Chinese colonisation; renunciation that resulted in a 'huge wave' of settlers. (E.E. Iashnov 'Sel'sko-khoziaistvennoe razvitie Severnoi Man'chzhurii', *VM*, 1925, Nos 1–2, p.18.) Much of this movement of people was controlled by the northern provincial authorities and the warlords.
3. For a full description of this process and the territories' character before the advent of the CER, see Iashnov, op. cit., p.18.
4. Ibid., p.19.
5. Figures for 1887 and 1914 are from E.E. Iashnov 'Sel'sko-khoziaistvennoe razvitie Severnoi Man'chzhurii', *VM*, 1925, Nos 1–2, p.19; that for 1930 is from the South Manchuria Railway's *Third Report on Progress in Manchuria*, Mukden, 1932, p.13.
6. Ibid.
7. Ibid., p.18.
8. Ibid. The evidence of settlements such as *Ozero* (see Chapter 3) would certainly support such an analysis.
9. Ibid., p.19.
10. A detail that perhaps explains why Russians and the Barguts, for example, for many years were in fierce competition in the wool industry (J. Gibbes in his report for July 1926 reports that the Russians engaged in the wool trade were 'in trouble again', conducting 'fierce competition' with local interests [J. Gibbes, Report, Manchouli, 6 August 1926]).
11. P.F. Konstantinov 'Zemledelie v Severnoi Man'chzhurii', *VM*, 1925, Nos 8–10 (cited in V.G. Shishkanov, 'Puti Razvitiia sel'skogo khoziaistva Severnoi Man'chzhurii', *VM*, 1929, No.3, p.32.). A. Gluvchinskii in his work on Manchurian agriculture takes this image further, describing how the methods employed by Chinese farmers involved shallow ploughing 'employing primitive methods,' with seeds scattered into furrows and then covered using a roller of 35–40 kilograms. Fertilisers, he continues, were rarely used on newly ploughed soils, and when they were (usually if the ploughing process was exceedingly lengthy), these would be in the form of diluted manure or mown grass. (A. Gluvchinskii, 'Sel'sko khoziaistvo Man'chzhurii', *Politekhnik*, No.10, 1979, p.212.) A.D. Voeikov in the diary he kept during a trip through the agricultural regions of Kirin Province in late 1929 wondered how well-suited some of the Chinese settlers were to the local conditions. In the Ninguta *uezd* of the province, he came across settlers who were cultivating vegetables and varieties of grain that were not suited to the soil there, 'but which they continue to cultivate through force of habit'. (A.D. Voeikov, 'Iz poezdki po Ningutinskomu uezdu', *VM*, 1930, No.2, p.58.) An experimental farm run by the Agricultural

Guild there received support, in the form of grains, vegetables and fruit 'tested' for its suitability to local conditions, from the CER experimental farm at Ekho. (ibid.) According to the Research Department of the SMR, only 54 per cent of the 1927 influx of Chinese into Northern Manchuria were equipped to work in the agrarian sector, and even then predominantly as labourers. (I.V. Pavlov, 'Pereselenie v Severnuiu Man'chzhuriiu', *VM*, 1928, No.7, p.47.)

12. A major result of this was the evolution of a most fragile, and inexplicably fluctuating, import market. This characteristic extended to most parts of the Chinese settler community. With the Sino-Soviet Conflict in 1929, for example, the sole agent for German sewing machines – whose business was largely with the Chinese sector of the market – saw sales drop from 200 machines per month to 3–4. (V.F. Shchepin, 'Severnaia Man'chzhuriia kak importnyi tsentr', *VM*, 1930, No.1, p.64.)

13. The fear held by the Chinese authorities regarding the 'underlying intentions' of any commercial project initiated by Russians resulted in many institutional hurdles being placed in the path of a rapid development of such an enterprise. Prime examples in this respect, and with regard to capital starvation too, were the attempts at diversification by larger entrepreneurial families such as the Skidelskys, Vorontsovs and Kovalskys (for the Skidelsky case, see Chapter 7).

14. See Vishniakova-Akimova's impressions of the various *émigré* political groupings, including the 'Musketeers'. (Op. cit, pp.113–14.)

15. G.K. Gins framed the dilemma that the CER faced by suggesting that '[s]hould the CER be unable to secure land concessions for the laying of feeder lines, its income may be saved only by a rapid colonization of the country and by the development of industry and trade'. (G.K. Gins 'Osnovnye cherty khoziaistva KVzhd', *VM*, 1927, No.2, p.21.) Due to political factors at play in the 1920s, the creation of feeder lines was difficult (see below, especially note 18 below); a result that left the railway with the task of continuing to shoulder its twin burdens. In addition to new areas of economic activity that were sponsored by the CER, the railway also devoted much capital to such projects as a wool-washing plant (with hydraulic presses for wool and skins) at Hailar, agronomical enterprises with attached experimental farms; agricultural laboratories, depots to house agricultural machinery and tractors that were leased to the population. (P.A. Shablinskii, 'Itogi eksportnoi kampanii v 1926/27 g. na Kitaiskoi Vostochnoi zheleznoi doroge', *VM*, 1927, No.10, p.1.) Shablinskii concludes that the CER '... considerably assisted in the development of the productive forces of the country and the attraction ... and creation of new commodities. A large amount of attention and money was given to the development and enlargement of such enterprises'. (Ibid.)

16. A.I. Gorshenin, 'Gruzooborot Man'chzhurii za poslednie gody I printsipy novogo zheleznodorozhnogo stroitel'stva', *VM*, 1926, No.6, p.37.

17. R.G. Athearn, *Union Pacific Country*, Lincoln, 1976, p.15.

18. The entire question of the expansion of the railway system in Manchuria invariably (but notably for Japan) became entangled with the politically sensitive issue of 'Parallel Lines' (or the ostensible duplication of existing lines). This frequently led Japan to invoke a 1905 protocol that had been intended to protect the SMR from encroachment in the early period of railway construction, but, as one authority on Chinese railways put it in 1932, this protocol was one which '... must now be considered as dead'. (N.O. Leitch, 'Additional Memorandum re Japanese Occupation of Manchuria', Tientsin, 4 April 1932, p.3, HIA, Pastuhov

Collection, Box 29.) Leitch overlooked one aspect in his otherwise sound analysis: that Japan invoked this protocol selectively, encouraging the Chinese railway system to look at ways in which it might compete with the CER.
19. The value of the railway was, of course, myriad. It provided a sense of permanence, stable presence to the Russian role in Manchuria. But the CER also allowed the continuous exertion of a form of political power, and thereby gave the Russians something of an 'official presence'.
20. See Iashnov op. cit., pp.24–5; Iashnov 'Severnaia Man'chzhuriia za tri goda', *VM*, 1927, No.10, p.9; G.K. Gins, 'Osnovnye cherty khoziaistva KVzhd', *VM*, 1927, No.2, pp.20–1.
21. P.A. Shablinskii, 'Itogi eksportnoi kampanii v 1926/27 g. na Kit. Vost. zhel. Dor.', *VM*, No.10, p.1.
22. In his 1927 survey of the CER, Gins summed up the problems that the investment pattern, and the railway's part in it, posed. In his article, he pointed out that the CER's auxiliary enterprises '…should be of no significant importance to railway'. He cited the sparse population and poorly developed industrial base in the region as reasons why no dramatic improvement was likely to have been seen in this situation. '[T]he majority of the enterprises', he continued, 'are of limited importance and do not pursue commercial aims'. Among their number, Gins singled out the railway's involvement in timber, coal and electricity generation projects. (Gins, 'Osnovnye cherty khoziaistva Kvzhd', op. cit., p.18.) In addition, he also brought a telling comparison to bear between the activities of the North Manchurian Telephone Exchange and Land Department (both of which functioned on a mixed state/private commercial basis, and therefore were in a position to bring in returns to the CER) and those attached to the SMR in Southern Manchuria. In the case of the former, the return was a mere half-million roubles annually, compared with '…the tens of millions of yen that the SMR raises through these sources'. (Ibid.)
23. See above, note 16.
24. The major weakness of river transport was its very short season. In the case of road transport (both by motor vehicle and cart), the limitations were numerous, not the least of which was the general absence of permanent roads. In addition, however, lorries, cars and carts were all vulnerable to attacks by bandits, imposition of numerous 'informal' duties by local authorities and the vagaries of weather. (For a discussion of transport problems in the hinterland, see J. Gibbes, Manchouli, Report for 1925.) Communication by motor vehicle between Harbin and the surrounding districts was limited to just 200 commercial vehicles by late 1930 (120 heavy vehicles, most of them buses, and 80 cars), owned by 14 different Harbin companies. The turnover for these in the 1929–30 period was just 120 000 Harbin Dollars; a sum lower than the previous year because of the economic downturn and the rise in banditry. (*Ekonomicheskii Biulleten'* [*EB*], No.4, 15 February 1931, p.12.)
25. Colonisation remained a major problem in provincial Northern Manchuria, with the populations of many towns and villages at times swelling and being depleted within the space of days. A major reason for this was the presence of large numbers of seasonal workers in the region. (For a discussion, see N.A. Sokolov 'Rasselenie pereselentsev v raionakh Severnoi Man'chzhurii (k pereselencheskoi kampanii 1930 g.)', *VM*, 1930, No.2, pp.36–45.) See also below, note 69 below.
26. Although by as early as 1924 Manchuria was the single largest destination for Japanese migrants (179484, or 30 of the total abroad [N.P., 'K kharakteristike

Iaponskoi emigratsii', *VM*, 1927, No.3, p.6]), such emigration was concentrated in the southern part of the region. Even by 1934, when the Japanese control of the whole of Manchuria had taken effect, the Japanese presence in Northern Manchuria was small. In Harbin, for example, there were only 13 696 Japanese and 7 338 Koreans living there in the latter year, while in Hailar the proportion was even smaller, with just 687 Japanese and 90 Koreans living there. (*Harbin Shimbun*, 16 November 1934) By comparison, the combined Russian populations (i.e. Stateless, Soviet and Chinese passport holders) at the two locations were 81 587 and 6335 respectively (figures taken from *VM*, 1934, No.9, p.37 & *Harbin Shimbun*, 16 November, 1934). Investment, on the other hand, showed a very clear Japanese predominance, even in the period before Japan took full control of Northern Manchuria. Japanese investments accounted for a total of 1 322 000 000 yen for the whole of Manchuria. Out of this sum, funds of purely Japanese origins accounted for 548 863 000 yen, with another 34 000 000 yen being of a mixed Japanese/Chinese origin. The remainder was made up of: loans by Japanese banks (286 192 000 yen); loans from the Japanese Oriental Development Company and other government-sponsored organizations (76 365 000 yen); various private Japanese loans (200 000 000 yen); various Japanese movable and immovable assets (146 634 000 yen). (*EB*, 1927, No.50, p.20.)

27. The following are figures for Russians living in Northern Manchuria by the early 1930s: 62 408 in the Harbin area (excluding the city of Harbin itself), 3246 on the Eastern Line of the CER, 4982 on the Western Line and 684 on the Southern Line. There were a further 85 in Kirin (out of a total population of 143 250!). The statistics are taken from *Manchuria Daily News* (6 September 1934).

28. By late 1934 *Trekhrech'e* had a Russian population of 10 015, of which 9763 were stateless Russian emigrants and 252 were Manchukuo citizens. There were *no* Soviet citizens there. (*Manchuria Daily News*, 6 September 1934.)

29. If in Soviet eyes *Trekhrech'e* represented a nest for counter-revolutionary activity, this image of independence and resistance to established political order continued to haunt the Japanese too when they took *de facto* control of Northern Manchuria. A major reason for this was the fact that, unlike Russians in the major settlements, the villagers here, as with the *Starovery* of the *Mudanzian-Pogranichnaia* area as a whole, were able to bear arms, and notably rifles. Although these weapons were used for hunting (a major occupation for Russians resident in the countryside), the suspicion was that these could quite easily be employed for military–political purposes too. Soviet forces disarmed as many of these small villages as they could locate in the course of the Soviet military incursion in 1929 (see Chapter 6). In the period 1937–38 the Japanese too called for a peaceful surrender of arms, but this was not heeded. After the villagers refused to obey this directive, the Japanese authorities, quite curiously, relented and replaced the surrender of arms with the requirement of a *registration* of the weapons instead. (Mr 'Katai', Interview, January 1981.)

30. Although the numbers of Soviet citizens in the provincial areas appeared greater (figures for the areas by the early 1930s were: 3246 Russians on the Eastern Line, of whom 2301 were Soviet citizens; 4982 on the Western line, of whom 3113 were Soviet citizens; 684 on the Southern line, of whom 634 were Soviet [*Manchuria Daily News*, 6 September 1934]), these were in the main people who worked for the CER in the immediate area of the railway. In the hinterland, the figures fell of dramatically (see, for example, the figures for the *Trekhrech'e* area, which show that there were no Soviet citizens there [note 28 above]).

31. In accordance to the terms agreed by the Russian and Chinese governments, the CER was provided with 55 000 *shan* of land on the Eastern Line and 126 000 *shan* on the Western Line from Manchuli to Harbin. A further 9500 *shan* on the Southern Line from Harbin to Changchun was under the control of the CER, although this had not officially been agreed to by Chinese authorities. Finally, another 10 394 *shan* of land around Harbin Station was also acquired by the CER. The railway set up a Land Department which was charged with the buying and selling of lands. (Tsao, op. cit., p.42.) In effect, therefore, this, the equivalent of 105 559 hectares, was the entire land fund that the railway had at its disposal, with the status of part of it remaining ambiguous.

32. If anything, the friction and sniping between the Soviet citizens and Russian *émigrés* were the source of considerable irritation for Chinese Republicans observing the situation in Manchuria. In the course of the Sino-Soviet crisis of 1929, a renewed Soviet charge that the authorities in Manchuria were collaborating with 'White Guardists' resulted in an uncharacteristically impatient, indeed exasperated, statement from a well-known Republican commentator: 'The attitude of the Chinese authorities is this: the Chinese-Russian crisis is Chinese business, and the Chinese troops are more than sufficient to protect Chinese territory and the employment of a handful of White Russians will only serve to complicate the situation'. (Hollington K. Tong, *Facts about the Chinese Eastern Railway Situation (with Documents)* Peiping (?), 1929, p.62.)

33. The greater the distance that the production was away from town centres and its buyers, the greater the number of local 'tax bands' (usually imposed by local authorities or the military) which either the seller or the buyer would have to deal with. (See Chapter 6 for an expansion of this point.)

34. *The North China Herald* (31 March 1929) summed up the situation well in referring to the result of the 1929 crisis: '...there will be many interesting readjustments of the balance of power between Russian [whether Red or otherwise], Japanese and Chinese "imperialism" in this territory which no one will ever be altogether satisfied to share with others since there are no natural boundaries but easily bridged rivers'.

35. See, for instance, the delicate negotiations that J. Gibbes, the head of Maritime Customs at Lahasusu, had to undertake in order to secure some land for official purposes. (S/O No.164, Lahasusu, 30 July 1930, pp.7–9.) Gibbes, when he was based at Manchuli, also reported on the antics and whims of the Chief of Police there. ('District Occurrences, July 1925' in his Report, August 1925.)

36. Gibbes writes of a lightning, blanket embargo on trade between Manchuli and Mongolia in 1926. When this was lifted, it was replaced by a highly policed regime for the traffic of goods out of that town. Goods had to be inspected at the local police station to see that the cargo tallied, and the Police were still at liberty to summarily seize the goods, or to withhold permission for their export. 'Manchouli,' Gibbes reported, 'is jubilant at even this limited concession'. (Report for November 1926, Manchouli, 5 December 1926.)

37. In an interview with Mr Gorbatenko (a Russian resident in Harbin since 1906, and an employee of the Russo-Asiatic Bank and later the CER), members of the Lytton Commission of Enquiry were given a detailed picture of the difficulties that many *émigrés* faced in surviving in Harbin without consular protection: '...various bureaus and officials...had to receive squeeze before a passport visa could be obtained by a Russian for a trip to Mukden for a few days of business. Every clerk exacted his share. There was no redress from ... the governor of

Kirin, who was anti-European in sentiment'. ('Interview at Harbin, 13 May 1932,' HIA, Pastuhov Collection, Box 3.)
38. The Russian solution is best summarised by V.F. Shchepin: 'If the CER is allowed, peacefully, to fulfil its role and spread its already very considerable economic influence deeper into N. Manchuria, the faster will be the development of the region, the faster its colonization and, as a consequence, the more rapid its growth as an import centre'. ('Severnaia Man'chzhuriia kak importnyi tsentr', *VM*, 1930, No.1, p.68)
39. Shen, op. cit., p.87.
40. This is shown by: (a) the competition with Harbin for freight, and (b) the attempts by the South Manchuria Railway (SMR) to secure large loans, presumably for capital construction purposes. (The SMR initiated talks twice: once with American interests, and before that with the Yokohama Specie Bank and the Hongkong & Shanghai Banking Corporation [HSBC] in London. [EB 1928, No. 20, p.14.])
41. Bean shipments through Vladivostok increased as follows: 1924–25 – 625 000 tons, 1926–31 – 1 190 000 tons. (*EB*, 1927, No. 50, p.18, citing the British newspaper *Commercial*). The article indicates that there was a co-ordinated, long-term policy in place to raise Vladivostok's rôle as a transshipment centre; a policy that was supported by the *Dal'bank's* dramatically enhanced activities in the region (see Chapter 6).
42. The June 1927 import figures for *Primor'e* stood at 111 509 tons; a considerable increase from the 65 356 tons recorded in June 1926. (*EB*, 1927, No.28, p.15.) However, the 1926 figures were themselves a 94 per cent increase over those of the previous financial year. (*EB*, 1926, No.24, p.15). While such figures may represent quite small levels of trade in absolute terms, their growth indicates more the *potential* that a more thoroughgoing economic integration of the two regions might have brought about; echoing strongly, thereby, the vision put forward by Witte concerning the peaceful symbiosis of Russian and Chinese economies.
43. Such a conclusion is represented vividly by the progress of the Soviet carrier *Transport* in the region: in early 1925 it opened an agency in Harbin; throughout that year it steadily expanded the number of branches and divisions in Northern Manchuria; by 1 June it had opened a branch in Hailar; finally, by the end of 1926, it concluded an agreement with the Rickmers Line of Hamburg to act as the latter's agent for the lucrative Vladivostok/European route. (*EB*, 1925, No. 6, pp.13–14; 1926, No. 22, pp.15–16; 1926, No. 48, p.9.)
44. G.K. Gins 'Osnovnye cherty khoziaistva Kvzhd', op. cit., p.20.
45. Ibid. Not only did the railway find itself without savings, but even the staff pension fund had been 'absorbed' by the company. For the important political ramifications of this policy, see Chapters 6 and 7.
46. Ibid, p.21.
47. Ibid., p.19. (Because of the abnormal status of its budget in the period of war and the revolution in Russia, a reorganisation of its entire economic system took place in that year. [Ibid.])
48. Iashnov, 'Sel'sko-khoziaistvennoe ...', op. cit., p.19. (Iashnov is, understandably, unable to provide exact figures, estimating the size of the shift of people on the figures for grain produced and transported in Northern Manchuria in the years after the war. The years 1905–11 show a steep rise in this regard, growing from 2.9 million *poods* in the former year to 45.6 million *poods* in the latter. By 1924,

the figure had risen to 114.6 million *poods*. [ibid. p.19.] Given the labour-intensive nature of cultivation in the region, such figures do represent a significant rise in the size of the population.)
49. HSBC Archives, Letter from H.C. Sanford to J.R. Jones, 30 November 1960. (The market worked on an intricate set of commercial co-ordinates, including prices on the London market, the Harbin market and a fairly sophisticated, if exploitative, 'futures' market run by Chinese soya bean buyers. [See V.G. Shishkanov 'Puti razvitiia sel'skogo khoziaistvo Severnoi Man'chzhurii', *VM*, 1929, No.3, p.32.)
50. HSBC, Letter/report from Ostrenko to Jones, 12 March 1955 (henceforth cited as: Ostrenko).
51. See *EB* reports on agriculture. A general picture is provided in the following statistics:
    1907  11.7 m. *poods* (100 per cent of 1907 prices)
    1926  62.2 m. *poods* (531 per cent)
    1927  165.0 m. *poods* (1410 per cent)
    (Taken from L.I. Liubimov, 'Dvadtsatiletie Man'chzhurskogo eksporta', *VM*, 1928, No.2, p.16.)
52. By 1925 prices for beans, bean-oil and bean cakes stood at 217 per cent, 271 per cent and 204 per cent respectively (1913 = 100 per cent), *VM*, 1927, No. 1, p.41.
53. Iashnov, 'Sel'sko-khoziaistvennoe...', op. cit., p.25. (Absolute numbers = 500 000 p.a. plus a very high birth rate. Population growth in Siberia at this time was only 1.5 per cent p.a.).
54. Iashnov, 'Severnaia Man'chzhuriia...', op. cit., p.8.
55. Ostrenko, op. cit.
56. *VM*, 1927, No. 2, p.46.
57. Shanghai, Hankow and Canton decline by 23 per cent, 45 per cent and 37 per cent respectively (the lowest since 1923, 1911 and 1920 respectively). Cited in K.P. Kursel', 'Dal'bank v 1927 g'. (*VM*, 1928, No. 4, p.18.)
58. Ibid.
59. Ibid. (according to local commercial organisations).
60. The Chinese Chamber of Commerce in Futiatien recorded an increase of about $\frac{1}{3}$ in registered firms alone. If unregistered companies are included, the figure would be much higher. (Cited in V.A. Kormazov, 'Rost naseleniia v Kharbine I Futsziadiane', *VM*, 1930, No. 6, p.6.)
61. 1924 – 427 636 tons; 1926 – 514 381 tons; 1928 – 616 821 tons.
62. Iashnov, 'Severnaia Man'chzhuriia ...', op. cit., p.8.
63. V.G. Shishkanov, 'Puti razvitiia sel'skogo khoziaistva Severnoi Man'chzhurii', *VM*, 1929, No. 3, pp.31–2.
64. L.E. Liubimov, 'Krizis sbyta bobov I poteri Man'chzhurskogo krest'ianina', *VM*, 1930, No. 6, p.6.
65. Ibid.
66. Shishkanov, op. cit., p.33. The reasons given for the difficulty in selling the ploughs: high costs and instability of the local dollar.
67. By 1929 the soya bean export trade was monopolised by the following companies: The East Asiatic Co. Ltd, The Siberian Co., *Dal'gostorg*, The Anglo-Chinese Eastern Trading Co., and Louis Dreyfus & Co. Of these the East Asiatic and Siberian were by far the largest purchasers (*Dal'gostorg*, the Soviet concern, captured a significant proportion of the market very late in the 1920s). For discussion of the collapse of the Siberian Co., see Chapter 7.
68. One of the main units in circulation in the Kirin and Tsitsihar provinces – the *Tiao* – was not bound by a regularised form of issue, resulting, according to some

authoritative sources, in the over-issue of this note by some 6 *milliard*. (A.I. Pogrebetskii, 'Denezhnyi rynok Kitaia I Severnoi Man'chzhurii', *VM*, 1925, Nos 3–4, p.89.) The somewhat suspect nature of this activity (which, in fact, drew the attention of the Mukden authorities in the mid-1920s) was to reveal itself in the reluctance of North Manchurian peasants to hold the *Tiao* which they received as payment for grain, preferring to immediately use the currency to buy items to be used on the farm, or, if they wished to save, to buy silver. (Ibid.) The purchase of large amounts of silver was in itself to cause trouble when, after the economic depression set in 1930–31, there was a sharp slide in the value of silver.
69. *EB*, 1929, Nos 15–16, pp.1–4. (No Chinese banks were engaged in the bean trade. See *VM*, 1930, No.2, p.83.)
70. Ibid. Not one bank of the 27 in operation in Northern Manchuria by 1929 was established specifically to finance industry. The most active in industry were the National City Bank and *Dal'bank*.
71. Sakhalian, a centre for administration and trade/industrial life for its entire region, is a good example: 'In the space of three years, 1926–28, from a "key" industrial commercial centre, the town has transformed completely; it has died (population: 1926 – 25 000; 1928 – less than 12 000). Reason given: eradication of contraband trade'. (V.A. Kormazov, 'Severnaia okraina Kheiluntsianskoi provintsii', *VM*, 1929, No. 6, p.72.)
72. Iashnov, op. cit., p.8.
73. Ibid.
74. *EB* reported 100 closures in one month of assorted Chinese firms in Harbin and Futiatien alone; others had to cut down the size of their work force, accounting for about 6000 workers. A Chinese newspaper reported 460 bankruptcies for the year (not including grain firms around Harbin) with a total indebtedness of $6 m (*EB*, 1931, No. 15, p.20.)
75. N. Sizov 'Ekonomicheskoe Polozhenie Severnoi Man'chzhurii,' *Novyi Vostok*, No. 6, 1924, p.147.
76. An indication of the numbers involved (and chaos present) may be seen in the following: between 1912 and 1918 the Russian population in China increased from 45 000 to 59 719. In 1919 that figure rose to 148 170, falling to 144 413 in 1920, 68 250 in 1921, and rising again to 96 727 in 1922, after which it remained at approximately 80 000. In 1919 and 1920 the total number of Russians in China rivalled closely the largest foreign population, that of the Japanese (171 485 in 1920). For Manchurian figures, see Quested, 'Matey Imperialists?', op. cit., pp.221–2, 276, 289.
77. HSBC S/O, K130.18.1, 174/7, Baker to Wood, 22 November 1922.
78. Witness the Soviet attempt (discussed earlier) to break the *émigrés* away from the CER through Order 94 (1 July 1925), which dismissed all employees who were not Soviet or Chinese citizens. For further discussion of this, see George E. Sokolsky, *Story of the Chinese Eastern Railway*, Shanghai, 1929, pp. 48–50.
79. Baykov. op. cit. pp. 7–17.
80. Exports from the Soviet Union increase from 8 612 000 Hk Taels in 1924 to 11 844 000 HkT in 1925 (or from 0.85 per cent to 1.25 per cent of total trade). (Marakueff, op. cit. pp. 66–7.)
81. K.P. Kursel', 'Itogi deiatel'nosti Dal'nevostochnogo Banka v Kharbine za 1923–26 gg. (Po materialam inspektsii Dal'banka)' *VM*, 1927, No.5, p.36.
82. Ibid.
83. The China Coast press was quick to pick up the slightest bit of evidence to suggest ulterior motives for Soviet commerce. In the summer of 1923, for example,

the Hong Kong newspaper *South China Morning Post* published an article about *Tsentrosoiuz* being more a political institution disseminating 'violent Bolshevik propaganda' than a co-operative trading society. The HSBC, which had financed a small shipment of furs to New York for them, made its position plain: 'One reason [for business with] them last year was that they were reported to me as keeping out of politics in Harbin, and I have not heard otherwise since. Probably there is too much chance of trouble with the Whites. We have on occasions to deal with Bolsheviks... but we don't want to have anything more to do with the militant type than we can help'. (HSBC S/O, K130.18.1, 174/7, Baker to Knox, 5 June 1923.)
84. Reports on marketing of manufactures, *EB*, 1925–26.
85. Just how far some Soviet officials were integrated into capitalist society in the North-Eastern provinces is shown by the Geitsman case (see Chapter 3).
86. HSBC S/O, vol. 91, Report, Wood to de Courcy, 26 July 1929.
87. Liubimov, in *Ekonomicheskie Problemy*, concludes that only the development of the Maritime Province, in industry or agriculture, would satisfy the needs of the Ussuri Railway (p.11). The province's industry was too weak, however, to allow the railway to turn in a profit (between 1922 and 1925 the number of firms in the region rose from 110 to 176, all small). (ibid., p.47.)
88. Its main function was to serve the Manchurian export market (in beans). But as Liubimov remarked, rolling stock filled with North Manchurian surpluses reaching Vladivostok would return to Suifenho empty. Dairen had captured much of the Manchurian import traffic. (Ibid. p.11.)
89. In 1928 alone exports were up by 38 per cent and imports by 33 per cent. (*EB*, 1929, no. 1, p.3.)
90. E. E. Iashnov, 'Kriziz sbyta I Man'chzhurskoe sel'skokhoziaistvo', *EB*, 1931, no. 2, pp.5–7.
91. Henry W. Kinney, Memorandum, Dairen, 18 December 1930, pp.1–2. HIA, Pastuhov Collection, Box 21.
92. By 1928, Soviet exports stood at $US5 000 000, and for 1929 the figure had risen to $US7 100 000. (I.I. Dombrovskii 'Vneshniaia torgovlia Kitaia v 1933 godu' *VM*, 1934, No.7, pp.104–5. The latter figure was reached despite the Sino-Soviet crisis which began in the middle of that year and brought trade to a full standstill for the remaining six months of 1929. Had the crisis not intruded into trade, the likelihood was for a doubling of 1928 figures. Export trade from Primor'e showed very sharp growth: between 1925 and 1926 alone, exports grew by 186 per cent (a total of 7 342 501 poods), *EB*, No.18, p.13.
93. This is represented in numerous ways, but none of these more distinctly than in the struggle over CER employment. In the course of 1929, the contest over the Russian positions see-sawed between *émigré* and Soviet interests, with the former supported by Manchurian authorities. The crushing blow that Soviet forces delivered to their Manchurian counterparts at the end of that year led, as *émigré* sources described it, to the 'vanquishers' returning to the railway with '... all their adherents whom they paid their salaries for the whole period of the conflict'. (S.A. Poperek 'To the Inquiry Committee of the League of Nations from the Delegation of discharged employees of the CER', 9 May 1932, HIA, Pastuhov Collection, Box 3). Their return, the letter continued, resulted in sustained 'bloodletting', with all those who had continued working, despite a Soviet boycott, during the crisis '... hav[ing] been considered enemies to the business and have been discharged from work'. (Ibid.) The animosity persisted, and indeed

grew, in subsequent years. See also Chapter 6 for a fuller discussion of the implications of this episode.
94. Kinney sums this up well when, in observing Soviet commercial activities in the late 1920s, he writes that some foreigners and Russians in Harbin '… feel that Soviet Russia is now trying to accomplish industrially and economically what she has failed to accomplish politically in China, and that she will be able to drive out the foreigner, at least to a great extent, by depriving him of the trade which is the reason for his being in China'. (Kinney, op. cit., p.2.) Such suspicions are to some extent also to be seen in the Chinese response to Soviet attempts to broaden their commercial presence. In 1926, for example, an informal Sino-Soviet conference was held to discuss a new commercial treaty between the two countries. The Soviet side attempt to remove the ceiling on personnel housed in their consulates (which restricted the presence to 10 per consulate) and to convince the Chinese government to allow Soviet foreign trade bureaux to be housed in the consulates was met with a frosty response. (*The Hankow Herald*, 9 February 1926.)
95. See, for example, Kinney report (op. cit., pp.2–3); regular reports on the healthy growth of Soviet industry were also to be found in *VM* and *EB*, and especially so after 1931, when the economic depression had bitten deep into the Manchurian and international economies. (See *EB*, 1931, pp.21, 22–3. Interestingly, until this year both *VM* and *EB* represent the Soviet Union's role and achievements in a far more modest light.) The image of Soviet Union as an economic power gained further prominence as the economic crisis grew more severe. The Soviet Union, after all, had gained in at least three ways from the depression: the growth in the export of gold, whose value had increased as a result of the collapse of silver prices; enhanced access to credit (Western financiers being willing to channel funds into the Soviet Union in proportions that the latter could not have hoped for without the economic depression in the West); the opportunity to 'import' thousands of Western specialists who could not find work in their own economies. (G. Grossman, Interview, San Francisco, 3 July 1979.)

# 6 The 1929 Crisis

1. B.G. Tours, the British Consul General at Mukden, reported that as early as August 1929, Chang Hsüeh-liang had begun to 'lose interest' in the crisis over the railway, preferring '… to devote all his attention to "movie-tone" pictures, which are being demonstrated to him by special agents of the American Fox Company'. (Tours to Lampson, No.50, Mukden, 2 August 1929, FO 371/13954-632.). There is also evidence of his unpopularity with Russians in Northern Manchuria. (See Skidelsky comments, Chapter 7.)
2. A measure of the political change that was in progress at this time is provided by the developments in the CER, whose staff, despite Mukden's efforts to ensure an *émigré* presence, was steadily becoming Soviet in make-up (Otto Mossdorf records that by the start of the crisis 22 000 out of a total of 28 000 CER employees were Soviet citizens. 'der mandschurische Konflikt der Jahres 1929'. [The Manchurian Conflict of 1929] *Zeitschrift für Politik*, Berlin, vol. 20, 1931, p.50).
3. Tang, *Russian and Soviet Policy*, op. cit., p.258.
4. E.H. Carr, *The Russian Revolution from Lenin to Stalin, 1917–1929*, London, 1979, p.183.

5. Christopher writes: 'The Sino-Soviet crisis and border war of 1929 have generally been given much less than their real importance in studies on international relations between the two world wars. The conflict has been overshadowed in retrospect by the Sino-Japanese crisis of 1931, which involved a challenge to the League of Nations, intruded into the forefront of world affairs, and formally diminished Chinese sovereignty by the creation of the new puppet state of "Manchukuo". The crisis of 1929, on the other hand, produced no appeal to the League of Nations, no permanent Russian military occupation of Manchuria and no formal breach of China's sovereignty'. And he then goes on: 'Since the Washington Conference no foreign power had invaded Chinese territory beyond the limits of the foreign settlements and concessions in order to impose terms on the Chinese government; by being the first to do so, anti-imperialist Soviet Russia showed herself more ready, instead of more reluctant, than the "imperialist" powers to coerce China on account of purely material national interests. Her success in the use of force (with the acquiescence or even approval of the rest of the world) was a major factor in encouraging the Japanese militarists to draw the sword, likewise, two years later and use it in a much larger way'. (J.W. Christopher, *Conflict in the Far East: American Diplomacy in China from 1928–1933*, New York, 1970, p.71; this is a reprint edition of a 1950 publication.) However, where christopher fails to pick up sufficient nuance from the events in Manchuria is in concluding that the Soviet handling of the 1929 crisis was nothing more than an example of the politics of crude imperialism. While the superficial evidence certainly suggests this, the position that the Soviet Union found itself in was far more complex than Christopher concludes was the case. Perhaps the most surprising shortcoming in this respect is G.A. Lensen's otherwise most impressive work *The Damned Inheritance: The Soviet Union and the Manchurian Crisis, 1924–1935* (Tallahassee, 1974) which, while it employs a broad array of British, American, Russian and Japanese sources in painting a vivid picture of the troubled region (the depiction below of the 1929 crisis, indeed, owes much to his study), nonetheless falls far short of giving the crisis its due weight (see Lensen, chs 2–5). Perhaps its chief shortcoming is by seemingly taking Japanese motives in the region too much at face value, which means, of course, that Japan would be seen as being fully behind the Soviet Union in the conflict (see especially his conclusion concerning the crisis on p.171). This tends to underplay Japan's own role in the region, and the impact of the crisis on its thinking regarding the geostrategic implications of the crisis and subsequent conflict. In this last respect, Lensen simply observes that the Japanese came to regard the Red Army as a 'definite military menace'. (Ibid.)
6. Tang, op. cit., pp.69–72, *passim*.
7. McCormack, op. cit. pp.4–5. In my interview with Swan, she observed that the appellation Three North-Eastern Provinces came to the fore only under Chiang Kai-shek. Otherwise the region was consistently – and historically – known as Manchuria. Indeed, as she pointed out, even the Japanese simply adapted the existing name in creating the polity of Manchukuo (by introducing the title *Man-chu*-di-go, where *di-go* stands for empire). (Swan, Interview, August 1981.) Similarly uncompromising views have been expressed to me by Russians and Chinese alike, although often without the detailed argument provided by Swan.
8. See, for example, US Army, Lt L.L.Williams (ed.), *15th Infantry Annual, May 4, 1924–May 4, 1925*, Tientsin, 1925. In one of the frequent periods of unrest between the northern warlords, a member of 'K' Company recorded how '[w]e

watched some 120 000 Wu Pei Fu soldiers, en route to Shanhaikuan pass through Tongshan ... and waited to see what would happen if Chang [Tso-lin] drove them back. In such a contingency the maelstrom which might hit us had grave possibilities'. (p.85) The Americans' regard for the warlords' forces was considerable: '[we] witnessed some stirring military sights, Cavalry, efficient and disciplined, trotted into town in perfect order, passed on west, went into camp or boarded trains in a manner that was a delight to any military man'. (Ibid., p.86.)
9. See Chapter 1 for a discussion of the nature of Manchuria. It must be said, of course, that by the 1920s the Manchus had in large measure been assimilated by the Chinese, to the extent that Mrs Swan, a linguist, never heard the Manchu dialect spoken in her time in Manchuria (she was unlikely to have, as its pure form was by then virtually a dead language, with a spoken form limited to a very small number of Manchus in the frontier districts of Tsitsihar and Kirin provinces, whilst the written language was restricted to a few tribes in Shahar, where it was used in correspondence. 'Notes on Several Conversations held by Dr Schnee during the Commission's Stay in Harbin', pp.1–2, HIA, Pastuhov Collection, Box 43). However, the distinctiveness of the Manchu minority remained, even in the linguistic area: their multi-syllabic language had *mutated*, adapting the monosyllabic form of the Chinese language, forming a readily identifiable, if curious, amalgam. (Swan, Interview, August 1981.)
10. I.I. Serebrennikov, 'The Historical Trend of Russian Policy in Outer Mongolia and Northern Manchuria', n.p, n.d., pp.14–15, HIA, Pastuhov Collection, Box 9. Originally, the problem in Barga was the hostile response that came from its indigenous people to the Chinese government's policy of 'strengthening the frontiers' and creating a Chinese element there, '[f]earing that the Chinese aggression would gradually lead to the extinction of their national individuality ... '. (Ibid.) In this respect, Barga was experiencing very similar pressures to the ones exerted on Outer Mongolia.
11. 'Notes on Several Conversations held by Dr Schnee during the Commission's Stay in Harbin', op. cit., p.1.
12. Ibid.
13. Ibid. (The 'new state' the Manchu leader refers to is the puppet state of Manchukuo, formed in 1932.)
14. See Tong (op. cit.), Shanghai Bureau of Industrial and Commercial Information. International Relations Committee, *The Sino-Russian Crisis: The Actual Facts Brought to Light*, Nanking, 1929. (Similar outpourings came from a large number of scholars and overseas Chinese organisations, in condemning – albeit in carefully constructed legal terms – Japanese aggression in 1931/32. Although the latter was a considerably more emotive issue, the case was still argued on the basis of this being an action against Chinese sovereignty. Given that the majority of those who made these appeals had no direct connection with Manchuria, one has to wonder how close to their hearts they held the more ambiguous outlook of those who had originally populated the sparsely peopled region of Manchuria. See, for example, *China and the Trouble in Manchuria: What it means to China, Japan, Russia and the World*, Sydney, 1931.)
15. *Sovetsko-Kitaiskii konflikt 1929 g.: Sbornik dokumentov*, Moscow, 1930, pp.3–4.
16. See Kingman, op. cit., especially pp.61–70.
17. Ibid., p.75.

182  Notes

18. Over a year after the conflict had run its course, 'White' Russian captains of steamers on the river system would hand over the ships to their Chinese seconds after they had cleared the Lahasusu Customs point and the vessels were ready to continue on the Amur portion of their trip, '[The captains] themselves remaining on the Sungari, ready to take over their ships on their return'. (Gibbes, *Memorandum on Trade*, Lahasusu, September Qr., 1930, p.3.)
19. HSBC, vol. 91, Wood to de Courcy, Harbin, 11/12.7.29; Tsao, op. cit., p.121; Lensen, op. cit., p.54.
20. 'Oblastnik', *Statia KVzhd (O Kitaiskoi Vostochnoi zheleznoi doroge)*, n.p. (Harbin?), n.d. (1929?), pp.13,16. GARF, 5869, No.1, Khr. No.9.
21. Department of State, *Papers Relating to the Foreign Relations of the United States*, 1929, vol. II, Washington: 1943 [FRUS], pp.264–5.
22. 'Oblastnik', op. cit., p.12.
23. FRUS, op. cit., p.274.
24. V. Dushen'kin *ot soldata do marshala*, Moscow, 1964, p.178. The text of the order for the formation of the force can be found in *Sovetsko-Kitaiskii konflikt 1929 g.*, op. cit., pp.37–8. (For an amplification of the circumstances leading to the formation of the army, see Chapter 3 in the present study.)
25. Badham-Thornhill to Lampson, Peking, 24 September 1929, 'Secret,' FO 376/13955.
26. Ibid.
27. FRUS, op. cit., pp.337–8. Similar reports exist for other northwestern areas: at Bukhedu Station, between Tsitsihar and Hailar, Soviet planes bombed Chinese encampments on 28–29 November (see below), causing an immediate rash of looting and violence as the troops made their chaotic retreat. ('Delegates of the European population of the District of Station Boohedoo C.E.Rly' to the Lytton Commission of Enquiry, 11 May 1932, p.1, HIA, Pastuhov Collection, Box 52.)
28. Dushen'kin, op. cit., pp.182, 194–5.
29. FRUS, op. cit., p.338.
30. For an account of the Red Army's tactics against Japanese forces in Manchuria, see G.A. Lensen, *The Strange Neutrality: Soviet–Japanese Relations during the Second World War, 1941–1945*, Tallahassee, 1967, pp.156–73.
31. Lensen, *The Damned Inheritance*, op. cit., pp.62–5.
32. Russian troops filmed this bizarre spectacle, showing it to the population of Manchuli and, some time later, in Moscow. (Kinney to Pratt, 3 February 1930, FO 371/14700.)
33. 'Delegates of the European Population ...', op. cit., p.1.
34. Badham-Thornhill to Lampson, Peking, 13 January 1930, 'Secret,' FO 371/14700.
35. FRUS, 1929, II, pp.392–3; *Sovetsko-Kitaiskii konflikt*, op. cit., p.86. There was a brief hiccough with respect to Mukden, with Chang Hsüeh-liang accepting all points with the exception of a return of Emshanov and Eismont to senior positions in the CER. After a Soviet threat of a resumption of hostilities, including the bombing of Tsitsihar, Chang finally came around to accepting the return of the two men, but, upon his having given in on this point, Narkomindel (the Soviet Commissariat of Foreign Affairs) soon replaced them as General and Assistant General Managers (with Rudyi and Denisov). [Ibid. p.397; *Sovetsko-Kitaiskii konflikt*, p.87.]
36. *Izvestiia*, 23 December 1929. (Also, all employees who had been dismissed were to be reinstated, or pensioned off if they were unwilling to resume their work; all former Russian subjects – not citizens of the USSR – hired by the CER during

the conflict were to be dismissed; White Guard detachments were to be disarmed by the Chinese and their organisers and leaders deported from the Three Northeast Provinces; diplomatic links were left to the Moscow Conference to consider, however Soviet consulates in the provinces and Chinese consulates in the Russian Far East were opened immediately.)

37. V. M. Kulagin and N.N. Iakovlev, *Podvig Osoboi Dal'nevostochnoi*, Moscow, 1970, p.124. This slogan was, by all accounts, adhered to, with gratitude being expressed by Chinese civilians for the treatment they received from the soldiers of the Red Army. (See, for example, the vote of thanks from the Chinese Municipal Council of Hailar, Dushen'kin, op. cit., pp.194–5.) Similar treatment, according to one account, was accorded to captured Chinese soldiers, with whom Red Army personnel shared bread, tobacco and sugar. (Ibid., p.194.)
38. Kulagin & Iakovlev, op. cit., p.124. The directives appear to have been obeyed: 'We received not so much as one complaint about the conduct of our soldiers with the civilian population', reported Bliukher upon completion of the military action. (Dushen'kin, op. cit., p.194.)
39. Kulagin & Iakovlev, op. cit., p.124. It is interesting to observe that the policies of non-interference and non-exploitation employed by the Red Army in Northern Manchuria in 1929 anticipated by a number of years the very successful political methods (subsumed under the body of theory known as the 'Yenan Way') introduced by Mao Tse-tung to the People's Liberation Army after the Yenan period.
40. Lensen, *The Damned Inheritance*, op. cit., p.64.
41. Kulagin & Iakovlev, op. cit., pp.158–9.
42. Ibid., p.166.
43. Ibid., p.164.
44. Ibid., pp.164–5.
45. The conduct of the operations in Manchuria conforms well to this definition, offered by S.P. Ivanov and A.I. Evseev in their article 'Voennoe iskusstvo', *Sovetskaia voennaia entsiklopediia*, 1976, Vol. 2, p.211.
46. A.A. Svechin 'Strategy and Operational Art', taken from the 2nd edition of *Strategiia*, Moscow, 1927 (in H.S. Orenstein (tr.) and D.M. Glantz (foreword & introductions) *The Evolution of Soviet Operational Art, 1927–1991: The Documentary Basis*, London, 1995, vol. 1, p.10). The Manchurian campaign, and Bliukher's contribution to it, eschewed the notion of a linear strategy, with its 'sweeping forward movement' and the simultaneous use of all effort; a long-accepted form derived from the writings of von Clausewitz. Instead, it appeared to conform to the new prescription that viewed the von Clausewitz formula as being suitable for the Napoleonic Wars, but not so for warfare in the twentieth century, '... when the operation became a multi-act phenomenon and spread out in a series of successive operational efforts into the depth'. (G. Isserson, 'The Evolution of Operational Art', ibid., p.70.). The origins of this may be found in General M.N. Tukhachevsky's Deep Operation Theory (see S. Naveh, 'Mikhail Nikolayevich Tukhachevsky' in H. Shukman (ed.) *Stalin's Generals*, New York, 1993, pp.255–73. Isserson was a close friend of Tukhachevsky's.)
47. The campaign seemed to present a consciously constructed alternative to the strategy of attrition that had been employed so successfully by the Japanese command against the Russian army in the war of 1904/1905. (For a discussion of the latter strategy, see Svechin, op. cit., pp.15–16.) This link was not an accidental one, given that Svechin himself was an ex-tsarist general staff officer and important military thinker, who had both participated in, and written a major

study on, the Russo-Japanese War. He, together with N. Varfolomeev (who was also an ex-tsarist officer serving in the Red Army (from 1918) as chief of an army staff and deputy *front* chief-of-staff), were important figures in the Frunze Academy's Department of Strategy. (Glantz, in Orenstein & Glantz, op. cit., p.3.)
48. Cf. Chapter 7 for the radio broadcasts; for propaganda, see *China Weekly Review*, Shanghai, 11 January 1930, No.6.
49. M. Lampson to Henderson, No.930, 2 July 1930, FO 371/14699.
50. A British banker at Harbin made the following observation of the Soviet Union's initial actions in Northern Manchurian crisis: '[The] Soviet Union as the champion of foreign rights in China is something very strange and totally unexpected. ... It would be a splendid thing if the Chinese Eastern Railway could be internationally controlled ... '. (HSBC, vol. 91, Wood to de Courcy, 26 June 1929.)
51. Although much was made of the imparity between the military equipment possessed by the two sides (*China Weekly Review*, Shanghai, 11 November 1930, No.6), the decisive factor was undoubtedly the new conception of the operational level of war arrived at by Soviet military thinkers (See Naveh, op. cit., pp.271–2 for a summary of this.)
52. While the Chinese government frequently invoked the pact, signed just a year earlier (27 August 1928), in the course of the crisis, the Soviet Union was able to negate the thrust of these complaints by referring to the Chinese incursions onto its own territory; raids which were much-publicised by Soviet media. Thus, the Soviet Union was not engaging in war-like action, but rather adopting measures essential to repel an aggressor, it argued. (*China Weekly Review*, 11 January 1930; For examples of Galen's contributions to strategy, see also Dushen'kin, op. cit., pp.179–85.)
53. FRUS, op. cit., p.263; Christopher, op. cit., pp.110–11. For a further description of the ragged Chinese diplomatic effort, see 'Kto otvetstvenen za razryv?' (Translated from *Weekly Review*, 25 January 1930) GARF, Fond 5878, no.1, Khr. no.173. Sun Fo was Sun Yat-sen's son.
54. Christopher, op. cit., p.111.
55. See Chapter 7 for details of the transfer.
56. Voroshilov, who became Commissar in 1925, showed his characteristically weak grasp of theory, it might be argued, in espousing such a position.
57. Christopher, op. cit., pp.99–100.
58. Ibid.
59. V.F. Shchepin 'Severnaia Man'chzhuriia kak importnyi tsentr', *VM*, No.1, 1930, p.68.
60. G. Isserson, 'Evoliutsiia operativnogo iskusstva', *Voina i revoliutsiia*, 5–6, 1932, pp.25–52. in Orenstein and Glantz, op. cit., p.76.
61. Ibid. The supreme irony in this analysis is that it was published in the same year as the Soviet Union began to see the untenable situation it had brought upon itself after 1929.
62. If anything, the competing forms of propaganda (the Chinese authorities countered Soviet efforts in this area) must have been the cause of considerable confusion for the civilian population watching the conflict from the sidelines. One Russian, who was an engineering student at *KhPI* (the Harbin Polytechnical Institute) at the time, remembered a particularly confusing example of the Chinese propaganda. The Chinese authorities had, he said, sent up an aeroplane with the large markings *Pekin-Moskva* on it, with the intention of using it as the 'vanguard for Chinese forces in their thrust towards Moscow'. The plane

managed to get as far as the border, where Soviet aircraft forced it to land. (B. Koreneff, Interview, Sydney, 13 March 1981.)
63. Gins, 'Osnovnye cherty...', op. cit., p.21. Gins, a professor of economics in Harbin, was especially critical of the CER's refusal to run a sinking fund when, at the same time, it had gone into debt to its own employees' Savings Fund (see previous chapter for a full discussion of this perspective).
64. HSBC, Ostrenko, op. cit..
65. Harbin market reports for the first half of 1930 show a very sharp decline across the board, but notably in soya bean trade. *EB* for 1 June 1930 showed that crop prospects for the first half of the year were very good, but that the European market had 'almost altogether' stopped purchasing Manchurian beans. (No.10, pp.11–14.) Later in the same month, an All-Manchurian Conference of Chinese Commercial Associations began to hold emergency sessions in Mukden in order to find ways in which to protect Manchurian trade and industry. (Ibid., 8 August 1930, No.14, pp.1–3.)
66. *EB*, 1931, No. 2, pp.1–5.
67. Hailar, an agricultural centre, in 1930: only 68 per cent of wool supply (compared with the previous year's figures) and a 50 per cent fall in the price of hay. (*EB*, 1930, No. 5, pp.19–20.)
68. Figures for those despatched from Dairen, for example: 1928 – 73 983; 1929 – 48 724; 1930 (first five months) – 9717. *EB*, 1930, No. 7, p.7.
69. *EB*, 1930, No. 3, p.27.
70. *EB*, 1929, Nos 15–16, p.20.
71. See, for example, 'Harbin Market Review', *EB*, 1930, No. 7, pp.14–18.
72. N.M. Dobrokhotov, 'Ekonomicheskiie zatrudneniia v Kharbine', *VM*, 1930, No.6, p.12.
73. L.I. Liubimov, 'Krizis sbyta bobov i poteri Man'chzhurskogo krest'ianina', *VM*, 1930, No.6, p.6.
74. Between 30 September 1929 and May 1931 prices in Harbin fell from 104 to 82 *Sen* per pood. Cited in ibid., p.7.
75. Dobrokhotov, op. cit. p.13.
76. *EB*, 1931, No. 5, p.14. On 1929 figures (1924 population = 92 000).
77. *EB*, 1931, No. 16, pp.10–12. In late November-December, London prices were not quoted at all. (See *EB*, No. 22, pp. 7–9.)
78. Ostrenko, op. cit.
79. Ostrenko, op. cit.
80. HSBC Annual Report, 1910.
81. Ostrenko, op. cit.
82. Ibid.
83. Ibid.
84. Ibid.
85. Only in 1930 did the Bank of China begin to compete seriously with European and Japanese banks for the financing of local exports. (*EB*, 1932, No. 8, p.9.)
86. A.I. Pogrebetskii, 'Denezhnyi rynok Kitaia i Severnoi Man'chzhurii', *VM*, 1925, Nos 3–4, p.99. This article, written in 1925, marks the transition to growing competition; at that time 'exchange' was still at the head of foreign banks' list of priorities.
87. *EB*, 1927, Nos 23–4, pp.16–17. (Refers to Kirin Province.)
88. HSBC, M.W. Wood to J.R. Jones, 16 November 1954.
89. Ostrenko, op. cit. The question of management and business technique is a complex one. It is undeniable that Knox's attitudes were innately conservative, while

Wood did display a far more imaginative approach, possibly being the result of the latter's experience in the Vladivostok Agency (which survived as long as it did almost wholly through his enterprise, tenacity and ability to find business just as Head Office's axe was about to fall on the entire operation) where opportunity had to be recognised, seized and exploited quickly and fully. In this respect, Ostrenko's comments concerning Wood and Knox are superficially borne out. Yet it would be wrong to conclude, as Ostrenko does, that Knox was a safer banker than Wood. The latter undoubtedly wished to see the HSBC base in Northern Manchuria broadened and the Harbin Office made more competitive. However, it was Wood who sensed very early on that increased involvement with the Siberian Company was a perilous undertaking; Knox, on the other hand, had been instrumental in drawing the Bank into deeper water with the latter concern because he regarded highly its management in Harbin, and because it was a European-based firm (see also Chapter 7).

90. Ibid.
91. Comments from a translation of an article from *Russkoe Slovo*, (undated) incorporated into a report written by the Assistant in charge of Sub-port, Lahasusu, 25 August 1927.
92. 'Petition to the Commission of Enquiry of the League of Nations' (from the depositors of the Russo-Asiatic Bank in Harbin), 1932, HIA, Pastuhov Collection, Box 3. For the political ramifications, see Chapter Seven. (See also Appendix 1 for a summary version of the petition.)
93. *EB*, 1929, Nos 15–16, pp.1–4. (Information comes from Mr Ishiga, the Assistant Director of the Bank of Chosen.)
94. A.V.M., 'Eksport Man'chzhurskikh bobov i ego finansirovanie' *VM*, 1928, No. 3, p.10.
95. Kursel', op. cit., p.20.
96. *EB*, 1927, No. 46, p.19.
97. *EB*, 1927, No. 46, p.19.
98. The meeting was held in mid-January 1930. Present were: representatives of the Bank of China, the Chinese Chamber of Commerce, the Federation of Banks and the Chinese Stock Exchange. At this meeting, a directive was issued abolishing the *Tael* as from 1 July 1930, the Chinese Dollar thereby becoming the sole currency. In A.I. Pogrebetskii, 'Na puti k zolotomu standartu', *VM*, 1930, No. 2, p.8.
99. *VM*, 1930, No. 2, p.83. The banks taking part in this action were: Chosen, Yokohama Specie, HSBC, Dal'bank (Harbin Office), National City, and, later, the Standard Chartered (but on a small scale).
100. *EB*, 1928, No. 32, p.17.
101. *VM*, 1930, No. 8, p.20.
102. *EB*, 1931, No. 3, p.21.
103. Dobrokhotov, op. cit., p.14.
104. The average rate was 8 per cent per month.
105. Ostrenko, op. cit. (refers to the HSBC in Harbin.)
106. *EB*, 1931, No. 19, p.21.
107. Ostrenko, op. cit.
108. *Politekhnik*, Sydney, 1979, No. 10, p.22. The various branches of the company's operations suffered considerably from the twin effect of the political/military and economic crises, forcing them into an even more difficult financial situation. With the deepening of the economic crisis in the early 1930s, the HSBC

found that there was no option left but to take over the company completely, thereby removing it from Russian hands.
109. Ostrenko, op. cit.
110. Zanozin was working for a fur company in Mongolia in 1929. The owner of the company had, in Zanozin's words, transformed '…from a millionaire to a pauper, but a pauper with accumulated debts'. Zanozin himself found out about the collapse when he attempted to buy some goods on credit, but discovered that his company had not paid its existing debts. Finally, after queries from his Chinese customers, he travelled to Kalgan (where the head office was based) only to find an empty office, with a cold stove. There was insufficient money left even to heat the office. Zanozin's stock of furs had for some time been sold off to local Chinese buyers, who sewed hats from the most exotic of furs, replacing the cheap fabric caps worn in the area. (Zanozin, Interview, 5 March 1981.)
111. Numerous retail businesses in Harbin were forced to run their operations on skeleton staff of 1–2 employees, shedding the remainder in the course of 1929/1930. (See Harbin Market Reports, *EB*, 1930, No. 9 – 1931, No. 1.; A.M. Pagudin, Interview, San Francisco, 7 July 1979.)
112. Pagudin, Interview, July 1979.
113. Pagudin, Interview, July 1979. The sharp slump in trading figures would have encouraged companies to transfer their operations. One report (for early 1930) observes that the activities of trading companies in the region had fallen to 40 per cent of those recorded for the same period in 1929. (N.M. Dobrokhotov 'Depressiia na Man'chzhurskom rynke', *VM*, 1930, No. 3, p.13.). There would, of course, also have been a knock-on effect at play here.
114. Tsao notes that '[a]side from seizure and damage to its rolling stock, the Railway also suffers the loss of huge revenue, which, according to the yearly rate of increase, should have surpassed that of preceding years during corresponding periods to a very great extent'. (op. cit., p.78. A detailed account of the extensive damage to the CER lines and rolling stock can be found on pp.90–9.)
115. Ibid., p.78.
116. S.A. Poperek, 'To the Inquiry Committee of the League of Nations from the Delegation of discharged employees of the CER', op. cit.
117. Ibid, p.4. The plight of the former employees is confirmed by a number of other sources, including the oral testimony of Koreneff, who, despite his view that the 1929 crisis was not quite as apocalyptic as it has generally been depicted (although his response to this question was based on the effect that it had on his own immediate life, which was minimal), viewed this aspect of the conflict as being 'very serious'. Many of the former employees had to resort to the Chinese court system for redress (the same court system, indeed, as the creditors applied to for money owing from the CER, see Chapter 7), which Koreneff depicted as biased and the processes costly, as each of the ex-employees had to initiate an individual action against the railway, thereby providing only the Russian lawyers representing them with a certain amount of windfall profit. Koreneff's own father was a case in point. Koreneff Senior was a company doctor based at Manchuria Station (the township). He was overworked and, when he asked for assistants to be hired to help him, had to face frequent refusals from the company. He was sacked in 1930, and died from typhus contracted after an epidemic struck the settlement in that year. The legal proceedings, which eventually resulted in a successful outcome, continued for two

years and two initial verdicts against the family. Koreneff Jr remembers 1929–31 as being 'particularly grave' for those who had lost their jobs. (Koreneff, Interview, March 1981.)
118. Poperek, op. cit., p.5.
119. Ibid.
120. Savchik, Interview, February 1981.
121. Petition from the Ukrainian Association to the Lytton Commission (May 1932), HIA, Pastuhov Collection, Box 3. After 20 years of existence, the club was closed by Chinese authorities because of reported 'disputes' between club members and the discovery of Bolshevik propaganda on its premises. (Ibid., Appendix, 28 April 1932, p.1.)
122. *Kharbinskii komitet pomoshchi Russkim bezhentsam* [Harbin Committee for Aid to Russian Refugees], Survey, p.6, HIA, Pastuhov Collection, Box 3.
123. Ibid., p.7.
124. Ibid., p.7. (The report suggests that it was difficult to estimate under whose abuse the refugees suffered more: 'the tyranny and violence of the Bolsheviks, or that of the Chinese authorities and soldiers'. [Ibid.]). Reports on specific incidents involving the seizure of refugees' property by Chinese soldiers is to be found in *On the Condition of Russian Emigrants in Northern Manchuria*, Submission to the Lytton Commission, 6 May 1932, No. 1850, Pastuhov Collection, Box 3, Hoover Institution Archives.
125. Ibid.
126. Patrikeeff, Interview, September 1975.
127. Patrikeeff, Interview, June 1986.
128. *Kharbinskii komitet pomoshchi*, op. cit., p.8, HIA. Regarding the forced repatriation of Russians, one case, that of General K.M. Aslamov, especially stands out: the man in question was returned to the Soviet Union on the pretext of bearing an expired passport (*On the Condition of Russian Emigrants in Northern Manchuria*, Submission to the Lytton Commission, 6 May 1932, No. 1850, HIA, Pastuhov Collection, Box 3.)
129. *Kharbinskii komitet pomoshchi*, op. cit., p.8.
130. Atrocities are focused upon by Tang, op. cit., pp.226–7. V.I. Ivachev, the head of the Russian emigrants' group at *Trekhrech'e*, reported on the excesses and explicit cruelty of both Soviet and Chinese forces. (*On the Condition of Russian Emigrants*, op. cit.)
131. Items seized by the local authorities included boats and steamers belonging to private individuals and the CER, a local telephone company, premises of the Museum of OIMK (*Organizatsiia izuchennie Manchzhurskago kraia* [Organisation for the Study of the Manchurian Region], a Russian think-tank engaged in social, economic and historical research) and even the Russian Red Cross. 'All had been arbitrarily seized by former representatives of local authorities,' a report stated, with there being little chance of their return, despite strenuous protests and repeated requests (*On the Condition of Russian Emigrants*, op. cit.)
132. The evolution of full control, which this in effect appeared to be, took various forms. The *KhkpRb* recommended to Chinese authorities as early as December 1929 that suitable plots of land be transferred to displaced refugees in order that the latter might be able to 'freely engage' in hunting, forestry, fishing, mining etc. Its efforts, however, were fruitless. (Survey of the activities of the *Kharbinskii komitet pomoshchi Russkim bezhentsam*, n.d. [1931?], Pastuhov Collection, Box 3, HIA.) The same organisation went on to list a large number

of steps that Chinese authorities had taken in order to inhibit Russian economic activity in the region. These ranged from restrictions on freedom of movement (the issuing of a local passport depended on Russians having photographs taken by a *designated* photographer, with only one being made available in each area to *all* Russians), to the prohibition of new enterprises in the provinces (permission to open power-stations, for example, was consistently refused because these might upset the sovereignty of the region, despite the fact, as the *KhkpRb* points out, that a monopoly on electricity production did not exist, nor were there municipal restrictions of this). Ibid., *Economic Situation*, Appendix 1.

133. Survey of the activities of the *Kharbinskii komitet pomoshchi Russkim bezhentsam*, n.d. (1931?), HIA, Pastuhov Collection, Box 3.
134. Vespa, op. cit., p.25.
135. I. Wallerstein 'The Rise and Future Demise of the World Capitalist System: Concepts for Comparative Analysis' in Wallerstein (ed.) *The Capitalist World-Economy*, Cambridge, 1979, p.25.
136. In *World Development*, vol. 6 (1978), pp.925–36
137. Ibid. p.925.
138. Confusion concerning the nature of the relationship between China and Manchuria, as well as the *stage* of development each had achieved, is evident in early Soviet work on the subject. See *inter alia* V. Avarin's *Imperializm i Man'chzhuriia: etapy imperialisticheskoi bor'by za Manchzhuriiu*, Moscow, 1931(?) and his 'K voprosu o klassovoi strukture Manchzhurskoi derevni' in *Problemy Kitaia*, 1933, No.12, pp.148–202.
139. Williams, op. cit., p.928.
140. For a full discussion of the ideological and conceptual problems faced by the Soviet Union at this time, see Richard B. Day, *The 'Crisis' and the 'Crash': Soviet Studies of the West (1917–1939)*, London, 1981 (especially chs 1 and 2).

# 7 Decline into Oblivion, 1930–31

1. 'Kto otvetstvenen za razryv?' translated from *Weekly Review*, 25 January 1930 (GARF, Fond 5878, No.2, Khr.173.). It was in the foreign powers' interests to support the Soviet Union's position with regard to the seizure of the railway. Indeed, as the author of this article puts it, many of the powers with interests in the country would have wanted Soviet Russia '…to teach China in such a way' as to force it to forget about the renunciation of extraterritorial and navigation rights. 'Many hoped, in fact,' the author went on, 'that a full war might be declared, which would lead to the complete defeat of China and [bring with it] political changes in Russia, which, in turn, would place the latter amongst the ranks of the imperialist powers once again'. (Ibid.) In 'O vosstanovlenii Sovetskogo vlianiia v S. Man'chzhurii', *China Weekly Review*, 11 January 1930, No.6, its author reports that a variety of nationalities were used in China alone to disseminate information on the Soviet side of the conflict (in Manchuria, the article observes, Japanese, English and Korean agents were employed, whilst in Central and Southern China Americans and Germans were used). [GARF, Fond 5878, No.1, Khr.173.]
2. Feng, who had once been in alliance with Chang Tso-lin, quarrelled with the latter in 1926, moving closer to the Soviet Union in the process. Borodin, in an

190  Notes

interview with a Danish journalist in Moscow in early 1928, described the General as '...a genius, but [one who] manages an asylum for beggars'. (*South China Morning Post*, 7 March 1928.) The Sino-Soviet conflict, according to one interpretation, had allowed Chiang Kai-shek to discredit some of his political foes, including Feng himself. ('Kto otvetstvenen za razryv?' op. cit.)
3. 'Otnosheniia mezhdu Kitaem i Sovetskoi Rossiei vstupaiut v novuiu fazu', summary translated from *China Weekly Review*, 3 May 1930, No.10. (GARF, Fond 5878, No.2, Khr.173.)
4. Ibid.
5. Ibid.
6. Ibid.
7. Ibid.
8. Ibid.
9. Discussed at length in Chapter 2.
10. The re-establishing of Soviet influence in Manchuria, the tightening of the hold over the Mongols and the securing of the borders with Northwest China (the Sinkiang region) had begun to resemble a most formidable front, bound together by a railway system that ran along, and linked, this complex series of borders. So formidable did this front appear that Kinney, in one of his regular reports, argued that '[t]he railway striking out from the Trans-Siberian Railway to Tashkent, following closely the Sino-Russian border line along Sinkiang, offers a tremendously important base for the extension of Soviet influence over the rich provinces of Western China, and many competent observers believe that these may follow in the way of Outer Mongolia'. (H.W. Kinney, Confidential Report, Dairen, 27 April 1931, p.1, Pastuhov Collection, Box 21, HIA.)
11. 'Kto otvetstvenen za razryv?', *Weekly Review*, 25 January 1930. (GARF, Fond 5878, No.2, Khr.173.)
12. Ibid.
13. 'O vosstanovlenii Sovetskogo vlianiia v S. Man'chzhurii', *China Weekly Review*, 11 January 1930, No.6. (GARF, Fond 5878, No.1, Khr.173.)
14. The *Weekly Review* of 25 January 1930 argues that the broad assistance supplied by the Japanese was '... for their own reasons, connected with their position in South Manchuria'. (GARF, Fond 5878, No.2, Khr.173.)
15. 'Kto otvetstvenen za razryv?', op. cit. By mid-1931, there were thought to be anywhere between 750 000 and 'well over a million' Koreans living in Manchuria, many of them in the border regions (including the older settlements in the Chientao district near the Korean border) and '... included political malcontents, as well as undesirable elements which found that well policed Korea did not offer the same scope for illegal activities as did Manchuria where banditry has become almost a recognized occupation in many regions'. (H.W. Kinney, Confidential Report, Mukden, 10 August 1931, pp.1–2, HIA, Pastuhov Collection, Box 21.)
16. 'O vosstanovlenii Sovetskogo vlianiia v S. Man'chzhurii', *China Weekly Review*, 11 January 1930, No.6 (GARF, Fond 5878, No.1, Khr.173.)
17. See U.S. Army, Williams (ed.), *15th Infantry Annual*, op. cit., p.86, *passim*.
18. According to one contemporary, whose family had close relations with the two Changs, the elder Marshal was '...a very impressive man, and much admired – unlike his successor Chang Hsüeh-liang'. (B. Skidelsky, Interview, London, 6 April 1981.)
19. Kinney, in one of his intelligence reports to the United States Government in late 1931, painted a bleak picture of the situation faced by the Japanese in the wake

of Chang Tso-lin's assassination. By 1930/31, the cases of banditry along the SMR line in Southern Manchuria were rising steeply (258 cases over virtually the entire spread of the rail network in 1930, rising by over 20 per cent by the mid-1931), as were instances of sabotage of the railway line (59 by late September 1931). And while his report suggests a maximum of restraint being exercised by Japanese troops and authorities in Manchuria, this appeared to have in itself been testing the patience of the Japanese public and, more importantly, the increasingly hardline right-wing elements in the Japanese political system. (H.W. Kinney, Confidential Report, Mukden, 25 September 1925, pp.2–3, HIA, Pastuhov Collection, Box 21.) Although Kinney attributed the increasing lawlessness to the change in generation between the older, more conservative leaders under Chang Tso-lin and the younger men under Chang Hsüeh-liang, with their 'fierce hatred of Japan' (Ibid. p.1), it is difficult to imagine that at least part of the reason was not the loss of control over the middle- to high-strata of the Chinese leadership by a less than impressive young Marshal's leadership.

20. By September 1931, bombs had been thrown at the Bank of Korea, Japanese Consulate-General, the house of the resident Japanese military officer, the office of a Japanese newspaper and other Japanese buildings in Harbin. Although, as Kinney observes, '[t]his was inexpert work, and no great damage was done,' the attacks resulted in calls from Harbin's Japanese residents for Japanese troops to be sent in to deal with their situation. (Kinney, Confidential Report, Mukden, 25 September 1925, op. cit., p.5) Any positive response to such a request would have, quite naturally, placed the Soviet Union's own interests in Harbin on guard and given rise to increased tension between the Japan and the Soviet Union. The Japanese would, no doubt, have been keenly aware of the view circulating at the time – although perhaps one that was quite misguided (see below) – that while the Chinese may have feared the Soviet Russians, they did not necessarily hate them. (Ibid.)

21. Kinney reports that Harbin burglaries and robberies 'had increased considerably'. Attacks by armed bandits, he continues, '...often [involving] murder, have become distressingly common and even the main streets are no longer considered safe at night'. Well-armed and large bands of so-called 'Partisans' (made up of Russian *émigrés*) had also begun to appear on the streets of Harbin. (H.W. Kinney, Confidential Report, Dairen, 27 April 1931, p.10, HIA, Pastuhov Collection, Box 21.)

22. Kinney in his report of 27 April 1931, for example, concludes that '...the time may not be so very far off when Soviet Russia will be by far the predominating Power in China, both commercially and politically'. (H.W. Kinney, Confidential Report, Dairen, 27 April 1931, p.1, HIA, Pastuhov Collection, Box 21.) Kinney also cites Chinese press reports concerning Soviet troop concentrations developing on the Soviet–Manchurian border and the expansion of 'the Soviet military establishment' in Siberia. (Ibid., p.6.)

23. Japanese authorities in Southern Manchuria, even if they wished to act more forcefully against the steady stream of seemingly provocative acts perpetrated by the Chinese military, would have found themselves in a considerable dilemma. The indications from Japan itself suggested that attitudes there were on the verge of shifting steadily rightward, in fact in the direction of the view that Japan should no longer make measured responses to such provocative acts, but take stronger action more in line with its status as a 'great power'; a view encouraged by the Japanese population of Manchuria itself. (See H.W. Kinney,

Confidential Report, Mukden, 25 September 1931, pp.1–2, HIA, Pastuhov Collection, Box 21.) On the other hand, any action of a forceful nature that was taken against the Chinese soldiery would be repaid with interest through the anti-Japanese propaganda which would be generated as a result.
24. In this period, Chang Hsüeh-liang, although with markedly less skill or success than his father, attempted to play a complicated political game with his twin 'overseers'. Despite the fact that his position was very much beholden to his Japanese allies, Chang began to show signs of ' ... sacrific[ing] Manchuria's interests for the sake of the *beaux yeux* of General Chiang Kai-shek'. (Edwin Haward 'The Manchurian Medley', Shanghai: 1931, p.21, Pastuhov Collection, HIA, Box 21. Kinney too observes that KMT officials had begun to move their 'friendship' northward. [H.W. Kinney, Confidential Report, op. cit., 27 April 1931, p.13]) On the other hand, as Kinney notes in his report of September 1931, Chang also gives the impression that he is seeking to re-establish friendly relations with the Soviet Union in order, seemingly, to enlist the latter's support against the Japanese. (H.W. Kinney, Confidential Report, Mukden, 25 September 1931, p.6, HIA, Pastuhov Collection, Box 21.)
25. V. Bratskii 'Kitaiskaia Vostochnaia Zheleznaia Doroga', *Vol'naia Sibir*, n.d. (1931?) (GARF, Fond 5869, No.1, Khr. No.8, p.7.)
26. See H.W. Kinney, Confidential Report, Dairen, 27 April 1931, p.5, HIA, Pastuhov Collection, Box 21. (Russians with Chinese passports had been discharged in spite of great length of experience or unquestioned skills, as were Russians holding Soviet passports. Ibid.)
27. Gorbatenko considered that the development of Japanese commercial interests in Northern Manchuria, and notably Harbin, began in earnest as early as 1924, the year in which Japanese banks first provided mortgages on land in the area. (HIA, Pastuhov Collection, Box 8, p.2.). This may have been the case, but they started from a very low level. Out of more than 50 bean oil mills in Harbin in that year, for instance, only three belonged to the Japanese. (K. Adachi, *Manchuria: A Survey*, New York, 1925, p.71.) Furthermore, competition within Harbin itself was still very much between Russian and Chinese entrepreneurs, with the latter steadily gaining the upper hand in the wake of the political changes in Russia. (Ibid.) By 1932 Japanese investment in commercial activities in Northern Manchuria had reached 60 000 000 yen (compared with the Soviet Union's 59 000 000 yen). Japanese bank capital there was by then 25 000 000 yen, which outstripped the Soviet Union's (15 000 000 yen) and that of all other nationalities (a total of 20 000 000 yen). [A. 'Inostrannye investitsii v Sev. Man'chzhurii', *VM* 1932, No.1, p.106.] Equally telling of the shift in balance between the Soviet Union and Japan were the trade figures in the post-crisis period. In 1929 itself, Soviet figures were 90 per cent of those that Russia achieved in 1913, whilst comparable figures for Japanese trade showed a 280 per cent rise over those of 1913. (I.D. & A.P., 'Vneshniaia torgovlia Man'chzhurii I ee mesto v torgovle Kitaia', *VM*, 1931, No.5, p.35.). For a survey of the companies that Japan created and heavily invested in by 1940, see *Special Companies in Manchukuo: Their Mission and Activities*, Hsinking(?), 1940. Total Japanese investment in Manchukuo for the years 1932–36 was more than 1 165 000 000 yen, plus a further 1 067 000 000 yen ' ... to cover the expenses of the Manchurian Incident and its aftermath'. (*Manchurian Economic Review*, Harbin, 1 November 1937, from HSBC Archives, H.180.6.)
28. Bratskii, op. cit.

29. Bratskii reported that the new forms of Chinese/Japanese competition had brought a '...very bad year' for the October–June 1930/31 export season, with about a million tons in cereal exports from Northern Manchuria finding their way from the CER/Ussuri lines, and their port of Vladivostok, to the ports of Dairen, Hankow and Tsingtao (all serviced by Chinese and/or Japanese freight facilities). [Ibid., p.7.]
30. Jorgenson, a Harbin-based merchant (he was head of the East Asiatic Company) and the Danish Consul at Harbin, in an interview with the Lytton Commission in 1932 confirmed the squeeze being exerted on the CER in the aftermath of the events in 1929, but added that Japanese interests in Northern Manchuria were making life very uncomfortable for foreign business as a whole in Harbin. (Interview, Harbin, 13 May 1932, HIA, Pastuhov Collection, Box 12.)
31. The links between petty Russian officials and the bands of the *Hunghutze* (discussed in Chapter 4) is a case in point. The Japanese, as it was argued, were to have little success in creating any links whatsoever with the bandits. It should be added, however, that other foreigners also found it difficult to create the necessary conditions for their commercial activities to function smoothly beyond the railway zones themselves (the case of BAT's activities in the region, as recounted by Zanozin, is one such example).
32. Extraterritoriality was a principle whereby foreigners who lived in China, and whose governments subscribed to the treaty system, enjoyed the privilege of not being subject to Chinese law, but tried or sued in their own consular courts and according to their own bodies of law. It is important to note too that even when the Soviet Union established some rights and elements of protection from Chinese law and intrusion into its affairs, these were far short of the comprehensive scheme of political and legal shelter possessed by other foreigners. Moreover, while the Soviet Union would, clearly, act in defence of its own full citizens, it would be far more reluctant – if at all interested, in fact – in looking after its second-class passport holders and, even more to the point, Russian *émigrés*. The latter, as a result, were often forced to live by their wits. Hapless *émigrés* who fell into the hands of corrupt members of the Chinese police force could be arrested and held without being charged until 'squeeze' was paid. It was said that the head of the Harbin force would sell 'White' Russians to Soviet authorities for five local dollars (League of Nations Commission of Enquiry, Interview with Mr Gorbatenko, Harbin, 13 May 1932, op. cit., p.3.). Fear of arbitrary behaviour on the part of local authorities gave rise – among Harbin Russians who could afford it – to the phenomenon of '"near" Americans, "near" Italians, "near" English, "near" French, and "near" Irishmen'. Russian children were sent to 'adopted' countries for education and, coincidentally, the securing of nationality too. The children would then return to Manchuria, register with the local consulate and, finally, see their parents' property signed over to them. Family and property would then be afforded the rudiments of extraterritoriality. (C.C. Wang, 'The Dispute between Russia and China', n.p., n.d.(1930?), pp.7–8, HIA, S.K. Hornbeck Collection, Box 101.)
33. Letter from Baron Ungern to General Lu Chang-Kuu, Urga, 15 February 1921, in *Letters Captured from Baron Ungern in Mongolia*, op. cit., pp.13–14. (Lu was Commander of the Asiatic Cavalry Division.)
34. Baron Ungern to General Lu Chang-Kuu, Urga, 2 March 1921, No.489, ibid., p.11.
35. Ibid., p.12.

194  Notes

36. Fujisawa Chikao, 'Manchukuo and a Renaissance of the Oriental Political Philosophy', n.d. (1931?), p.23, HIA, Pastuhov Collection, Box 20.
37. Ibid., p.25.
38. Von Ungern Sternberg's closeness to his adopted cultural setting was reflected in his language, dress, style of life and, importantly, the fact that he was married to a Chinese (Iuzefovich, op. cit., p.236). Borodin's milieu was very different. His closest friend and confidant in the KMT and Republican Government was Eugene Chen, who himself could not speak Chinese (he was of Cantonese descent, but born in Trinidad and educated in Britain, moving to China only in 1912) and showed decidedly Western habits. (Chen, op. cit., p.99. Elsewhere in his memoirs, his son observes that '[Eugene Chen's] chef always served an excellent European-style dinner, for my father never ate Chinese food'. Ibid., p.105.)
39. *Rossiiskaia emigratsiia – Velikaia Man'chzhurskaia Imperiia*, Harbin, n.d. (1942?), p.321.
40. Ibid., p.324.
41. These codes were reinforced by the activities of individuals such as Valentin Vasil'evich Ponomarev, originally from the Perm Guberniia who first reached Harbin in 1922. There, he completed a degree with the *Iuridicheskii Fakul'tet* there, following which he served for a time as inspector of the *Pervoe Kharbinskoe Russkoe real'noe uchilishche*, before becoming the Director of the charitable organisation of *Russkii Dom* (which ran a number of churches, orphanages and schools in Northern Manchuria). In the early 1940s, the principles and moral codes he espoused found a published form, thanks to the help of his editor/publisher K.V. Rodzaevsky, the head of the First Section of the Bureau, and the Chief of the Fascist Party of Harbin. The publication, *Pravila dlia vospitannikov* (Harbin, 1942), contains three main sections: the Russian hymn, rules governing discipline, education and the proper socialisation of children, and a paean to *Gosudar' Naslednik Tsarevich*. Similar functions (although nowhere near the extremism displayed by the views of individuals such as Ponomarev) appear to have been served, ironically, by the many national associations and groups that were based in Harbin (such as those of the Armenians, Georgians, Tatars, Poles, Lithuanians, Latvians and Estonians). As one former resident of the city observed of a visit of some Harbin Russians to the house of a non-Russian Harbinite in Sydney: 'how pleasant it was to hear his words: "we are all from the one town of Harbin, with its unifying Russian culture'. (S.I.Z., 'Natsional'nye gruppy v Kharbine', *Politekhnik*, 1979, No.10, p.243.)
42. *Rossiiskaia emigratsiia*, op. cit., p.301.
43. For a depiction of life in Harbin under the Japanese, see Vespa, op. cit. The Japanese authorities in Manchuria placed great emphasis on the Bureau in the efforts to unify and pacify the Russian population. Under the control of the Japanese, the Bureau was given the opportunity to broadcast on Manchurian airwaves for propaganda purposes. (V.G. Savchik, Interview, Sydney, 14 February 1981. Savchik remembers that the broadcasts were in the form of daily half-hour slots.) One Russian commentator put the situation in the Japanese period in the following succinct way: 'The Japanese organized a totalitarian state in Manchuria without the totalitarian idea…'. (T. Butov, *Manchuria: 1945–1950*, n.p., n.d. (1960?), p.6. [Columbia University Library].)
44. With the Main Bureau of Russian Emigrants' Affairs (as the bureau was formally known) as the political hub, a large number of associations and unions were formed after 1934 (for example: the Union of Bakery Owners [1934]; Association

of 'Russian Transport' [1935]; Association of Restaurant Owners [1937]; Union of Confectionery-Chocolate Factories [1940]; Association of Dairy Firms [1940]), *Velikaia Man'chzhurskaia Imperiia*, op. cit., pp.301–4.

45. Examples of these include: the Association for Aid to Invalids [1919] (a Union of Russian Military Invalids was created under Manchukuo authority to complement it); a Russian House (*Russkii Dom*) [1920 – its characteristics are discussed above]; *Dom Miloserdiia* (House of Mercy). More politically orientated organisations included a Union of Soldiers and Union of Cossacks; *Kruzhok port-arturtsev* (Circle of Port-Arthurites) [1920]; the Refugee Committee [1920]; and the Youth Organisation. *Velikaia Man'chzhurskaia Imperiia*, op. cit., pp.304–11.

46. The Asano Brigade was a full military force (formed in the early part of 1938) made up of Russians who enlisted to engage in armed struggle against the Comintern, as well as to defend Manchukuo, and its Russian community, against attack by foes of Japan. In the closing stages of the war with Japan, many of the Russian volunteers were marched out of Harbin in their units and 'disposed' of (the majority either shot or bayonetted) for fear that they might switch sides. So complete was the loyalty and the trust that these men placed in their Japanese commanders that the victims offered no resistance to their Japanese executioners. (Patrikeeff, Interview, Sydney, February 1981. The latter described how his young brother-in-law was marched away by only a handful of armed Japanese regulars; a number small enough for the Asano-ites to have successfully overwhelmed.) For a brief history of the Asano Brigade, see J.J. Stephan *The Russian Fascists: Tragedy and Farce in Exile, 1925–1945*, New York., 1978, pp.196–9.

47. The new political order encouraged activities of the Armenian, Georgian, Turko-Tatar and Ukrainian National Associations, as well as the Jewish community's organisations. All were to enjoy freedom of worship and cultural practices. *Velikaia Man'chzhurskaia Imperiia*, Harbin, op. cit., pp.312–20. (See also above, note 41.)

48. Interestingly, the Manchurian community was able to preserve even the language of the old Russia (Manchurian Russians to this day use the word *krestaslovitsa* for 'crossword puzzle' rather than the anglicised – and generally accepted – *krossvord*; just one of a number of examples of the creative use of the Russian mind rather than the simpler process of 'borrowing').

49. The economy's share of the national budget went up from 2 800.4 million roubles in the fourth quarter of 1930, to 16 506.8 million roubles in 1931. In 1932, the year the negotiations over the future of the CER were first broached, this figure had grown to 24 781.6 million roubles. (R.A. Clarke, *Soviet Economic Facts 1917–1970*, London, 1972, p.33.)

50. In the first year of the Five-Year Plan, currency emission had increased by a third. In the fist eleven months of the second year of the Plan, it had risen by a further 80 per cent (i.e. 638 million and 1762 million roubles respectively). From October 1928 to September 1930, the Soviet currency had been multiplied by 2.5 times. Despite these sharp rises, the Soviet Union asserted that it still had 'firm cover' for the rouble (that is, foreign currency reserves and gold covering at least 25 per cent. of emission) [H.R. Knickerbocker, *The Soviet Five Year Plan and its Effect on World Trade*, London., 1931, p.228]. Such an assertion, of course, appeared less and less credible in international financial circles; a problem that, in turn, had severe implications for the Soviet Union's ability to maintain its considerable levels imports from the outside world (between 1923 and

mid-1930, Soviet imports from the United States alone had amounted to $US518 million, while sales to America were only $147 million [Ibid., p.244]). In late 1930, the Soviet Union had only 47.252 million Roubles in foreign exchange, and needed to produce at least $US50 million in gold *per annum* in order to maintain suitable backing for its currency (to give the reader a sense of scale in this last respect – the latter figure was $2 million more than the entire gold production of the United States [including Alaska] for 1928). [Ibid, pp.229–30.]
51. For a detailed discussion of this question with respect to exports of Soviet grain, see Knickerbocker, op. cit., pp.194–201. Given the sensitivity of the world market due to the onset of economic depression, it is perhaps fitting that the author should conclude his discussion by writing: '[n]ecessity apparently is the mother of dumping, in the "bourgeois" as well as the Communist world'. (Ibid. p.201) In building the edifice of the Planned Economy, the Soviet Union's sense of urgency in building up its exports would doubtless have easily matched that of the depressed economies of the capitalist world in seeking outlets for their respective output.
52. From a high point of 3219 million roubles in exports and 3690 million roubles in imports in 1929, the Soviet Union's dealings with the international economy had declined to 1.458 million and 810 million respectively by 1934, and dipped further still to 462 million and 745 million in 1939. (Clarke, op. cit., p.37)
53. Narkomindel statement on an interview between the Japanese Ambassador and the Vice-Commissar for Foreign Affairs for Manchuria, 29 February 1932, reproduced in J. Degras (ed.) *Soviet Documents on Foreign Policy, Volume II, 1925–1932*, Oxford, 1952, pp.524–6.
54. Tass, 11 December 1932, published in Soviet Union Review, January 1933 & cited in Degras, op. cit., pp.549–50.
55. The dilemma that the Soviet Union faced in dealing with the problem of what to do with the CER became clear when, in December 1931, there were rumours that the southern part of the railway had been offered to Japan; reports denied by the Soviet News Agency Tass (ibid., p.522), but which make some sense in terms of what the Soviet Union had to do resolve the knotty problem it faced in Manchuria.
56. For a full account of the sale of the CER, see Lensen, op. cit., chs 7–10; Bratskii, op. cit., pp.4–18.
57. A.W. Serapinin 'Kak Iuzhno-Man'chzhurskaia zheleznaia doroga rasplachivaetsia s kreditorami byvshei Kitaiskoi Vostochnoi zheleznoi dorogi', Tientsin, letter to P.N. Miliukov, 29 June 1937, p.4, GARF, Fond 6845, No.1, Khr. No.226.
58. Ibid., pp.13–14.
59. Ibid., p.1.
60. From reports published in *Manchuria Daily News*, Dairen (14.3.35), the figure presented at the talks was 10 million gold roubles, while the actual sum was 100 million gold roubles (the mistake was later attributed to 'careless bookkeeping' by the Soviet authorities. Ibid., p.5.)
61. *Manchuria Daily News*, Dairen (the edition for 8 March 1935) had already indicated that there was something wrong, when it was reported that the Soviet Union had earmarked only 5 691 811.18 gold roubles for payment to 'private parties' (of these, the MDN said, almost all were either 'dead souls' or institutions and businesses that no longer existed. Ibid.).
62. Ibid., pp.6–9.

63. By the end of June 1933, the Soviet Union had offered the railway to the Japanese for 250 000 000 gold roubles, while the latter had made a counter-offer of 20 000 000. After the Soviet authorities had reduced their 200 000 000, the Manchukuo government stepped in to 'assist' the bargaining process by launching a spate of arrests of Soviet citizens employed by the CER. These brought the talks to an abrupt halt. In February 1934 the talks were resumed, with the revised Soviet figure being 67 500 000 gold roubles. This offer was refused by Japanese representatives to the talks. Eventually, a final compromise figure of a little over 60 000 000 gold roubles was arrived at, but even this was to include 10 000 000 gold roubles to be distributed by the Soviet Union as severance pay to its CER employees. (Balakshin, op. cit., Vol. II, pp.167–8.) A curiosity here – and something that indicates how unworldly the operation of the railway had become – was that the gold rouble was a measure used by the railway itself, existing nowhere else. Ironically, its use for the calculation of freight rates had helped to scare away a considerable amount of business from the railway in years past. (Bratskii, op. cit., p.3.)
64. See above for discussion on CER debts.
65. Serapinin, op. cit., p.14. (There were over 1000 legal actions in a variety of stages of progress inherited by the Manchukuo government. [Ibid. p.4])
66. Serapinin suggests that payments and settlements in the Soviet period (i.e. after 3 September 1924, when Soviet participation was formally incorporated into the CER management) were managed on the basis of a political calculation regarding their benefits to the Soviet Union. (Ibid., p.3.)
67. Legal procedures were inordinately protracted and frustrating, even for those whose claims were open-and-shut (for example, suppliers of coal, firewood, timber and other uncontroversial goods and services). Part of the problem here was that, with Mukden's and Moscow's agreement, the courts hearing these cases had been provided by the CER with a 500 000 Harbin-dollar subvention towards their operating costs! (Ibid., p.3) Actions which had reached the High Court level, and won there, would – at the behest of the Soviet lawyers for the CER – be reviewed by the courts, delaying any settlement even more. Ultimately, even after these reviews had been completed, a successful litigant would be directed to the CER for a bargaining session in which discounts and deferred payments might be arranged. (Ibid.).
68. After tenacious agitation by the creditors, the Manchukuo authorities created a 'Bureau for the Settlement of Old Business Affairs of the NMR/CER' at Harbin (into this bureau were merged the Liquidation/Settlement and Juridical Departments, as well as the CER Archives). After initial optimism at this move, disappointment set in when it was discovered that its job was not to settle outstanding debts, but rather to seek easy, and cheap, ways of disposing of claims against the CER. One of the first acts of the Bureau was for its head, General Arita, to respond to even the most uncontroversial of claims a stock note: 'The sum owed to you is not contained in the list of debts of the railway, as supplied by the Soviets in advance of the transfer of its rights. As a result, unfortunately, a payment cannot be made'. Any further contact from creditors was met by a bargaining process in which NMR clerks would attempt to discount the debts by 20–50 per cent , and even then only if these were sums did not exceed 2000–3000 *gobi* (a small sum in the new Manchukuo currency). Amounts in excess of this sum were to remain suspended indefinitely. (Ibid., pp.18–20.) The methods employed by the Bureau elicited a uniform view from

Harbin newspapers, ranging from the popular *Zaria* (Dawn) to the more limited readership of the Fascist *Nash Put'* (Our Path), as those of a '*moshennika-kommersanta*' [businessman-cheat]. (Ibid., p.20.)
69. Ibid., p.15. He notes that, as the new administration spoke nor read any Russian, all pre-23.3.35 affairs were for a time treated '... as if they did not exist'. (Ibid., p.17.)
70. Ibid., pp.16–17.
71. The inactivity of the CER with respect to its running debts was in itself sufficient to affect the work of over 1000 firms – most of them Russian – on Harbin's financial market. (Ibid., p.18.) In addition, the economic downturn resulting from the confluence of political and economic crisis after 1929 meant that many smaller Russian firms had gone out of business altogether. (In Hailar, by mid-1930 the number of firms had been reduced by 50–60 per cent. *EB*, No.14, pp.14–15.)
72. The Skidelsky business (known as *nasledniki L.S. Skidelskogo*) was established by the Skidelsky Snr (he died in 1916), the son of a *kupets* (merchant), who came from European Russia to Eastern Siberia shortly before the construction of the Trans-Siberian Railway. He moved there originally to construct roads, but soon ran into trouble with his workers, who deserted him. Skidelsky approached the Governor of the province and the latter provided him with convicts (*katorzhniki*) to complete the initial projects. The company quickly expanded, and especially so with the completion of the Trans-Siberian and Chinese Eastern Railways. By the time of the Revolutions of 1917, the family business was involved in a broad spectrum of commercial activities, ranging from timber concessions, to a plywood factory outside of Vladivostok and ownership of the Grand Hotel in that city. By 1918, the Skidelsky enterprises were worth an estimated $200 000 000. With the rise of the Bolsheviks in Russia, the company had already moved part of its operations to Manchuria (the company was by then run by the elder Skidelsky's four sons, of whom Solomon was the head of the Manchurian business, while Simon was in charge of the Vladivostok operation. Of the other two brothers, one died early, and the other, Moses, declined to take part in the active running of the business. After the Skidelskys were forced out of Russia, the business became consolidated under Solomon's headship). (Boris Skidelsky, Interview, London, 6April 1981.)
73. The origins of the Skidelsky involvement in these areas is important to our understanding of the methods that Russian commerce employed in the region. The Manchurian concessions were secured by Solomon Skidelsky through his love of poker, a passion he shared with Marshal Chang Tso-lin. Solomon at an early stage had seen this mutual interest as a way of broaching the subject with the Marshal, but in preparation for the posing of this request, Solomon had to play and lose to the latter on 'numerous occasions'. At the final session, Solomon posed the question, and handed Chang a draft contract prepared in Chinese. The Marshal agreed in principle, but demanded that a number of clauses be altered. Solomon, together with his advisers and lawyers, sat up all night revising – again, in Chinese – the unsuitable terms. The final agreement took the form of a 50/50 participation, with the Mukden authorities providing the land, whilst the Skidelsky family was to supply the necessary finances for its exploitation. (Skidelsky, Interview, April 1981.) This need for capital proved to be of crucial importance, as the Chinese authorities consistently refused to provide any financial assistance to the joint venture. But as important was the establishment of the

links with the CER. Boris Skidelsky, Solomon's son, recounted how informal – and vulnerable – the nature of doing business was amongst the Russians of Northern Manchuria. 'A business contract,' he explained, 'might be as simple as: "How much for a *pood* of coal?" "Nine dollars" would come the reply, "Alright, begin supplying"'. This was, Skidelsky noted, precisely the form of 'contract' that his father had with General Khorvat for the supply of coal to the CER. (Ibid.) When Ostroumoff replaced Khorvat as the head of the CER, he declared that the price agreed upon by his predecessor was too high, and so terminated the 'contract'. 'Solomon was so incensed,' Skidelsky remembered, 'that he initiated legal proceedings against the railway. By the time the action had ended, it had cost [us] about $1 Million, and had virtually crippled the company, but he won'. (Ibid.) Shortly after the loss of this dispute, Ostroumoff lost his position and emigrated. (Ibid.)
74. The Skidelskys held the Mulin concession on a thirty-year lease (1924–54). It was a rich vein of coal, producing between 70–90 million tons in all. Unfortunately, it was only one metre thick and difficult to extract. (Skidelsky, Interview, April 1981). The problem of extraction appears to have further contributed to the Skidelskys' financial difficulties.
75. Skidelsky, Interview, April 1981.
76. The collection contained work of all the Russian masters. For some years it was held by the HSBC (as security for the Skidelskys' debt to the bank and, for a time, displayed at Churin's, Harbin's prestigious department store, which itself had been acquired by the bank – see below). It was removed by the Soviet forces when they captured Harbin from the Japanese. (Skidelsky, Interview, April 1981.)
77. The beggar, a Chinese man nicknamed Misha, was one day approached by Simon Skidelsky, who asked him how he was. Misha responded, as always, 'plokho, ochen' plokho' (bad, very bad) and then, after receiving a customary handout, asked why he had not seen Simon in a long time. Simon replied that he was working at the family's office in Pristan', and added politely: 'why don't you come there?' 'What,' retorted Misha, 'all the way to Pristan' for 25¢?' (Skidelsky, Interview, April 1981.) The anecdote is indicative of the easy-going relationship that Russians were able to strike with the Chinese, and at all levels of the social scale.
78. HSBC, S/O Files, Memo, H.O. to Wood, Vladivostok (24.8.22).
79. HSBC, S/O Files, vol. 319, Baker to MacLennan, 31 January 1921). 'Goose' is a pun on Portuguese (i.e. singular: 'Portugoose').
80. In a memo of March 1921, Baker wrote the following to Macintyre at Shanghai: 'I am confidentially informed that they [the CER] had issued Yen 3 million in short term notes up to 8th inst. Of these, the Specie hold Yen 6 lacs, the Russian 4 lacs, the Chinese American Bank of Commerce 7 lacs, Banque Industrielle de Chine (Peking?) 6 lacs, private parties 7 lacs. The latter include S.L. Skidelsky and two or three others. I believe the notes have been discounted with the banks at 15 per cent or higher'. (HSBC, S/O Files, vol. 319, Baker to Macintyre, 17 February 1921.)
81. It is interesting to reflect that even Solomon Skidelsky's move to become the Portuguese Consul at Harbin – referred to so disparagingly in Baker's memo – had a shrewd motive behind it: Solomon, as a result of his elevation to this nonsensical status, was providing himself and his business with some insurance against any drastic turn in the politics of the region.

82. Of particular note in this respect is the reference to the monies owed to the CER by '...certain Allied Governments', an oblique reference to the railway's part in the allied intervention during the Russian Civil War (Similarly, the Bank appears to have been employed as a conduit for the salaries of troops fighting in Siberia at that time; at least partially explaining why it should have kept its Vladivostok office open as late as 1923.)
83. The Russo-Asiatic Bank, founded in 1896 (and renamed the Russo-Chinese Bank in 1905), had been the financial instrument via which the funding of the CER took place. With its headquarters in Paris (much of the initial capital for the project had been raised there), the closure of its operations through insolvency represented a further major blow to the members of Harbin's Russian business community who had their funds lodged with it. An appeal was formally presented to the Lytton Commission in 1932. See Appendix.
84. 'Petition to the Commission of Enquiry of the League of Nations' (from Depositors of the Russo-Asiatic Bank at Harbin), op. cit., HIA, Pastuhov Collection, Box 3.
85. Ibid.
86. Ibid.
87. Boris Skidelsky mentioned that, even after the Japanese had taken control of politics in Harbin in 1932, he himself had carried a revolver when going out, and had a Chinese bodyguard armed with a rifle walk in front of him. (Skidelsky, Interview, April 1981.)
88. I.Ia. Churin & Co. was formed in 1867 by Siberian trader Ivan Iakovlevich Churin, an 'immensely gifted trader, with natural talent, a keen mind, and a warm Russian soul'. The operation, which first started business in Harbin in 1898, quickly spread its retail trade across Manchuria and into China proper, '...carr[ying] out a tremendous amount of work in the introduction of Russian goods and in the establishment of light and heavy industry [throughout Manchuria]'. Later, it diversified its operations into import–export business. (Byvshii Churinets, 'Torgovye i kommercheskie predpriiatiia', *Kharbinskaia Starina*, 1936 Issue, reprinted in *Politekhnik*, 1979, No.10, p.222.) The firm, which employed many Russians, '...in harmonious way built up a well-deserved authority for Russian firms on Chinese soil'. (Ibid.) The company had begun taking loans from HSBC in the latter half of the 1920s, when its business had taken a distinct turn for the worse. (HSBC Archives, Wood to Brent, 20 December 1928). The 1929 crisis drove it deeper and deeper into debt (see HSBC Archives, Correspondence, S/O Files from Harbin, 1928–31, Vols 91, 92.); a situation from which it could not recover. It was taken over by the HSBC in early 1931 (Ibid., Roe to Gillingham, 2 April 1931). Correspondence on V.F. Kovalsky, another firm with a solid reputation in Harbin, indicates that it too was suffering severely from shortages of capital during this period; a situation that the HSBC was reluctant to act upon. (See HSBC Archives, S/O to Harbin, vol. 319, Finance WP/CEH, the H. & S. Bank Ltd, London [10.10.29]; Jones to H.B. Roe, Harbin [11.10.29].)
89. The head of the company, Misha Lopato, eventually went to work for BAT itself. (B. Skidelsky, Interview, London, 6 April 1981.) Boris Skidelsky, who might have taken over the family business, went to work for Caltex and, finally, at the Royal Opera House, Covent Garden.
90. The collapse of the Siberian Co. is an interesting one, but lies beyond the scope of this study. The company's high profile in Manchuria and (until its sudden declaration of insolvency in early 1930) very active business in the bean market

had a two-fold effect on the North Manchurian economy. First, its collapse left an industry that had already been battered by the Sino-Soviet conflict in an even weaker state, with no other local company in a position to take up the slack. Second, the scale of the debts that the Siberian Co. left was to have a considerable impact on the local capital market (HSBC correspondence from March 1930 shows that three banks were left with sizeable 'shortages' in Harbin: the the National City and Chartered Banks, as well as the HSBC itself). The situation was further aggravated when, in May 1930, HSBC and Chartered Bank sold their holdings of 35 000 tons of soya beans (left with them by the bankruptcy of the Siberian Co.) on the London market '... at a considerable sacrifice,' thereby further weakening the Harbin market. (Ibid., vol. 319, Jones to Roe, 19 May 1930.) The combination of factors ensured that the Harbin bean market remained depressed for some 18 months in advance of the international economic depression gripping Northern Manchuria in its full severity.

91. HSBC, S/O Files, vol. 319, Head Office to A.E. Baker, Harbin, 25 January 1921.
92. B. Skidelsky recounted how he discovered that his household's Russian watchman had been reporting to the Bureau of Emigrants, who, in turn, reported to the Japanese authorities. The last, he came to know, kept a full dossier on all foreigners '... down to a party on such-and-such a night in 1935. We learnt to keep our mouths shut, never mentioning anything anti-Japanese or even mildly pro-Soviet. It was, to put it simply, a police state'. (Skidelsky, Interview, April 1981.)

## 8 Manchuria and the Geopolitics of Myth

1. For a detailed treatment of this subject, see my 'Geopolitics of Myth: Interwar Northeast Asia and Images of an Inner Asian Empire' in D. Christian & C. Benjamin (eds), *Realms of the Silk Roads: Ancient and Modern*, Turnhout, 2000.
2. See, for example, the discussion of the thought of Russia's foremost Sinologue V.P. Vasil'ev in A. Malozemoff, *Russian Far Eastern Policy, 1881–1904: With Special Emphasis on the Causes of the Russo-Japanese War*, Berkeley & Los Angeles, 1958, pp.42–3. Vasil'ev, who was active in the late 19th century, depicted Russia's role in the East as that of a 'cultural missionary' (*Kulturträger*), with Russians advancing as 'liberators' of peoples deep in '... internecine strife and impotency.' (Ibid.)
3. H.J. Mackinder, *Democratic Ideals and Reality* (edited & with introduction by A.J. Pierce), New York, 1962, pp.259–60.
4. For an exploration of this theme, see F. Patrikeeff, 'Russian and Soviet Economic Penetration of North-Eastern China, 1895–1933' in J.W. Strong, *Essays on revolutionary Culture and Stalinism*, New York, 1990.
5. Ibid. p.16.
6. For an analysis of this process, see R.K.I. Quested, *Sino-Russian Relations: A Short History*, Sydney, 1984, pp.71–7.
7. The northern, and largest portion, bordering on Russia (including the richest, most densely populated areas of Persia) became the latter's sphere of influence. The southern region (largely barren desert, but containing the strategically important roads to India), on the other hand, became the British 'sphere'. Between these broad and most readily defined regions lay another; a central neutral region (which included the head of the Persian Gulf), that allowed neither side to claim concessions without consultation with other party. Reinforcing this broad delineated 'arrangement' in the 'Great Game' were the

Anglo-Afghan Agreement, governing the border between Afghanistan and British India (the so-called Durand Line) as well as the Anglo-Japanese Treaty of 1902 and the Franco-Japanese Treaty of 1907. (For an engaging account of the 'Great Game,' see P. Hopkirk, *Setting the East Ablaze: Lenin's Dream of an Empire in Asia*, Oxford, 1984.).

8. Interestingly, Hopkirk indicates that his work on the 'Great Game' '... is primarily a story about people' (op. cit., p.5), and the game itself best depicted as a 'secret' or 'shadowy, undeclared' war (ibid., pp.3, 95). The combination creates a sense of players with their moves and counter-moves on a sweeping chess board. The environment associated with it remains opaque for Hopkirk, and the indigenous ideologies unidimensional.
9. A most useful exposition of this point can be found in Black *et al.*, op. cit., pp.10–11. They conclude: 'The key to Inner Asian politics in traditional times was the empire builder. A repeated pattern saw an individual use military prowess to attain leadership of a tribe, and make his tribe the leading group in a confederation that would then conquer sedentary areas.' (p.10).
10. For a vivid depiction of empire formation in the region, see J. Curtin, *The Mongols: A History*, Boston, 1908 (Reprinted Pennsylvania: Combined Books, 1996), pp.62–112; see also Black, op. cit., pp.10–12.
11. For a summary of the sweeping changes brought in by the new emperor Meiji, see M. Montgomery, *Imperialist Japan: The Yen to Dominate*, London, Christopher Helm, 1987, pp.68–9.
12. W.H. Chamberlin, better known for his work on Soviet Russia, presents a compelling, immediate image of the pressures Japan feels at this time in his *Japan Over Asia*, London, Duckworth, 1938, pp.17–26.
13. F. Patrikeeff, 'Prosperity and Collapse: Banking and the Manchurian Economy in the 1920s and 1930s' in F.H.H. King (ed.), *Eastern Banking: Essays in the History of the Hongkong & Shanghai Banking Corporation*, London, Athlone Press, 1983, p.265.
14. Fears of such alliances are evident in Japanese intelligence circles. In an interview held between General Araki (the Japanese Minister of War) and the Lytton Commission of Enquiry in 1932, the former indicated how worried Japanese authorities were in finding that the Manchurian warlord Chang Tso-lin and Kuomintang leader Chiang Kai-shek had created common ground between them, even if this was done to stem the 'red tide' of Communist influence perceived as sweeping through Peking and Canton (Hoover Institution Archives, Pastuhov Collection, Box 29, Folder 3, pp.9–10).
15. Chamberlin, op. cit., represents the shift as one in which the military drove 'liberalism and pacifism into the background' through its actions in Manchuria in 1931, but that this was not the only cause of the militarists gaining decisive advantage, given the 'many unsettled economic disputes with China,' as well as the strengthening relations between the warlord government of Manchuria and central Chinese authorities, and the need to check Soviet 'expansionism' in East Asia (p.26). For a more recent study of the Japanese perspective, see L. Young, *Japan's Total Empire: Manchuria and the Culture of Wartime Imperialism*, Berkeley & London, 1998, pp.3–20.
16. For an incisive discussion of the dilemmas that confronted the Japanese *body politic*, see Chamberlin, op. cit., chs I, II.
17. Recent treatments of the Soviet Union's relations with Mongolia can be found in Elena Boikova', 'Aspects of Soviet-Mongolian Relations, 1929–1939' and Bruce A. Elleman's, 'The Final Consolidation of the USSR's Sphere of Interest in

Outer Mongolia'. (Both in S. Kotkin & B.A. Elleman [eds], *Mongolia in the Twentieth Century: Landlocked Cosmopolitan*, Armonk & London, 1999.]
18. The Japanese garrison of the interventionist forces was by far the largest (some 70 000 men), and was also, coincidentally, the last to leave Russian soil (in October 1922). In the time that it was active in Siberia and the Russian Far East, the Japanese forces appeared to be angling for a more protracted part there. This included its negotiations with the authorities in the Russian Far East, and its financial support for the various 'White' armies and bands. For a discussion of the political web that some of these relations resulted in, see W.S. Graves, *America's Siberian Adventure, 1918–1920*, New York, 1941. In some cases, the Japan not only provided material support for the 'White' armies, but even 'volunteers' for their rank and file (see, for instance, 'On the 26th Anniversary of Ataman G.M. Semenov's Opposition to the Communists' in *Luch Azii*, 1944, p.53).
19. For an account of this complicated episode, see H. Carrére d'Encausse, 'Civil War and New Governments' in E. Allworth (ed.), *Central Asia: A Century of Russian Rule*, New York & London, 1967, pp.224–8.
20. See H.W. Kinney, Confidential Report, Dairen, 27 April 1931, p.1, Hoover Institution Archives, Pastuhov Collection. Box 21 (The place of socialist ideology in the regional equation is an interesting one. It could be said that Communism, both in its Soviet and Chinese incarnations, represented another 'myth' which competed with the heartland, espousing, in the earlier part of the period, what was essentially an advanced, urban-based political credo for application to a largely undeveloped terrain, while Mao Tse-tung's 'Yenan Way' of the late 1930s brought the Communist vision closer to local realities. I am grateful to Greg de Cure for our discussions on this question).
21. For an analysis of the Soviet Union's policies, see F. Patrikeeff 'Russian and Soviet Economic Penetration of Northern China, 1895–1933' in J.W. Strong (ed.), Essays on Revolutionary Culture and Stalinism, Columbus, Ohio, 1990, pp.63–6.
22. By mid-1931, there were thought to be anywhere between 750 000 and 'well over a million' Koreans living in Manchuria, many of them in border regions (including the older settlements in the Chientao district near the Korean border). H.W. Kinney Confidential Report, Mukden, 10 August 1931, pp.1–2, Hoover Institution Archives, Pastuhov Collection, Box 21. For a detailed study of the Korean presence in Manchuria, see Yi Hun-gu, *Korean Immigrants in Manchuria*, Korea, 1931(?).
23. Chamberlin, in his attempt to explain Japan's readiness to justify military and naval aspirations, refers to 'the will of heaven' as being the one which comes with greatest ease (op. cit., p.27).
24. Sun Yat-sen's republicanism arguably represented a departure from the traditionalism of empire, bringing with it many of the characteristics of Western statehood, couched in notions of nationalism and political rebirth. However, under Chiang Kai-shek, more traditional forms of Chinese identity and isolationism resurfaced. In part, these were the result of the brutal nature of the struggle between the Kuomintang and Chinese Communists, in which assertion of 'Chineseness' were placed in bright contrast to the 'internationalism' of the Communists, or for that matter foreigners as a whole. On this last point, see O. & E. Lattimore, *The Making of Modern China*, London, 1945, p.138.
25. Fujisawa Chikao, 'Manchukuo and a Renaissance of the Oriental Political Philosophy', Tokyo, n.d. (1932?), p.23, Hoover Institution Archives, Pastuhov Collection, Box 20 (author's emphases).

26. Fujisawa Chikao, *Japanese and Oriental Political Philosophy*, cited in Chamberlin, op. cit., p.27.
27. A quotation from Major-General Kenji Doihara, one of Japan's leading military diplomats at the time, in an issue of *Dai Asia Shugi* (a journal devoted to the elaboration of Pan-Asian ideas), cited in Chamberlin, op. cit., p.28.
28. For a fascinating account of the inner workings of this logic, see Murakami Hyoe, *Japan: The Years of Trial, 1919–52*, Tokyo, 1982. In some important respects, the influences that shaped the outlook of some of the Japanese military leaders concerned with the region were not dissimilar to those that played a part in developing Baron Ungern-Sternberg's outlook (for a discussion of the latter, see below). Lieutenant Colonel Ishihara Kanji, who is regarded as one of the masterminds of the Japanese seizure of Manchuria built his reputation on his skills as a military strategist, and a strange blend of military philosophy based on his research of Frederick the Great, Napoleon, World War I and on a strong faith in the prophecies of the 13th century Japanese priest Nichiren, the founder of the Nichiren Buddhist sect. (Ibid. pp.31–2). Nichiren sought to suppress other beliefs and practices, depicting himself as the 'pillar of Japan, the eyes of Japan, the Great Ship of Japan' (L.R. Rodd 'Nichiren' in I.P. McGreal [ed.], *Great Thinkers of the Eastern World*, New York, 1995, pp.327, 329)
29. These were on the extreme wing of the Slavophile movement, placing little (if any) emphasis on the notion of Pan-Slavism, instead looking to the Orient as the region most akin to Russian culture. This group, its ideology most fully enunciated by Ukhtomskii, came to feel that Russia's 'historical mission' was to merge with the Orient by incorporating it into the Russian empire. (For a full discussion of this movement, see Malozemoff, *Russian Far Eastern Policy 1881–1904…*, op. cit., pp.41–50).
30. A. Malozemoff, 'The Ideology of Russian Expansion' in G.A. Lensen (ed.), *Russia's Eastward Expansion*, New Jersey, 1964, p.92.
31. Cited in Malozemoff, 'The ideology of Russian Expansion', 1964, p.93.
32. Despite the abundance of literature that speaks of the importance of 'socialist internationalism' in the Soviet Union's dealings with the region (not least, of course, the country's own extensive propaganda on the subject), the reality was somewhat different. Stalin's world view (which dominated much of the period in question), irrespective of internationalist outpourings that came form Moscow, was an explicitly statist one. Attempts to marry the professedly utopian and the visibly pragmatist are depicted in such essays as N.S. Timasheff's anti-Soviet diatribe 'Russian Imperialism or Communist Aggression' [sic] in W. Gurian (ed.), *Soviet Imperialism: Its Origins and Tactics*, Indiana, 1953 (reprinted, Conneticut, Greenwood Press, 1975), pp.17–42.
33. See, for example, 'White Russian Tools of Japan Play Game of China's Ravishers in North' in *China Weekly Review*, LXXXIX, 1939, p.208 (A detailed study of the relations between the Japanese army and 'White' Russian groups in Manchuria is provided by J.A. Smith, *White Russian Emigrants and the Japanese Army in the Far East*, typescript, 1950, HIA).
34. A.J. Beveridge, *The Russian Advance*, New York, 1903, pp.9–10, 16–17, *et seq.*

# Select Bibliography

## Archival material

Canberra, ACT, Australian Archives
  AA, ACT, A458/1, C156/3, Immigration – Russians
  AA, ACT, A981/1, Soviet Union 42, Pt 1
Hong Kong, Hongkong and Shanghai Banking Corporation Archives.
  Vols 90, 91, 319
  S/O K130.18.1 174/7 (25.6.23–22.9.26)
  S/O K130.18.1 174/7 Correspondence (Manchuria)
London, Public Records Office
  FO 371/13891-638
  FO 371/13954-632
  FO 371/13955
  FO 371/14699
  FO 371/14700
Moscow, Gosudarstvennyi arkhiv Rossiiskoi Federatsii (GARF)
  Fond 5869
  Fond 5878
  Fond 6845
Oxford, J. Gibbes Papers
  Chinese Maritime Customs Reports, Lahasusu
  Chinese Maritime Customs Reports, Manchouli
  Assorted clippings
Soviet Documents on Foreign Policy, Vols I & II (ed. by J. Degras),
  Oxford: 1951 & 1952
Stanford, Hoover Institution on War, Revolution and Peace
  Boris Vladimirovich Annenkov Collection
  A. Bogdanov Collection
  Frederick E. Fuhrman Collection
  Liubov' V. Golitsyna Collection
  George C. Guins Collection
  Stanley K. Hornbeck Collection
  Jay C. Huston Collection
  Dmitrii Leonidovich Khorvat Collection
  Anatolii Markov Collection
  Boris I. Nikolaevsky Collection
  Vladimir D. Pastuhov Collection
  Grigorii Semenov Collection
  Ivan I. Serebrennikov Collection
  Jack A. Smith Collection
  Roman F. Ungern-Shternberg Collection
  Vladimir Aleksandrovich Zubets Collection
Washington, Department of State
  Papers relating to the Foreign Relations of the United States, 1929–31

## Interviews

Chang Fu-yun, San Francisco, 1 July 1979
Freeman, Magaret, Boston, 23 May 1979
Gibbes, George, Oxford, 3, 12 September 1980
Grossman, Prof. Gregory, Berkeley, 3 July 1979
'Katai', Mr, Hong Kong, 8 January 1981
Koreneff, Boris, Sydney, 13 March 1981
Levaco, Ben, New York, 1 June 1979
Lutai, Shura, Sydney, 19 February 1995
Malakhoff, Anisa, Oxford, 18–19 September 1981
Pagudin, Aleksei Matveevich, San Francisco, 7 July 1979
Patrikeeff, Petr Nikolaevich, Sydney, September 1975; February 1981; June 1986
Savchik, Vladimir Grigorievich, Sydney, 14 February 1981
Skidelsky, Boris, London, 6 April 1981
Slobodchikoff, Nicholas A., San Francisco, 11 July 1979
Swan, Margerita, London, 9 August 1981
United Nations Refugee Organization, Hong Kong office, Interview with case workers, 15 December 1987
Zanozin, Alexei Petrovich, Sydney, 28 January; 2,5,12 March 1981

## Unpublished papers

Bix, Herbert P., 'Japanese Imperialism and Manchuria, 1890–1931', unpublished thesis, Harvard University, 1972.
Benson, George Stewart, 'Interest of Foreign Powers in Manchuria', unpublished MA thesis, University of Chicago, 1931.
Bresler, B., 'Harbin Jewish Community (1898–1958): Politics, Prosperity, Adversity', Symposium on Jewish Diasporas in China: Comparative and Historical Perspectives, John K. Fairbank Center for East Asian Research, Harvard University, 16–18 August 1992.
Bunting, Helen M., 'Manchuria in International Affairs, 1911–1922', unpublished MA thesis, University of Chicago, 1929.
Butov, Professor T. *Manchuria: 1945–1950*, n.p., n.d. (1960?), Columbia University Library.
Levaco, Ben, 'My 35 Years in the Far East – 1915/50', New York, 1979.
Lustig, Raymond J., '*Tokumu Kikan*: Intelligence Service of the Japanese Army, 1900–1945' unpublished paper, Washington and Southeast Regional Seminar on Japan, February 1979.
*Memorandum on the Plans for the Solution of the Manchurian Problem*, n.p., n.d. [1932?], Columbia University Library.
Pan, S.C.Y., *American Diplomacy Concerning Manchuria*, PhD dissertation, Catholic University of America, 1938.
Savvides, K.H., *Benevolent Imperialists? The United States and the Changing Balance of Power in Eastern Asia, 1882–1900*, Master of International Studies thesis, Sydney University, 1998.

## Serials

The China Weekly Review
Chinese Economic Bulletin
Chinese Economic Journal
Chinese Economic Monthly
Contemporary Japan
Far Eastern Review
The Hankow Herald
Harbin Shimbun
Izvestiia
Japan Advertiser
Jerusalem Post, International Edition
Krasnyi Arkhiv
Manchuria Daily News
Na Putiakh
The North China Herald
The North China Daily News
Novyi Vostok
The Peking Leader
Politekhnik [Sydney]
Problemy Dal'nego Vostoka
Problemy Kitaia
Put' Emigranta
Rubezh
Russkoe Obozrenie
South China Morning Post
Vestnik Azii
Vestnik Man'chzhurii
Vpered

## Secondary sources

A., 'Inostrannye investitsii v Sev. Man'chzhurii', *VM*, 1932, No.4.
Adachi, Kinnosuké, *Manchuria: A Survey*, New York, 1925.
'Agriculture in North Manchuria', *The Chinese Economic Bulletin*, Vol. XV, No.2, 13 July 1929.
Aikhenval'd, A., *O takticheskoi linii Kominterna v Kitae*, Moscow, 1927.
A.K., 'Bor'ba za vlast' v Kitae', *VM*, 1925, Nos 3–4.
Akagi, R.H., *Understanding Manchuria: A Handbook of Facts*, 3rd edn, New York, 1932.
Aldcroft, Derek H., *From Versailles to Wall Street, 1919–1929*, London, 1977.
Allison, A.P., 'Siberian Regionalism in Revolution and Civil War', *Siberica*, 1(1).
'American Recognition of the U.S.S.R.', *The Chinese Affairs*, 1933 (November), Vol. V, 12.
Andorgskii, A.I., 'Puti k razresheniiu tikhookeanskoi problemy', *VM*, 1925, Nos 5–7.
——, *Puti k razresheniiu tikhookeanskoi problemy*, Harbin, 1926.
Anuchin, Vsevolod Aleksandrovich, *Geograficheskie ocherki Man'chzhurii*, Moscow, 1948.
Asakawa, Kanachi, 'Japan in Manchuria', n.p., 1908.
Athearn, R.G., *Union Pacific Country*, Lincoln, 1976.

## 208 Select Bibliography

Avarin, V., 'K voprosu o klassovoi strukture Manchzhurskoi derevni' in *Problemy Kitaia*, 1933, No.12.
——, *Imperializm i Manchzhuriia: etapy imperialisticheskoi bor'by za Manchzhuriiu*, Moscow, 1931(?).
A.V.M., 'Eksport Man'chzhurskikh bobov i ego finansirovanie', *VM*, 1928, No.3.
Avdoshchenkov, A. Ia. 'Osnovnye problemy iapono-man'chzhurskikh ekonomicheskikh otnoshenii', *VM*, 1933, No.13.
Avenarius, G.G. 'K tridtsatiletiiu Kharbina', *VM*, 1933, No.13.
——, 'Promyshlennye predpriiatiia Kharbina', *VM*, 1933, Nos 14–15.
Azovtsev, N.N. et al., *Istoriia grazhdanskoi voiny*, Moscow, 1938–60.
Balakshin, P. P., *Final v Kitaii*, Vols 1 & 2, Munich, 1958
Balawyder, A., 'Russian Refugees from Constantinople and Harbin, Manchuria enter Canada (1923–1926)', *Canadian Slavonic Papers*, Vol. 14, 1972.
Baranov, I.G. 'Administrativnoe ustroistvo Severnoi Man'chzhurii', *VM*, 1926, Nos 11–12.
Bartlett, C.J., *The Global Conflict: The International Rivalry of the Great Powers, 1880–1990*, London, 1994.
Baykov, Alexander M., *Soviet Foreign Trade*, Princeton, 1946.
Bektiashinskii, N.S., 'Munitsipalitet g. Kharbina', *VM*, Nos 5–7.
Beloff, Max, *The Foreign Policy of Soviet Russia, 1929–1941*, Vols 1 & 2, 1947, 1949.
Beveridge, A.J. *The Russian Advance*, New York, 1903.
Bix, Herbert P. 'Japanese Imperialism and the Manchurian Economy', *China Quarterly*, 1972, Vol.51.
Black, C.E. et al., *The Modernization of Inner Asia*, Armonk & London, 1991.
Blagodatov, A.V., *Zapiski o Kitaiskoi revoliutsii, 1925–1927*, Moscow, 1975.
Boloban, A.P., *Zemledelie i khlebo-promyshlennost' Severnoi Man'chzhurii*, Harbin, 1909.
Bonavia, D., *China's Warlords*, Hong Kong, 1995.
Bradley, J.F.N., *Civil War in Russia, 1917–1920*, London, 1975.
Brandt, C., *Stalin's Failure in China, 1924–1927*, Cambridge, Mass., 1958.
Braun, Otto A., *Comintern Agent in China, 1932–1939*, Stanford, 1982
BRF [KVO], *Istoriia Rossiiskago fashistkago dvizheniia*, Harbin, 1936.
Byvshii Churinets, 'Torgovye i kommercheskiie predpriiatiia', *Kharbinskaia Starina* (1936 issue), reprinted in *Politekhnik*, No.10, 1979.
Carr, E.H., *The Russian Revolution from Lenin to Stalin, 1917–1929*, London, 1979.
Carrére d'Encausse, H., 'Civil War and New Governments' in E. Allworth (ed.), *Central Asia: A Century of Russian Rule*, New York & London, 1967.
CER Economic Bureau, Harbin, *Statisticheskii ezhegodnik*, Harbin, 1926, 1931.
Chamberlin, W.H., *Japan Over Asia*, London, 1938.
——, *The Russian Revolution: 1917–1921*, New York, 1965.
Channon, J., 'Siberia in Revolution and Civil War' in A. Wood (ed.), *The History of Siberia: From Russian Conquest to Revolution*, London, 1991.
Chen, Percy, *China Called Me: My Life Inside the Chinese Revolution*, Boston, 1979.
Chen, Wei-ping, *Manchuria or Manchukuo?: The Effect of Three Years of Japanese Aggression*, Sydney, 1934.
Cherniakov, Iu., *Diplomaty, chinovniki, I drugie: sovetskie ministrpy inostrannykh del (1917–1991)*, New York, Azimuth Publishers, 1996.
Ch'i Hsi-Sheng, *Warlord Politics in China, 1916–1928*, Stanford, 1976.
*China and the Trouble in Manchuria: What It means to China, Japan, Russia and the World*, Sydney, 1931.

Chinese Academy of Science, Kirin Provincial Branch, Institute of Historical Research, *A History of the People's Revolutionary Movement in the Northeast in Modern Times*, Changchun, 1960.
'The Chinese Eastern Railway and the Development of North Manchuria', *The Chinese Economic Monthly*, No.2, 1923 (November).
Chinese National Salvation Publicity Bureau, *The Tanaka Memorial*, San Francisco, 1932(?).
Christopher, J.W., *Conflict in the Far East: American Diplomacy in China from 1928–1933*, New York, 1970.
Chu Hsiao, *Manchuria: A Statistical Survey of Its Resources, Industries, Trade, Railways and Immigration*, Tientsin, 1929.
Clarke, R.A., *Soviet Economic Facts 1917–1970*, London, 1972.
Condliffe, J.B. (ed.), *Problems of the Pacific*, Chicago, 1929.
Conolly, Violet, *Soviet Asia*, London, 1942.
——, *Soviet Trade: From the Pacific to the Levant*, London, 1935.
Conway, J.F., 'Agrarian Petit-Bourgeois Responses to Capitalist Industrialisation: The Case of Canada', in Frank Bechhofer & Brian Elliott, *The Petit Bourgeoisie: Comparative Studies of an Uneasy Stratum*, London, 1981.
Cooper, Russell M., *American Consultation in World Affairs: For the Preservation of Peace*, New York, 1934.
'The Currency Situation in Manchuria', *The Chinese Economic Journal*, Vol. 1, No.2 (May 1927).
Curtin, J., *The Mongols: A History*, Boston: 1908 (reprinted Pennsylvania: Combined Books, 1996).
*Daikan'en no Kaib* Mukden, 1941(?).
Dallin, D.J., *The Rise of Russia in Asia*, New Haven, Conn., 1949.
——, *Soviet Russia and the Far East*, New Haven, Conn., 1948.
Day, R.B., *The 'Crisis' and the 'Crash': Soviet Studies of the West (1917–1939)*, London, 1981
Demidov, A.P., *Sovremennyi Kitai i Rossiia*, Paris, 1931.
Dennett, Tyler, *Roosevelt and the Russo-Japanese War*, Washington, 1924.
Deutscher, I., *Prophet Unarmed: Trotsky, 1921–1929*, London, 1959.
Dickinson, Goldsworthy Lowes, *Letters from a Chinese Official: Being an Eastern View of Western Civilization*, New York, 1928.
Dobrokhotov, N.M., 'Depressiia na Man'chzhurskom rynke', *VM*, 1930, No.3.
——, 'Ekonomicheskiie zatrudneniia v Kharbine', *VM*, 1930, No.6.
Dombrovskii, I.I., 'Tseny Kharbinskogo rynka za 1931 god', *VM*, 1932, No.2.
Dridzo, S.A., *Revoliutiia i kontr-revoliutsiia v Kitae*, Moscow, 1927.
Dushen'kin, V., *Ot soldata do marshala*, Moscow, 1964.
Eddy, Sherwood, *The World's Danger Zone*, New York, 1932.
'Ekonomicheskaia khronika SSSR', *VM*, 1927, No.2.
Elleman, B.A., *Diplomacy and Deception: The Secret History of Sino-Soviet Relations, 1917–1927*, New York & London, M.E. Sharpe, 1997.
Engel'fel'd, V.V., 'Kitaiskie politicheskie partii', *VM*, 1925, Nos 3–4.
——, 'Posledniaia grazhdanskaia voina v Kitae i ee itogi', *VM*, 1925, No.1.
Erickson, J., 'Military and Strategic Factors' in A. Wood (ed.), *Siberia: Problems and Prospects for Regional Development*, London, 1987.
Ermachenko, Irina Sergeevna, *Politika man'chzhurskoi dinastii Tsin v iuzhnoi i severnoi Mongolii v XVII v*, Moscow, 1974.
Ershov, M.N., 'Natsionalisticheskoe dvizhenie v Kitae', *VM*, 1929, No.6.

Ershov, M.N., *Novyi Dal'nyi Vostok; sovremennye khoziaistvennye, kul'turnye I mezhdunarodnye otnosheniia na tikhom okeane*, Harbin, 1931.
Etherton, T.P. & H.H. Tiltman, *Manchuria, the Cockpit of Asia*, New York, 1932.
Fairbank, J.K. et al., *East Asia: Tradition and Transformation*, London, 1973.
Federation of British Industries, *Report of Mission to the Far East, August–November 1934*, London, 1935(?).
'Flour Market in North Manchuria', *CEB*, Vol.XI, No.33 (1927).
Footman, David, *Ataman Semenov* (St Antony's Papers on Soviet Affairs), Oxford, 1955.
Forsyth, James, *A History of the Peoples of Siberia: Russia's North Asian Colony, 1581–1990*, Cambridge, 1992.
Fritsendorf, M., *Severnaia Man'chzhuriia: ocherki ekonomicheskoi geografii*, Khabarovsk, 1930.
Gamberg, V., 'Ekonomicheskii Krizis v Kitae', *Problemy Kitaia*, No. 3, 1930.
——, 'Uglublenie ekonomicheskogo krizisa v Kitae', *Problemy Kitaia*, Nos 6–7 (1–2), 1931.
*General Survey of Conditions in Manchukuo, with Special Emphasis on Economic Developments* (Second Revision), Hsinking, 1936.
Gerrare, Wirt, *Greater Russia: The Continental Empire of the Old World*, London, 1904.
Gerasimov, A.E., *Kitaiskie Nalogi v severnoi Man'chzhurii*, Harbin, 1923.
——, 'Ocherki ekonomicheskogo sostoianiia rainov verkhovev r. Sungari', *Vestnik Man'chzhurii*, No.10, 1929.
Geyer, Dietrich (trans. B. Little), *Russian Imperialism: The Interaction of Domestic and Foreign Policy, 1860–1914*, Leamington Spa, 1987.
Gins, G.K., 'Osnovnye cherty khoziaistva KVzhd', *VM*, 1927, No.2.
Gluvchinskii, A., 'Sel'sko khoziaistvo Man'chzhurii', *Politekhnik*, Sydney, No.10, 1979.
Go, Toshi (Manager, SMR), *Report on Railway Situation*, New York, 30 March 1927.
Golub, P.A., *Revoliutsiia zashchishchaetsia: Opyt zashchity revoliutsionnykh zavoevanii Velikogo Oktiabria, 1917–1920*, Moscow, 1982.
Gordeev, M.K., *Lesa i lesnaia promyshlennost' Severnoi Man'chzhurii*, Harbin, 1923.
Gorshenin, A.I., 'Gruzooborot Man'chzhurii za poslednie gody i printsipy novogo zheleznodorozhnogo stroitel'stva', *VM*, 1926, No. 6.
Gorman, G.W., *Two Millions to Manchuria*, Shanghai, 1928(?).
Graves, W.S., *America's Siberian Adventure, 1918–1920*, New York, 1941.
Green, O.M., *The Story of China's Revolution*, London, 1938(?).
Gul', Roman, *Krasnye Marshaly: Tukhachevskii, Voroshilov, Bliukher, Kotovskii*, Moscow, 1990.
Haslam, J., *Soviet Foreign Policy 1930–1933: The Impact of Depression*, London, 1983.
Hazard, John N., 'Post-War Government and the Politics of the Soviet Far East', *The Journal of Politics*, Vol.9, No.4, 1947 (November).
Hidaka, Nobru (ed.), *Manchukuo-Soviet Border Issues*, Hsinking(?), 1938.
Hopkirk, P., *Setting the East Ablaze: Lenin's Dream of an Empire in Asia*, Oxford, 1984.
'Household Industries in Harbin', *The Chinese Economic Bulletin*, Vol.XV, No.8, 24 August 1929.
*How 'Manchukuo' Came Into Being*, Peiping, 1932.
Hsü, Shuhsi, *An Introduction to Sino-Soviet Foreign Relations*, Shanghai, 1941.
——, *China and Her Political Entity (A Study of China's Foreign Relations with Reference to Korea, Manchuria and Mongolia)*, New York, 1926.
——, *Manchuria at Kyoto*, Peiping, 1929.
Hunt, Michael H., *Frontier Defense and the Open Door: Manchuria in Chinese–American Relations, 1895–1911*, New Haven, Conn., 1973.

'Iaponskie kapitaly v Man'chzhurii', *VM*, 1927, No.12.
Iashnov. E.E., 'Kitaiskoe i Russkoe krest'ianskoe khoziaistvo na dal'nem vostoke', *VM*, 1926, No.9.
——, 'Krizis sbyta Man'chzhurskoe sel'skokhoziaistvo', *EB*, 1931, No.2.
——, 'Sel'sko-khoziaistvennoe razvitie Severnoi Man'chzhurii', *VM*, 1925, Nos1–2.
——, 'Severnaia Man'chzhuriia za tri goda', *VM*, 1927, No.10.
——, 'Tikhookeanskaia problema (mysli i fakty)', *VM*, Nos3–4.
'Import and Export Trade on the Ussuri and the South Manchuria Railway', *The Chinese Economic Bulletin*, Vol. XV, No. 11, 4 September 1929.
'The Inner Mongolia Situation', *The Chinese Affairs*, 1933 (October), Vol. V, 9.
Intelligence Office, Council Board, Manchukuo Government, *First Report on the Plots to Disturb N. Manchuria*, Changchun, 1937.
IPR 3rd Conference, Kyoto 1929, *Documents of the Third Conference*, Nos 10–11, 13, Kyoto, 1929.
Iriye, Akira, *The Origins of the Second World War in Asia and the Pacific*, Harlow, 1987.
Isaacs, H., *Re-encounters in China: Notes on a Journey in a Time Capsule*, New York, 1985.
——, *The Tragedy of the Chinese Revolution*, 2nd Revised edn, Stanford, 1961.
Iuzefovich, L., *Samoderzhets pustyni: fenomen sud'by barona R.F. Ungern-Shternberga*, Moscow, 1993.
Ivanov, S.P. & A.I. Evseev, 'Voennoe iskusstvo' in *Sovetskaia voennaia entsiklopediia*, Moscow, 1976, Vol.2
Jacobs, Daniel N., *Borodin: Stalin's Man in China*, Cambridge, Mass., 1981.
Jacobson, Jon, *When the Soviet Union Entered World Politics*, Berkeley, 1994.
'Japanese Annexation of Manchuria and Abolition of the Puppet "Manchukuo"', *The Chinese Affairs*, 1933 (October), Vol. V, 9.
Johnstone, William Crane Jr, *The Shanghai Problem*, Stanford, 1937.
Jones, F.C., *Manchuria Since 1931*, London, 1949.
Kartunova, A.I., *V.K. Bliukher v Kitae, 1924–1927 gg.: Dokumentirovannyi ocherk, dokumenty*, Moscow, 1970, 1979.
Kawakami, K.K., 'Russia's Sinister Plot to Exploit China' in *Current History*, Vol. XXIII, No.6 (October 1925–March 1926).
——, 'The Russo-Chinese Conflict in Manchuria' in *Foreign Affairs*, Vol. 8, No.1 (October 1929).
Kantorovich, Anatolii Iakovlevich, *Iaponskii kapital v Manchzhurii*, Moscow, 1932.
Kharbinskii Birzhevoi Komitet, *O polozhenii russkoi torgovli i promyshlennosti v Man'chzhurii*, Harbin, 1913.
Kharbinskii Komitet Pomoshchi Russkim Bezhentsam, *Otchet: Kharbinskago Komitet Pomoshchi Russkim Bezhentsam, o ego deiatel'nosti v Severnoi Man'chzhurii (Kitai) v 1930 god*, Harbin, 1931.
Khodorov, A.E., 'Manchzhurskaia Problema (Pis'mo iz Kitaia)', *Novyi Vostok*.
Kingman, Harry L., *Effects of Chinese Nationalism upon Manchurian Railway Developments, 1925–1931*, Berkeley, 1932.
Kinney, Henry W., *Manchuria and the South Manchuria Railway Company*, Dairen, 1927.
——, 'Manchuria in 1927', *Chinese Economic Journal*, Vol. II, No.2, 1928 (February).
——, *Manchuria Today*, Dairen, 1930.
——, *Modern Manchuria and the South Manchuria Railway Company*, Dairen, 1928.
——, *Some Observations of the Present Manchurian Situation*, Dairen, 1933.
Kirby, E.S. (ed.), *Contemporary China*, Vol.I & V, Hong Kong, 1956, 1963.
Klepinkov, Flegont, *V Plenu u Kitaitsev*, Vladivostok, 1921.

Knickerbocker, H.R., *The Soviet Five-Year Plan and Its Effect on World Trade*, London, 1931.
Konstantinov, P.F., 'Zemledelie v Severnoi Man'chzhurii', *VM*, 1925, Nos 8–10
Koo, V.K., Wellington, *Memoranda Presented to the Lytton Commission*, Vols 1–2, New York, 1932.
Korablev, Iu.I. *et al.* (eds), *Zashchita Velikogo Oktiabria*, Moscow, 1982.
Kormazov, V.A., 'Rost naseleniia v Kharbine i Futsziadiane', *VM*, 1930, No.6.
——, 'Severnaia okraina Kheiluntsianskoi provintsii', *VM*, 1929, No.6.
——, 'Trekhrech'e (za period 1924–1933 gg.), *VM*, 1934, No.5.
Kotkin, S. & B.A. Elleman (eds), *Mongolia in the Twentieth Century: Landlocked Cosmopolitan*, Armonk & London, 1999.
K–skii, V., 'Doklad chlenov sledstvennoi komissii po delu o shankhaiskikh sobytiiakh', *VM*, 1926, Nos 3–4.
Kulagin, V.M. & Iakovlev N.N., *Podvig Osoboi Dal'nevostochnoi*, Moscow, 1970.
K'ung, T.P., *The Tragic Death of Chang Tso-lin: A Documentary Survey of a Prelude to the Japanese Invasion of Manchuria*, Peiping, 1932.
Kursel', K.P. 'Dal'bank v 1927 g.' *VM*, 1928, No.4.
——, 'Itogi deiatel'nosti Dal'nevostochnogo Banka v Kharbine za 1923–26 gg. (Po materialam inspektsii Dal'banka)', *VM*, 1927, No.5.
'K voprosu o bezrabotitse v Kitae i Man'chzhurii', *VM*, 1931, No.4.
Lattimore, Owen, *Manchuria, Cradle of Conflict*, New York, 1932.
——, O. & E., *The Making of Modern China*, London, 1945.
League of Nations, *Appeal by the Chinese Government. Report of the Commission of Enquiry* Geneva, October 1932.
Lee, Edward Bing-Shuey, *Two Years of the Japan–China Undeclared War and the Attitude of the Powers*, (2nd edn,) Shanghai, 1933.
Lei, K.N. (ed.), *Information and Opinion Concerning the Japanese Invasion of Manchuria and Shanghai from Sources other than Chinese*, Shanghai, 1932.
Lensen, George Alexander, *The Damned Inheritance: The Soviet Union and the Manchurian Crises, 1924–1935*, Tallahassee, 1974.
——, *The Strange Neutrality: Soviet–Japanese Relations during the Second World War, 1941–1945*, Tallahassee, 1967.
Leo, T.Y., *How Japan Has Maneuvered to Satisfy Her Manchuria-Hunger*, New York, 1931.
——, *The Manchuria-Hunger of the East Asiatic 'Boches'*, New York, 1931.
Leong Sow-Theng, *Sino-Soviet Relations: The First Phase, 1917–1920*, Canberra, 1971.
——, *Sino-Soviet Diplomatic Relations, 1917–1926*, Canberra, 1976.
Leshko, O., *Russkie v Man'chzhugo*, Shanghai, 1937.
'Lesnaia promyshlenost', 1900–1932 gg.', *Politekhnik*, Sydney, No.10, 1979.
*Letters Captured from Baron Ungern in Mongolia [Reprinted from Pekin and Tientsin Times]*, Washington, 1921.
L.I., 'Ekonomicheskii krizis i interesy derzhav v Man'chzhurii', *VM*, 1931, No.9.
Liang Chin-tung, *The Sinister Face of the Mukden Incident*, New York, 1969.
Li Chi, 'Manchuria in History', *Chinese Social and Political Science Review*, Peiping, July 1932, Vol.16.
Lidin, N., 'Russkaia Emigratsiia v Shankhae', *Russkiia Zapiski: Obshchestvenno-Politicheskii i Literaturnyi Zhurnal, Annales Russes*, Vol. II, 1937.
Lilliestrom, T.L. & A.G. Skerst, *North Manchuria and the Chinese Eastern Railway*, Harbin, 1924.
Limanoff, E.G., 'The Soviet-Mukden Conference and the Chinese Eastern Railway', *VM*, 1926, No.5.

Lin'kov, I.I. et al., *Deiateli Rossii XIX – nachala XX V.: Biograficheskii spravochnik*, Moscow, 1995.
Liubimov, L.I., 'Krizis sbyta bobov i poteri Man'chzhurskogo krest'ianina', *VM*, 1930, No.6.
——, 'Iaponskie banki v Man'chzhurii', *VM*, 1931, No.1.
——, 'Man'chzhurskaia derevnia, kak potrebitel' importnykh tovarov', *VM*, 1933, No.12.
——, 'Mirovoi krizis i biudzhet man'chzhurskogo krest'ianina', *VM*, 1931, No.9.
——, 'Rynok severnoi Man'chzhurii v 1932 godu', *VM*, 1933, No.1.
Liubimov, Nikolai Nikolaevich, *Ekonomicheskie problemy Dal'nego Vostoka (Vostochnaia Kitaiskaia Zheleznaia Doroga)*, Moscow, 1925.
Löwenthal, Rudolf, 'The Jewish Press in China', *Nankai Social & Economic Quarterly*, Vol. X, No. 1, 1937 (April).
Luk, M.Y.L., *The Origins of Chinese Bolshevism: An Ideology in the Making, 1920–1928*, Hong Kong, 1990.
Lum Ying-wun, *A Brief Study of the Manchurian Question*, Chicago, 1931.
Mackinder, H.J., *Democratic Ideals and Reality* (edited & with introduction by A.J. Pierce), New York, 1962.
Malitskii, V.S. 'Kustarnaia promyshlennost' Kharbina', *VM*, 1929, No.2.
Malozemoff, A., *Russian Far Eastern Policy, 1881–1904*, Berkeley, 1958.
——, 'The Ideology of Russian Expansion' in G.A. Lensen (ed.), *Russia's Eastward Expansion*, New Jersey, 1964.
Malraux, A., *The Conquerors* (tr. A. MacDonald), London, 1983.
——, *Man's Estate* (tr. S. Becker), London, 1968.
Mancall, Mark, *China at the Center: 300 Years of Foreign Policy*, New York, 1984.
——, 'The Kiakhta Trade' in C.D. Cowan (ed.), *The Economic Development of China and Japan*, London, 1964.
——, & G. Jidikoff, 'The Hung Hu-tzu of Northeast China' in J. Chesneaux (ed.), *Popular Movements and Secret Societies in China, 1840–1950*, Stanford, 1972.
Manchukuo Department of Foreign Affairs, *General Survey of Conditions in Manchukuo, with Special Emphasis on Economic Developments*, Hsinking, 1935.
——, *A General Outline of Manchukuo*, Hsinking, 1932.
——, *The Independence of Manchukuo*, Hsinking, 1932.
——, *Manchukuo Government Information Bulletin*, Nos 1–50, Hsinking, 1932–33.
*Manchukuo: The Founding of the New State of Manchuria*, New York, 1933.
*Manchukuo–Soviet Union Border Questions*, Tokyo, 1938.
*Manchuria, Treaties and Agreements*, Washington, 1921.
*The Manchuria Year Book (1931)*, Tokyo, 1931.
'Man'chzhurets', *Russkaia kazna na Kitaiskoi Doroge*, St Petersburg, 1910.
Marakueff, A.V., *Foreign Trade of China and Its Place in World Trade*, Harbin, 1927.
——, 'The Foreign Trade of China and its Place in the Total Commerce of the World', *VM*, 1927, No.6.
Marks, S.G., 'The Burden of the Far East: The Amur Railroad Question in Russia, 1906–1916', *Sibirica*, Vol. 1, No. 1, 1993.
Martykov, E.I., *Rabota nashikh Zh/d del'tsov v Manchzhurii*, Moscow, 1914.
Mawdsley, Evan, *The Russian Civil War*, London, 1987.
McCormack, Gavan, *Chang Tso-lin in Northeast China, 1911–1928: China, Japan and the Manchurian Idea*, Stanford, 1977.
Melikhov, G.V., *Rossiiskaia emigratsiia v Kitae (1917–1924 gg.)*, Moscow, 1997.
*Memorandum on the Plans for the Solution of the Manchurian Problem*, n.p., n.d., 1932(?).

McGreal, I.P. (ed.), *Great Thinkers of the Eastern World*, New York, 1995.
Miao Chu-huang, *Kratkaiia Istoriia Kommunisticheskoi Partii Kitaia*, Moscow, 1958.
Mif, P., 'Kitaiskaia revoliutsiia i nekapitalisticheskii put' razvitiia', *Problemy Kitaia*, Nos 8–9 (3–4), 1931.
Millard, Thomas F., *The ABC's of the Manchurian Question*, New York, 1921.
Ministerstvo Torgovli i Promyshlenosti, Otdel Torgovli, *Po voprosu o polozhenii russkoi torgovli i promyshlenosti v Man'chzhurii*, Harbin, 1913.
Mitchell, Janet, *Spoils of Opportunity: An Autobiography*, London, 1938.
M.N. Er—v. 'Ekonomicheskoe proniknovenie Iaponii v Man'chzhuriiu', *VM*, 1931, Nos 11–12.
Montgomery, M., *Imperialist Japan: The Yen to Dominate*, London, 1987.
Moon, Parker Thomas, *Imperialism and World Politics*, New York, 1927.
Mossdorf, O., 'der mandschurische Konflikt der Jahres 1929', *Zetschrift für Politik* Berlin, Vol.20, 1931.
Mughal, Nazir A. *China and World Powers: A Case Study of the Manchurian Crisis, 1931–33*, Karachi, 1975.
Murakami Hyoe, *Japan: The Years of Trial, 1919–52*, Tokyo, 1982.
Nasyrov, V.M., *KVzhd k sobytiiam 1929 goda*, Khabarovsk, 1929.
Naveh, S., 'Mikhail Nikolayevich Tukhachevsky' in Harold Shukman (ed.), *Stalin's Generals*, New York, 1993.
Neopihanoff, A.A., 'The Development of North Manchuria', *CEJ*, Vol. II, No.3, 1928 (March).
Nikiforov, P.M., *Zapiski prem'era DVR*, Moscow, 1974.
Nilus, E.Kh. (ed.), *An Abridged Outline of the Historical Survey of the Chinese Eastern Railway*, Harbin, 1923 (?).
Northeast Asian Affairs Research Institute, Peking, *How 'Manchukuo' Came into Being*, Peiping, 1932.
——, *Some More Lights on Manchuria*, Vol.2 ('Japan's Responsibility for Banditry in the Three Eastern Provinces'), Peiping, 1932.
N.S.-v., 'Ocherki ekonomicheskogo sostoianiia pristantsionnykh raionov Vostochnoi linii KVzhd', *VM*, 1929, No.9.
Obshestvo Izucheniia Man'chzhurskogo Kraia (OIMK), *Khlebnaia torgovlia I mukomol'naia promyshlennost' v sev. Man'chzhurii*, No.2, Harbin, 1923.
Parlett, Sir Harold, *A Brief Account of Diplomatic Events in Manchuria*, London, 1929.
Parvus, *Sprawa Wschodnia (zatrag japonsko-rosyjski)*, Krakow, 1904.
Patrikeeff, F., 'Geopolitics of Myth: Interwar Northeast Asia and Images of an Inner Asian Empire' in D. Christian & C. Benjamin (eds), *Realms of the Silk Roads: Ancient and Modern*, Turnhout, 2000.
——, 'Lashevich, Mikhail Mikhailovich' in H. Shukman (ed.), *The Blackwell Encyclopedia of the Russian Revolution*, Oxford, 1994.
——, 'Prosperity and Collapse: Banking and the Manchurian Economy in the 1920s and 1930s' in F.H.H. King (ed.), *Eastern banking: Essays in the History of the Hongkong & Shanghai banking Corporation*, London, 1983.
——, 'Revolution in Northern China' in H. Shukman (ed.), *The Blackwell Encyclopedia of the Russian Revolution*, Oxford, 1994.
——, 'Revolution in Siberia' in H. Shukman (ed.), *The Blackwell Encyclopedia of the Russian Revolution*, Oxford, 1994.
——, 'Russian and Soviet Economic Penetration of Northern China, 1895–1933' in J.W. Strong (ed.), *Essays on Revolutionary Culture and Stalinism*, Columbus, Ohio, 1990.
Pavlov, I.V., *Na Dal'nem Vostoke v 1905 godu; iz nabliudenii vo vremia voiny s Iaponiei*, St Petersburg, 1907.

——, 'Peresilenie v Severnuiu Man'chzhuriiu', *VM*, 1928, No.7.
Pavlovich, M., 'Iaponskii imperializm na dal'nem vostoke', *Novyi Vostok*, No.2, 1922.
Pegov, N.M., *Dalekoe-blizkoe: vospominaniia*, Moscow, 1982.
Pereira, N.G.O., 'White Power during the Civil War in Siberia (1918–1920): Dilemmas of Kolchak's "War Anti-Communism"', *Canadian Slavonic Papers*, 29(1).
——, 'Regional Consciousness in Siberia Before and After October 1917', *Canadian Slavonic Papers*, 30(1).
Petrov, Viktor, *V Man'chzhurii . . . razskazy*, Shanghai, 1937.
Pickens, Robert Sylvester, *Storm Clouds over Asia*, New York, 1934.
Pogrebetskii, 'Denezhnyi rynok Kitaia i Severnoi Man'chzhurii', *VM*, 1925, Nos 3–4.
——, 'Finansovye meropriiatiia Man'chzhurii', *VM*, 1932, No.4.
——, 'Inostrannye interesy v Kitae', *VM*, 1931, No.10.
——, 'Na puti k zolotomu standartu', *VM*, 1930, No.2.
——, 'Osnova Tarifov na KVzhd ("zoloto" ili "serebro"?)', *VM*, 1926, No.5.
Polner, T.I., *Obshchezemskaia organizatsiia na dal'nem vostoke*, Tom I & II, Moscow, 1908, 1910.
Pratt, John T., *War and Politics in China*, London, 1943.
*The Present Condition of China with Reference to Circumstances Affecting International Relations and Good Understanding Between Nations upon which Peace Depends – Document A* – (revised edn), Washington, 1932.
*The Present Manchurian Tangle*, New York, 1932(?).
*Pre-war Diplomacy: The Russo-Japanese Problem*, London, 1920.
Pye, L.W., *Warlord Politics: Conflict and Coalition in the Modernization of Republican China*, New York, 1971.
Quested, R.K.I., *The Expansion of Russia in East Asia, 1857–1860*, Kuala Lumpur, 1968.
——, *'Matey' Imperialists? The Tsarist Russians in Manchuria, 1895–1917*, Hong Kong, 1982.
——, *The Russo-Chinese Bank*, Birmingham, 1977.
——, *Sino-Russian Relations: A Short History*, Sydney, 1984.
Raeff, M., *Russia Abroad: A Cultural History of the Russian Emigration, 1919–1939*, New York & Oxford, 1990.
Rahul, Ram, *Politics of Central Asia*, India (Curzon Press), 1974.
Ravenstein, E.G., *The Russians on the Amur*, London, 1861.
*The Record in China of the British–American Tobacco Company Ltd 1925(?)* [Sokolsky Collection, Hoover Institution Library].
Rea, George Bronson, *What American [sic] Don't Know About 'The Open Door'*, Shanghai, 1932.
Rea, Kenneth W. (ed.) *Canton in Revolution: The Collected Papers of Earl Swisher, 1925–1928*, Boulder, col. 1977.
'Report of Mr Chang Kia-ngau, General Manager of the Bank of China, for the Year ended 31st Dec., 1930', *Chinese Economic Journal*, Vol. VIII, No.6 1931 (June).
Robinson, Nehemiah, *The Jewish Communities of China in Dissolution*, New York, 1954.
Romanov, B.A., *Russia in Manchuria*, Ann Arbor, 1952.
*Rossiiskaia emigratsiia – Velikaia Man'chzhurskaia Imperiia*, Harbin, 1942(?).
Runin, Sergei, *V Man'chzhurii*, St Petersburg, 1904.
Russkii dom imeni Naslednika Tsarevicha i Velikogo Kniazia Alekseia Nikolaevicha, *Pravila dlia vospitannikov*, Harbin, 1942.
Safarov, G., 'Avtoportret vtorogo internatsionala, ili Emil' Vandervel'de v gostiakh u Kitaiskoi kontrrevoliutsii', *Problemy Kitaia*, Nos 6–7 (1–2), 1931.
Sakamoto, N., *L'Affaire de Mandchourie*, Paris, 1931.
Sale, G.S., *Impressions of a Visit to the Far East*, Sydney, 1938.

'Sale of C.E.R. Further Protested', *The Chinese Affairs*, 1933 (June), Vol. V, 2.
Sannikov, V., *Pod znakom voskhodiashchego solntsa v Man'chzhurii: Vospominaniia*, Sydney, 1990.
Schimmelpenninck van der Oye, D., *Toward the Rising Sun: Russian Ideologies of Empire and the Path to War with Japan*, DeKalb, Il.: 2001.
——, 'Russia's Ambivalent Response to the Boxers', *Cahiers du Monde russe*, Vol. 41, No. 1, January–March 2000.
'Second Note Against C.E.R. Sale', *The Chinese Affairs*, 1933 (July), Vol. V, 4.
Serebrennikov, I.I., *Albazintsy*, Peking, 1922.
——, *Moi vospominaniia, Tom I & II*, Tientsin, 1937, 1940.
Setnitskii, N.A., 'Vneshniaia torgovlia Sev. Man'chzhurii', *VM*, 1927.
Shablinskii, P.A., 'Itogi eksportnoi kampanii 1925/26 g. Na KVZhD', *VM*, 1926, No.8.
——, 'Itogi eksportnoi kampanii v 1926/27 g. Na Kitaiskoi Vostochnoi zheleznoi doroge', *VM*, 1927, No.10.
Shanghai Bureau of Industrial and Commercial Information, International Relations Committee, *The Sino-Russian Crisis: The Actual Facts Brought to Light*, Nanking, 1929.
Shchepin, V.F. 'Severnaia Man'chzhuriia kak importnyi tsentr', *VM*, 1930, No.1.
Shen, Mo, *Japan in Manchuria (An Analytical Study of Treaties)*, Manila, 1960.
Shishkanov, V.G., 'Import Severnoi Man'chzhurii i rol' v nem Rossii', *VM*, 1925, Nos 5–7.
——, 'Krizis torgovli v Severnoi Man'chzhurii', *VM*, 1931, No.9.
——, 'Puti razvitiia sel'skogo khoziaistva Severnoi Man'chzhurii', *VM*, 1929, No.3.
Shishkin, P.P., *Bol'shevism v Kitae, chast' 1-ia; obzor deiatel'nosti Severo-Man'chzhurskoi kommunisticheskoi partii* Shanghai, 1930.
Shteinfel'd, Nikolai, *Russkoe delo v Man'chzhurii*, Harbin, 1910.
——, *Chto delat' s Man'chzhuriei?*, Harbin, 1913.
Shukman, Harold (ed.), *Blackwell Encyclopedia of the Russian Revolution*, Oxford, 1994.
——, *Stalin's Generals*, London, 1993.
Siiakin, N.D., 'Biudzhet Man'chzhurskikh provintsial'nykh vlastei do 1931 goda' *VM*, 1933, Nos 18–19.
Sibirskii Kazak, *Nashe proshloe do Velikoi voiny 1914 goda*, Harbin, 1934.
*The Sino-Japanese Question relating to China's Three Eastern Provinces (Manchuria), 1931–1932: Extracts from the Lytton Report and Press Comments*, Sydney, 1933.
'Sino-Russian Trade', *The Chinese Economic Monthly*, Vol. III, No.6 (June 1926).
S.I.Z., 'Natsional'nye gruppy v Kharbine', *Politekhnik*, No.10, 1979.
Sizov, N., 'Ekonomicheskoe Polozhenie Severnoi Manchzhurii', *Novyi Vostok*, 1924, No.6.
Skliarov, D., *Ekonomicheskaia politika iaponskogo imperializma v Manchzhurii*, Moscow, 1934.
Skvirskii, F.V., 'Tsarskaia avantiura na Dal'nem Vostoke', *VM*, 1931, No.1.
Smele, J. & D. Collins (eds), *Kolchak i Sibir*, New York, 1988.
Smith, S., *The Manchuria Crisis, 1931–1932: A Tragedy in International Relations*, New York, 1948.
Sokolov, N.A. 'Rasselenie pereselentsev v raionakh Severnoi Man'chzhurii (k pereselencheskoi kampanii 1930 g.)', *VM*, 1930, No.2.
Sokolsky, George E., *The Story of the Chinese Eastern Railway*, Shanghai, 1929.
——, *The Tinder Box of Asia*, New York, 1933.
South Manchuria Railway, *Report on Progress in Manchuria, 1–2 (1929–31)*, Mukden, 1930, 1931.

——, *Third Report on Progress in Manchuria*, Mukden, 1932.
*Sovetsko-Kitaiskii konflikt 1929 g.: Sbornik dokumentov*, Moscow, 1930.
'Soviet's Non-Aggression Policy and China', *The Chinese Affairs*, 1933 (November), Vol. V, 11.
*Sovetsko–Kitaiskii Konflikt 1929g.: Sbornik Dokumentov*, Moscow, 1930.
*Special Companies in Manchukuo: Their Mission and Activities*, Hsinking(?), 1940.
Spector, I., *The First Russian Revolution: Its Impact on Asia*, New Jersey, 1962.
Spirin, L.M., *Klassy i partii v grazhdanskoi voine v Rossii*, Moscow, 1968.
Stalin, J., *Marxism and the National and Colonial Question*, London, 1936.
Stauffer, Robert Burton, *Manchuria as a Political Entity: Government and Politics of a Major Region of China, Including Its Relations to China Proper*, Ann Arbor, 1954.
Stephan, John J., *The Russian Far East: A History*, Stanford, 1994.
——, *The Russian Fascists: Tragedy and Farce in Exile, 1925–1945*, New York, 1978.
——, 'Russian Soldiers in Japanese Service: The Asano Brigade', *Shikan*, No. 95, March 1977.
Stewart, J.R., *Manchuria Since 1931*, New York, 1936.
Stimson, H.L., *The Far Eastern Crisis: Recollections and Observations*, New York, 1936.
Stokes, G. & S., *The Extreme East: A Modern History*, Hong Kong, 1964.
*A Study of Manchuria: Papers Presented before Anti-Cobweb Society*, Foochow, 1933.
Suleski, Ronald, *The Modernization of Manchuria: An Annotated Bibliography*, Hong Kong, 1994.
Sumner, B.H., 'Tsardom and Imperialism in the Far East and the Middle East, 1880–1914' (Raleigh Lecture on History), *Proceedings of the British Academy*, Vol.XXVII (1940).
Sun Jui-chin, *Chinese Public Opinion as Reflected in Leading North China Newspapers Concerning League Commission of Inquiry*, Peiping, 1932.
Sun, Kungtu C., *The Economic Development of Manchuria in the First Half of the Twentieth Century*, Cambridge, Mass., 1969.
Surin, E.E., 'Tikhookeanskaia problema i Severnaia Man'chzhuriia', *VM*, 1926, Nos 1–2.
Surin, V.I., *Zheleznye dorogi v Man'chzhurii i Kitae: Materialy k transportnoi probleme v Kitae i Man'chzhurii*, Harbin, 1932.
——, *Lesnoe Delo v Man'chzhurii*, Harbin, 1930.
——, 'Lesnye rynki Man'chzhurii', *VM*, 1930, Nos 11–12.
——, *Man'chzhuriia i ee perspektivy*, Harbin, 1930.
Svechin, A.A., 'Strategy and Operational Art' (from 2nd edn of *Strategiia* Moscow, 1927) in H.S. Orenstein & D.M. Glantz, *The Evolution of Soviet Operational Art, 1927–1991: The Documentary Basis*, Vol.1, London: 1995.
Tang, Peter S.H., *Russian and Soviet Policy in Manchuria and Outer Mongolia, 1911–1931*, Durham, 1959.
Tairov, M., 'Pristan' i novyi gorod', *Politekhnik*, No.6., Sydney, 1974.
Taskina, E.P. (ed.), *Russkii Kharbin*, Moscow, 1998.
Tavokin, S.N., *K voprosu o "zheltoi opasnosti"*, St Petersburg/Kiev, 1913.
Terentev, N., *Iaponskii kapital v Manchzhurii*, Moscow, 1932.
Thomas, James A., *A Pioneer Tobacco Merchant in the Orient*, Durham, 1928.
Thorne, Christopher, *The Limits of Foreign Policy: The West, the League and the Far Eastern Crisis of 1931–1933*, London, 1972.
Timasheff, N.S., 'Russian Imperialism or Communist Aggression' in W. Gurian (ed.), *Soviet Imperialism: Its Origins and Tactics*, Indiana, 1953 (reprinted, Conneticut, Greenwood Press, 1975).
Tishenko, P., 'K voprosu ob inostrannykh munitsipalitetakh v Kitae', *VM*, 1926, No.5.

Tong, Hollington, *Facts About the Chinese Eastern Railway Situation (With Documents)*, Peking(?), 1929.
Tretchikov, N.G., *Bibliografiia finansov Kitaia (knigi i zhurnal'nye stat'i na russkom i angliiskom iaz. po 1929 god vkliuchitel'no)*, Harbin, 1930.
Tsao, L.E., 'The Chinese Eastern Railway', *The Chinese Economic Journal*, Vol. IV, No.4, April 1929.
Tsao Lien-en, *The CER: An Analytical Study*, Shanghai, 1930.
'Tsitsihar', *Chinese Economic Journal*, Vol.III, No.4, October 1928.
Tul'skii S., *Manchzhuriia – platsdarm dlia napadeniia na SSSR*, Moscow, 1934.
Uldricks, Teddy J., *Diplomacy and Ideology: The Origins of Soviet Foreign Relations, 1917–1930*, London, 1979.
US Army, Lt L.L. Williams (ed.), *15th Infantry Annual, May 4, 1924–May 4, 1925*, Tientsin, 1925.
US Dept of State, Division of Far Eastern Affairs, *Proposed Establishment by the Chinese Eastern Railway Company of a Municipal Administration at Harbin*, Washington, 1909.
Ustrialov, N.V., *Poniatie o gosudarstve*, Harbin, 1931.
——, *Problema progressa*, Harbin, 1931.
Velidov, A.S. et al. (eds), *Politicheskie deiatelii Rossii 1917: bibliograficheskii slovar'*, Moscow, 1993.
Vernadsky, George., *Political and Diplomatic History of Russia*, Boston, 1936.
Vespa, Amleto, *Secret Agent for Japan: A Handbook to Japanese Imperialism*, London, 1938.
Vilenskii-Sibiriakov, V., *Chzhan-tszo-lin: Man'chzhurskaia problema*, Moscow, 1925.
Vishniakova-Akimova, V.V., *Dva goda v vostavshem Kitae, 1925–1927: Vospominaniia*, Moscow, 1965.
*The Voice of the People of Manchukuo*, Hsinking, 1931.
Voeikov, A.D., 'Iz poezdki po Ningutinskomu uezdu', *VM*, 1930, No.2.
Voitinskii, G., *KVzhd i politika imperialistov v Kitae*, Moscow, 1930.
Volkogonov, Dmitrii M., *Trotsky: politicheskii portret, Kniga 2*, Moscow, 1992.
Vl. R., 'Voprosy kommercheskoi raboty KVzhd', *VM*, 1931, No.4.
Vradii, V.P., *Geograficheskii, etnograficheskii i ekonomicheskii ocherk Manchzhurii*, St Petersburg, 1905.
Waley-Cohen J., *The Sextants of Beijing: Global Currents in Chinese History*, New York & London, 1999.
Wallerstein, I., 'The Rise and Future Demise of the World Capitalist System: Concepts for Comparative Analysis' in Wallerstein (ed.), *The Capitalist World-Economy*, Cambridge, 1979.
Wang, Whitehall (ed.), *Wanpaoshan Incident and the Anti-Chinese Riots in Korea*, Nanking, 1932.
Weigh, Ken Shen, *Russo-Chinese Diplomacy, 1689–1924*, Maine, 1928.
Wells, D. & S. Wilson (eds), *The Russo-Japanese War in Cultural Perspective, 1904–05*, New York & London, 1999.
'Where Stands Moscow?', *The Chinese Affairs*, 1933 (June), Vol. V, 2.
Williams, Gavin, 'Imperialism and Development: A Critique', *World Development* 1978, Vol.6.
Willoughby, Westel W., *The Sino-Japanese Controversy and the League of Nations*, New York, 1968.
White, J.A., *The Siberian Intervention*, Princeton, 1950.
Whiting, A.S., *Siberian Development and East Asia: Threat or Promise?*, Stanford, 1981.
——, *Soviet Policies in China, 1917–1924*, Stanford, 1968.

Wilbur, C. Martin & J. Lien-ying How (eds), *Documents on Communism, Nationalism, and Soviet Advisers in China, 1918–27*, New York, 1972.
Witte, S.Iu., *Vospominaniia, Tom II*, Moscow, 1960.
Wolff, D., *To the Harbin Station: The Liberal Alternative in Russian Manchuria, 1898–1914*, Stanford, 1999.
Wood, A., 'From Conquest to Revolution: The Historical Dimension' in A. Wood (ed.), *Siberia: Problems and Prospects for Regional Development*, London, 1987.
——, (ed.) *Siberia: Problems and Prospects for Regional Development*, London, 1987.
Woodhead, Henry George W., *A Visit to Manchukuo*, Shanghai, 1932.
Yi Hun-gu, *Korean Immigrants in Manchuria*, Korea: 1931(?).
Young, C.W., *Chinese Colonization and the Development of Manchuria* Honolulu, 1929.
——, 'Economic Bases for New Russian Railways in Manchuria', *The Chinese Economic Journal*, Vol. 1, No. 4, 1927.
Young, L., *Japan's Total Empire: Manchuria and the Culture of Wartime Imperialism*, Berkeley & London, 1998.
*Zaiman Hakkei Rojin no Kazakku Ngy*, Tokyo, 1936(?).
Zhiganov, V.D., *Russkie v Shankhae*, Shanghai, 1936.
Zimonina, V.P. (ed.), *Konflikt na Kvzhad: Iz istorii Sovetskikh Vooruzhennykh sil*, Khabarovsk, 1989.
Zumoto, Motosada, *Sino-Japanese Entanglements, 1931–32 (A Military Record)*, Tokyo, 1933(?).
Zürcher, E. '"Western Expansion and Chinese Reaction." A Theme Reconsidered' in H.L. Wesseling (ed.), *Expansion and Reaction*, Leiden, 1978.

# Index

Afghanistan, 6, 202n.
Agricultural Guild (Manchuria), 170–1
Aigun, Treaty of, 5, 136
Alaska, 81
Albazin, 4
Alexander I, Tsar, 5
Alexander II, Tsar, 5
Alexander III, Tsar, 6
All-Manchurian Conference of Chinese Commercial Associations, 185
Amur, River, 3, 4–5, 84, 136, 140, 144, 150, 182
Anarcho-syndicalisation, 163
An'da Station, 19
Anglo-Afghan Agreement, 202
Anglo-Chinese Trading Co., The, 176
Anglo-Japanese Treaty (1902), 202
Ankuochün, The (Army of National Pacification), 34, 152
Annam, 135
Annenkov, Ataman, 24, 54, 55, 145, 146, 149, 161, 162
Antonov-Ovseenko, V.A., 50
Araki, General (Japanese Minister of War), 169, 202
Argun, River, 31, 136
Arita, General, 197
*Artel's* (co-operatives), 32
Asano Brigade, 195
Asiatic Petroleum Co., 19
Assistant of Chief Liquidator (Russo-Asiatic Bank), 132
Association for Aid to Invalids, 195
Association of Dairy Firms, 195
Association of Restaurant Owners, 195
Association of 'Russian Transport', 195
Australia, 30, 151
Austria, 6

Badmaev, Dr, 6, 137
Baikal, Lake, 23
Bakich, General, 145
Balkans, 6
Banditry, 74, 172, 190
Bank of China, The, 185, 186

Bank of Chosen, 186
Bank of Korea, 191
Banque Industrielle de Chine, 199
Barga, 105, 181
Barguts, 81, 170
Bashkirs, 23
Basmachi guerillas, 126
Beikker, 83
Belov, General, 145
Berlin, 87
*Betar*, 61
Beveridge, Senator Albert J., 130–1
*Bezalabernyi* Imperialism, xiii, 14–15
Bezobrazov clique, 16, 18
Blacher (Manager, Russo-Asiatic Bank, Pristan' Branch), 120
Black Earth region (Russia), 31
Black market, 20
Black Ring, The, 60–1
Black Sea, The, 148
Blagoveshchensk, 167
Bliukher, V.K. (Galen), 26, 36–7, 40, 43, 83, 105, 147, 148, 153, 183, 184
Boldyrev, General, 83
Bolsheviks, The, 22–3, 26–7, 29, 33, 111, 126, 139, 143, 147, 160, 163, 188, 198
  agitation in Manchuria (1905), 139, 142
'Bolshevization of China', 126, 154, 158, 164
Bonavia, D., 154
Borders
  China and, 8, 42, 76
  Japan and, 148
  Lenin and, 29–30
  Manchuria and, 32, 52, 106
  Russia and, 122
  Soviet Union and, 24–5, 28, 129, 190
Border Patrol (Harbin), 11
Borodin, Mikhail, 36–7, 40, 42, 43, 44, 46, 47, 105, 153, 154, 155, 157, 189–90, 194
Borzaia, capture of, 147
Boundary inspections, 5

220

## Index

Boxer Rebellion, The, 7, 148
Bren, 133
Bresler, Boris, 60, 165
Brinkley, Captain F., 157
Britain, 7, 88, 137
British–American Tobacco Company (BAT), 62, 193, 200
British Concession (Shanghai), 41
Briukhanov, N.P., 88, 89
Bukharin, Nikolai, 36
Bukhedu, 84, 100, 182
Buriatia, 144
Burma, 135
Bureau for the Settlement of Old Business Affairs of the NMR/CER, 197–8
Bureau of Emigrants, 112, 113, 194, 201

Canada, 30, 32, 33, 149, 201
   Immigration and Colonization Office, 150
Canton, 14, 34, 35, 42, 63, 149, 152, 153, 158, 176, 202
Capitalist world system, 103, 140
Carr, E.H., 80, 88n.
Catherine I, Empress, 5
Catherine II, Empress, 5
Chalainor, 83, 84, 100
Changchun, 174
Chang Fa-kuei, General, 153
Chang Hsüeh-liang, Marshal, 26, 46, 64, 80, 85, 87, 106, 107, 169, 179, 182, 190, 192
Chang Tso-lin, Marshal, 4, 34–5, 36, 45, 49, 52, 61, 62, 63, 67, 106, 111, 136, 146, 152, 154, 165, 169, 181, 189, 190, 198, 202
   assassination of, 63–4, 106–7, 191
Chang Tsung-ch'ang, General, 33
Channon, J., 143
Cheka, 43
Chernykh (Soviet chargé d'affaires), 42
Chen, Eugene (Minister for Foreign Affairs, China), 41, 154, 155, 194
Chen, Percy (Eugene Chen's son), 154, 155, 194
Chen Kung-po, General, 153
Ch'en Pao, 152
Chicherin, Georgii (Commissar of Foreign Affairs), 147

Chiang Kai-shek, 35, 40, 43, 63, 152, 155, 157, 169, 180, 190, 192, 202, 203
Ch'ien-Lung, Emperor, 2
Chientao, 190, 203
Chin Dynasty, 1
China, xiii, 1–8, 9, 11, 14–15, 17, 18–19, 24, 25, 26, 27–8, 29, 33–51, 60, 61, 63, 65, 66, 69–71, 74, 75–7, 78, 80–1, 82–3, 87–90, 96, 102–3, 105–6, 109–10, 111n., 123–4, 125–6, 127–8, 129–30, 136, 137–8, 140, 141, 144, 146, 147, 148, 153, 154, 155, 156, 158, 162, 165, 179, 180, 189, 190, 191, 193, 200, 202
   and Manchuria, 81, 102, 189
*China Advertiser*, The, 41
China coast press, 37–8, 40, 42, 45, 155, 168
*China Weekly Review*, The, 37, 160, 184, 189
Chinese American Bank of Commerce, The, 199
Chinese Chamber of Commerce, The (Futiatien), 176
Chinese Commercial Organisation of Harbin and Futiatien, 96
Chinese Communist Party (CCP), 35–6, 38, 158, 203
Chinese court system, 187n.
Chinese Eastern Railway (CER)
   auxiliary enterprises 172
   CER Zone, 28, 29, 63, 75
   debt question, 53
   employment controversies, 182–3
   mixed administration of, 108, 145–7, 158, 161
   Pension Department, 99
   sale of, 88, 113–16, 195, 196–7
Chinese law, 29, 193
Chinese Maritime Customs, The, 43, 67, 83, 156, 174
Chinese nationalism, 50, 82, 86
Chinese peasantry, 66, 74
Chinese Stock Exchange, 186
Chinese Treasury, 133
Ch'ing Dynasty, 1–2
Chita, 6, 21, 23, 85, 130, 144, 159, 168
Chol'sk Concession, 151
Christopher, J.W., 80, 180

Chung Wo Tong, The (Hong Kong triad organisation), 166
Churin, Ivan Iakovlevich (I.Ia. Churin & Co.), 97, 120, 186–7, 199, 200
Cigarette trade in Manchuria, 15
Citizenship, Russians and, 51, 52–3
Civil War (Chinese), xii, 109, 145
Civil War (Russian), xiii, 21–8, 57, 105, 122, 143, 145, 147, 200
Clausewitz, C.P. von, 183
Coleman (American representative in Latvia), 88
*Collectanea Commissionis Synodalis*, 164
Comintern, The, 36, 37
Constantinople, 33
Constituent Assembly, The, 22, 143, 162
Conversion programme, 136
Cossacks, 5, 23, 168
   Cossack expeditions, 4, 136
   Orenburg, 23
   Ural, 23
Curtis, Mr (representative of the International Banking Corporation, Harbin), 94
Customs duties, 9, 18–19, 20, 138, 143, 159, 172
Czech Legion, The revolt of, 22

Dairen, 7, 20, 71, 78, 141, 185, 193
*Dal'bank*, 77, 83, 95–6, 97, 175, 176, 177, 186
*Dal'gostorg*, 77, 176
Deep Operation Theory (Tukhachevsky), 183
Denikin, General A.I., 50
Denisov (Assistant General Manager, CER), 182
Directory, The, 23
Diterikhs, General M.K., 23, 146
*Dni* (Days), 63, 64
Doihara Kenji, Maj.-Gen., 204
*Dom Miloserdiia* (House of Mercy), 195
Durand Line, The, 202
Dutov, Ataman, 24, 144

'East Asian Siberia' (defined), 144
East Asiatic Co. Ltd, The, 94, 176
Eastern Siberia, 31, 71, 105, 117, 127, 137
Egan, W.J. (Deputy Minister of Immigration and Colonization, Canada), 149, 150

Eismont, A.A., 82, 182
Eitington, Naum (Leoinid), 156
Ekaterinoslav, 44
*Ekho* (Location of CER experimental farm), 171
Elleman, B.A., 38
Emshanov, A.I. (General Manager, CER), 53–4, 82, 158, 182
Entente, The, 147
'Eurasian Empire', 144–5
Extraterritoriality, 29, 110, 132, 193
   Russians and, 193

Far Eastern Crisis, The (1931), 78
Far Eastern Republic, The (FER), 23, 59, 145, 147
Farghana Khanate, 126
Federation of Banks, The (China), 186
Feng Yü-hsiang, Marshal, 104, 152, 154, 158, 189–90
Fengtien Party, The, 45
Fengtien Province, 136
First Five-Year Plan (Soviet Union), 113–14, 195
Formosa, 2
Forestry, 31, 32, 75, 97, 117, 151, 172, 188, 198
France, 6, 132
Franco-Japanese Treaty (1907), 202
Frederick the Great, 145, 204
French Consul (Harbin), 134
Frunze, M.V. (Soviet Minister of War), 152
Frunze Academy (Department of Strategy), 184
Fuchin, 84
Fujisawa Chikao, 111, 194, 203, 204
Fur trade, 3, 31, 32, 48, 100n., 187
Furman, F.A., 142
Futiatien, 96, 168, 176, 177

Geitsman (Soviet Consul, Manchuli), 48, 159, 178
Geneva, 150
Germany, 6
   diplomatic representative, 83
Geopolitics, xiv, 21, 104, 105, 131
Gibbes, J., 48–9, 156, 159, 170, 172, 185
Gins, G.K., 91–2, 98, 171, 172, 175, 185
Glavkov, Polkovnik, 145
Glebov, General, 146

## Index

Gobi Desert, The, 36,
Golitzin, Prince Alexander V. (Commissioner of the Russian Red Cross, Harbin), 32, 149, 150
Gorbatenko, Mr, 174, 192
Gould, Randall (correspondent for United Press), 34
Grand Hotel, The (Vladivostok), 198
Graves, William S. (General), 147
Great Depression, The, 177, 179, 187, 196
  and the Soviet Union, 201
Great Game, The, 123
*Great Manchurian Empire, The*, 112–13, 130
Greater East Asian Co-prosperity Sphere, The, 129
Green, O.M., 152

Haas, Robert, 155
Hailar, 11, 12, 32, 100, 145, 150, 160, 173, 175, 182, 185
  Chinese Municipal Council of, 183
Hankow, 41, 42, 43, 45, 176, 193
*Hankow Herald, The*, (cited), 154, 155, 156, 158, 179
'Happy Khorvatia', 144
Harbin, 3n., 8, 9, 10, 13, 14, 17, 18, 26, 30, 32, 45, 57, 58, 59, 62, 71, 74, 83, 84, 99, 106, 108, 114, 116, 117, 132, 138, 139, 140, 142, 145–6, 149, 151, 152, 163, 166, 167, 173, 174, 175, 177, 178, 191, 192, 194, 195
  as 'Paris of the North', 60
  Chinese population of, 9–10
  Jewish life in, 60–1, 165, 195
  municipal administration (*Zemstvo*), 9, 139
  origins of, 7–11
  Polytechnical Institute (KhPI), 162, 184
  press, 64, 161
  role of gossip and rumour in, 140
*Harbin Observer, The*, 64
Harbin Relief Committee of Russian Emigrants in North Manchuria (China), 112, 185–9
*Harbin Shimbun*, 173
Harbin Stock Exchange Committee, 17, 19
Hassis, M. (Soviet Vice-Consul, Canton), 44, 157

Heiho region, 141
Heilin, 114
Heilungkiang, 158
Hell's Kitchen (New York), 60
Hirota, Koki (Japanese Ambassador to the Soviet Union), 115
Hiyama, E., 148
Ho Lung (Chinese Communist leader), 52–3
Hong Kong, 155
Hongkong & Shanghai Banking Corporation (HSBC), 18, 20, 73, 77, 93–4, 96, 97, 118–19, 120, 142, 174, 178, 184, 192, 200
  Vladivostok Agency, 118, 186
Honjo, General S. (Commander, Kwantung Army & adviser to Chang Tso-lin), 169–70
Hsinmintun, 4
Hu Lan River, 3
Hunghutze (Red Beards), 61–2, 106, 124, 166–7, 168, 193
Hunting, 32, 151, 173, 188

Iakutia Oblast, 165
Imianpo, 114
I Ho Ch'uan (the Righteous and Harmonious Boxing Order) [The Boxers], 7
Ilous, The, 135
Imperialism & development, 102–3, 143, 174, 189
India, 6, 201
Industry, 71, 72, 74–5, 97–98, 121, 185n., 200
  collapse of the Siberian Company and, 200–1
  early development, 14–20
  political strife and, 74
  Maritime Province and, 77–8
  Soviet industry, 79, 179
Inner Asia, 144
Inner Mongolia, 105
Intelligentsia, 22n.
International Banking Corporation (later The National City Bank), 94
International Refugee Organisation (Hong Kong), 164
Intervention, Allied, 24–5, 27, 125, 142, 145, 200, 203
Ioffe, Adolf, 153

Irkutsk, 21, 144
Ishiga, Mr (Assistant Director, Bank of Chosen), 186
Isserson, G.S., 89–90
Iudenich, General, 50
Iuridicheskii Fakul'tet (Faculty of Law, Harbin), 57, 162, 194
Ivachev, V.I. (Head, Russian Emigrants' Group, Trekhrech'e), 188
Ivan the Terrible, 130
Ivanov, A.N. (General Manager, CER), 52, 53–4, 116, 158

Jacobs, D.N., 47
Japan, xiv, 3, 6–7, 8, 28, 88, 101, 103, 107, 109, 111, 114–15, 120, 122–3, 125–6, 128, 129, 139, 144, 147–8, 157, 169, 171, 180, 195, 203
*Japan Advertiser, The*, 148
Japanese Army Intelligence, 62, 148, 168, 189
Japanese Concession (Hankow), 41
Japanese Diet, The, 148
Japanese Embassy, Washington, 166
Japanese intervention (Russian Civil War), 145, 203
Japanese policies in Manchuria, 62–3, 190, 191, 194, 204
Jen Te-chiang (Chinese Communist leader), 152
Jewish Commercial Bank, The, 119
Jewish National Bank, The, 119
Jorgenson (Head of the East Asiatic Company & Danish Consul at Harbin), 193
*Journal de Pekin*, 164

'K' Company, 180–1
Kadets, The, 22
Kaigorodov, Ataman, 145
Kalgan, 62
Kalinin, M.I., 88
Kalmykov, Ataman I.P., 24, 147
Kamchatka, 144
Kang-hi, Emperor, 4
Kanji, Lieutenant Colonel Ishihara, 204
Karakhan, Lev Mikhailovich
(Deputy Commissar of Foreign Affairs), 36–7, 39, 40, 43, 82, 83, 105, 146, 153, 158

Karakhan Declarations, The (1919), 28, 49
Karakhan Note, The, 160
Kato, R., 130
Kazagrandi, Ataman, 145
Kazantsev, Ataman, 145
Kellogg Pact, The, 87
Genghis Khan, 1
Kennan, G.F., 30
Kerosene, 19, 74
Khabarov, Erofei, 4, 136
Khabarovsk, 41, 84, 104, 105, 144, 168
Khabarovsk Protocol, The, 85, 104
Kharbinskii komitet pomoshchi Russkim bezhentsam (Harbin Committee for Aid to Russian Refugees) [KhKpRb], 101
*Kharbinskoe Vremia* (The Harbin Times), 33
Khorvat, General Dmitrii, 23, 27, 57, 58, 59–60, 138, 144, 146, 147, 164, 199
Khreshchatitskii, General, 164
Kiakhta System, 14
Kiakhta Treaty, The, 14, 140
Kiangsu, 169
Kidnapping, 61–2
Kinney, H.W., 179, 190–1, 192
Kirin Province, 2, 16, 18, 170, 173, 175, 176–7, 181
Kislitsin, General V.A. (Head of Bureau of Emigrants, Harbin), 112
Knox, E.M., 94, 186
Kokand government, 126
*Kokuryūkai* Society (the Amur, or 'Black Dragon', society), 168
Kolchak, Admiral A.V., 23, 24, 27
Komatsubara, Col. (Chief of Harbin Special District), 158
Komsomol, 60–1, 85, 86, 165
Konstantinov, P.F. (agronomist), 66
Korea, 6, 23, 127, 135, 144, 146
Korean agents, 189
Korean settlers, 31, 131, 173, 190, 203
Koreneff, B., 187–8
Kovalskys, 116, 133, 151, 171, 200
*Krasnyi Kitaiskii soldat* (The Red Chinese Soldier), 86
Krougloff, 134
*Kruzhok port-arturtsev* (Circle of Port-Arthurites), 195

Kudashev, Prince Nikolai (Russian Ambassador to China), 147, 148
Kuomintang (KMT), 35, 36, 38, 109, 152–3, 154, 155, 202, 203
Central Executive Committee of, 35
*Kung Pao*, 158–9
Kuropatkin, General A.N., 7–8, 13, 137
Kwantung Army, The, 27–8
Kwantung Province, 169

Lahasusu, 83, 84, 174, 182, 186
Lampson, Sir Miles W., 86–7, 88n.
Lashevich, M.M. (Soviet Vice-President of the CER), 50–1, 160
funeral of, 51
Lattimore, Owen, 2, 13
League of Nations, The, 180
Lenin, V.I., 12, 29–30
Leningrad Opposition, The, 50
Lensen, G.A., 180
Li Chi, 1
Li Hung-chang, 6
Liang Ch'i-chao (Chinese nationalist), 65
Liaotung Peninsula, 2, 5, 6
Linevich, General, 12, 139
Limits of Empire, 126
Litvinov, M.M. (Commissar for Foreign Affairs), 88
Liuchu Islands, 135
Liushkov, G.S. (Head, NKVD, Far Eastern Region), 148
Lobanov-Rostovskii, Prince, 6
London, 12n.
Lopato, Misha, 200
Louis Dreyfus & Co., 176
Lu Chang-Kuu, General (Commander, Asiatic Cavalry Division), 193
*Luch Azii* (Light of Asia), 203
Lytton Commission of Enquiry, 132, 155, 174, 188, 200, 202

Mackinder, Halford, 201
MacMurray (American consular representative), 83
Main Administration of the Three Eastern Provinces, 96
Malraux, A., 155
Mancall, Mark, 140
Manchu Court, 2

Manchu Empire, 4, 45, 65
Manchukuo, 111, 113, 115, 116, 120, 161, 180, 181, 195
Manchuli (*see* Manchuria Station)
Manchuria
agriculture in, 31, 66–7
banking in, 18, 74–5, 177
Chinese colonisation of, 2–3, 4, 66, 69, 72, 170–1, 172
capital formation in, 3–4
commercial agriculture, 3
differentness of, 81, 169, 189
duality of power, 8
economic development of, 3–4
industry, 75, 78, 92, 93–8, 141–2
Japanese investment in, 192
Japanese population growth in, 167, 169, 172–3
manufacture in, 4
population growth in, 138
Russian/Soviet trade with, 13, 16–17, 19, 72, 110, 120, 140, 156, 165
soya bean trade, 74–5, 76, 77
*Manchuria Daily News*, 196
Manchuria Station (*see* Manchuli)
Manchurian Guard, 106
Manchurian steppe, 66
Manchuli, 20, 48, 83, 156, 159, 160, 168, 174, 182
Manchus, 1, 2, 3, 4, 81–2, 181
Manila, 151
Mao Tse-tung, 183, 203
'Yenan Way', 183, 203
Marx, 49, 102
Marxism, 37, 102, 148
*Marxism and the National and Colonial Question*, 30
Matsievskii, General, 145
Meiji Restoration, 125, 202
Mel'nikov, Boris (Soviet Consul General at Harbin), 83
Mergen, 5
MacGrath, Captain Robert P. (Executive Secretary, Russian Refugee Relief Society of America), 32, 149
Middle East, 6
Mikoyan, A.I., 88
Ming Dynasty, 1
Ministry of Foreign Affairs, Peking, 38

Ministry of Trade & Industry (Soviet Union), 16
Mitarevskii, N.A., 164
McLure, F.J. (Passenger Manager, Robert Reford Shipping Company), 30
Modiagou, 11, 167
Mohos, The, 135
Mongolia, 24, 54n., 105, 110, 146, 149, 155, 174, 187, 202–3
Mongolian People's Republic, 28
Mongols, 145, 190
Monroe Doctrine, The, 169
Moscow, 23, 36, 39, 41, 44, 45, 104, 108, 114, 155, 157, 160, 182
Mudanzian-Pogranichnaia, 173
Mukden, 39, 45, 46, 63, 64, 108, 109, 167, 174, 182, 185
Mukden government, 52, 61, 82, 87, 106, 160, 177, 179
Mukden Incident, The (1931), 27, 28, 152
Mulin concession, 133, 199
Muraviev, Nikolai Nikolaevich, 5, 136, 137
Mutual Credit Bank, The, 119

Nagatsu, Lieutenant Colonel (Adviser to Marshal Chang Hsüeh-liang), 169
Nanchang (Kiangsi Province), 35, 152
Nanking, 82
  government, 83, 104
Napoleon, 204
Napoleonic Wars, 183
Narkomindel, 37, 182
Narym (Western Siberia), 160
*Nash Put'* (Our Path), 198
Natarov, Mikhail, 112
National City Bank, 94, 95, 97, 177, 186, 201
National Revolutionary Army, The, 145
Nationalisation of Trade (Soviet Union), 76
Navigation on Manchurian rivers, 71
  rights, 189
Nepal, 136
Nerchinsk, Treaty of, 4–5, 136, 140
Nichiren, 204
Nicholas I, Tsar, 5, 145
Nikolaevsk, 168
Nikol'sk-Ussuriisk, 77, 85, 142

Ninguta, 170
Niomura, M, 130
1929 Crisis, xiii, 27, 116
Nonni River, 84
*North China Daily News, The*, 153
*North China Herald, The*, 174
*North China Standard, The*, 87
Northeast Asia, 27–8, 111, 121, 123, 127–8
  images of politics in, 124
  Lenin on, 12
  political topography of, 122
Northern Manchuria
  agriculture, 75
  banking in, 75, 93–8, 177, 185–6
  communist activities in, 158
  crisis & conflict and the economy of, 77–9, 90–4, 98–102, 117–20
  defined, 138
  economy of, xiii, 15–20, 68–79, 92–7, 102, 116–20, 172
  flow of illegal immigrants to, 73
  Japan and, 62–63, 78, 101, 120, 127–29, 168, 173
  Japanese presence in, 69, 167–8
  Red Army in, 86–7, 183
  restoring balance of power in, 85
  Russian civil war and, 25–7
  Russian migration into, 13–14
  Russian society in, 12–13, 21, 23, 49, 56–7, 62, 88, 100–1, 109, 113, 116, 121–2, 163, 194
  Russian trade policy, 19
  significance of 1929 crisis to, 121
  Soviet economic interests in, 75–9, 113–16, 161
  Soviet political activities in, 46–9, 52–4, 55–7, 78, 102–3, 120, 122, 161
  world economy and, 102–3
Novonikolaevsk (Novosibirsk), 21
Novyi Gorod (New Town), 11, 99
Nuchens, The, 135

Octobrin, 49
Omsk, 21, 23
Omsk-Cheliabinsk partisan division, 145
*On the Condition of Russian Emigrants in Northern Manchuria*, 188

*Organizatsiia izuchennie Manchzhurskago kraia* (Organisation for the Study of the Manchurian Region) [OIMK], 188
*Osobaia Dal'nevostochnaia armiia* (ODVA), 26–7, 28, 83, 84
Transbaikal Group, 84
Ostrenko (HSBC Agency), 97, 185–6
Ostroumoff, B. (General Manager, CER), 97, 115, 199
*Otmol'tsy* (Komsomol in Harbin), 145
Outer Mongolia, 105, 181
Ozero (Lake), 31–2, 150

Pan-Slavism, 204
*Papirosy* (Russian cigarettes), 15–16
'Parallel lines' question (railway system in Manchuria), 171–2
Paris, Treaty of (1856), 5
Partisan activity
  'red', 23
  'white', 146, 152, 191
Pavlovsk Military Academy, 50
Peking, 24, 29, 34, 39, 59, 63, 158, 163, 165–6, 167, 202
  Treaty of, 136
Peking Commission, The, 34
Peking government, 170
Peking Metropolitan Police Headquarters, 152
Peking-Mukden Line (Railway), 63
Peking University
  Baron Staal'-Gol'shtein at, 60
  Karakhan lectures at, 153
People's Commissariat of Commerce and Industry (later Commissariat of Foreign Trade), 76, 154
Pepeliaev, General, 146, 165
Peraulov, 145
Perm Guberniia, 194
Peter the Great, 4, 5
Petition to the Commission of Enquiry of the League of Nations, 132–4, 200
Petrograd, 138
Piatnitskii, I.A., 88–9
Pick, Captain Eugene, 41, 42, 155
Pizarro, 136
Plehve, V.K. von (Minister of the Interior), 141

Podvoisky, N.I., 50
Poiarkov, Vasilii, 4, 136
Poland, 29, 59
Ponomarev, Valentin Vasil'evich, 194
Port Arthur, 6, 18
Porstmouth, Treaty of, 9, 114
Pratt, Sir John, 153–4
*Pravda*, 34
*Pravila dlia vospitannikov* (Harbin, 1924), 194
Preobrazhensky, E., 153
Primor'e, 168, 175
Profintern, 37
Proletarian Movement, The (article), 148
Pristan' (The Quay), 10, 139, 199
Provisional Government, The, 20, 138
Provisonal Siberian Government, The (PSG), 22–3
Przhevalsky, Nikolai, 137
Puteloff, 95
P'u Yi, 81
Putilov, 147
Pye, L.W., 145

Quested, R.K.I., 14, 21

Radek, K., 153
Ravenstein, E.G., 1, 4, 5, 8n., 13n., 136
Red Army, The, 23, 24, 80, 84, 88, 104, 144, 150, 182
  propaganda in Northern Manchuria, 85–6, 183
Red Army Command, The, 24–5, 157, 180
Refugee Committee, 195
Refugees, Russian, 13, 30–5, 76, 149, 150, 159, 163–4, 188–9
Republican Executive Committee, 138
Reuter Agency, 45
Reval (Tallin), 145
Revoensovet, 50
Revolutionary Military Council (RMC), 50, 83, 160
Rickmers Line (Hamburg), 175
Robert Reford Shipping Company, 30
Rodzaevsky, K.V., 194
Roosevelt, President Theodore, 169
*Rubezh* (The Border), 151, 152
Rudyi Iu. (General Manager, CER), 116, 182

Rudzutak, Ia. E., 88
*Rupor* (The Megaphone), 168
Russian advisers, 67
Russian Embassy, Peking, 7
Russian Far East, The, 15, 23, 24–5, 26, 54, 105, 126, 128, 142, 144
Russian House (*Russkii Dom*), 195
Russian peasantry, 66, 143, 146, 150
Russian Red Cross (Harbin), 32
Russian Refugee Relief Society of America, Inc., 32, 149, 150
Russian Revolution (1905), 12, 124, 138, 139
Russian Revolutions (1917), 9, 18, 21–7, 28, 29, 32, 39n., 45, 57, 146
Russian settlers, 69–70, 89
Russian Social-Democratic Labour Party (RSDLP, also RSDRP), 142, 160
Russian Soviet Federative Socialist Republic (RSFSR), 23
Russian Spiritual Mission, 164
*Russikii Golos* (The Russian Voice), 59
*Russkoe Slovo* (The Russian Word), 33, 186
Russo-Asiatic Bank (*see* Russo-Chinese Bank)
Russo-Chinese Bank (later the Russo-Asiatic Bank), 6, 17, 95, 120, 132–4, 137, 174, 186, 200
 liquidation of, 132–4
Russo-Japanese War (1904–1905), 3, 8–9, 10, 12, 14, 16, 17, 71, 86, 105, 107, 125, 136, 138, 157, 169, 183–4

Sage King, 111
Sakhalin, 144
Sakhalian, 168, 177
Sanchagou, 168
Sanyu Bank, 4
Sanyu Grain Company, 4
Sanyu Pawnshop, 4
Sanyu Public Oil Company, 4
Schnee, Dr N., 181
Semenov, Ataman Grigorii, 23, 24, 25, 144, 145, 146, 147, 164, 203
Serebrennikov, I.I. (Supply Minister with the Provisional Government of Autonomous Siberia), 58–9, 60, 146, 149, 164, 165, 166
Shcherbin Distillery, 19

Shahar, 181
Shanghai, 9, 42, 58, 138, 146, 149, 164, 165, 166
 police, 152
Shanghai Volunteer Corps, 152
Shanhaikwan, 181
Shantung Province, 152
Shantung workers, 140
She-ki Company, 32
Shengking, 2
Shevchenko, 151
Shirani Takeshi (Kwantung Civil Governor), 4
Siberia, 15, 20, 21–2, 23, 54n., 89, 117, 122, 136, 140, 143, 144, 147, 163
Siberian Company, The, 92, 120, 176, 186, 200–1
Siberian Military District, The (SMD), 26
Silver (price of), 93
Simanovskii (representative of the Foreign Commissariat, Khabarovsk), 85
Simonoseki, Treaty of, 6
Sinkiang, 2, 145, 190
Sino-Japanese Crisis (1931), 180
Sino-Japanese War (1894–95), 3, 6
 Treaty, 13
Sino-Russian relations, 137, 147, 174
Sino-Soviet Conflict, The (1929), xii, 28, 92n., 101n., 146, 147, 158, 171, 174, 178, 180, 182, 187
Sino-Soviet Treaties (1924), 29, 38–40, 46, 54, 63, 82
Skidelsky & Successors, 198
Skidelskys, 116, 117, 118, 133–4, 151, 171, 200, 201
Slavophile movement (Russia), 204
Smidovich, P.G., 88, 89
Smirnov, A.P., 88, 89
Socialism in One Country, 113
Socialist Revolutionaries (SRs), 22
*Soiuz Mushketiorov* (The Union of Musketeers), 67, 171
South China Mission, Intelligence Division (Soviet), 152
*South China Morning Post, The* (SCMP), 155, 178
South Manchuria, 13, 19, 107
South Manchurian Railway (SMR), 8, 17, 72, 107, 169, 170, 171, 172, 175

South Manchurian Railway Research Bureau, 148
Sovereignty, Chinese, 180, 181
Soviet advisers, 36–51, 152, 155
Soviet Consular Corps, 161
Soviet Consulate (Canton), Raid on (1927), 34–5, 152, 155
Soviet Consulate (Harbin), 164
  Raid on (1929), 34, 46, 82, 158–9
Soviet Consulate-General (Shanghai), 42
Soviet Embassy at Peking, 43
  raid on (1927), 34, 35, 62, 152, 155, 155–6
Soviet Military Academy, 88–9, 104, 157
Soviet Operational Art, 86, 89–90, 183
Soviet policies in Northeast China, xiii–xiv, 28, 34, 35–8, 44–7, 52, 54, 78–9, 80, 114, 179
Soviet of Workers' and Sailors' Deputies, 160
Soviet passports/citizenship, 52, 192
Soviet propaganda, 155, 178, 184, 204
Soviet Union, The, 26–8, 30, 33, 35, 37–9, 44–5, 56, 65, 70, 71, 76, 78–9, 80–2, 88, 91, 100, 102–3, 104–5, 108–9, 126–7, 152, 161, 163, 184, 189, 202–3
Soviet Outer Mongolian Republic, The, 24, 27
Soya beans, 73, 74–5, 91, 92, 95–6, 141, 175, 176, 178, 185, 201
Spain, 136
Special Far Eastern Army, The (*See Osobaia Dal'nevostochnaia armiia* [ODVA])
Stalin, 30, 36, 89, 204
  plot to assassinate, 148
  Stalin-Bukharin Faction, 36
St Petersburg, 6, 8, 139, 157
Staal'-Gol'shtein, Baron, 60
Standard Chartered Bank, The, 96, 186, 201
Standard Oil, 13
Starovery (Old Believers), 31, 100, 150, 173
Staryi Kharbin (Old Harbin), 10
Stimson, Henry (American Secretary of State), 83
Sushens, The, 135
Suifenho (Pogranichnaia), 77, 178

Sun Fo (Minister of Railways), 87
Sun Yat-sen, 40, 43, 203
Sungari Mill, 97, 133
Sungari, River, 10, 84
Supply Committee, Ministry of Commerce and Industry, 76
Sushens, The, 135
Svechin, A.A., 183

Taiga, The, 32
Taiping Rebellion, 3
Tang, Peter S.H., 88n.
Tashkent, 190
*Tass* (Soviet News Agency), 196
Tatars, 194
Tax
  in Manchuria, 19, 138, 174
  in China, 9, 138
Three Northeastern Provinces, The, 81
Thrift Corporation Bank, 96
*Tiao*, 176–7
Tibet, 2, 145
Tientsin, 41, 163
Timasheff, N.S., 204
Tobolsk province, 59, 60
*Tokumu Kikan* (Army Special Service Organisation), 167
Tokyo, 167
Tomsk, 21
Tongshan, 181
Toshihachirō, Banzai Lt-General (Adviser to Yuan Shih-kai), 167
Tours, B.G. (British Consul-General, Mukden), 179
Transbaikal Army, 6
Trans-Siberian Railway, 6–7, 137, 190
*Transport* (Soviet carrier), 175
Treaty ports, 9, 140
*Trekhrech'e* (Three Rivers), 31, 100, 101, 150, 159, 175, 188
Triad societies, 166
Triple Alliance, The, 6
Trotsky, Leon, 29, 36, 39, 45, 153, 156
  The New Course, 35–6
Trotskyite Opposition, 160
Tsai Yun-sheng (Commissioner of Foreign Affairs, Mukden), 83, 85
Tsarism, 21
*Tsentrosoiuz*, 146, 178
Tsingtao, 58, 198

Tsitsihar, 5, 11–12, 84, 182
  Province, 176–7, 181
Tukhachevsky, M.N., 183
Turkey, 148

Ufa Conference (September 1918), 23
Ukhtomskii, Prince Esper Esperevich, 129, 204
Ukrainian Association (Harbin), 188, 195
Ungern-Sternberg, R.F. von, 23, 24–5, 110–11, 124, 144, 145, 146, 193, 194
  capture of, 164
  Order No. 15, 145
Union of Bakery Owners, 194
Union of Confectionery-Chocolate Factories, 194
Union of Russian Military Invalids, 195
Union of Soldiers and Union of Cossacks, 195
Union of Soviet Railway Workers, 195
United Front, The, 44–5, 157
United Nations Refugee Organisation (Hong Kong), 164
United States, The, 24, 32, 68, 81, 164, 169
Urals, The, 23
Urga (Ulan-Bator), 23, 145
Uriankhai, 145, 193
Urumchi, 62
Ussuri Railway, 77, 142, 178
Ussuri Region, 136
Ussuri River, 1, 3
Ustrialov, Professor, 57, 162, 163

Varfolomeev, N., 184
Varges, A.L., 156
*Vasia Kariavyi* (Vasia the Pockmarked), 166–7
Verkhneudinsk, 145
Vishniakova-Akimova, V.V., 42
Vladivostok, 20, 21, 23, 24, 71, 77, 118, 142, 158, 175, 178, 193, 198–9, 200
*Voennoe iskusstvo* (military art), 86, 183n.
Vologda province, 160
Volga, River, 144
  region, 31, 160

Volgin (*Dni* Correspondent in Harbin), 64, 169
Vorontsov Brothers, 32, 150, 151, 171
Voroshilov, K.I. (Commissar of War), 88, 184
*Vostochniki* (Easterners), 129, 130
Vostretsov, Stepan S., 84

Wall Street Crash (1929), 91, 117–18
Wallerstein, I., 102
'Wandering Russian', The, 33
Wan Fu-lin, General, 84
Wang, C.T. (Chinese Minister of Foreign Affairs), 83, 87–8
Warlords, 3, 80, 81, 125, 129, 154
Washington, 87
Western Siberia, 31, 59
Westphalia, Treaty of, 124
Whampoa Academy, The, 40
White Guard, 26–7, 33–4, 42, 114, 125–6, 146, 174, 182–3
White Siberia, 25
Whiting, Allen S., 37–8, 47
'Will of Heaven', 203
Williams, G., 102
Witte, Sergei Iul'evich, 6–8, 16–17, 121, 137, 140, 175
Wood, M.W., 118, 186
Wool industry, 21, 32, 92, 100, 170, 171
World War I, 15, 19, 20, 160n., 204
World War II, 102, 120
Wu P'ei-fu, 181
Wuhan Government, 41

Yahuda, M., 157
Yakutia, 144, 157
Yanagita, General (Head of Japanese Military Mission), 112
'Yellow Russia', 14
Yokohama Specie Bank, 175, 186, 199
Youth Organisation, 195
Yuan Shih-k'ai, 167

Zaamur Province, 58, 152
Zabaikal, 24, 152
Zanozin, A.P., 54–6, 162, 187, 193
*Zaria* (Dawn), 198
Zemstvo, 163
Zorge, R., 156